THEMES
of
ADULTHOOD
Through
LITERATURE

THEMES
of
ADULTHOOD
Through
LITERATURE

SHARAN B. MERRIAM, Editor

Northern Illinois University

Teachers College
Columbia University
New York and London 1983

Published by Teachers College Press, 1234 Amsterdam Avenue,
New York, N.Y. 10027

Library of Congress Cataloging in Publication Data

Main entry under title:

Themes of adulthood through literature.

   Bibliography: p.
   Includes index.
   1. Adulthood—Literary collections.   2. Literature,
Modern.   I. Merriam, Sharan B.
PN6071.A36T48   1983   808.8'0354   82-19608

ISBN 0-8077-2731-8

Manufactured in the United States of America

96 95 94 93   9 8 7 6 5

CONTENTS

6. Adult Learning

PREFACE

In reflection of a widespread and growing emphasis on the concept of adult development, colleges and universities are offering an increasing number of courses and degree programs that focus on adulthood and adult developmental stages and tasks. Various textbooks are now available that present overviews of the entire life span, compilations of research about adulthood, or in-depth discussions of one stage of adulthood, such as old age. There is, however, a need for a mode of presentation that promotes a level of understanding not easily obtainable from texts on adult development. Presenting adult development and aging through literature has the potential of bringing concepts to life in a manner that students can readily relate to themselves and to the lives of people they know. This book, through its fictional selections, offers real life encounters with the basic themes and issues of adulthood.

The themes of adulthood and the selection of related literary works presented in this text evolved from the editor's research and extensive reading in adult development and in literature, and from classroom experiences in using literary works to study adult development and aging. The themes stressed in this volume recur throughout the literature on adult development and aging. The poems, short stories, and parts of novels and plays were selected for their illumination of the topics, their literary merit, and their readability. Certainly many works could have been chosen, and several examples of works not included here are mentioned in the introductory discussions of each theme. Also, readers will soon realize that particular pieces selected to illustrate one theme could just as easily have been used to explicate others.

With regard to the organization of the readings, two structures were considered: chronological and thematic. In the first, the readings could

have been organized under the major periods of adulthood: young adulthood, middle age, and late adulthood. This is in fact the pattern of several
texts on adult development. The second structure, thematic, was chosen
for this anthology because it was felt that such an organization better pre-
serves the essential notion of adult development—that of change over
time. Six themes, or central issues in adulthood, are presented. They are:
The Need for Intimacy, The Family Life Cycle, Identity in Adulthood, The
World of Work, Physical Development, and Adult Learning. Each theme is
illustrated by literary selections reflecting the way in which the theme
emerges at the major chronological stages of adulthood. For example, being able to establish an intimate relationship with another adult in young
adulthood is a task bounded by social norms and expectations and personal considerations different from those found in mid-life. Likewise, the need
for intimacy, for the presence of a "significant other," in old age has its
special and unique aspects. As a second example, the world of work moves
from establishing a career or getting a job as a young adult, to a sense of
maturity or perhaps malaise in middle age, to coping with retirement and
declining influence and power in later life.

Each of the six adult development themes is introduced in a short es-
say that precedes the group of selections chosen to illustrate that theme.
In these essays discussion of the literary works is deliberately kept brief in
anticipation that students of adult development and other readers will be
able to glean significant insights as they relate the readings to their own individual life experiences.

The editor would like to thank the many people who had a part in
making this volume possible. Three people in particular deserve special
recognition. Edward V. Jones, a personal friend and faculty member at
George Mason University, Fairfax, Virginia, had a major role in the concep-
tualization of the project. His encouragement and support have been felt
throughout. William Russell, a doctoral student at Northern Illinois University and a former editor, spent many hours assisting in securing permis-
sions for the literary selections in this text. His care and thoroughness in
this task are appreciated. Finally, thanks go to Dorothy Jossendal for finding time to type the manuscript.

INTRODUCTION
Using Literature to Study Adult Development

Compared with childhood and adolescence, adulthood is a relatively new area of scholarly interest. Only within the past few decades have educators and developmental psychologists begun to chart the patterns of growth and development that occur as an individual moves from young adulthood through middle age into later life.

The recent emergence of adulthood as a period of life to be explored and charted is reflected in both academic and popular literature. Daniel Levinson's *Seasons of a Man's Life* (1978), George Vaillant's *Adaptation to Life* (1977), Roger Gould's "Transformations During Early and Middle Adult Years" (1978), *Four Stages of Life*, by Marjorie Lowenthal, Majda Thurnher, and David Chiriboga (1975), and Gail Sheehy's best-selling *Passages: The Predictable Crises of Adult Life* (1976) are examples of comprehensive studies in this area. In addition, various aspects of adult life have received attention in popular books, magazines, television documentaries, and talk shows. Particular focus has been accorded such topics as alternative lifestyles, mid-career change, mid-life crisis, and adjustment to retirement.

The study of adulthood can focus upon a particular stage of growth or upon the process of development itself. Focusing upon a particular stage or stages of adulthood leads to descriptive information, that is, information that shows how adults of one stage or age in life are similar to and different from other groups of adults. A study conducted by Lowenthal,

1

Thurnher, and Chiriboga (1975) is a good example of this approach. In this investigation, people representing four transitional stages of life — high school seniors, newlyweds, empty-nest parents, and pre-retirees — were interviewed and asked to describe their lives. In contrast to focusing upon a particular stage of life, researchers also investigate the nature of development in adulthood itself by charting the patterns of change and stability over time. The Grant Study of ninety-five Harvard graduates who were followed over a period of forty years is an example (Vaillant, 1977).

For some developmental psychologists, the term *development* involves the notion of progressing from simple to complex behavior, from a less developed to a more "mature" state. Others see development as the changes or transformations that occur within individuals as they interact with their environment. Whatever a particular researcher's definition of development, the common endeavor of all who study adulthood is to observe, describe, and measure changes in behavior through the life span.

To observe and measure change as an individual ages involves taking account of the passage of time. But this is both a complex *and* complicating variable. Neugarten and Datan identify three types of time that have an effect upon human development: *life time*, or chronological age, is the most frequently used index of change, although it fails to be a meaningful predictor of much social and psychological behavior; *social time* refers to the age-grade system of a particular society, that is, culture determines the appropriate time for certain behaviors, and different societies have different sets of age expectations not necessarily related to chronological age; *historical time* "shapes the social system, and the social system, in turn, creates a changing set of age norms and a changing age-grade system which shapes the individual life cycle" (1973, p. 57). Historical time includes both long-term cultural processes such as industrialization, and specific historical events such as the moon landing that persons experience. Keeping the various dimensions of time in mind, Neugarten and Datan (p. 69) assert that the essence of developmental psychology is "to study sequences of change for the purpose of determining *which ones* are primarily developmental (in the sense of being tied to maturational change) and *which ones* are primarily situational — if indeed, this distinction can be made at all."

Studying changes over time to determine which ones are truly developmental requires sophisticated research methodologies that have only recently been developed. Furthermore, studying adulthood in all of its dimensions has been beyond the scope of the most comprehensive investigations. Rather, the approach has been to concentrate on one area such as cognitive ability, physical growth, personality, or interpersonal behavior and chart the changes with age. Studies focused on particular aspects of adulthood, and a few recent large-scale investigations, have provided the current knowledge base of the field of adult development.

From the accumulation of knowledge to date, several generalizations can be made about adulthood in contemporary America:

There are predictable patterns of development in adulthood. Various researchers have delineated and labeled phases or stages of adulthood, each with its characteristic tasks and challenges. While there is much similarity between the various theoretical frameworks proposed (indeed, they can be loosely meshed with each other), there is disagreement on several points. First, some feel that the stages of adulthood occur at very specific ages. Middle age, for example, is said to begin at age thirty-five, forty, or forty-five, depending upon the particular study. But chronological age may no longer be a reliable index of development. As one writer points out, "An adult's age no longer tells you anything about that person's economic or marital status, style of life, or health. Somewhere after the first twenty years, age falls away as a predictor" (Neugarten, in Hall, 1980, p. 66). Other areas of debate center on the differences in developmental patterns of men and women and whether or not stages of adulthood are linear or hierarchical (Troll, 1975; Knox, 1977); that is, do adults go from one phase to another different phase, each phase having its own specific tasks and concerns, or do adults move to higher levels of the same basic structure?

Adulthood consists of periods of stability and periods of transition. It was once thought that people did not change very much once they became adults, until perhaps the very end of life. Researchers have found, however, that adults go through many changes or transitions, all of which require adjustment and self-evaluation. These changes may be brought about by planned events such as marriage or by unplanned occurrences such as a late-life pregnancy. There are also periods of stability when adults consolidate and enhance what Levinson has called the "life structure" or framework that underlies each individual's relationship to the self and the surrounding world (1978).

Adult behavior is determined more by social than by biological events. Adult behavior is very much a product of the societal norms in the culture in which one lives. Each culture determines appropriate behavior and social roles for its members. What is regarded as "appropriate" behavior is often a function of age and stage of life. Most adults marry and start families in young adulthood, for example, and a man is expected to be well into a career by mid-life. Such events are part of an adult's "normal" developmental pattern. Unexpected events that break the normal pattern can be disconcerting to the adult who experiences them. Being widowed at seventy is expected and so is being employed until around sixty-five. But being widowed at thirty or jobless at forty is unexpected; the event did not occur at the anticipated time. Such off-timing of events can lead to a crisis or dramatic behavioral change (Neugarten, in Schlossberg and Entine, eds., 1977, p. 45).

There are recurrent themes in adulthood. Freud has been quoted as saying that maturity is measured by the capacity to work and to love. Work and interpersonal relationships are two central themes of adulthood. As an individual moves from youth to middle age to old age, the nature, intensity, and manner of one's working and loving change. The changing nature of relating to other people has also been explored under the theme of intimacy.

Identity is another recurrent theme in adulthood. A young adult is concerned with forging an identity; a middle-aged person evaluates who he or she has become; and an older person must accept who he or she has been. Thus the developmental tasks of different stages or phases of adulthood can be seen as the unfolding of recurrent themes such as work, love, or intimacy, and identity.

These, then, are some of the major concepts, issues, and themes in the study of adulthood. Most of what is known about adults has been derived from intensive case studies, biographies and autobiographies, interviews, and field studies. Occasionally fiction has been used to illustrate some aspect of adult growth and development. However, the potential value of literature for uncovering and conveying understanding about adulthood has not been fully realized. The power inherent in a work of fiction to reveal the human condition often far exceeds that which is obtainable from research studies and textbooks.

Fictional literature in the form of a novel, play, short story, or poetry may be read solely for recreation. Fiction has also been used to illuminate for readers various historical periods, social mores and institutions, psychological processes, and aspects of the human condition. In the study of adulthood, literature has been employed both as a medium for uncovering new insights and as an illustrative device.

As a source of illustrations, the use of fictional literature is popular in schools and universities, church groups, and informal seminars. There are numerous collections of fiction available that illustrate themes such as death, sports, love, or stages in life such as childhood, adolescence, or old age. Some writers have even offered guidelines for making the best use of literary materials in social science courses. For example, Channels (1971) has devised a "dialogue duo" approach in which students work together in understanding family life through novels; Somerville (1971) provides a list

of ten questions to consider when using fiction to illuminate death and be-
reavement.

There are several reasons why fictional literature offers an exciting
medium for understanding the human condition, and adult development
in particular. To begin with, literary artists are among our most disciplined
observers and effective communicators. They are often master psychologists whose work provides us with knowledge about the workings of the
human psyche. Their deep introspection, as well as their analytic abilities,
help them to identify the crucial issues of the human condition. As James
Baldwin states in *Nobody Knows My Name,*

> The questions which one asks oneself come at last to illuminate the world and
> become one's key to the experience of others. One can only face in others
> what one can face in oneself. Upon this confrontation depends the measure
> of our wisdom and compassion (1961, p. xiv).

McKenzie (1975) underscores this point in an article urging the use of fiction as a source of information about human development:

> A large number of creative artists have much to say about adult development
> and learning. What they have to say is based on their experience, on excep-
> tional perceptions of life, and on penetrating insights and profound intui-
> tions. The author of a . . . novel offers to the researcher a conceptual model
> of human development and a theory of the factors that shape human behav-
> ior and direct human development. This conceptual model, derived from the
> novelist's experience, is embedded in the novel (p. 215).

In contrast to social scientists, whose investigations are guided by
"objective" methodologies, the picture of development in adulthood that
literary artists give to readers is often imaginative, colorful, and multi-
dimensional. In the study of adulthood the importance of a full perspective is particularly apparent. Adult developmental stages and tasks are
influenced by total life experience. Literature, through the presentation of
episodes from real life, not only presents the events in which individuals
are involved but has the potential to convey understanding of the full impact of these events upon people's lives—what they mean and how they
feel to people who live them. Because we readers can get "inside" the
characters, our insights are often much more powerful, more real, than
those that can be obtained from factual data.

The impact of historical, chronological, and social time is depicted in
the many fictional works (particularly novels) that cover extended periods
of time. It takes researchers years to observe and measure age-related
changes in human subjects. Literary works, on the other hand, "freeze" as

much as whole life spans. The authors give us life histories or eyewitness accounts of behavioral changes over time. The longitudinal data found within literary works can thus be observed and analyzed without waiting for the passage of time.

Those who advocate the use of literature to study human development are sometimes met with the charge that literary works deal with imaginary characters and situations. This fact does not detract from the truths and insights that literature contains, however. Shakespeare's *King Lear* is a good case in point. As an overdrawn portrait of an old man, it is hardly descriptive of the great majority of older persons. But the play's universal and timeless appeal lies in its expression of certain salient issues of old age. Thus even when an aspect of the human condition is exaggerated, fiction can still provide universal insights.

What Shakespeare and other literary artists such as those represented in this volume have done is to communicate truths in works and contexts that millions of readers can understand and relate to. Such writers have earned recognition precisely because their skills in observing and communicating convey to us truths that we can feel in ourselves. Their observations about adult development and human nature have been verified and validated by millions of readers. Whatever contrivance there is in fiction does not obscure the sound insights about life that good literature contains. As Berger (1977) has observed,

> Such insights are convincing and worthy of further investigation for several reasons. First, they ring true; that is, they conform to the readers' general sense of things, to their common sense about themselves as social beings. Frequently insights also follow from the events and characters the novelist describes, from the premises in the story, all of which are felt to resemble real experience in some way. Readers thus accept the novelist's conclusion from his premises as applying to social life outside as well as inside the story (p. 161).

Literature offers a mode for understanding adult development not readily accessible through conventional social science materials. Sensitive and perceptive literary artists portray themes of human experience in ways that allow us to understand, to see our own lives with greater clarity and order:

> The best stories, as far back as we can trace the tales, myths, and dramas of man, sweep us out of our world into a new, intriguing setting, yet in the final analysis they return us to our present lives by reminding us of truths, character types, and patterns of experience we already recognize in our own existence (Gasarch and Gasarch, 1972, p. xiii).

Thus literary works can bring to life the knowledge uncovered to date by developmental psychologists, and social science findings can provide a framework for understanding the human truths depicted in literature. Both sources comment on human behavior, both borrow from "the stock of knowledge that human beings have about their own behavior," and "both the novel and social science use familiar notions, rephrase them, and try to add to one's understanding" (Berger, 1977, p. 159). A young adult can be told as a fact that a shift in time perspective occurs in mid-life or that coping with the death of a spouse in old age is a difficult adjustment. But to be in the mind of a middle-aged protagonist as he or she experiences the shift, notices the body aging, and feels time running out, or to follow an elderly person through the grieving process is to more fully appreciate the impact of such occurrences on the lives of those who experience them. Literary works thus become a valuable teaching aid in facilitating an in-depth understanding of adult developmental processes.

1

THE NEED FOR INTIMACY

If maturity is measured by one's capacity to work and to love, as Freud has said, then forming and maintaining close interpersonal relationships is a task all adults must at some point grapple with. Relating to others, whether it be in a marriage, a friendship, a love relationship, or some combination of these, allows for growth and development throughout adulthood. Though the need for intimacy is ever present, the ways in which the need is fulfilled may change as one moves from young adulthood to middle age to old age.

IN YOUNG ADULTHOOD

Erik Erikson (1950) has postulated that the major task in young adulthood is to establish intimacy. A person who cannot achieve an intimate relationship will suffer a sense of isolation and loneliness. Being able to reach out from oneself to another requires a sense of one's own identity. A person who has achieved a sense of identity is able to enter a relationship without fear of losing the self; rather, interaction with other people serves to strengthen this independent identity.

Intimacy, for Erikson, means more than physical love. It includes friendship, in which there is concern and caring for one another. The concept of intimacy is thus broad enough to include many ways of relating at each stage of adulthood. Much of young adulthood is spent exploring the many facets of intimacy. In Stephen Tracy's "The Potato Baron and the Line," a young cohabiting college couple discovers that they have drifted apart from one another and that living together perhaps calls for more responsibility and commitment than either is ready for. The story is a study in the testing out of an intimate friendship in young adulthood.

Selecting a marriage partner is probably the most common expression of intimacy in young adulthood. It is one of the social norms of our culture, somewhat in flux, but one that still exerts enormous pressure on young men and women. The single young man in Gregory Corso's poem "Marriage" battles against the social pressure to get married, tries to imagine himself in that state, and in general expresses the vacillation and indecision that confronts all who grapple with this major developmental task.

Sometimes a young adult enters an intimate relationship unprepared for the commitment and responsibility that it requires. In the short story "Others," by Robley Wilson, Jr., Philip is pulled between the freedom his artistic friends represent and a sense of caring and responsibility for his pregnant wife. The tension reaches a breaking point the night his wife unexpectedly goes into labor. The last-ditch effort of Philip's "friends" to pry him away from what they view as repressive responsibility at first succeeds. In the end, however, he breaks from them and joins his wife and new daughter. In accepting the responsibility of marriage and parenthood, he has grown, but not without realizing what freedom has been lost. In the final scene, Philip watches a young man ride by on a bicycle: "Watching the single rider glide out of sight, he feels a sense of loss that is entire — and not to be defined by any familiar word."

IN MID-LIFE

Middle age is a period when an individual evaluates his or her life to date. It involves the realization that half of one's life is over and that there is only a finite number of years left to accomplish goals or realize the dreams set forth in young adulthood. One takes stock of career achievements, physical condition, and interpersonal relations, and one either accepts what has occurred or tries to make adjustments before it is too late. In the poem "The Love Song of J. Alfred Prufrock," by T. S. Eliot, the middle-aged protagonist takes stock of his life and his success in relating to others. It soon becomes clear that this is a "love song" never to be sung or heard, for Prufrock has been unable to achieve any measure of intimacy in his life and despairs of ever doing so. He is awkward in social settings ("Do I dare to eat a peach?"), self-conscious about his looks ("Shall I part my hair behind?"), and afraid to reach out to others ("And should I then presume?/

And how should I begin?"). Bored and lonely, he measures out his life "with coffee spoons." The poem ends with his realization that there will be no songs sung to him and that he is doomed to "drown" in his own ineptitude.

Couples who have been busy building a life together sometimes find themselves emotionally depleted in mid-life as they attempt to maintain meaningful relationships with each other, their children, parents, and friends. An intimate relationship can become grossly distorted in this stage of life, or it can fade into a pattern of coexistence without emotional bonding. Readers may recall George and Martha, the well-known couple in Edward Albee's play *Who's Afraid of Virginia Woolf?*, who play games with each other's strengths and weaknesses. It is a relationship in which the boundaries between love and hate are no longer clear. It represents an intimacy both vital and destructive, passionate and ruthless.

By contrast, the twenty-year marriage portrayed in Daniel Curley's "The Eclipse" has become sterile and boring. Man and wife are so distant from each other that the husband lives at home, almost unnoticed, while the couple is getting a divorce. It is his intimate relationship with a younger woman that allows him to feel alive, to interact with other people, to appreciate aspects of life that had long been forgotten. Intimacy in mid-life, then, cannot be assumed simply because one is married, older, or involved with people at work. It is as fragile at mid-life as it is tentative in young adulthood.

IN OLD AGE

The need for intimacy does not diminish with age. Research, in fact, tells us that a support network of friends and family relations is a crucial factor in an older person's adjustment to aging and the many losses one is likely to encounter in this stage of life. The availability of an intimate other provides a resource one can call upon to negotiate the crises of adult life. It has even been suggested that a person's ability to form intimate relationships might be associated with life expectancy (Jourard, 1964). Two selections illustrate the role of a significant other in an older person's life. In the poem "Isaac and Archibald," by Edwin Arlington Robinson, we see two old men who care about each other and enjoy each other's company. Each gives to the other a purpose for existing. Because their lives are mutually dependent and mutually satisfying, each worries about losing the other. The poem presents a touching portrayal of mature, intimate friendship. In Patricia Highsmith's story "The Cries of Love," we meet another elderly pair of friends, Alice and Hattie. They too are dependent upon one another. Their daily routine, which offers them a purpose in life, centers on each other. The need for companionship is so great that they endure, perhaps enjoy, the somewhat sadomasochistic nature of their interaction.

As noted earlier, intimacy may or may not include physical contact. Unfortunately our society has stereotyped older persons as sexless and physically unattractive. The capacity for sexual activity extends well into late life, however, and the desire for physical contact with other human beings does not disappear with age. Two poems, "Minnie Remembers," by Donna Swanson, and "What Lips My Lips Have Kissed," by Edna St. Vincent Millay, illustrate this need. Minnie, an old woman, appreciates all that her family does for her but yearns for the one thing they do not give — their touch. In the second poem, the protagonist remembers the days when she had lovers and grieves for the loss of human affection.

The last selection, "Old Man Minick," by Edna Ferber, illustrates yet another facet of intimacy in old age — that of relating to the younger generation. In this story Minick's wife dies, and he goes to live with his son and daughter-in-law in their five-room apartment. Efforts are made on both sides to make the arrangement work, but their life-styles and their idiosyncrasies do not allow for a comfortable interaction. Minick finds much more camaraderie and intimacy when he meets friends his age in the park. It is only with them that he is able to rid himself of the loneliness and isolation he feels when he is trying to relate to his son and daughter-in-law and their friends. Certainly some multigenerational living situations work well, but it is more typical to find tension resulting from the differing class values, outlooks, and life-styles of two generations who were raised in two different eras. Older persons thus generally seek friendship with peers as perhaps the most rewarding avenue for achieving intimacy in late life.

Intimacy, then, is an important recurring theme during adulthood. It refers to close human relationships with other people: children, lovers, friends, spouses, parents. The depth and intensity of involvement with others varies with time, but the need remains: "Our love relationships are always in one or another position in a cycle that is organized and driven by the inexorable need to grow" (Gould, in Smelser and Erikson, eds., 1980, p. 233).

THE POTATO BARON AND THE LINE

Stephen Tracy

> *My own melancholy is often remedied by the house.*
> *. . . I am a mustachioed potato baron, once more*
> *basking in the aura of power.*

Straight across the bay from Monterey is Santa Cruz, the last hazy bit of shoreline you can see across Monterey Bay on a clear day. Back when sardines and anchovies made Monterey a booming fishing center, Santa Cruz's southern exposure and long white beaches made it a resort, with its own boardwalk and merry-go-round and roller coaster. My father grew up in Santa Cruz just before it began its decline into a shabby retirement town, with hotels and mansions transformed into condominiums and boarding houses. I grew up in turn in Monterey after the fish had disappeared and the city's businessmen had taken over Steinbeck's Cannery Row, making steakhouses, theatres, bookstores, and quaint wine-tasting rooms out of what had been huge whitewashed warehouses permeated with the stench of fish—a vague putrescence that used to give the fog an acrid, substantial character. Now, at nineteen, I'm back in Santa Cruz, which is suffering a renaissance as a university town. I have a room off campus in a peeling gray mansion built around the turn of the century by a potato baron, who, with his fortune, wife and children, silk vest, and gold pocket watch, left the Midwestern plains for the Pacific Coast, where he built his home.

13

Originally standing beside the beach, the old house was subsequent-
ly moved up the hill to its present site above the city, where it has assumed
a slightly hunched attitude, as if its sagging walls hoped to expand with
one last, deep breath, in spite of termite-riddled timbers and attic beams
that were left charred by some long-ago fire. Sometimes prospective buyers appear and tour the premises, but I think they are just curious or looking for entertainment. My own melancholy is often remedied by the house.
I take strolls through the ground-floor rooms when the sliding doors are
open, so that huge, high-ceilinged rooms are formed, and I can imagine it
as it was originally decorated—plush and crowded, the pastel ceilings
trimmed in gold, the walls dark mahogany, the windows draped with
velvet, and the blazing chandelier lights creating movement in the woodwork. I am a mustachioed potato baron, once more basking in the aura of
power that young capitalism brings to those who believe. There is more
opportunity here on this great West Coast than Wall Street can imagine,
Horatio—more than can be inferred from some silken debutante's sparkling eyes. This country here will grow. Opening the stained-glass windows
in the tower-like cupola, I can look out and see its expansive potential.

Now, however, the house is filled with students. It is owned by a Mrs.
Thurgood, who is a sociology professor. She has rented the place to un-
dergraduates while she attempts to sell it. The floors are eternally scuffed,
and some of the rooms have been painted obscenely bright colors. Expensive stereos have replaced the delicate consonance of a harpsichord. As the
youngest potato baron, I am upset by all this. Things are fading; the potato is not as popular as it once was. There are termites in the cupola, and,
not far away, the brown pelican and the blue whale are being exterminat-
ed. We are all concerned. In this house, peopled with students of biology,
ecology, and mathematics, concern is an important part of us—a glint of
urgency in our otherwise dull eyes, an almost subversive inflection in our
usually monotonous tone of conversation. I think we are growing out of it.
Already, our concern lacks imagination; we sometimes spend a weekend
registering Democrats.

Jessica is the woman who lives with me in my room, our room. Together, we share the finest room on the first floor, and at night we huddle
in bed watching the fire writhe in the tiny fireplace cage, framed by hand-
made tile and a carved-woodwork mantel, which one visitor guessed would
be worth a great deal by itself in any antique market. Our room was once
the library, and the bookshelves still remain, rising the entire fourteen
feet to the ceiling. Many of the prospective buyers who are being shown
the house think it is a shame that students are allowed to live here, be-

cause it is such a fine old house. At times, I share their dismay and contempt, but usually I am busy studying. I am studying calculus and the fundamentals of chemistry, so that when the crops give out and I am no longer a baron I will be able to do something useful and relevant, something other than simply studying or playing the violin. I will take organic chemistry, then genetics, physics, and a great deal of biology. Eventually, I will be a doctor, my curly brown hair tousled in the wind as I make my way through the streets of an impoverished neighborhood of Chicago, New York, or Los Angeles. I will be a doctor for the poor, whom I can help with my knowledge and ply with my care. Jessica, after some thought, told me that this was, at least, a rational plan.

For this logical trend in my own thinking I thank calculus. At the same time, I can feel a new complexity cropping up in me because of my habit of having to shape everything before it can be used—taking usable equations off a curve that knows no stopping, no self-reflection, but simply continuance. There is, of course, a power in one's ability to stop the continuity for a moment in order to get a glimpse of the slope and the direction of the entire line. Too often, I feel events scurrying off on their own straight paths while I am left with an imaginary construct, an elaborate framework—this crooked house and a crooked smile. With mathematical training, however, I am beginning to see more and more the workings of a mathematical divinity. Whenever I complain of being a mindless, bodiless vector moving unsteadily away from a point of origin through squares of no coordinates across the Cartesian plane, Jessica accuses me of being theatrical and says that this is the way life is supposed to be arranged and that I should stop complaining. Jessica was married for a while. At the age of seventeen, she worked as a bookkeeper to support her husband and herself during their stay together, and she is still very good at work requiring order, straight-line thinking, and discipline. But me, I'm growing soft on Communism; I remember children's stories and the green emerald on my mother's hand.

For most purposes, Jessica and I are a self-contained unit and spend most of our time together, in the same room. But there are other students in the house. In fact, it was the others who found the house at the beginning of summer, and we moved in only after they had already painted the ceilings, sanded the floors, and varnished some of the old wood, and had forced Mrs. Thurgood to repair the plumbing. Tom and Jim, both blue-eyed, blond, and eager, apparently did most of the work, and they still feud about how the kitchen is to be repaneled or whether or not the house money can be used to repair the dishwasher. After an especially devastating argument, Tom will retreat to his lab up on campus, where he is doing undergraduate research on plant development, and Jim will spend a day or two programming computers, although his declared major is political science. If the disagreement is relatively minor, Jim, a member of the university chorus, will spend an hour or two singing at the top of his lungs. These two share a room on the second floor.

The second floor also houses Jane, a thin, sweet girl with a permanent closed-mouth smile and arms that are freckled like cream-of-mushroom soup. Also Susan, a short and jolly senior in biology, who occasionally bakes us a sheet of very rich chocolate-chip cookies. Both have graduation as their primary concern. Wade, another second-floor resident, seems to have dismissed the idea of graduating and has dropped out for the fall quarter, occupying himself with photography and the acquisition of a girlfriend who has no objections to modelling in the nude. At one time or another, all the girls in the house have endured his pleading stare, which is magnified by thick-rimmed glasses. Sharon and Mary-Ann complete the original house population, sharing the first floor with Jessica and me. Sharon, with large wrists and deep voice, is a sloppy but energetic cook, who keeps a steady flow of bread, cakes, and gritty, massive salads coming from the kitchen. Mary-Ann, a senior in chemistry, spends the largest portion of her time pining away for her fiancé, stationed in Germany, who is only a rare phone call in the house. In all, there are nine of us living in seventeen rooms. For the most part, we are compatible. The size of the house allows escape into the attic or an empty room, but the distances we keep affect us; we become strangely and suddenly gentle, touching each other at times with a genuine kindness, an almost exploratory compassion.

I have been shut up in my room for an entire cold gray afternoon studying for the mid-December finals, and I begin to feel that the separations imposed by the house have become a permanent part of me, breeding a cold, gray melancholy. The house is quiet and there is no evidence of anyone else as I make a pot of coffee, but then, coming out of the kitchen, I notice Mary-Ann stretched out on the front-room rug. With my coffee, I stand in the doorway a moment, watching the place where her legs meet. They are big legs, and smooth. Rather like bananas, I imagine.

"Tired?" I ask.

She nods and says her neck is tight. She has been studying for her comprehensives in chemistry. I sit down beside her on the floor and take her neck in my hands, beginning an adventure beyond the established relationship. We have laughed together over dinner with the others and

have joined in wild food throwing, in juggling glasses, in circus fantasies.
Once, she got milk for a cup of coffee I was drinking, but we have never
touched each other. I never thought of her as something to touch. So
there is a strangeness to it, and an excitement in feeling the blond hair on
her neck become sweaty with the warmth of my hand as I squeeze there
and press and then relax and again push the muscles together until they
are no longer tense. I try to think of other things, of things my hands have
touched—cracked granite while building a retaining wall, sand, cold
rusted metal protruding from the winter beach, jellyfish, mosaic table-
tops, the waxberries of a neighbor's hedge, the soft feathers of a parakeet's
breast, steel-wound gut violin strings, bread dough. Mary-Ann's neck is
softer now.

I leave her sleeping on the shag carpeting, and I think how comfortably we all live here, our individual dreams uninterrupted by the revolution, all of us well-fed and healthy, and the house preserving us within its
aura. Jessica, with whose warmness I sleep (sometimes a leg extending its
own private warmth across my own), is the best cook. She prepares blue-
berry cheesecake, pancakes, loaves of whole-wheat bread, and spaghetti
with cream cheese and herb sauce. Her delicately flavored soups are served
quietly and with formality, as if the whole sometimes vulgar collection of
us were a group of tiny Orientals in this fading house. Jessica has had offers to live with others, because of her cooking and because she has hair
the color of wheat and dark skin setting off blue eyes. She laughs at the
proposals. There seems to be no question about us—perhaps because I am
still the potato baron, perhaps because I can still pretend that this deriva-
tive and comfortable stopping of our lives will not change someday into
something lifeless and joyless. Perhaps because I can pretend in bed that
we are whales on the verge of extinction, floating just beneath the surface
as we make love, singing the low whale songs.

In truth, it is beginning to seem as if the whole of my life is an exercise, a strenuous test of my imagination. Even in this house, in which time
moves so slowly, limits manifest themselves again and again. The day
comes to an end gradually as the talk in the kitchen dwindles and the people wander off into their rooms, leaving me, the only one up, studying
calculus out of a thick book bound with integral tables. I have memorized
most of them and can graph almost any algebraic function. I can find the
first, second, and third derivatives, and soon, I see, noticing the heading
of a future chapter, I will be able to do work with transcendental functions,
which I imagine as extending off the graphed paper and through the win-

dows, or up the old walls, along the beams, and up into the attic, worming their way across the silver planks there, where they sit for a moment on the cupola windowsills, and then finally leaping into the night sky and integrating themselves into the far-off glimmerings and the smoky odor of night—a continuous river of soaring equations pouring into velvet stratosphere.

In our room, Jessica takes the bedcovers in both hands and sleepily pulls them over her head. I am increasingly tempted to join her, to sleep and legitimately dream, instead of grappling with this calculus, but the math, I remind myself, is something useful, scientific, and physical. Nevertheless, I am affected by limits: the blankets, the bookcases, and the doors, always necessarily at some point of being opened or closed. Late at night, when I can feel that calculus can exist without my understanding, doors and their definite positions bother me. When I sleep, Gertrude Stein haunts me. She is leading a small encounter group and talking it into nonexistence. ''We must be aware of our nonexistence,'' she says to me. ''We must meet it head on.''

The landlady, never a popular figure in fiction or in this house, is making a move that may put an end to the stagnation that I have begun to feel here. Mrs. Thurgood is generally soft-spoken and sometimes motherly; she likes to refer to us as her ''affluent brood.'' At one time she was quite a political figure here, running for office on Socialist Party tickets during the Depression, and she still keeps up a radical front, in spite of what we see as her exploitation of students. She is now in her late fifties, and freshly divorced. There is a property dispute with her ex-husband, who has threatened to come in and make off with the velvet curtains and the luxurious carpeting in the living room. All this is the cause of the first instability to threaten our lives here, for Mrs. Thurgood, who apparently believes her husband capable of anything, has decided to take up the carpet herself.

Jessica, a veteran of and deserter from the ranks of the married, sees all this as proof of the mess people get into when they accept marriage as any kind of ratification of an essentially personal relationship. ''The government should build highways and hospitals, and leave people alone,'' she says.

And so the house slips into December. The school quarter will end on the fifteenth; today is the fifth, and the landlady was here for rent. I have gone to the market, a few blocks from the house, to buy tangerines and groceries for the rest of the household, whom I find gathered around the stove in the kitchen when I return. She has done it—taken up the carpet and left the bare floor, carpet nails, and this subdued fury. Tom points out that, together, we probably pay five times more than Mrs. Thurgood's mortgage payments on the house and that the removal of the carpeting is not going to mean a reduction in our rent. Tom uses the words "one iota."

"Not one iota," Jim says, in echo, "and now we don't have a rug in the living room."

Sharon comes stamping in. She has just finished taking down and hiding all the velvet curtains—an act of retribution. Now it is decided that we will move out "en masse" in a combination rent strike and exodus, possibly taking the curtains as spoils.

"Before we vacate, perhaps we should attempt some sort of negotiation," I suggest. But no one is going to be persuaded at this point.

"Well, then, how about an obscene phone call or a bomb threat?"

I am hoping to become a part of the mood, but they ignore me, their backs up against the drainboards and counters, rancor in their eyes. It is going to be a revolution without humor. Damned if I'll support such a dull venture! I hide my tangerines against the coming unheaval and notice that the sugar is running low in the pantry but that there is plenty of salt. Three cartons of half-gallon cans of whole beets seem to be an omen of grim days ahead. I had hoped that things wouldn't converge until the quarter was over, and that I could play a more significant part in the revolution, but history is always out of people's control.

Here in the kitchen—in headquarters, now that the decision has been made—reliable sources regard the mood as tense. The initial surge of self-righteousness has been followed by a lot of activity involving calls home and to real-estate agents. We'll soon be homeless, and, standing in the kitchen after hiding my tangerines, I see that the tenants are suffering; almost everyone is either down with a cold or just getting over the flu. It is the rainy season here, and the roof is leaking badly; the ceiling of the second floor let loose an island of plaster this morning. Looking out the kitchen window, I feel the stillness of the house. It stands quiet as the rain begins again, and the clouds turn pink in the dusk. The whole house is beginning to float. I leave the kitchen and find Jessica.

"At least it feels like Christmas," she says, peeling one of my carefully hidden tangerines.

" 'What would Christmas be without presents?' said Jo," I say. "And what's Christmas vacation going to be like if we have to spend it looking for a place to live?"

We huddle together on the bed. Jessica squeezes a section of tangerine into her tight lips, spits out a seed, and sniffles. "I'm beginning to feel unstable again," she says. "I thought we had a place where we could stay awhile, but this place is crumbling. The paint's cracking, and tomorrow we do the whole thing with the newspaper and telephone calls, the 'Are you a student? I'm sorry, we don't rent to students' routine. God."

"I'll do the calling then. I'll just be firm and confident. 'Hello, I'm a potato baron. I need a winter place by the ocean. A big back yard, furnished and large enough for me and my concubine.' 'What?' 'Concubine —you know, a potato-picking machine. A large garage will do fine.' There must be some old people who will show proper respect for the aristocracy. What ever happened to the University that is Mankind, the vast Studentdom?"

Jessica, unimpressed, unrolls some of the toilet paper we keep in the room, wipes her nose, and goes upstairs. I light my pipe and look out the window, where the yellow sour-grass flowers are being beaten down by the rain. Damn her.

We're tired. The future is usurping things; our energy is no longer ours. At one time, when we first moved in together, just seeing Jessica getting up from bed and walking to the closet through the shadows—two white crescents of buttocks and the comfortable arch of her back moving away—filled me with warm excitement. Now I feel we are pushed together too often by having to sleep in the same bed, share the room, and make plans as a unit. The unique intimacy is becoming habit. But we don't talk about it. I have begun reading magazines, especially the advertisements —calculations in fine wool, spotless complexions, rich smiles, and long fingers. How would they look in this old room, those long women making their way to the closet from this brass bed? It is a vision filled with energy, and I am in need of energy. I have become a house-hunter, and it is lonely.

House-hunting is put aside during the next week, the week of finals, and each of us again attempts his own miraculous academic pupation, from which we hope to emerge with shining new wings and brighter colors. Wade, with no courses and nothing to worry about, wanders around the house exclaiming, "What the hell has happened to you people?"

After finals, we continue to tighten our schedules, reducing alternatives and inhibiting tangents. It is musical chairs; we are trying to find a new place before the music stops. Michael, my first-year roommate, tells us of a small apartment—shower, tiny kitchen, and bedroom—that Jessica and I can rent for forty-five dollars a month.

We call the place, and an old voice answers. I ask if there is an apartment for rent.

"Well, maybe," the voice replies. "Are you a student?"

"Yes, I'm a biology major," I say, exuding uprightness, cleanliness, dedication, and reverence.

At the other end, she clears her throat. "How many of you are there?"

"There's one of me, and I have one friend. A young lady."

"A friend? Are you married?"

"Not at the moment."

She pauses. "You'd better talk to my sister. It's her house. I don't have anything to do with it."

"Hello?" her sister says. "Actually, we're looking for a single working man. No couples. It's just too small. No, I don't think that we want to rent to a couple."

"There's a possibility I might be living alone. Do you suppose I could come over and look at it?"

"You're not a hippie, are you?"

"No, I'm a biology major."

I hang up and put on a clean shirt and clean pants. Jessica and I walk the few blocks to the house, go up the front steps, and knock on the screen door. A lady, in curlers and jowls, meets us without a greeting.

"It's strictly for one person, you know," the woman says. "You can go around back and talk to my husband, if you want."

The door closes. Behind the lace curtains of a side window, a shadowy mass watches us—the sister. The entrance to the apartment is at the back of the house, and the apartment itself, it turns out, is in the basement. Inside, the husband has just finished repainting the shower. He shows us his work, complaining about the condition in which the place was left by the former tenants. "I cleaned the oven, too," he says. "Those three people left everything a mess."

"Three?"

"Yah. Of course, they were all boys. For you two, I'll move in a double bed. Maybe you want a desk, too? I've got a couch you could look at."

Jessica and I nod. We have decided to take the place, in spite of the old lady. We all go back outside.

"That'll be eighty dollars a month for the two of you," the man says, rubbing his scruffy chin with the back of his hand. He looks up at the sky, the telephone wires. Finally, he has to look back at us. "That too much?"

We shrug vaguely.

''All right. Because you're young and she's so pretty, sir, I'll let you have it for seventy. How's that?''

Smiling, we agree to it and shake hands. The door of the main house creaks open behind us. The man's wife leans her head out, her pudgy fingers on the latch. She says one word, ''Telephone,'' and a magnificent wave of dread sweeps over the moment. The man goes into the house.

''Jessica, I think our plans are about to be hacked asunder,'' I say.

After a few minutes, the wife extends her head. Her grimace might be construed as a grin.

''I'm awfully sorry,'' she says, ''but that was a single working man. You know—just what we wanted.'' She retracts her head and the door swings shut. We stand in the driveway for a few minutes, staring at the door, and then shuffle out of the yard.

I think somewhere in some chemistry book I might be able to find a formula for a bomb that would lift the white boredom out of that sagging house and fill it with the grand heat of vengeance. At the same time, I wish that instead of being a potato baron I could be a Single Working Man.

With Christmas only a week away, the melancholy seems to be deepening, as more and more of our various house-hunting ventures are unsuccessful. Wade, in an effort to cheer us up and still convey the epidemic nature of the despair, has christened the mood ''melancholera.'' The rest of us are not comforted, but we are organizing our defenses. We are planning an extravaganza for the old house—something to fray the thread of our future, stretching from here to the beginning of next month, when the rent is due.

''It has to be *extravagant*,'' says Jim. As a first step, he invites the entire university chorus. On the day of the party, a keg of beer arrives and is dutifully tapped and tested. Sheets of cookies are turned out by our domestic faction, Susan and Sharon. A few of these cookies survive the strenuous test instituted by the rest of us. Emissaries are visiting the neighbors, borrowing their tablecloths and extending invitations. By this time, most of us have recovered from finals, but serious plans for the future are not possible until after the party. Tonight, the night of the party, a household resolution has been passed banning all serious talk and any further visits from ''prospective buyers.''

The guests, most of them chorus members, start arriving late in the evening, knocking at the door, rattling the old stained glass. Their Christmas concert was a success, and they are still singing. The party develops very much as I once imagined college parties to be. I walk about, watching it all—the fast drinking, the small contests and intense laughter, red faces, hands holding and moving. A bearded fellow I've never seen before has his arm around Sharon's big middle, and she is smiling sweetly. Sure that no one will miss us, Jessica and I retreat to our room waiting for the arrival of our own friends. Perhaps we have never been part of the household, but I'm not sure now that any of us were. Perhaps it was just a house.

Jessica and I build a fire in the fireplace cage and watch it through the gold effervescence of our beer. Michael, my old roommate, makes his entrance and introduces his guest, Anne, a violinist. Her chin is almost double, but she is still invested with a kind of controlled beauty. Michael, who sometimes used to play duets with me, tells us she is a *real* musician, one who warms up with the Tchaikovsky Violin Concerto. She has a slight blond mustache.

"Hello," she says. "Michael has told me about you. I understand we are all violinists."

"To some extent or another," I reply. She seems poised, damnably poised, and is probably fascinatingly disciplined.

Wade evidently had a successful finals week, for now he comes into our room with a new girlfriend, Elizabeth. We all make our way up to the cupola with a half gallon of white wine and several mugs of beer. Anne, it turns out, is not drinking. I take large swallows of wine and watch the lights of Santa Cruz through an open cupola window. Occasional doors slam in nearby houses, and there is a kind of music to the motors of the cars on the streets below—high octave stoppings and diminuendos at red lights, and a slow grumbling crescendo of the same motors as they begin again. Tonight, Jessica seems such little company. Sitting across from her in the cupola, I see no communication or strength in her tight little smile. How can this be? There is no interest there, and watching her fills my stomach with dry dust. I take another mouthful of wine, no longer tasting it, and I begin to think what it would be like to live with someone who could force herself to practice the violin five or six hours a day. I have decided that we all have intense passions and that it is endurance that finally makes the difference.

Anne, submerged now in a polite boredom, slightly tightening her lips and folding her hands in her lap, projects an air of two parts refusal and one part transcendence. With a nonchalant deliberation, I am getting drunk. I watch the blue veins in my hands.

Anne whispers to Michael about an early appointment in the morning, and together they rise to go, Michael a little embarrassed and Anne thanking Jessica for the wonderful time. They apologize for leaving so early. I stand also, consciously steady, and walk with them downstairs, seeing them out. There are mumbled good nights, and the door shuts softly. The car is starting, and in a kind of spasm of dejection I pull the door open again and scramble out to them before they pull away.

Anne rolls down the window.

"What is it?" Michael asks.

Ignoring him, I mumble something and take Anne's face in my hands, kissing her lips gently but drunkenly.

"Must taste like wine and beer," I say. "Awful."

"Not too bad," she says smiling a little. Michael says good night, and the car pulls away. From the cupola, Wade and Jessica yell down. I don't know if they saw.

Michael comes back at six the next morning and wakes me up. We have an old appointment to go to Monterey for a violin lesson. The distant knocking at the glass front door comes as a shock; I feel a little like rattled glass myself. Rolling out of bed in a panic, unsteady and weak, I remember four of us on my bed, and me taking Elizabeth, Wade's friend, and holding her face tightly between my hands, I kissed her desperately. I couldn't feel my hands but I could feel her cheeks, and I had to connect my face with what I could feel of hers. Jessica was trying to dissuade me, saying that the only thing she wanted was me. Sometime after that, she made her way to the closet, slipped into my Army-surplus overcoat, and left the room, and sometime after that I was sick.

Now Jessica is sleeping on our bed, but I don't remember her returning. I pull on my pants, nearly losing my balance as I painfully hop about on the cold wood. I take my violin and let Michael in the door. He asks if I feel well enough for a lesson.

"Almost." I fix a cup of black instant coffee. The kitchen is filled with froth-crusted beer mugs and there is a pot of cold, stiff noodles. Michael is silent.

Later, in his Volkswagen, Michael turns his eyes from the road and glances at me nervously. "Could I ask you something?" he says.

I nod.

"What did you mean last night? I mean, you don't have to answer if you don't want to, but were you serious?"

I look at him for a moment. He has thick, Biblical hands, like Moses' hands in Michelangelo's marble.

"I'm sorry, Michael," I say. "I was drunk. I didn't have anything in mind. She seemed so disciplined, so sure."

He looks straight ahead.

"You both seemed older," I say, "and I felt that the only thing left to do was kiss her. Actually, I don't think I would even like her. She seems so set and confident, and I can't stay drunk all the time, can I?"

"I was just curious," Michael says. "But you're right—she is hard. And aggressive. You're lucky to have someone like Jessica."

"I guess it's just difficult to do anything all the time. Being with someone all the time. Or practicing every day, putting your life in order."

The Volkswagen is rattling, but it relaxes me. Calculus formulas begin to re-form in my head, like green sprouts recovering from a flood. The drunkenness is wearing off. I am exhausted.

I think maybe Jessica will find a place by herself for the next quarter, maybe a house in the woods in the Santa Cruz mountains that she can share with someone else. I think I will move back on campus, to the colorless, comfortable dorms. On this simple gray Saturday, I think that I will move into a dormitory room, where there will be less confusion, less to worry about, and more time to study the violin, calculus, and chemistry.

MARRIAGE

Gregory Corso

Should I get married? Should I be good?
Astound the girl next door with my velvet suit and faustus hood?
Don't take her to movies but to cemeteries
tell all about werewolf bathtubs and forked clarinets
then desire her and kiss her and all the preliminaries
and she going just so far and I understanding why
not getting angry saying You must feel! It's beautiful to feel!
Instead take her in my arms lean against an old crooked tombstone
and woo her the entire night the constellations in the sky—

When she introduces me to her parents
back straightened, hair finally combed, strangled by a tie,
should I sit knees together on their 3rd degree sofa
and not ask Where's the bathroom?
How else to feel other than I am,
often thinking Flash Gordon soap—
O how terrible it must be for a young man
seated before a family and the family thinking
We never saw him before! He wants our Mary Lou!
After tea and homemade cookies they ask What do you do for a living?
Should I tell them? Would they like me then?

Say All right get married, we're losing a daughter
but we're gaining a son—
And should I then ask Where's the bathroom?

O God, and the wedding! All her family and her friends
and only a handful of mine all scroungy and bearded
just wait to get at the drinks and food—
And the priest! he looking at me as if I masturbated
asking me Do you take this woman for your lawful wedded wife?
And I trembling what to say say Pie Glue!
I kiss the bride all those corny men slapping me on the back
She's all yours, boy! Ha-ha-ha!
And in their eyes you could see some obscene honeymoon going on—
Then all that absurd rice and clanky cans and shoes
Niagara Falls! Hordes of us! Husbands! Wives! Flowers! Chocolates!
All streaming into cozy hotels
All going to do the same thing tonight
The indifferent clerk he knowing what was going to happen
The lobby zombies they knowing what
The whistling elevator man he knowing
The winking bellboy knowing
Everybody knowing! I'd be almost inclined not to do anything!
Stay up all night! Stare that hotel clerk in the eye!
Screaming: I deny honeymoon! I deny honeymoon!
running rampant into those almost climactic suites
yelling Radio belly! Cat shovel!
O I'd live in Niagara forever! in a dark cave beneath the Falls
I'd sit there the Mad Honeymooner
devising ways to break marriages, a scourge of bigamy
a saint of divorce—

But I should get married I should be good
How nice it'd be to come home to her
and sit by the fireplace and she in the kitchen
aproned young and lovely wanting my baby
and so happy about me she burns the roast beef
and comes crying to me and I get up from my big papa chair
saying Christmas teeth! Radiant brains! Apple deaf!

God what a husband I'd make! Yes, I should get married!
So much to do! like sneaking into Mr Jones' house late at night
and cover his golf clubs with 1920 Norwegian books
Like hanging a picture of Rimbaud on the lawnmower
like pasting Tannu Tuva postage stamps all over the picket fence
like when Mrs Kindhead comes to collect for the Community Chest
grab her and tell her There are unfavorable omens in the sky!
And when the mayor comes to get my vote tell him
When are you going to stop people killing whales!
And when the milkman comes leave him a note in the bottle
Penguin dust, bring me penguin dust, I want penguin dust—

Yet if I should get married and it's Connecticut and snow
and she gives birth to a child and I am sleepless, worn,
up for nights, head bowed against a quiet window, the past behind
      me,
finding myself in the most common of situations a trembling man
knowledged with responsibility not twig-smear nor Roman coin soup—
O what would that be like!
Surely I'd give it for a nipple a rubber Tacitus
For a rattle a bag of broken Bach records
Tack Della Francesca all over its crib
Sew the Greek alphabet on its bib
and build for its playpen a roofless Parthenon

No, I doubt I'd be that kind of father
not rural not snow no quiet window
But hot smelly tight New York City
seven flights up, roaches and rats in the walls
a fat Reichian wife screeching over potatoes Get a job
And five nose running brats in love with Batman
And the neighbors all toothless and dry haired
like those hag masses of the 18th century
all wanting to come in and watch TV
The landlord wants his rent
Grocery store Blue Cross Gas & Electric Knights of Columbus
Impossible to lie back and dream Telephone snow, ghost parking—
No! I should not get married I should never get married!
But—imagine If I were married to a beautiful sophisticated woman

tall and pale wearing an elegant black dress and long black gloves
holding a cigarette holder in one hand and a highball in the other
and we lived high up in a penthouse with a huge window
from which we could see all of New York and ever farther on clearer
          days
No, can't imagine myself married to that pleasant prison dream—

O but what about love? I forget love
not that I am incapable of love
it's just that I see love as odd as wearing shoes—
I never wanted to marry a girl who was like my mother
And Ingrid Bergman was always impossible
And there's maybe a girl now but she's already married
And I don't like men and—
but there's got to be somebody!
Because what if I'm 60 years old and not married,
all alone in a furnished room with pee stains on my underwear
and everybody else is married! All the universe married but me!

Ah, yet well I know that were a woman possible as I am possible
then marriage would be possible—
Like SHE in her lonely alien gaud waiting her Egyptian lover
so I wait—bereft of 2,000 years and the bath of life.

OTHERS

Robley Wilson, Jr.

At first the word is a passion in Philip's mind. It cries out in fevered images in the shadows of rooms. It glitters in the delirium of rain on dark window panes. It allies itself with voices and drinking and difficult movement from place to place. It is incessant.

Though it is only a word it has become, with time, so real that Philip often sits, as now, in an attitude suggesting pain, with his eyes shut and his hands over his ears. This is an absurd pose for him to strike in the tiny room of a German hotel at midnight; the silence is almost absolute, and he is not even alone.

He tries to relax. He puts his hands away from his head, and opens his eyes. The word goes away. He lights a cigarette. He sees Cathy, his wife, lying in bed against a pair of pillows, reading a magazine. She has pulled the quilted comforter over her knees; a pale blue sweater is arranged across her shoulders. As if his glance were an abrupt, physical touch, she looks up.

"What is it?" she says. The bedside lamp lights one side of her face and shades the other. She is half smiling.

"It just happened again," he tells her. "I must be worn out."

"Maybe you're not used to being on land. They say that bothers people right after a crossing."

"I guess that's it."

"Sally told me she was land-sick." The single corner of her smile turned upward: "Isn't that just like Sally?"

"Just." Sally is one of the others.

"You ought to get some sleep."

Philip stands up. "I think I will."

He goes to the wash basin and runs water on the cigarette butt. He drops it into the wastebasket and begins to undress. He thinks it is true that he does not feel well; his throat aches and an odd languor informs his arms and legs. He suspects he may be running a temperature.

"This room is like an ice-box," his wife says.

"I told the others we should have waited until April."

"But then you'd have had to leave me home."

Philip sits, naked, on the edge of the bed. "I forgot," he says, truthfully. "Is everything all right?"

"You know I've been fine since the fourth month," she says.

"I'm showing concern," he answers. He leans across the bed to kiss her. She lets the magazine fall and clings to him with a familiar compulsiveness. He draws away too soon.

"What's the matter?"

"I feel rotten," he says. He sits shivering beside her. "Really rotten."

"You get under the covers." She arranges the pillows and moves nearer the light to make room. "You're like ice."

Philip lies next to her under the heavy puff, stretching out his legs and hugging the warm pillow. He stops trembling. He tries to think what he will do if he is genuinely sick in the morning. He pictures the disgust of the others: Damon, Jenny, Chris, Sally. They will condemn his weakness when there is still travel ahead of them. They will damn him; he dares not be in poor health.

"Phil?"

"I'm fine," he says.

"Phil, don't be that way. Don't feel obliged to be sympathetic with me, just because I'm pregnant."

"I don't feel obliged."

"I wish you wouldn't force yourself," she insists. "I know you resent the idea, but don't force yourself not to."

He puts out his hand to touch her—her throat, her small breasts, the full, hard mound of her belly. "I don't resent anything," he says, "only I don't know what to expect."

"We'll know in a month." She rests her hand on his, stroking his fingers gently. "I'm sure it's going to be a boy. I dream about little boys, and you know how strong the heartbeat is. Masculine strength."

"Spare me," Philip says. She often misunderstands.

"Poor Phil." She raises her head from the pillow and kisses his eyelids. "Your cheeks are so flushed, dearest."

"I'll be better in the morning."

"Please do be," she says. She releases his hand and turns out the light.

Philip lies on his stomach and tries to think of nothing. He makes himself acutely sensitive to his surroundings—the movements of his wife as she settles down to rest, the echo of his own heart at his temples, the rattle of the March rain at the windows. He is wide awake, but he does not think.

"Phil," says his wife, and her voice is barely audible above the weather, "when you talk about what to expect, that isn't what you mean, is it? Not the things I say to you."

"Not exactly."

"Boy or girl doesn't matter."

"I don't think so."

"I'm sorry, Phil."

"For God's sake, Cathy!"

He is exasperated, and pushed into thinking. It is like her to apologize for chance. It is like her to plead guilt for every misfortune. It has been like her, from the moment of their vows, to assume all responsibilities and make room for them in the honeycomb of her conscience. She seizes the blame for poems he lacks patience to finish, teaching jobs he cannot hold, fellowships he always loses. His mind rummages through her perverse martyrdoms. Now, and for the rest of her life, she will have the baby as a burden endlessly to be forgiven her. Forever and ever she will be a falsetto saint. It is an image impossible to dwell on.

He pulls himself upright in bed and hammers the pillow with his fist.

"Are you all right, Phil?"

"Hell, yes, I'm in the pink." It is too late to prevent the reflex of his voice. "I'm in rare good health." Then he feels her hand touch his cheek with a delicacy that shames him. "It's all right," he says, "only it's hard to get to sleep."

Her fingers move to his brow and caress his temples. "It doesn't feel as if you have a temperature."

"No." He is impatient. "Come on; get some rest."

She withdraws her hand and lies quietly. Philip feels better, calmer, like the thrum of the rain.

"Please don't go to sleep in a mood, Phil. Be jolly."

"Get some rest," he says. "Remember, you're sleeping for two." It is absurd to be jolly.

"Phil." She giggles like a child. "What a silly thing."

Soon after he has said it, she is asleep. For the rest of the night the very presence of his wife close by him, breathing evenly, nags at his peace.

He gets out of bed at noon, feeling light-headed and unrefreshed. He dresses and smokes a cigarette, sitting wearily by a window where he can look out on the streets. He hears Cathy get up, wash, rustle about the room in her nightgown.

"It's chilly," she says.

He does not look around. He takes no pleasure from seeing his wife dress, though once this was ritual with him. He believes she is ashamed of her ripeness, and he thinks he is more offended by her shame than by her body.

"Shall I pack your briefcase?" she asks.

"No. I'm going to try and work."

She leaves the room. Philip pushes open the window, takes a last drag from his cigarette and tosses it into the street. The view is barren. Across the gray cobbles is a broad meadow filled with buildings caved into their foundations; further off stands the Gothic spire of a gutted church, spindly gulls wheeling about it; the sky is drab. Philip finds paper and pencil and sits studying the church. He writes nothing. He has not written anything for seven months; everything eludes him. He is grateful for a knocking at the door.

"It's Chris," says a voice. Chris comes in, carrying a bottle of beer. A grotesque, bearded man with skinny hands.

"What's on?" Philip says.

"Party." Chris sprawls on the bed and sets the bottle on the floor. "The *Berlin* sails at two-thirty, and Damon got visitor's passes last night from a seaman. You coming?"

"Damon going to be there?"

"It's his party."

Philip nods: it is all Damon's party. "What about the train?"

"Ten tonight. Twenty-two hours, the Krauts say." He picks up the bottle and gulps from it, spilling. "You working?"

"Trying to, but not."

"You should have gone out with us. We've just been back here a couple of hours."

"I was bushed," Philip says.

"This town's full of bars and whores. I could retire here and expatriate my brains out."

"Are we going to Switzerland?"

"Damon says. We change trains in Bremen and Basel."

"Then?"

Chris sucks at the neck of the bottle and shrugs. "I guess Rome. Damon's got friends there. Maybe I'll get to the Vatican."

Cathy comes in quietly. She greets Chris with what starts as a smile, then turns to dislike at one corner of her mouth.

"Kate the mate," Chris says loudly. "You look more obscene every day."

Cathy neglects answering. She pushes a handful of toilet articles into a corner of her suitcase, slams the lid and locks it.

"You're dusty all over with the rich glow of motherhood."

Philip stands up. "Look," he says, "we'll meet you at the boat." He is still showing concern.

Chris looks from the woman to the man and grins foolishly. Propping his bottle between the two pillows he launches himself to his feet with an impact that rattles the bedlamp.

"Sure," he says. He winks at Cathy and ducks out the door.

"What is it this time?" Cathy says.

"Farewell party. The *Berlin*."

"Farewell for who?"

"Nobody."

Cathy slips the blue cardigan over her shoulders and fastens one button at her throat. She is not wearing lipstick, but she compresses her lips as if she has just put some on.

"It's a farewell party for Phil Willing, the big poet," she says. "Goodbye, dreams."

Philip picks the bottle off the bed, dumps the rest of the beer down the sink and the bottle into the wastebasket. He rinses his hands and dries them on the threadbare towel by the sink. Cathy is waiting in the hall.

"Better hurry," she says.

He does hurry, apprehensive about repeating old arguments. His mouth is dry from anger—or desperation—suppressed in him.

"You're not wearing a coat," he tells Cathy.

"I know. I don't own one I can button."

She is first downstairs; when he has left the key at the desk she is already sitting in a taxi. He gets in beside her and instructs the driver.

"It's aimless," Cathy says.

He is resolved not to answer, but broods, smoking, as the cab rattles past monotonous gray apartment houses on the way to the docks. At the customs gate the car stops; an American soldier leans down to the window.

"We're seeing some friends off on the *Berlin*," Philip says.

The soldier touches his cap and passes them through. Ahead, at the end of a dirt road, is the cement bulk of the Columbus Bahnhof—where Philip and the others docked the day before. A passenger train is half-devoured by the building; a loading crane moves ponderously beyond and above it.

The car stops near the edge of the quai; Philip pays the driver and gets out. As he helps Cathy, she says:

"It's all right for Sal and Jenny. They aren't married."

She keeps his hand and squeezes it gently. Philip tolerates the pressure to lead her aboard the ship.

As they pause in a mirrored, marbled corridor outside the third-class lounge of the *Berlin*, Cathy turns toward him. She puts her hands to her belly.

"I can't go in there," she says. "They'll trample me."

Philip urges her into the room. "Don't be silly," he tells her. She lets herself move sullenly ahead of him.

The lounge is jammed. It is dark, gloomily paneled, lighted now by scores of faces, noisy with laughter and talk mostly in German. It is as if half of Germany is beginning a voyage to North America, and the other half has come to cheer. Three bartenders pour liquor and dispense beer. There is a continual movement toward the bar of men with heads low, shoulders hunched, empty glasses in their fists. Away from the bar moves an equal current of men, heads and shoulders stiffly back—sometimes with elbows close to their chests and the filled glasses riding at cheek level, sometimes with arms raised so the drinks barely clear the light fixtures. The center of the room is open for traffic; small tables and chairs are along the walls.

"This is a peach of a time for an abortion," Cathy says. She is trying to smile—to make up with him.

They push to one side of the lounge, skirting tables and chairs. No one moves out of their way, no one objects to their shoving. A face—Damon's, thin and rabbity—suddenly appears.

"Sweets!" he cries. He is looking at Philip, but kisses Cathy roughly on the forehead. "The girls are in the corner." He gestures over his shoulder and twists his body to let her past. Philip lets her go.

"Big party," he says.

"A brawl," Damon answers. "Come help with the liquor."

Philip follows Damon to the bar.

"What are you drinking? Scotch?"

"Sure," Philip says.

Damon buys six whiskies and passes three of them back to Philip. They begin the precarious trip to a table with the drinks held high over their heads.

"Cathy doesn't drink Scotch." Philip shouts this.

"These are for us," Damon calls back. He stops abruptly, pointing; Philip sees two vacant seats at a littered table. Damon lunges into one of the chairs, and Philip sits across from him, feeling whisky dribbling over his fingers. Damon clears the table simply, sweeping his arm across it; the fall of glass and debris is scarcely audible.

"You owe me a mark-fifty," Damon says. He arranges his three glasses in a line and appraises them. "You can pay me on the train."

"What comes after Rome?"

"I'm not certain. Take a drink," Damon orders.

Philip gulps his first whisky; it clears the lounge smoke from his throat and he feels awake for the first time today.

"I thought about Athens," Damon is saying. "It's a real thing now to lap up the Golden Age. And it's cheap."

"I don't know," Philip says vaguely.

"What don't you know?" Damon's green eyes study him with a special brightness—drunkenness, but with no loss of energy.

"All this flitting around."

"That what Cathy thinks?"

"Yes," Philip says. She is convenient for blame.

"Have a drink," Damon repeats.

"And me, too," Philip adds. He drinks the second Scotch and sets the empty glass inside the first. "I have to stop somewhere and do a little work."

"You think we don't know that?"

"No. No, I think *you* do." He begins to feel sheepish.

"We just got here," Damon says. He sips his liquor slowly, not taking his eyes off Philip. "Maybe you should go back to teaching, huh?"

"I don't miss that," Philip says. He thinks of Cathy. "All this drifting," he begins, but fails to finish.

Over the noise behind him he can hear the metallic accents of a loudspeaker. He does not know what is said, or what language it is said in, but he guesses it has to do with the sailing. There is a drift of people toward the exits. He looks to Damon, but Damon dismisses the unspoken idea of going ashore by a wave of his hand.

"Just tell me one thing," Damon says. "What does a poet want?" If he is drunk, he asks the question soberly.

"How should I know?" Philip answers. He is annoyed.

"What do *you* want?" Damon puts his hand on Philip's arm and holds on. "You write a lot of junk, Phil, but you write a little poetry. I don't care a damn about the junk."

Philip shrugs.

"A reputation?"

"I never write a single line with the least shadow of public thought." Philip spins out the borrowed words; a feint, a defense. Damon's grip is painful, and the hurt jumps to his brain, where it throbs and makes him dizzy. It is the whisky, and smoke, and being commanded to say the passionate word.

"What the devil do you want?" Damon repeats.

"Not the name," says Philip, "but the remembering of it." He wrenches the arm away and folds his hands under the table. Leaning forward, he says: "It scares me, Damon. It scares me I'll never get it."

Damon shakes his head, pitying. "Fame." He pronounces it with an odd laugh. "Poor old fame."

"Let's forget it," Philip says. Sorry to have forced the word, he stands up scowling and turns away. He catches sight of Cathy in a far corner of the room; she is at a table with Jenny and Sally and Chris—yet she is alone. The other three are arguing; Cathy sits apart, looking vaguely about her. When Philip succeeds in meeting her eyes, she shakes her head and glances away.

"You ought to be scared," Damon is saying. He drinks a whisky and drops the glass on the floor. "There's no immortality in the Twentieth Century—not even for the Immortals."

Philip nods and sits down, as if he agrees. In fact, he is uncertain. He remembers that Damon is going to reform the world—with art, with poetry, with a Golden Age—and he keeps silent. The lounge gradually empties; all the visitors have left the ship, and the travelers are lining the rails to weep and wave farewells. The six Americans and the two German bartenders are left.

"Let's get off," Philip says.

They band together. Cathy takes Philip's arm and clings harder than she needs to. Chris smirks. Sally and Jenny whisper together.

On deck they are confronted with an unbroken barrier of railing. The covered gangplank is pulled away from the side of the ship.

"Canada, here we come," Damon says.

"Oh, God," Cathy murmurs.

Chris whirls on a white-jacketed officer nearby. "How do we get off?" He points at the shore. "Off this silly ship."

The officer understands. He beckons and they follow him aft—Damon and Jenny in the lead, Chris and Sally, Philip and Cathy last. They are led down a series of narrow metal companionways which the German officer negotiates at incredible speed.

"Don't go too fast," Cathy says on each ladder. "Don't pull me."

"I'm not," Philip says. "I'm not."

They find themselves deep in shadow, looking toward a rectangle of daylight. The officer points; Damon thanks him.

"It's the crew's gangway," Damon says.

"Like a railroad," says Jenny, "without the tracks."

"Be careful," Cathy says.

"*You* be careful," Philip replies.

He is behind her as they make their way down the narrow plank studded with crosspieces. Only a few paces from the end of it, Cathy stumbles. She catches at his sleeve, loses her grasp, and before he can reach out or shout for Chris to turn, she has gone sprawling onto the cobbled quai.

Later, Philip will not remember that she cries out—only that as she strikes the ground she twists her body violently to lie on her side, and that she draws her knees close to her. He kneels beside her and speaks her name.

Her eyes are open; her lower lip is white under her teeth. "Get a doctor," she says, breathless. "Please, Phil."

Philip looks up at the others.

Damon says: "Chris, better call an ambulance."

"Where should I call one?"

"At a hospital. Maybe there's an army hospital."

Chris jogs away.

"It'll be all right, sweetie," Sally says.

"Phil?" Cathy draws his hand to her face. "You won't leave me here?"

"Don't be silly." He can think of nothing gentle.

She forces a smile, her eyes still astonishingly open. "We should have gone to Canada," she says in a thin voice.

Chris is back in minutes. "You were right," he says. "The army's got a hospital, and I ordered an ambulance."

"Did they say how long?" Philip asks.

"Quick." Chris turns to Damon. "I also got us a cab."

"Do you need us?" Damon asks.

"No," says Philip. "No, go ahead."

Damon bends over the woman. "It's going to be okay, Cathy," he says. "Don't you worry."

"I'm all right," Cathy says. She puts her lips against her husband's hand.

Damon squeezes Philip's shoulder. "See you at the train; ten o'clock." He straightens up and leads the others away. Chris is saying: "I had a hell of a fight with that Kraut payphone. It was like a slot machine."

As he crouches alone beside his wife, Philip feels as if he is in an enormous arena. Behind him the *Berlin* is moving away from the dock, tugboats nudging at bow and stern. Before him the second-story railing of the *Bahnhof* is lined with bandsmen playing, and with people weeping, waving, cheering the departure. It is the cheering that particularly unsettles him, and makes him think the waiting is more tedious than it ought to be.

What finally does come for Cathy is a boxy, olive-drab sedan-truck with red crosses flamboyant on its panels. It skids to a stop beside Philip; two men in army fatigues and field jackets launch themselves out of the cab and run to him.

"What's up?" one of them asks.

"She fell," Philip says.

"Any bones broken?"

"I don't think so. She's going to have a baby."

The second soldier has opened the rear doors of the van and dragged out a stretcher. He puts it on the ground by Cathy.

"Don't you worry, Mrs.," he says. "We got very good doctors."

"Help me move her," the first soldier says. "You'll have to let go his hand, lady, just till we get you in the vehicle."

Philip feels his hand released, cool. Cathy puts her own hands against her mouth and closes her eyes.

"She don't want to go on her back," one of the men says.

"Put her on just like she is. Don't do anything clumsy."

They ease her onto the stretcher, still on her side. As they slide the stretcher into the van, she moans—the first animal sound Philip has heard her make.

"Give her something," the first soldier tells his partner inside the ambulance. He holds the doors open while Philip climbs in, then he shuts and latches them.

There is small light in the van; Philip fumbles his way to a narrow bench dropped down from a side wall and sits at one end of it. The soldier moves away from the woman, shoves a small bag under the bench, and settles himself at the other end. He raps at the tiny window into the cab, finds and lights a cigarette. The ambulance lurches.

Cathy does not ask for the return of Philip's hand, nor does he offer it. He sits uneasily while the truck bounces and rattles toward a hospital he hopes is close by.

"I gave her a little something," the soldier tells him. "Not a drug or anything—just a kind of tranquilizer."

Philip nods.

"She's preggy, huh?"

"Yes."

"How far along?"

"Eight months, about."

"Well," the soldier drawls, "she is sure going to have it."

Philip sits with his elbows on his knees, his hands folded, looking down at Cathy. She has taken one handle of the stretcher in both her hands and holds it hard.

"You army?" the soldier asks.

"No."

"Special Services?"

"No. Tourist."

"Hell of a way to see Germany," the soldier says. He grinds the cigarette under his heel and slumps into the corner.

Philip is looking at Cathy, but his thoughts are of the others. He does not blame them for leaving him at the dock: his family trials are none of their concern, and their particular uses of freedom are none of his. He feels guilty for what has happened. He wonders how much he will upset the planning which has brought them to Europe, and he wonders how this day of his life will affirm or destroy Damon's ambition for them all. On this impulse he reaches into his coat pocket and draws out his billfold. It is fat with the money he and Cathy have saved for the trip—most of it in traveler's checks, the rest in hundred-dollar bills. He counts out three of the bills and puts the money into the breast pocket of his shirt behind the pack of cigarettes.

The soldier has been watching. "You got any greenbacks?"

"What?" Philip says. He is sweating, for no reason he can imagine. His voice is hollow in the narrow van.

"U.S. currency. You got any with you?"

"A little."

"I can get you five marks on the dollar for greenbacks," the soldier says.

"No thanks."

"I can maybe get you five-twenty. That's better than you can do for yourself," the soldier says. "Same deal on traveler's checks—so long as they're not signed."

Philip shakes his head. The soldier sighs and smokes again.

Then the ambulance stops, backs, stops again. The doors open, flooding in light. Philip jumps to the ground; the two corpsmen jostle the stretcher out of the van.

"This way," the driver says.

The truck has come under a narrow arch and into a paved courtyard. The hospital, a half-dozen floors of red brick, surrounds the court on three sides. Philip follows at some distance as the two men carry his wife into one of several entrances. By the time he reaches the building, Cathy is nowhere to be seen, and he is in a high ceilinged lobby looking down an empty corridor.

"Sir?" A small, dark nurse stands up from a desk in one corner of the lobby.

"They just brought my wife in," he says, gesturing vaguely.

"Yes, sir. They've taken her up." She turns, motioning Philip to follow. "Would you sit here, please?"

She returns to the desk. He sits before her, watching as she goes through a ritual of opening drawers, taking out cards and papers, arranging them.

"Your full name?" she says, poising a fountain pen.

"Philip Willing."

"And your wife?"

"Catherine." He spells the name.

"Are you a civilian?"

"Yes." He fumbles after a cigarette and lights it. "We've just arrived here."

"Then you are not personnel assigned to this port?"

"No."

"I see." Everything she says disowns communication. "Your age?"

"Thirty-one."

"Your wife's?"

"Twenty-eight."

And so on. It is a tedious cross-examination, endless. By now the liquor he has drunk earlier is wearing off, and his lips and throat are dry. He is fidgeting, licking his lips and swallowing hard, when a tall figure approaches from the corridor. The nurse swings around in her chair.

"Doctor Magnus," she says, "this is the woman's husband."

Magnus stops beside the desk. He is a tall, incredibly straight man, slender but not thin, with severe features. His manner is military as he takes up the admission forms to read.

"I'm almost finished," the nurse says.

"Quite so," Magnus tells her, "but I will complete them in my office." He surveys Philip. "Mr. Willing?"

"Doctor." The word scratches his throat.

"Come with me, if you would be so kind."

Philip follows into a small room off the lobby. The office smells of pipe tobacco. The furnishings are of leather and dark wood; casement windows overlook the courtyard.

"Please sit," Magnus says. "I have put your wife in the care of Major Morris. He is American, excellent with mothers."

"Thank you," Philip says.

Magnus sits at his desk. "These forms," he says, sorting them on the desk-top. Philip keeps quiet; the doctor looks at him, through him. "You should have to wait not long," he says. "It will be a normal birth; more difficult, but normal."

"I'm glad to know that." The doctor's brittle attention and precise English unnerve him.

"A terrible experience," Magnus concludes. He takes a mechanical pencil from the breast pocket of his coat and lays the point against the papers. "Have you been long in Germany?"

"Since yesterday," Philip answers. He glances toward the windows, sees the flat gray color of a sky that is neither morning nor evening, and becomes unexpectedly confused. "No, no," he stammers, "the day before yesterday."

"Which?" says Doctor Magnus.

The doctor's eyes are yellow, like a cat's, with enormous pupils that exploit every shred of light in the dim office. Looking into them, Philip feels confusion mastering him. "Thursday," he says hoarsely. It is the limit of his ability to commit himself.

"That is yesterday," says Magnus, making a note.

"Yes. Yesterday. Around noon."

Magnus writes. He is busy for a long time. Philip sits uneasily in the leather chair, listening to sounds from the corridor of heels, empty-place voices, the click and echo of doors; he wonders what the doctor is doing to the simple fact of his arrival, yesterday, around noon.

"Are there more questions?" Philip asks.

Magnus stops working and taps the pencil on the desk.

"Do you have to ask any more questions?" Philip repeats.

"There are a few," the doctor says, "for the sake of the records." He makes more pencil marks. "You are American?"

"Yes."

"And your work? Your vocation?"

"Writer." After seven months, is it a lie?

"I see."

"And teacher," Philip adds. A hedge.

"Of course. And who should be notified, in the event of problems touching upon your wife's accident?"

Philip is startled by the question. Anger occurs to him; it is poised in his mind as he says: "*I* am her husband."

"*Natürlich*," says Magnus. An indulgent smile flickers on his features, and he taps the pencil once, twice, against the knuckles of his left hand. "We like also another name. Your wife's parents, perhaps. Some permanent address."

"I don't see why—"

"It is not so important, Mr. Willing."

Magnus secures the pencil in his pocket and pushes his chair away from the desk. When he stands, he tucks his hands into the pockets of the long coat and walks toward the windows. He seems interested in the dull sky.

"The Americans in Bremerhaven have a joke," he says irrelevantly, "that last year spring was a Friday afternoon."

Philip waits.

"I should like to ask you questions which have nothing to do with records," Magnus says. "Will you take offense?"

"No," says Philip, not knowing.

"In America, did your wife have a doctor to consult?"

"Yes."

"She is how many months pregnant?"

"About eight."

"And the doctor? He called your attention to the dangers of a long journey? Fatigue. Unusual movement. The possibility of risk in unfamiliar surroundings?"

"We didn't discuss our plans with the doctor."

Magnus sits, stiffly, on a corner of the desk. "But the steamship agents? They raised a question, did they not?"

"It was a fairly large ship," Philip says. "Adequate."

"And from here, where were you going?"

"A number of places. Switzerland. Italy."

"I presume by train."

"Yes."

"You are foolish," Magnus says. He leans over to open the top desk drawer and brushes the papers into it. "You are a foolish man, and an incomprehensibly lucky one."

Philip gets up, feeling shaky. "Is that all?" he asks.

Doctor Magnus shrugs. "If you wish," he replies. He is once more interested in the sky as Philip leaves the office.

In the lobby Philip stops at the reception desk. The nurse looks up expectantly.

"Do you have an envelope?" he asks her.

"Yes, certainly." She rummages until she finds one. Philip takes the three hundred dollars from his shirt and puts the money into the envelope; he seals it and writes *Catherine Willing* across the front of it. "Would you keep this for me?"

The nurse takes the envelope and reads the name.

"The fact is," Philip hastens to lie, "I didn't bother to buy traveler's checks when we left New York. I'm going out to get something to eat, and I don't want to lose this."

She smiles. "Of course, Mr. Willing. I'll have Doctor Magnus lock it up for you."

She goes directly to the office he has just left, before Philip can find the voice to call her back. He does not wait for her reappearance.

Outside the hospital arch he hails a cab and goes directly to the hotel. It is a trip of several miles; the fare takes the last of the few German coins he has, and by the time he gets his key and goes to his room a heavy bell nearby is tolling seven. He switches on the light and goes back to close the door; in the hall he finds the desk clerk, looking apologetic, holding out a folded paper.

"This," the clerk says. He seems to want to say more.

Philip takes the paper. "Thank you very much," he says, and closes the door gently. The note is in Damon's bad hand. It reads: *Next door— come drink.*

Philip crumples the paper into the wastebasket. He wants no party. It is a novelty to be alone and free, and he tries—finding a stubby pencil on the floor beside the bed and the empty folder for the steamer tickets in his pocket—to write a poem about himself and his freedom. Failing—because he is out of practice, or because he has chosen a bad subject—he puts his materials aside and stretches out on top of the bed. He puts a cigarette to his lips, realizes he does not want to smoke, and falls asleep. He has no useful dreams.

He is awakened some time later by the furious pressure of hands at his shoulders. Chris, reeking of beer, hovers over him.

"Where you been?" Chris says.

"Here," Philip answers. His head throbs and his mouth tastes like sleep. "The hospital, then here."

"Damon wants you."

"I can't, Chris. I can't drink now."

"Who said drink?"

"That's what it always is."

"Maybe he wants to talk."

"No," Philip says, and he tries to lie down. Chris takes him under the arms and pulls him upright beside the bed.

"Look," he says, "are you with us?"

Philip is wholly awake; he picks up his coat, and follows Chris down the stairs and out of the hotel. Outside, Chris punches him playfully on the arm. "Relax," he says; he stops in front of a barroom, opens the door and gestures Philip inside.

It is a small room, poorly lighted, with a short, mirrored bar against the far wall, and under the windows to the left a long, shallow aquarium boiling with green water and tiny fish darting in and out of algae and coral castles. A fat bartender, enormously jowled and red in the face, waves to

Philip. Damon and the two girls are at a round table close by the bar; he seems to be playing solitaire while Jenny and Sally look on.

Chris pushes Philip forward. "See what I found."

Damon glances up from his cards. "Philip Willing," he says. "Philip Willing come liquor-swilling."

"I fell asleep," Philip says.

"Likely," Damon answers. He kicks a chair out from the table; Philip sits down. Damon shuffles the cards and begins dealing them face up around the table. "Jacks," he says.

The deal continues. The first knave turns up in front of Chris. "Triple cognac," he says. He signs to the bartender.

The second jack comes to Jenny. She takes the drink from the counter and touches it briefly to her lips.

The third jack falls to Philip. He protests: "I don't want to start drinking again."

Philip drains the glass. The brandy is hot, welcome. He coughs self-consciously and puts the glass on the table.

Chris accepts the fourth jack, and pays. The deal passes.

For two hours the game goes on, and during it nothing is said about Cathy, or about a train to Basel, or about a choice between them. Damon does not tease Philip about fame, or chide him over responsibilities, or preach to him about art. Only much later does it occur to Philip that the third jack is usually his, and that most of the drinks are multiple shots of cognac. Once he excuses himself to go to the men's room, and there he leans dizzily over the urinal, his hands against the discolored wall tiles supporting him while he vomits and tries to remember where he is. When he comes out, ready in an automatic, mindless way to resume the drinking game, Damon and Chris are in wait outside the door.

"Train time," Chris says.

"Listen," Philip says. "No, no." When he pulls free he loses his balance and starts to fall.

"The road to Athens." Damon says, catching him.

Of the chaos to follow, Philip will remember a blurred glimpse of the bartender's chins trembling over cognac glasses, and the shimmering street, and his face cool under a light rain. There is a taxi—small and absurdly uncomfortable. He rides in the rear seat, his head against a window, his feet hung over the front seat between Damon and the driver. When the cab reaches the railroad station he is dragged feet-first out of the car. He waits, unsteady, his mind sluggishly pursuing the idea that he is keeping an appointment. Damon is beside him, taking his arm, magically holding his briefcase out to him.

"Here's your work," Damon says.

Philip takes it; it seems weightless. He stumbles along beside Damon, who opens a door for him. They pass through a noisy, musty waiting room where people and benches are fuzzy under a haze of smoke. On the platform the air is cleaner and cooler, and the confusion behind him is diminished to a whisper high up in the curved darkness. The train is ahead of them.

Their tickets are for a third-class carriage, a spare, wooden interior lit violently by bare bulbs. The benches are occupied by plump old women in kerchiefs, gray men in seamen's caps, children with uncovered, stunning blond hair. Philip sits by the aisle and pushes his briefcase under the seat. Now he is aware of reflections in the window glass, and of objects moving beyond the reflections. He feels his hand touched.

"It'll be fine, Phil," he hears Jenny say.

The train lurches ahead. Feeling the movement, gradually comprehending it, he forces himself to stand.

"I'm sick," he says. He wonders if he really is.

He gropes gracelessly up the aisle and stops between cars. It is noisy, and he tastes a slowly growing draught of air; the side door has not yet been shut; the gray station pavements slip past. Philip plunges forward, down three narrow steps, and for an instant hangs poised in the opening. He guesses that the train has passed out of the station, and then he lets go. As he comes to the ground, limp and tumbling, he thinks he hears his name.

"WILLING!"

The voice might be Damon's—it sounds much like it, a strong shout over the noise of the train. But life is all loud; he thinks this as he falls, feeling his senses smothered by the train, by the word that might be his own name, by the dull throb of drink against his skull. It is difficult to separate things; he cannot decide which is the murmur of continuous movement, which the whispered suggestion of fame, which the pulse of alcohol. Rolling down the wet embankment, feeling grass and gravel coarse against his hands and face, he looks up to see the train lurching past, creaking and piping loud. Its lighted windows one by one blur before his eyes. In the windows are the faces of the others, distinct but scarcely aware of him; as the last lights vanish he stops falling and passes out in the dark and the silence of drenched earth.

When next he opens his eyes Philip is lying on a padded leather table. The surroundings seem familiar—a small room furnished with a desk of dark wood, a walnut coat rack, a low table with a metal sterilizer glistening on it. He smells pipe tobacco. Raising himself on one elbow he sees light outside the narrow casement windows; dawn or dusk—he does not know which.

His head aches. His neck muscles are stiff and his whole body feels vaguely as if has lain a long time on a bare floor. He discovers that his suit is streaked with dirt; a three-corner tear is open at the knee of one trouser leg. When he tries to remember, the events of his boarding and leaving the train seem improbable.

A door opens. He sits up slowly. "Doctor Magnus," he says.

"I'm delighted you are awake," Magnus says. "We were disturbed."

"I guess I had myself a night," Philip says. He is embarrassed. "I had this peculiar . . . accident." Magnus extends a pack of American cigarettes. Reaching out to take one, Philip notices that his hand is bandaged. "How did I get this?"

"Your peculiar accident. A small thing."

"Stupid," Philip says. He talks around the cigarette. "I left something on a train. Do you suppose I'll get it back?"

"Money?"

Philip puts his hand to the inside pocket of his jacket; he is relieved to feel the billfold.

"No," he says. "Not money."

Magnus pretends a smile. "It is hard to know what will happen with trains."

"I know." It occurs to him that Damon will have the briefcase—that he will likely not mail it back.

"One can only tell the authorities," Magnus says.

Philip is annoyed. Since entering the room, Magnus has stood in one place, watching, studying. If the doctor intends a medical pronouncement, why doesn't he get to it? Except for the nagging of his bruised muscles, Philip feels well. He feels, surprisingly, better than he has for some months. Still, good health aside, Philip is irritated by the German. He wonders if Magnus knows what is in the envelope locked in this room.

"I am most pleased to find you recovered," Magnus repeats, "to remind you of your wife. She is in the delivery room."

Something—fatigue, or drink, or design—has made Philip forget about the baby.

Magnus turns his back. "Major Morris is with her."

"May I talk with her?"

"Later, after the child is delivered." Doctor Magnus pauses at the door. "If you wish," he ends formally.

"Certainly I wish." Philip is trembling, partly from anger, partly from the curious guilt this man forces upon him.

"It is the third floor. There are chairs."

Philip slides down from the table; his left knee hurts and he stands unevenly. "Please show me," he says.

Taller than Philip, the doctor responds from what seems a level of divine condescension. "Of course, Mr. Willing."

Limping slightly, Philip follows him along the corridor into a roomy stairwell. The light is harsh yellow after the dimness of the office. Soft-drink and candy machines stand along one wall; a German janitor is swinging a damp mop over the tiled floor. At the bottom of the stairs Philip steps over a sallow young man in army fatigues reading a tabloid. The man glances up; his expression conveys contempt for the doctor, indifference to Philip.

At the second landing, out of breath and frowning from the ache in his knee, he follows Magnus down the disinfected hall to the door of the delivery room. Three chairs stand in a neat row along the wall. Magnus motions Philip into one of them.

"You will wait here," he says.

Philip sits down, gladly, his legs weak from climbing. Magnus raps at the door, goes inside, and reappears at once.

"Soon," he says, and goes away.

Philip folds his arms. Alone, without cigarettes, he finds the waiting tedious. There is nothing in the corridor to look at; nothing to do with his hands; nothing but the boredom of sitting still. He listens for Cathy—for a groan, a cry, some message of pain from behind the closed door. He hears nothing, only interior, early-morning silence.

In this perfection of inactivity it is easy for him to read meaning into the actions of the others—to know that Magnus's coldness measures his irresponsibility, that Damon's impatience deplores his weakness as artist, that Catherine's distress cries her domesticity and his failure to minister to it. He is astonished that in his own half-intentioned actions he finds no meaning at all. It is true, what he has told Cathy, that he does not know what to expect. He has never known. Life is not susceptible to him; it holds back answers. Even his poetry is an evasion, a synthetic stronger than fact but more fragile than philosophy, an escapist rewording of the hard problems.

He is roused from waiting by a woman's voice saying his name. A nurse—old, capless, in a soiled white uniform—is beckoning to him. By the time he reaches the delivery room she has gone inside, then emerges, pushing ahead of her a cart that bears his wife and his new child. Nothing in this new vision of Cathy is calculated to please him; she lies with one hand awkwardly palm-up over her belly, the other half-clasping the baby; her head lolls to one side, her eyes are swollen; small white accretions of salt cling to her cheeks; a line of dried blood rims the inside of her lower lip, and flakes of blood show on her teeth; the dark hair at her brow is matted from sweat.

Beside her, its head cradled against her throat, the baby lies like some pathetic, found animal, a creature of incredibly tiny features and fists. Without hair, eyebrows, lashes, its skin vaguely yellow save for tinges of pink throbbing at its temples and smears of thick blood on its shoulders and head, it looks like soft clay twisted into a clumsy imitation of childness and put aside to be fired. Both mother and baby are swaddled in layers of dingy gray linens.

Cathy puts out her hand to him.

"Say hello to your new daughter," she whispers.

"Is everything all right?"

"Yes," Cathy says. "Oh, yes."

An odd thought comes to Philip. "I envy you," he says.

"I kept telling them it had to be a boy. The doctor said you wouldn't mind."

"I don't."

"Did the doctor tell you that?"

"I haven't seen him."

"He said you wouldn't mind." She turns her head so her cheek touches the baby's forehead. "You really don't mind?"

"No."

"She's perfect, Phil. I counted her fingers and toes—that was the first thing I did. I was scared that she wouldn't be perfect, but she is. She's beautiful, isn't she?"

He kisses Cathy on the forehead, as if answering.

"I saw everything," she murmurs. "I was never out. They kept telling me to push harder and the doctor said, 'Come on, you can do better than that,' and all at once he held her up for me to see. He laid her across my stomach while they sewed me up, and then they took her away to wash some of the blood off. More than six pounds, the doctor thought.'' She presses Philip's hand. ''God, Phil, I'm so tired.''

The old nurse comes back into the hall. ''I must take the baby now,'' she says.

''They'll come get me, too, in a minute,'' Cathy says. ''Will you be all right in that hotel room by yourself?''

''Why not?''

''Wasn't it marvelous she could be born in an American hospital? Even the doctor was American.''

''We were lucky,'' Philip says. He looks down at Cathy's pale face slack with fatigue; he tries to think of something affectionate to say. ''The others are on the way to Italy,'' he reports finally. ''I saw them off last night.''

''I'll miss them. I thought you might leave me here and go with them.''

''I didn't.''

''Forgive me, Phil, for even imagining a thing like that.''

He kisses her once more, then takes his hand from hers. ''You'd better get some rest,'' he says. He knocks at the door of the delivery room; it opens and a second nurse looks out. ''You can take her back in now,'' Philip tells the nurse.

''Come this afternoon,'' Cathy says. ''We have to pick out a perfect name. And bring my little overnight case.''

By way of answer he puts his fingers to his lips, signifying fondness across the growing distance between them as his wife is taken away.

He limps to the end of the hall, looking out a window pushed open on the damp morning. Over the rooftops of Bremerhaven he sees the long sheds and the angular loading cranes of the docks, far off against a dim horizon he imagines to be the North Sea. The wet spring wind carries in to him the reed voice of a train whistle; it reminds him of the lost manuscripts and of his own name ringing in his ears as he rolled over and over into the gully alongside the tracks. Below him, in a street shiny with cobblestones, a young man rides past on a bicycle, bobbing his head in time to a music Philip cannot hear. Watching the single rider glide out of sight, he feels a sense of loss that is entire—and not to be defined by any familiar word.

THE LOVE SONG
OF J. ALFRED PRUFROCK

T. S. Eliot

> *S'io credessi che mia risposta fosse*
> *a persona che mai tornasse al mondo,*
> *questa fiamma staria senza più scosse.*
> *Ma per ciò che giammai di questo fondo*
> *non tornò vivo alcun, s'i'odo il vero,*
> *senza tema d'infamia ti rispondo.*

Let us go then, you and I,
When the evening is spread out against the sky
Like a patient etherised upon a table;
Let us go, through certain half-deserted streets,
The muttering retreats
Of restless nights in one-night cheap hotels
And sawdust restaurants with oyster-shells:
Streets that follow like a tedious argument
Of insidious intent
To lead you to an overwhelming question . . .
Oh, do not ask, 'What is it?'
Let us go and make our visit.

In the room the women come and go
Talking of Michelangelo.

The yellow fog that rubs its back upon the window-panes,
The yellow smoke that rubs its muzzle on the window-panes,
Licked its tongue into the corners of the evening,
Lingered upon the pools that stand in drains,
Let fall upon its back the soot that falls from chimneys,
Slipped by the terrace, made a sudden leap,
And seeing that it was a soft October night,
Curled once about the house, and fell asleep.

And indeed there will be time
For the yellow smoke that slides along the street
Rubbing its back upon the window-panes;
There will be time, there will be time
To prepare a face to meet the faces that you meet;
There will be time to murder and create,
And time for all the works and days of hands
That lift and drop a question on your plate;
Time for you and time for me,
And time yet for a hundred indecisions,
And for a hundred visions and revisions,
Before the taking of a toast and tea.

In the room the women come and go
Talking of Michelangelo.

And indeed there will be time
To wonder, 'Do I dare?' and, 'Do I dare?'
Time to turn back and descend the stair,
With a bald spot in the middle of my hair—
(They will say: 'How his hair is growing thin!')
My morning coat, my collar mounting firmly to the chin,
My necktie rich and modest, but asserted by a simple pin—
(They will say: 'But how his arms and legs are thin!')
Do I dare
Disturb the universe?

In a minute there is time
For decisions and revisions which a minute will reverse.

For I have known them all already, known them all—
Have known the evenings, mornings, afternoons,
I have measured out my life with coffee spoons;
I know the voices dying with a dying fall
Beneath the music from a farther room.
        So how should I presume?

And I have known the eyes already, known them all—
The eyes that fix you in a formulated phrase,
And when I am formulated, sprawling on a pin,
When I am pinned and wriggling on the wall,
Then how should I begin
To spit out all the butt-ends of my days and ways?
        And how should I presume?

And I have known the arms already, known them all—
Arms that are braceleted and white and bare
(But in the lamplight, downed with light brown hair!)
Is it perfume from a dress
That makes me so digress?
Arms that lie along a table, or wrap about a shawl.
        And should I then presume?
        And how should I begin?

                . . . . .

Shall I say, I have gone at dusk through narrow streets
And watched the smoke that rises from the pipes
Of lonely men in shirt-sleeves, leaning out of windows? . . .

I should have been a pair of ragged claws
Scuttling across the floors of silent seas.

                . . . . .

And the afternoon, the evening, sleeps so peacefully!
Smoothed by long fingers,
Asleep . . . tired . . . or it malingers,
Stretched on the floor, here beside you and me.
Should I, after tea and cakes and ices,
Have the strength to force the moment to its crisis?

But though I have wept and fasted, wept and prayed,
Though I have seen my head (grown slightly bald) brought in upon a
    platter,
I am no prophet—and here's no great matter;
I have seen the moment of my greatness flicker,
And I have seen the eternal Footman hold my coat, and snicker,
And in short, I was afraid.

And would it have been worth it, after all,
After the cups, the marmalade, the tea,
Among the porcelain, among some talk of you and me,
Would it have been worth while,
To have bitten off the matter with a smile,
To have squeezed the universe into a ball
To roll it towards some overwhelming question,
To say: 'I am Lazarus, come from the dead,
Come back to tell you all, I shall tell you all'—
If one, settling a pillow by her head,
        Should say: 'That is not what I meant at all.
        That is not it, at all.'

And would it have been worth it, after all,
Would it have been worth while,
After the sunsets and the dooryards and the sprinkled streets,
After the novels, after the teacups, after the skirts that trail along the
    floor—
And this, and so much more?—
It is impossible to say just what I mean!
But as if a magic lantern threw the nerves in patterns on a screen:
Would it have been worth while
If one, settling a pillow or throwing off a shawl,
And turning toward the window, should say:
        'That is not it at all,
        That is not what I meant, at all.'

        . . . . .

No! I am not Prince Hamlet, nor was meant to be;
Am an attendant lord, one that will do
To swell a progress, start a scene or two,
Advise the prince; no doubt, an easy tool,
Deferential, glad to be of use,

Politic, cautious, and meticulous;
Full of high sentence, but a bit obtuse;
At times, indeed, almost ridiculous—
Almost, at times, the Fool.

I grow old . . . I grow old . . .
I shall wear the bottoms of my trousers rolled.

Shall I part my hair behind? Do I dare to eat a peach?
I shall wear white flannel trousers, and walk upon the beach.
I have heard the mermaids singing, each to each.

I do not think that they will sing to me.

I have seen them riding seaward on the waves
Combing the white hair of the waves blown back
When the wind blows the water white and black.

We have lingered in the chambers of the sea
By sea-girls wreathed with seaweed red and brown
Till human voices wake us, and we drown.

THE ECLIPSE

Daniel Curley

It was an awful day in a series of awful days. All morning—it was the fifth Wednesday morning in a row—Mason had sat in the courthouse lobby across from his wife, pretending to read in order to avoid meeting her eyes or seeming to listen when she talked with her lawyer. He tried to listen of course, but he could hear very little. He wondered what her lawyer was saying to her. When his own lawyer came out and talked to him, he still wondered what was being said. And when the two lawyers went back into the judge's chambers arm in arm, he wondered what they said to each other, what to the judge. He felt at times as if he were standing at a supermarket checkout, watching aghast as the clerk rang up an endless tape of items he hadn't intended to buy. Often they were alone in the lobby with the statue of Lincoln, a hand extended to each of them but eyes still fiercely on Stephen Douglas. She knitted row after row, upstaging him as usual. He could only bring a book, a solid respectable book, and make sure he had it right side up and kept his head bent over it.

His lawyer came out at noon and said, "That's all for today." Mason shrugged. He was no longer outraged.

The lawyer assumed a stance like Lincoln and said—probably with an eye on his biographer—" 'The hungry judges soon the sentence sign, / And wretches hang that jury-men may dine,' " He was a very literary sort of lawyer.

"Just so," Mason said. He started for the stairs.

"Next Wednesday," the lawyer called after him.

"Same time, same place," Mason said without turning.

"Just so," the lawyer said. It was his phrase after all.

Mason turned his back on his office and instinctively walked in the direction where he would meet open country the soonest. He chose back streets, mostly deserted, for he felt himself surrounded by a force field of gloom and despair, an object of loathing to himself and others. He knew they could feel what he was, and he didn't want to see it in their faces. That would be too much. Especially he didn't want to see it in Sandy's face.

"You aren't really like that, Mr. Mason," she had said. She was a kid then, a student at the university working part-time in his office.

"Like what?"

"Like the things you say."

"Such as what?"

"Such as, 'Most men live lives of quiet desperation.'"

"Don't they?"

"I don't believe it, and I don't think you do either."

"I think I do."

"You're putting yourself on," she said.

"Good lord," he said. "What a language."

"And you don't believe men's lives are 'nasty, brutish, and short' either."

"But if I think I believe it, how can you say I don't?"

"I just feel it."

"That's getting pretty esoteric for me," he said.

"It's just something I sense. I don't listen to you really."

"Well, thank you very much."

"You know what I mean, Mr. Mason."

"Of course I do, but it's all very tenuous." His vocabulary was very refined in those days.

"It's what I feel," she said. "I feel it very strongly." She walked out of the office one day and walked in again ten years later. Mason had thought about her from time to time, and after five years or so of thinking decided he should have fucked her. It would have been statutory rape then, and his wife might have had him thrown in jail. But then, she might have divorced him. Who knows?

"Hello, Mr. Mason," she said when she came back.

"Long coffee break," Mason said.

"I was trying for the record," she said.

"My wife set that," Mason said. "She went out in aught and fifty and isn't back yet. Still on the payroll. Twenty-two years. You're just a piker but I'm glad to see you."

"I'm glad to see you, too, Mr. Mason," she said.

"Perhaps we can drop that Mr. Mason stuff," Mason said.

"OK."

"Unless you're coming back to work, of course."

"No, I don't think so."

"Too bad."

"You might say we have some unfinished business, though," she said.

"You might say that," Mason said. So they finished—or began—it that afternoon. He had had a lot of time to think about it.

And that was what at last had brought him into court after twenty years—more—of marriage. He thought he had discovered what it was all about. He went around smiling at people. People even smiled at him. He thought he had discovered what he was really like. He wasn't Old Gruff-and-Grim after all. Not that he was exactly an enchanted prince, although he felt pretty fine most of the time. A weight that had been on his shoulders fell off—a house, a wife, children, a business, all fell off and rolled away somewhere out of sight. He straightened up and looked around him. He walked on the balls of his feet. A new man—a rediscovered man. At once he wanted to make an honest woman of Sandy, but she didn't see it that way at all.

"Marry?" she said. "After ten rotten years of rotten marriage? I'd have to be crazy."

"Oh," Mason said. He hadn't thought about it that way. He guessed he was an incurable romantic.

"I'm the incurable romantic," she said. "I keep thinking there's got to be something better than marriage."

The question proved to be academic in any case, because his wife laughed at the idea of divorce. "Keep your whore," she said. "I'm keeping the house and the car and the paycheck and the insurance and the retirement and the social security and Medicare and Medicaid and the eleventh *Britannica*."

"What do I get?" Mason said foolishly.

"Fair is fair," she said. "You get what you want, and I get what I want."

So there they sat week after week in court while the lawyers got what they wanted.

The street he was walking along was very quiet. It wasn't a through street. There were stop signs at every corner. The trees were large and old. In places the brick sidewalks were completely overgrown by grass. The small clapboard houses were close to the sidewalk but very private, with large vine-covered porches.

At first Mason had to go on living at home. His wife kept all the money, and he couldn't afford to live anywhere else. Sometimes Sandy took him out to dinner when her alimony check came in, but mostly he ate at home, which wasn't as bad as it might have been, because his wife rarely spoke to him and wouldn't eat with him. At least he didn't have to listen to her jaw click as she chewed. It wasn't perfect but it was still a lot better than before Sandy.

He was better. Even when fits of his old despair returned, he knew he was better. He laughed sometimes—he laughed a lot. It was like old times with his own family when he was little. There had been laughter then. Sandy had changed him completely. He positively radiated, and he could prove it by the girl with the flowers.

That was a rainy afternoon in winter. He was walking home through the park from Sandy's. He was just going to go in and eat whatever his wife set before him and hang on to that island of joy square in the middle of himself. He was walking along in the rain, hanging on, wearing his old army poncho with his head as hidden as a monk's. Vaguely he was aware of someone overtaking him, but he didn't pay any attention until he heard a woman say, "Hold out your hands." Without thinking, he disengaged his hands from his poncho and held them out. Like magic they cradled a bowl of flowers. "I could tell you would like them," she said and went on. "Thank you." he whispered. It *was* like magic. She had had only a shape-less mass to go on as she overtook him. It had to be pure feeling. A month ago she would have run past screaming.

His wife didn't think much of the flowers. "Flower Arranging I at the university," she said. "Any fool can see that. She probably had a roomful already."

"Perhaps," he said, but he couldn't believe less in the magic.

"Or did your whore give them to you to butter me up with? Ugly ar-rangement."

"Perhaps," he said.

"Or has your whore run off with a younger stud at last, so you bought them for me yourself? How touching."

"Perhaps," he said. He was hanging on for dear life, but he was hanging on.

He saw that he was about to pass an old VW bus parked at the curb. He recognized it now. He had walked here at night. There were two hounds that lived in the bus and sprang out as he passed. They scared him stiff. Now, he rather wished they would spring out. He'd like to see how they reacted. He must be giving off a really lovely stink—terror added to despair—but it was always possible that the dogs would sense something else, something even he couldn't be sure of. But the bus was empty, although the stench of the dogs sickened him as he passed. Maybe they only work at night, he thought, but he wasn't sure if he was relieved or disappointed.

"It's crazy," he said to Sandy. "This whole business is crazy. I can't sit down in the middle of a field without having a kitten in my lap within seconds. I'll bet if I tried to cross Times Square at 3 A.M. some nice old lady would grab my arm and see me across."

"That's a crock of shit," Sandy said.

"What's a crock of shit?" Mason said. Knowing her had done something to his vocabulary.

"That feeling business is a crock of shit."

"I learned it from you," he said.

"The body replaces each and every cell within seven years," she said. "I am not the person you learned it from."

"Oh," he said, "I thought it was you."

"You have a lot to learn," she said. She was right, of course. He could only be humble.

He had his own opinion, however. And things were improving. Not fast enough to suit him but definitely improving. Especially since the judge had allowed him to keep a little of his check, enough for a cheap apartment and a pound of hamburger now and then. He had thought it might be easier if he and Sandy pooled their hamburger, shared an apartment, but she wasn't ready to live with anyone. In a way he was grateful. He was grateful at night when he was too tired to be polite to anyone and when he needed the whole bed to toss in. He was grateful when he was too awful in the morning. And he was grateful when he just wanted to scratch himself and fart and go to sleep. He wanted to live with Sandy and would have sacrificed these luxuries for her, but he knew they were luxuries and enjoyed them. They were doing him good. Everything was doing him good.

Take the spacey old man in the supermarket. Space calling to space. Mason had been working all night—spending afternoons with Sandy had put him behind in his work. He thought he would just buy himself a little liver for breakfast—another luxury of living alone. His wife never gave him liver because she didn't like the smell. Everything was very clear and deep in the early morning light. He felt he was walking just a little off the floor, perhaps enough to slide a sheet of paper under the soles of his boots. He didn't think anyone would notice, but as he was struggling to free a grocery cart from the stack, an old man came up and said, "Howdy."

"Oh," Mason said, freeing his cart at last, "lovely morning, isn't it?"

The old man took a cart and came along. "A little cold," he said.

Mason was uneasy with people who said Howdy. Either they had you sized up or they were hiding behind it like a beard. The old man had a beard too, but he looked very much the real thing. "Seasonal," Mason said.

"Time to buy seed for my birds," the old man said. "They'll be back any day now."

"Yes indeed," Mason said, moving on.

"I must feed a hundred during the winter," the old man said, keeping pace. "They'll be back soon. The teal have gone. I saw two flights. They're the first."

"Early for geese," Mason said. He wondered how the old man knew that the one nice thing he took when he moved out of the house was his binoculars, his good bird glasses and the hand-made case he had designed himself.

"The geese hang on until the last minute," the old man said. He stopped beside the sacks of birdseed.

"Sometimes even after," Mason said. He stopped too. "I've seen some waxwings."

"What do you know?" the old man said. "I guess I missed them this year. Glad to hear of them, though."

"Have a good winter," Mason said. He went off toward the meats.

"Same to you," the old man called. "Lots of birds."

Mason waited at a corner for a car to pass, but it sat at the stop sign until he reluctantly looked at the driver and was waved ahead. Coincidence, he said to himself. Just a lonely old man wanting someone to talk to. There was no help there. It had been an awful day. He was awful.

"Would you like to see the eclipse?" someone said. Mason kept going. But he glanced at the sky involuntarily. The sky had cleared. There was going to be an eclipse, almost a total eclipse. It would be visible after all. There had been something about it in the paper, but he had paid little attention. Perhaps it was taking place right now. He knew better than to look at the sun, though.

"Take the glass," his mother said, "and hold it carefully by the edges. Don't rub the smoke off, or the sun will hurt your eyes." They were standing in the driveway between the two houses to keep out of the wind. The sun looked very strange through the dark glass. It was a dark disk with a bright crown. "This is very educational," his mother said. She put her arm around him and drew him tight against the cold fur of her coat. It was soft and smelled lovely like her closet.

"I say, would you like to see the eclipse?" the voice said again. Although it couldn't be speaking to him, Mason stopped. There was no one else who could be spoken to. There was no one who could be speaking. He looked all around carefully and was about to go on when he caught a slight movement among the vine leaves on the nearest porch. Then he saw an old man's face peering out at him. My God, he thought, am I getting to be a crazy old man myself? Can they smell me?

"Would you?" the old man said. He skipped down the steps.

"Why yes," Mason said. "I would. Yes," he said, "I really would."

"I've made a device," the old man said. "I saw how to do it in the paper." He was a thin straight old man, very shabby. Mason guessed a professor retired so long ago that his pension had become almost worthless. "Look," he said. He held up a cardboard box, long and narrow. It was rather like a periscope.

"Yes," Mason said. He handled it gently. He was impressed. He knew he could never make a periscope from directions in the paper. Sometimes he was discouraged by things like that, but now the old man's pleasure outweighed everything.

"Point the top at the sun and look down at the bottom." Mason studied the white paper at the bottom of the box, straining for something too faint for him to see. The old man placed both delicate hands on the device and moved it slightly. "Yes," Mason said. "Yes, there it is." And there it was, a small but perfect image of the sun with a small but perfect bite out of the side.

"It's wonderful," Mason said.

"Isn't it?" the old man said.

"I don't know how to thank you," Mason said. "I had forgotten all about it and would have missed it completely." He handed the periscope back to the old man, who received it lightly on his outstretched palms. "I must be getting on," he said. It was nearly time to call Sandy to report that nothing had happened again. It was only what they expected, but he had to hear her say it didn't matter.

The old man took another look at the sun. Mason looked, too. They said goodbye.

As he went back through the dappled shade, he thought, It *is* all right. It's not awful at all.

ISAAC AND ARCHIBALD

Edwin Arlington Robinson

To Mrs. Henry Richards

Isaac and Archibald were two old men.
I knew them, and I may have laughed at them
A little; but I must have honored them
For they were old, and they were good to me.

I do not think of either of them now,
Without remembering, infallibly,
A journey that I made one afternoon
With Isaac to find out what Archibald
Was doing with his oats. It was high time
Those oats were cut, said Isaac; and he feared
That Archibald—well, he could never feel
Quite sure of Archibald. Accordingly
The good old man invited me—that is,
Permitted me—to go along with him;
And I, with a small boy's adhesiveness
To competent old age, got up and went.

I do not know that I cared overmuch
For Archibald's or anybody's oats,
But Archibald was quite another thing.

From *Collected Poems* by Edwin Arlington Robinson. New York: Macmillan, 1922.

And Isaac yet another; and the world
Was wide, and there was gladness everywhere.
We walked together down the River Road
With all the warmth and wonder of the land
Around us, and the wayside flash of leaves,—
And Isaac said the day was glorious;
But somewhere at the end of the first mile
I found that I was figuring to find
How long those ancient legs of his would keep
The pace that he had set for them. The sun
Was hot, and I was ready to sweat blood;
But Isaac, for aught I could make of him,
Was cool to his hat-band. So I said then
With a dry gasp of affable despair,
Something about the scorching days we have
In August without knowing it sometimes;
But Isaac said the day was like a dream.
And praised the Lord, and talked about the breeze.
I made a fair confession of the breeze,
And crowded casually on his thought
The nearness of a profitable nook
That I could see. First I was half inclined
To caution him that he was growing old,
But something that was not compassion soon
Made plain the folly of all subterfuge.
Isaac was old, but not so old as that.

So I proposed, without an overture,
That we be seated in the shade a while,
And Isaac made no murmur. Soon the talk
Was turned on Archibald, and I began
To feel some premonitions of a kind
That only childhood knows; for the old man
Had looked at me and clutched me with his eye,
And asked if I had ever noticed things.
I told him that I could not think of them,
And I knew then, by the frown that left his face
Unsatisfied, that I had injured him.
"My good young friend," he said, "you cannot feel

What I have seen so long. You have the eyes—
Oh, yes—but you have not the other things;
The sight within that never will deceive,
You do not know—you have no right to know;
The twilight warning of experience,
The singular idea of loneliness,—
These are not yours. But they have long been mine,
And they have shown me now for seven years
That Archibald is changing. It is not
So much that he should come to his last hand,
And leave the game, and go the old way down;
But I have known him in and out so long,
And I have seen so much of good in him
That other men have shared and have not seen,
And I have gone so far through thick and thin,
Through cold and fire with him, that now it brings
To this old heart of mine an ache that you
Have not yet lived enough to know about.
But even unto you, and your boy's faith,
Your freedom, and your untried confidence,
A time will come to find out what it means
To know that you are losing what was yours,
To know that you are being left behind;
And then the long contempt of innocence—
God bless you, boy!—don't think the worse of it
Because an old man chatters in the shade—
Will all be like a story you have read
In childhood and remembered for the pictures.
And when the best friend of your life goes down,
When first you know in him the slackening
That comes, and coming always tells the end,—
Now in a common word that would have passed
Uncaught from any other lips than his,
Now in some trivial act of every day,
Done as he might have done it all along
But for a twinging little difference
That nips you like a squirrel's teeth—oh, yes,
Then you will understand it well enough.
But oftener it comes in other ways;

It comes without your knowing when it comes;
You know that he is changing, and you know
That he is going—just as I know now
That Archibald is going, and that I
Am staying. . . . Look at me, my boy,
And when the time shall come for you to see
That I must follow after him, try then
To think of me, to bring me back again,
Just as I was to-day. Think of the place
Where we are sitting now, and think of me—
Think of old Isaac as you knew him then,
When you set out with him in August once
To see old Archibald.''—The words come back
Almost as Isaac must have uttered them,
And there comes with them a dry memory
Of something in my throat that would not move.

If you had asked me then to tell just why
I made so much of Isaac and the things
He said, I should have gone far for an answer;
For I knew it was not sorrow that I felt,
Whatever I may have wished it, or tried then
To make myself believe. My mouth was full
Of words, and they would have been comforting
To Isaac, spite of my twelve years, I think;
But there was not in me the willingness
To speak them out. Therefore I watched the ground;
And I was wondering what made the Lord
Create a thing so nervous as an ant,
When Isaac, with commendable unrest,
Ordained that we should take the road again—
For it was yet three miles to Archibald's,
And one to the first pump. I felt relieved
All over when the old man told me that;
I felt that he had stilled a fear of mine
That those extremities of heat and cold
Which he had long gone through with Archibald
Had made the man impervious to both;
But Isaac had a desert somewhere in him,

And at the pump he thanked God for all things
That He had put on earth for men to drink,
And he drank well,—so well that I proposed
That we go slowly lest I learn too soon
The bitterness of being left behind,
And all those other things. That was a joke
To Isaac, and it pleased him very much;
And that pleased me—for I was twelve years old.

At the end of an hour's walking after that
The cottage of old Archibald appeared.
Little and white and high on a smooth round hill
It stood, with hackmatacks and apple-trees
Before it, and a big barn-roof beyond;
And over the place—trees, houses, fields and all—
Hovered an air of still simplicity
And a fragrance of old summers—the old style
That lives the while it passes. I dare say
That I was lightly conscious of all this
When Isaac, of a sudden, stopped himself,
And for the long first quarter of a minute
Gazed with incredulous eyes, forgetful quite
Of breezes and of me and of all else
Under the scorching sun but a smooth-cut field,
Faint yellow in the distance. I was young.
But there were a few things that I could see,
And this was one of them.—"Well, well!" said he;
And "Archibald will be surprised, I think,"
Said I. But all my childhood subtlety
Was lost on Isaac, for he strode along
Like something out of Homer—powerful
And awful on the wayside, so I thought.
Also I thought how good it was to be
So near the end of my short-legged endeavor
To keep the pace with Isaac for five miles.

Hardly had we turned in from the main road
When Archibald, with one hand on his back
And the other clutching his huge-headed cane,

Came limping down to meet us.—"Well! well! well!"
Said he; and then he looked at my red face,
All streaked with dust and sweat, and shook my hand,
And said it must have been a right smart walk
That we had had that day from Tilbury Town.—
"Magnificent." said Isaac; and he told
About the beautiful west wind there was
Which cooled and clarified the atmosphere.
"You must have made it with your legs, I guess."
Said Archibald; and Isaac humored him
With one of those infrequent smiles of his
Which he kept in reserve, apparently,
For Archibald alone. "But why," said he,
"Should Providence have cider in the world
If not for such an afternoon as this?"
And Archibald, with a soft light in his eyes,
Replied that if he chose to go down cellar,
There he would find eight barrels—one of which
Was newly tapped, he said, and to his taste
An honor to the fruit. Isaac approved
Most heartily of that, and guided us
Forthwith, as if his venerable feet
Were measuring the turf in his own door-yard,
Straight to the open rollway. Down we went,
Out of the fiery sunshine to the gloom,
Grateful and half sepulchral, where we found
The barrels, like eight potent sentinels,
Close ranged along the wall. From one of them
A bright pine spile stuck out alluringly,
And on the black flat stone, just under it,
Glimmered a late-spilled proof that Archibald
Had spoken from unfeigned experience.
There was a fluted antique water-glass
Close by, and in it, prisoned, or at rest,
There was a cricket, of the brown soft sort
That feeds on darkness. Isaac turned him out,
And touched him with his thumb to make him jump,
And then composedly pulled out the plug
With such a practised hand that scarce a drop

Did even touch his fingers. Then he drank
And smacked his lips with a slow patronage
And looked along the line of barrels there
With a pride that may have been forgetfulness
That they were Archibald's and not his own.
"I never twist a spigot nowadays,"
He said, and raised the glass up to the light,
"But I thank God for orchards." And that glass
Was filled repeatedly for the same hand
Before I thought it worth while to discern
Again that I was young, and that old age,
With all his woes, had some advantages.

"Now, Archibald," said Isaac, when we stood
Outside again, "I have it in my mind
That I shall take a sort of little walk—
To stretch my legs and see what you are doing.
You stay and rest your back and tell the boy
A story: Tell him all about the time
In Stafford's cabin forty years ago,
When four of us were snowed up for ten days
With only one dried haddock. Tell him all
About it, and be wary of your back.
Now I will go along."—I looked up then
At Archibald, and as I looked I saw
Just how his nostrils widened once or twice
And then grew narrow. I can hear to-day
The way the old man chuckled to himself—
Not wholesomely, not wholly to convince
Another of his mirth,—as I can hear
The lonely sigh that followed.—But at length
He said: "The orchard now's the place for us;
We may find something like an apple there,
And we shall have the shade, at any rate."
So there we went and there we laid ourselves
Where the sun could not reach us; and I champed
A dozen of worm-blighted astrakhans
While Archibald said nothing—merely told
The tale of Stafford's cabin, which was good,

Though "master chilly"—after his own phrase—
Even for a day like that. But other thoughts
Were moving in his mind, imperative,
And writhing to be spoken: I could see
The glimmer of them in a glance or two,
Cautious, or else unconscious, that he gave
Over his shoulder: . . . "Stafford and the rest—
But that's an old song now, and Archibald
And Isaac are old men. Remember, boy,
That we are old. Whatever we have gained,
Or lost, or thrown away, we are old men.
You look before you and we look behind,
And we are playing life out in the shadow—
But that's not all of it. The sunshine lights
A good road yet before us if we look,
And we are doing that when least we know it;
For both of us are children of the sun,
Like you, and like the weed there at your feet.
The shadow calls us, and it frightens us—
We think; but there's a light behind the stars
And we old fellows who have dared to live,
We see it—and we see the other things,
The other things . . . Yes, I have seen it come
These eight years, and these ten years, and I know
Now that it cannot be for very long
That Isaac will be Isaac. You have seen—
Young as you are, you must have seen the strange
Uncomfortable habit of the man?
He'll take my nerves and tie them in a knot
Sometimes, and that's not Isaac. I know that—
And I know what it is: I get it here
A little, in my knees, and Isaac—here."
The old man shook his head regretfully
And laid his knuckles three times on his forehead.
"That's what it is: Isaac is not quite right.
You see it, but you don't know what it means:
The thousand little differences—no,
You do not know them, and it's well you don't;
You'll know them soon enough—God bless you, boy!—
You'll know them, but not all of them—not all.

So think of them as little as you can:
There's nothing in them for you, or for me—
But I am old and I must think of them;
I'm in the shadow, but I don't forget
The light, my boy,—the light behind the stars.
Remember that: remember that I said it;
And when the time that you think far away
Shall come for you to say it—say it, boy;
Let there be no confusion or distrust
In you, no snarling of a life half lived,
Nor any cursing over broken things
That your complaint has been the ruin of.
Live to see clearly and the light will come
To you, and as you need it.—But there, there,
I'm going it again, as Isaac says,
And I'll stop now before you go to sleep.—
Only be sure that you growl cautiously,
And always where the shadow may not reach you.''

Never shall I forget, long as I live,
The quaint thin crack in Archibald's voice,
The lonely twinkle in his little eyes,
Or the way it made me feel to be with him.
I know I lay and looked for a long time
Down through the orchard and across the road,
Across the river and the sun-scorched hills
That ceased in a blue forest, where the world
Ceased with it. Now and then my fancy caught
A flying glimpse of a good life beyond—
Something of ships and sunlight, streets and singing,
Troy falling, and the ages coming back,
And ages coming forward: Archibald
And Isaac were good fellows in old clothes,
And Agamemnon was a friend of mine;
Ulysses coming home again to shoot
With bows and feathered arrows made another,
And all was as it should be. I was young.

So I lay dreaming of what things I would,
Calm and incorrigibly satisfied

With apples and romance and ignorance,
And the still smoke from Archibald's clay pipe.
There was a stillness over everything,
As if the spirit of heat had laid its hand
Upon the world and hushed it; and I felt
Within the mightiness of the white sun
That smote the land around us and wrought out
A fragrance from the trees, a vital warmth
And fullness for the time that was to come,
And a glory for the world beyond the forest.
The present and the future and the past,
Isaac and Archibald, the burning bush,
The Trojans and the walls of Jericho,
Were beautifully fused; and all went well
Till Archibald began to fret for Isaac
And said it was a master day for sunstroke.
That was enough to make a mummy smile,
I thought; and I remained hilarious,
In face of all precedence and respect,
Till Isaac (who had come to us unheard)
Found he had no tobacco, looked at me
Peculiarly, and asked of Archibald
What ailed the boy to make him chirrup so.
From that he told us what a blessed world
The Lord had given us.—"But, Archibald,"
He added, with a sweet severity
That made me think of peach-skins and goose-flesh,
"I'm half afraid you cut those oats of yours
A day or two before they were well set."
"They were set well enough," said Archibald,—
And I remarked the process of his nose
Before the words came out. "But never mind
Your neighbor's oats: you stay here in the shade
And rest yourself while I go find the cards.
We'll have a little game of seven-up
And let the boy keep count."—"We'll have the game,
Assuredly," said Isaac; "and I think
That I will have a drop of cider, also."

They marched away together towards the house
And left me to my childish ruminations
Upon the ways of men. I followed them
Down cellar with my fancy, and then I left them
For a fairer vision of all things at once
That was anon to be destroyed again
By the sound of voices and of heavy feet—
One of the sounds of life that I remember,
Though I forget so many that rang first
As if they were thrown down to me from Sinai.

So I remember, even to this day,
Just how they sounded, how they placed themselves,
And how the game went on while I made marks
And crossed them out, and meanwhile made some Trojans
Likewise I made Ulysses, after Isaac,
And a little after Flaxman. Archibald
Was injured when he found himself left out,
But he had no heroics, and I said so:
I told him that his white beard was too long
And too straight down to be like things in Homer.
"Quite so," said Isaac.—"Low," said Archibald;
And he threw down a deuce with a deep grin
That showed his yellow teeth and made me happy.
So they played on till a bell rang from the door,
And Archibald said, "Supper."—After that
The old men smoked while I sat watching them
And wondered with all comfort what might come
To me, and what might never come to me;
And when the time came for the long walk home
With Isaac in the twilight, I could see
The forest and the sunset and the sky-line,
No matter where it was that I was looking:
The flame beyond the boundary, the music,
The foam and the white ships, and two old men
Were things that would not leave me.—And that night
There came to me a dream—a shining one,
With two old angels in it. They had wings,

And they were sitting where a silver light
Suffused them, face to face. The wings of one
Began to palpitate as I approached,
But I was yet unseen when a dry voice
Cried thinly, with unpatronizing triumph,
"I've got you, Isaac; high, low, jack, and the game."

Isaac and Archibald have gone their way
To the silence of the loved and well-forgotten.
I knew them, and I may have laughed at them;
But there's a laughing that has honor in it,
And I have no regret for light words now.
Rather I think sometimes they may have made
Their sport of me;—but they would not do that,
They were too old for that. They were old men,
And I may laugh at them because I knew them.

THE CRIES OF LOVE

Patricia Highsmith

Hattie pulled the little chain of the reading lamp, drew the covers over her shoulders and lay tense, waiting for Alice's sniffs and coughs to subside.

"Alice?" she said.

No response. Yes, she was sleeping already, though she said she never closed an eye before the clock struck eleven.

Hattie eased herself to the edge of the bed and slowly put out a white-stockinged foot. She twisted round to look at Alice, of whom nothing was visible except a thin nose projecting between the ruffle of her nightcap and the sheet pulled over her mouth. She was quite still.

Hattie rose gently from the bed, her breath coming short with excitement. In the semi-darkness she could see the two sets of false teeth in their glasses of water on the bed table. She giggled, nervously.

Like a white ghost she made her way across the room, past the Victorian settle. She stopped at the sewing table, lifted the folding top and groped among the spools and pattern papers until she found the scissors. Then, holding them tightly, she crossed the room again. She had left the wardrobe door slightly ajar earlier in the evening, and it swung open noiselessly. Hattie reached a trembling hand into the blackness, felt the two woollen coats, a few dresses. Finally she touched a fuzzy thing, and lifted the hanger down. The scissors slipped out of her hand. There was a clatter, followed by her half-suppressed laughter. She peeked round the wardrobe door at Alice, motionless on the bed. Alice was rather hard of hearing.

With her white toes turned up stiffly, Hattie clumped to the easy chair by the window where a bar of moonlight slanted, and sat down with the scissors and the angora sweater in her lap. In the moonlight her face gleamed, toothless and demoniacal. She examined the sweater in the manner of a person who toys with a piece of steak before deciding where to put his knife.

It was really a lovely sweater. Alice had received it the week before from her niece as a birthday present. Alice would never have indulged herself in such a luxury. She was happy as a child with the sweater and had worn it every day over her dresses.

The scissors cut purringly up the soft wool sleeves, between the wristbands and the shoulders. She considered. There should be one more cut. The back, of course. But only about a foot long, so it wouldn't be immediately visible.

A few seconds later, she had put the scissors back into the table, hung the sweater in the wardrobe, and was lying under the covers. She heaved a tremendous sigh. She thought of the gaping sleeves, of Alice's face in the morning. The sweater was quite beyond repair, and she was immensely pleased with herself.

They were awakened at eight-thirty by the hotel maid. It was a ritual that never failed: three bony raps on the door and a bawling voice with a hint of insolence, "Eight-thirty! You can get breakfast now!" Then Hattie, who always woke first, would poke Alice's shoulder.

Mechanically they sat up on their respective sides of the bed and pulled their nightgowns over their heads, revealing clean white undergarments. They said nothing. Seven years of co-existence had pared their conversation to an economical core.

This morning, however, Hattie's mind was on the sweater. She felt self-conscious, but she could think of nothing to say or do to relieve the tension, so she spent more time than usual with her hair. She had a braid nearly two feet long that she wound around her head, and every morning she undid it for its hundred strokes. Her hair was her only vanity. Finally, she stood shifting uneasily, pretending to be fastening the snaps on her dress.

Alice seemed to take an age at the washbasin, gargling with her solution of tepid water and salt. She held stubbornly to water and salt in the mornings, despite Hattie's tempting bottle of red mouthwash setting on the shelf.

"What are you giggling at now?" Alice turned from the basin, her face wet and smiling a little.

Hattie could say nothing, looked at the teeth in the glass on the bed table and giggled again. "Here's your teeth." She reached the glass awkwardly to Alice. "I thought you were going down to breakfast without them."

"Now when did I *ever* go off without my teeth, Hattie?"

Alice smiled to herself. It was going to be a good day, she thought. Mrs. Crumm and her sister were back from a weekend, and they could all play gin rummy together in the afternoon. She walked to the wardrobe in her stockinged feet.

Hattie watched as she took down the powder-blue dress, the one that went best with the beige angora sweater. She fastened all the little buttons in front. Then she took the sweater from the hanger and put one arm into a sleeve.

"Oh!" she breathed painfully. Then like a hurt child her eyes almost closed and her face twisted petulantly. Tears came quickly down her cheeks. "H-Hattie—"

Hattie smirked, uncomfortable yet enjoying herself thoroughly. "Well, I do know!" she exclaimed. "I wonder who could have done a trick like that!" She went to the bed and sat down, doubled up with laughter.

"Hattie, you did this," Alice declared in an unsteady voice. She clutched the sweater to her. "Hattie, you're just wicked!"

Lying across the bed, Hattie was almost hysterical. "You know I didn't now, Alice . . . hah-haw! . . . Why do you think I'd—" Her voice was choked off by incontrollable laughing.

Hattie lay there several minutes before she was calm enough to go down to breakfast. And when she left the room, Alice was sitting in the big chair by the window, sobbing, her face buried in the angora sweater.

Alice did not come down until she was called for lunch. She chatted at the table with Mrs. Crumm and her sister and took no notice of Hattie. Hattie sat opposite her, silent and restless, but not at all sorry for what she had done. She could have endured days of indifference on Alice's part without feeling the slightest remorse.

It was a beautiful day. After lunch, they went with Mrs. Crumm, her sister, and the hotel hostess, Mrs. Holland, and sat in Gramercy Park.

Alice pretended to be absorbed in her book. It was a detective story by her favorite author, borrowed from the hotel's circulating library. Mrs. Crumm and her sister did most of the talking. A weekend trip provided conversation for several afternoons, and Mrs. Crumm was able to remember every item of food she had eaten for days running.

The monotonous tones of the voices, the warmth of the sunshine, lulled Alice into half-sleep. The page was blurred to her eyes.

Earlier in the day, she had planned to adopt an attitude toward Hattie. She should be cool and aloof. It was not the first time Hattie had committed an outrage. There had been the ink spilt on her lace tablecloth months ago, the day before she was going to give it to her niece . . . And her missing volume of Tennyson that was bound in morocco. She was sure Hattie had it, somewhere. She decided that that evening she should calmly pack her bag, write Hattie a note, short but well worded, and leave the hotel. She would go to another hotel in the neighborhood, let it be known through Mrs. Crumm where she was, and have the satisfaction of Hattie's coming to her and apologizing. But the fact was, she was not at all sure Hattie would come to her, and this embarrassing possibility prevented her from taking such a dangerous course. What if she had to spend the rest of her life alone? It was much easier to stay where she was, to have a pleasant game of gin rummy in the afternoons, and to take out her revenge in little ways. It was also more ladylike, she consoled herself. She did not think beyond this, of the particular times she would say or do things calculated to hurt Hattie. The opportunities would just come of themselves.

Mrs. Holland nudged her. "We're going to get some ice cream now. Then we're going to play some gin rummy."

"I was just at the most exciting part of the book." But Alice rose with the others and was almost cheerful as they walked to the drugstore.

Alice won at gin rummy, and felt pleased with herself. Hattie, watching her uneasily all day, was much relieved when she decreed speaking terms again.

Nevertheless, the thought of the ruined sweater rankled in Alice's mind, and prodded her with a sense of injustice. Indeed, she was ashamed of herself for being able to take it as lightly as she did. It was letting Hattie walk over her. She wished she could muster a really strong hatred.

They were in their room reading at nine o'clock. Every vestige of Hattie's shyness or pretended contrition had vanished.

"Wasn't it a nice day?" Hattie ventured.

"Um-hm." Alice did not raise her head.

"Well," Hattie made the inevitable remark through the inevitable yawn. "I think I'll be going off to bed."

And a few minutes later they were both in bed, propped up by four pillows, Hattie with the newspaper and Alice with her detective story. They were silent for a while, then Hattie adjusted her pillows and lay down.

"Good night, Alice."

"Good night."

Soon Alice pulled out the light, and there was absolute silence in the room except for the soft ticking of the clock and the occasional purr of an automobile. The clock on the mantel whirred and began to strike ten.

Alice lay open-eyed. All day her tears had been restrained, and now she began to cry. But they were not the childish tears of the morning, she felt. She wiped her nose on the top of the sheet.

She raised herself on one elbow. The darkish braid of hair outlined Hattie's neck and shoulder against the white bedclothes. She felt very strong, strong enough to murder Hattie with her own hands. But the idea of murder passed from her mind as swiftly as it had entered. Her revenge had to be something that would last, that would hurt, something that Hattie must endure and that she herself could enjoy.

Then it came to her, and she was out of bed, walking boldly to the sewing table, as Hattie had done twenty-four hours before . . . and she was standing by the bed, bending over Hattie, peering at her placid, sleeping face through her tears and her shortsighted eyes. Two quick strokes of the scissors would cut through the braid, right near the head. But Alice lowered the scissors just a little, to where the braid was tighter. She squeezed the scissors with both hands, made them chew on the braid, as Hattie slowly awakened with the touch of cold metal on her neck. *Whack*, and it was done.

"What is it? . . . What—?" Hattie said.

The braid was off, lying like a dark gray snake on the bed cover.

"Alice!" Hattie said, and groped at her neck, felt the stiff ends of the braid's stump. "Alice!"

Alice stood a few feet away, staring at Hattie who was sitting up in bed, and suddenly Alice was overcome with mirth. She tittered, and at the same time tears started in her eyes. "You did it to me!" she said. "You cut my sweater!"

Alice's instant of self-defense was unnecessary, because Hattie was absolutely crumpled and stunned. She started to get out of bed, as if to go to the mirror, but sat back again, moaning and weeping, feeling of the horrid thing at the end of her hair. Then she lay down again, still moaning into her pillow. Alice stayed up, and sat finally in the easy chair. She was full of energy, not sleepy at all. But toward dawn, when Hattie slept, Alice crept between the covers.

Hattie did not speak to her in the morning, and did not look at her.

Hattie put the braid away in a drawer. Then she tied a scarf around her head to go down to breakfast, and in the dining room, Hattie took another table from the one at which Alice and she usually sat. Alice saw Hattie speaking to Mrs. Holland after breakfast.

A few minutes later, Mrs. Holland came over to Alice, who was reading in a corner of the lounge.

"I think," Mrs. Holland said gently, "that you and your friend might be happier if you had separate rooms for a while, don't you?"

This took Alice by surprise, though at the same time she had been expecting something worse. Her prepared statement about the spilt ink, the missing Tennyson, and the ruined angora subsided in her, and she said quite briskly, "I do indeed, Mrs. Holland. I'm agreeable to anything Hattie wishes."

Alice offered to move out, but it was Hattie who did. She moved to a smaller room three doors down on the same floor.

That night, Alice could not sleep. It was not that she thought about Hattie particularly, or that she felt in the least sorry for what she had done —she decidedly didn't—but that things, the room, the darkness, even the clock's ticking, were so different because she was alone. A couple of times during the night, she heard a footstep outside the door, and thought it might be Hattie coming back, but it was only people visiting the W.C. at the end of the hall. It occurred to Alice that she could knock on Hattie's door and apologize but, she asked herself, why should she?

In the morning, Alice could tell from Hattie's appearance that she hadn't slept either. Again, they did not speak or look at each other all day, and during the gin rummy and tea at four, they managed to take different tables. Alice slept very badly that night also, and blamed it on the lamb stew at dinner, which she was having trouble digesting. Hattie would have the same trouble, perhaps, as Hattie's digestion was, if anything, worse.

Three more days and nights passed, and the ravages of Hattie's and Alice's sleepless nights became apparent on their faces. Mrs. Holland noticed, and offered Alice some sedatives, which Alice politely declined. She had her pride, she wasn't going to show anyone she was disturbed by Hattie's absence, and besides, she thought it was weak and self-indulgent to yield to sleeping pills—though perhaps Hattie would.

On the fifth day, at three in the afternoon, Hattie knocked on Alice's door. Her head was still swathed in a scarf, one of three that Hattie possessed, and this was one Alice had given her last Christmas.

"Alice, I want to say I'm sorry, if *you're* sorry," Hattie said, her lips twisting and pursing as she fought to keep back the tears.

This was or should have been a moment of triumph for Alice. It was, mainly, she felt, though something—she was not sure what—tarnished it a little, made it not quite pure victory. "I am sorry about your braid, if you're sorry about my sweater," Alice replied.

"I am," said Hattie.

"And about the ink stain on my tablecloth and . . . where is my volume of Alfred Lord Tennyson's poems?"

"I have not got it," Hattie said, still tremulous with tears.

"You haven't *got* it?"

"No," Hattie declared positively.

And in a flash, Alice knew what had really happened: Hattie had at some point, in some place, destroyed it, so it was in a way true now that she hadn't "got" it. Alice knew, too, that she must not stick over this, that she ought to forgive and forget it, though neither emotionally nor intellectually did she come to this decision: she simply knew it, and behaved accordingly, saying, "Very well, Hattie. You may move back, if you wish."

Hattie then moved back, though at the card game at four-thirty they still sat at separate tables.

Hattie, having swallowed the biggest lump of pride she had ever swallowed in knocking on Alice's door and saying she was sorry, slept very much better back in the old arrangement, but suffered a lurking sense of unfairness. After all, a book of poems and a sweater could be replaced, but could her hair? Alice had got back at her all right, and then some. The score was not quite even.

After a few days, Hattie and Alice were back to normal, saying little to each other, but outwardly being congenial, taking meals and playing cards at the same table. Mrs. Holland seemed pleased.

It crossed Alice's mind to buy Hattie some expensive hair tonic she saw in a Madison Avenue window one day while on an outing with Mrs. Holland and the group. But Alice didn't. Neither did she buy a "special treatment" for hair which she saw advertised in the back of a magazine, guaranteed to make the hair grow thicker and faster, but Alice read every word of the advertisements.

Meanwhile, Hattie struggled in silence with her stump of braid, brushed her hair faithfully as usual, but only when Alice was having her bath or was out of the room, so Alice would not see it. Nothing in Alice's possession now seemed important enough for Hattie's vengeance. But Christmas was coming soon. Hattie determined to wait patiently and see what Alice got then.

MINNIE REMEMBERS

Donna Swanson

God, my hands are old.
I've never said that out loud before
but they are.
I was so proud of them once.
They were soft
like the velvet smoothness of a
     firm, ripe peach.
Now the softness is more like
worn out sheets
or withered leaves.
When did these slender, graceful hands
become gnarled, shrunken claws?
When, God?
They lie here in my lap;
naked reminders of this worn out
body that has served me too well.

How long has it been since someone
     touched me?
Twenty years?
Twenty years I've been a widow.
Respected.
Smiled at.

Reprinted, with permission, from *Mind Song*, by Donna Swanson. Nashville, Tenn.: Upper Room. Copyright 1978 by Donna Swanson.

But never touched.
Never held so close that loneliness
was blotted out.

I remember how my mother used to hold
        me, God.
When I was hurt in spirit or flesh,
she would gather me close,
stroke my silky hair,
and caress my back with her warm
        hands.
Oh God, I'm so lonely!

I remember the first boy who ever
        kissed me.
We were both so new at that!
The taste of young lips and popcorn,
the feeling inside of mysteries to
    come.

I remember Hank and the babies.
How else can I remember them
but together?
For out of the fumbling, awkward attempts
of new lovers
came the babies.
And, as they grew, so did our love.
And, God, Hank didn't seem to mind
if my body thickened and faded a little.
He still loved it
and touched it.
And we didn't mind if we were no longer
        beautiful.
And it felt so good.
And the children hugged me a lot.
Oh God, I'm lonely!

God, why didn't we raise the kids
to be silly and affectionate

as well as dignified and proper.
You see, they do their duty.
They drive up in their fine cars.
They come to my room
to pay their respects.
They chatter brightly and reminisce.
But they don't touch me.
They call me Mom, or Mother
or Grandma.

Never Minnie.
My mother called me Minnie.
So did my friends.
Hank called me Minnie, too.
But they're gone.
And so is Minnie.
Only Grandma is here.

And God! She's lonely!

WHAT LIPS MY LIPS HAVE KISSED

Edna St. Vincent Millay

What lips my lips have kissed, and where, and why,
I have forgotten, and what arms have lain
Under my head till morning; but the rain
Is full of ghosts tonight, that tap and sigh
Upon the glass and listen for reply;
And in my heart there stirs a quiet pain
For unremembered lads that not again
Will turn to me at midnight with a cry.

Thus in the winter stands the lonely tree,
Nor knows what birds have vanished one by one,
Yet knows its boughs more silent than before:
I cannot say what loves have come and gone;
I only know that summer sang in me
A little while, that in me sings no more.

OLD MAN MINICK

Edna Ferber

His wife had always spoiled him outrageously. No doubt of that.
Take, for example, the matter of the pillows merely. Old man Minick
slept high. That is, he thought he slept high. He liked two plump pillows
on his side of the great, wide, old-fashioned cherry bed. He would sink into them with a vast grunting and sighing and puffing expressive of nerves
and muscles relaxed and gratified. But in the morning there was always
one pillow on the floor. He had thrown it there. Always, in the morning,
there it lay, its plump white cheek turned reproachfully up at him from
the side of the bed. Ma Minick knew this, naturally, after forty years of the
cherry bed. But she never begrudged him that extra pillow. Each morning, when she arose, she picked it up on her way to shut the window. Each
morning the bed was made up with two pillows on his side of it, as usual.

Then there was the window. Ma Minick liked it open wide. Old man
Minick, who rather prided himself on his modernism (he called it being
up to date), was distrustful of the night air. In the folds of its sable mantle
lurked a swarm of dread things—colds, clammy miasmas, fevers.

"Night air's just like any other air," Ma Minick would say, with some
asperity. Ma Minick was no worm; and as modern as he. So when they
went to bed the window would be open wide. They would lie there, the
two old ones, talking comfortably about commonplace things. The kind
of talk that goes on between a man and woman who have lived together in
wholesome peace (spiced with occasional wholesome bickerings) for more
than forty years.

"Remind me to see Gerson to-morrow about that lock on the basement door. The paper's full of burglars."

"If I think of it." She never failed to.

"George and Nettie haven't been over in a week now."

"Oh, well, young folks . . . Did you stop in and pay that Koritz the fifty cents for pressing your suit?"

"By golly, I forgot again! First thing in the morning."

A sniff. "Just smell the Yards." It was Chicago.

"Wind must be from the west."

Sleep came with reluctant feet, but they wooed her patiently. And presently she settled down between them and they slept lightly. Usually, some time during the night, he awoke, slid cautiously and with infinite stealth from beneath the covers, and closed the wide-flung window to within a bare two inches of the sill. Almost invariably she heard him; but she was a wise old woman; a philosopher of parts. She knew better than to allow a window to shatter the peace of their marital felicity. As she lay there, smiling a little grimly in the dark and giving no sign of being awake, she thought, "Oh, well, I guess a closed window won't kill me either."

Still, sometimes, just to punish him a little, and to prove that she was nobody's fool, she would wait until he had dropped off to sleep again and then she, too, would achieve a stealthy trip to the window and would raise it slowly, carefully, inch by inch.

"How did that window come to be open?" he would say in the morning, being a poor dissembler.

"Window? Why, it's just the way it was when we went to bed." And she would stoop to pick up the pillow that lay on the floor.

There was little or no talk of death between this comfortable, active, sound-appearing man of almost seventy and this plump capable woman of sixty-six. But as always, between husband and wife, it was understood wordlessly (and without reason) that old man Minick would go first. Not that either of them had the slightest intention of going. In fact, when it happened they were planning to spend the winter in California and perhaps live there indefinitely if they liked it and didn't get too lonesome for George and Nettie, and the Chicago smoke, and Chicago noise, and Chicago smells and rush and dirt. Still, the solid sum paid yearly in insurance premiums showed clearly that he meant to leave her in comfort and security. Besides, the world is full of widows. Every one sees that. But how many widowers? Few. Widows there are by the thousands; living alone; living in hotels; living with married daughters and sons-in-law or married sons and daughters-in-law. But of widowers in a like situation there are bewilderingly few. And why this should be no one knows.

So, then. The California trip never materialised. And the year that followed never was quite clear in old man Minick's dazed mind. In the first place, it was the year in which stocks tumbled and broke their backs. Gilt-edged securities showed themselves to be tinsel. Old man Minick had retired from active business just one year before, meaning to live comfortably on the fruit of a half-century's toil. He now saw that fruit rotting all about him. There was in it hardly enough nourishment to sustain them. Then came the day when Ma Minick went downtown to see Matthews about that pain right here and came home looking shrivelled, talking shrilly about nothing, and evading Pa's eyes. Followed months that were just a jumble of agony, X-rays, hope, despair, morphia, nothingness.

After it was all over: "But I was going first," old man Minick said, dazedly.

The old house on Ellis near Thirty-ninth was sold for what it would bring. George, who knew Chicago real estate if any one did, said they might as well get what they could. Things would only go lower. You'll see. And nobody's going to have any money for years. Besides, look at the neighbourhood!

Old man Minick said George was right. He said everybody was right. You would hardly have recognised in this shrunken figure and wattled face the spruce and dressy old man whom Ma Minick used to spoil so delightfully. "You know best, George. You know best." He who used to stand up to George until Ma Minick was moved to say, "Now, Pa, you don't know everything."

After Matthews' bills, and the hospital, and the nurses and the medicines and the thousand and one things were paid there was left exactly five hundred dollars a year.

"You're going to make your home with us, Father," George and Nettie said. Alma, too, said this would be the best. Alma, the married daughter, lived in Seattle. "Though you know Ferd and I would be only too glad to have you."

Seattle! The ends of the earth. Oh, no. No! he protested, every fibre of his old frame clinging to the accustomed. Seattle, at seventy! He turned piteous eyes on his son George and his daughter-in-law Nettie. "You're going to make your home with us, Father," they reassured him. He clung to them gratefully. After it was over Alma went home to her husband and their children.

So now he lived with George and Nettie in the five-room flat on South Park Avenue, just across from Washington Park. And there was no extra pillow on the floor.

Nettie hadn't said he couldn't have the extra pillow. He had told her he used two and she had given him two the first week. But every morning she had found a pillow cast on the floor.

"I thought you used two pillows, Father."

"I do."

"But there's always one on the floor when I make the bed in the morning. You always throw one on the floor. You only sleep on one pillow, really."

"I use two pillows."

But the second week there was one pillow. He tossed and turned a good deal there in his bedroom off the kitchen. But he got used to it in time. Not used to it, exactly, but—well—

The bedroom off the kitchen wasn't as menial as it sounds. It was really rather cosy. The five-room flat held living room, front bedroom, dining room, kitchen, and maid's room. The room off the kitchen was intended as a maid's room but Nettie had no maid. George's business had suffered with the rest. George and Nettie had said, "I wish there was a front room for you, Father. You could have ours and we'd move back here, only this room's too small for twin beds and the dressing table and the chiffonier." They had meant it—or meant to mean it.

"This is fine," old man Minick had said. "This is good enough for anybody." There was a narrow white enamel bed and a tiny dresser and a table. Nettie had made gay cretonne covers and spreads and put a little reading lamp on the table and arranged his things. Ma Minick's picture on the dresser with her mouth sort of pursed to make it look small. It wasn't a recent picture. Nettie and George had had it framed for him as a surprise. They had often urged her to have a picture taken, but she had dreaded it. Old man Minick didn't think much of that photograph, though he never said so. He needed no photograph of Ma Minick. He had a dozen of them; a gallery of them; thousands of them. Lying on his one pillow he could take them out and look at them one by one as they passed in review, smiling, serious, chiding, praising, there in the dark. He needed no picture on his dresser.

A handsome girl, Nettie, and a good girl. He thought of her as a girl, though she was well past thirty. George and Nettie had married late. This was only the third year of their marriage. Alma, the daughter, had married young, but George had stayed on, unwed, in the old house on Ellis until he was thirty-six and all Ma Minick's friends' daughters had had a try at him in vain. The old people had urged him to marry, but it had been wonderful to have him around the house, just the same. Somebody young around the house. Not that George had stayed around very much. But when he was there you knew he was there. He whistled while dressing. He sang in the bath. He roared down the stairway, ''Ma, where's my clean shirts?'' The telephone rang for him. Ma Minick prepared special dishes for him. The servant girl said, ''Oh, now, Mr. George, look what you've done! Gone and spilled the grease all over my clean kitchen floor!'' and wiped it up adoringly while George laughed and gobbled his bit of food filched from pot or frying pan.

They had been a little surprised about Nettie. George was in the bond business and she worked for the same firm. A plump, handsome, eye-glassed woman with fine fresh colouring, a clear skin that old man Minick called appetising, and a great coil of smooth dark hair. She wore plain tailored things and understood the bond buisness in a way that might have led you to think her a masculine mind if she hadn't been so feminine, too, in her manner. Old man Minick had liked her better than Ma Minick had.

Nettie had called him Pop and joked with him and almost flirted with him in a daughterly sort of way. He liked to squeeze her plump arm and pinch her soft cheek between thumb and forefinger. She would laugh up at him and pat his shoulder and that shoulder would straighten spryly and he would waggle his head doggishly.

''Look out there, George!'' the others in the room would say. ''Your dad'll cut you out. First thing you know you'll lose your girl, that's all.''

Nettie would smile. Her teeth were white and strong and even. Old man Minick would laugh and wink, immensely pleased and flattered. ''We understand each other, don't we, Pop?'' Nettie would say.

During the first years of their married life Nettie stayed home. She fussed happily about her little flat, gave parties, went to parties, played bridge. She seemed to love the ease, the relaxation, the small luxuries. She and George were very much in love. Before her marriage she had lived in a boarding house on Michigan Avenue. At mention of it now she puckered up her face. She did not attempt to conceal her fondness for these five rooms of hers, so neat, so quiet, so bright, so cosy. Over-stuffed velvet in the living room, with silk lamp-shades, and small tables holding books and magazines and little boxes containing cigarettes or hard candies. Very modern. A gate-legged table in the dining room. Caramel-coloured walnut in the bedroom, rich and dark and smooth. She loved it. An orderly woman. Everything in its place. Before eleven o'clock the little apartment was shining, spotless; cushions plumped, crumbs brushed, vegetables in cold water. The telephone. "Hello! . . . Oh, hello, Bess! Oh, hours ago . . . Not a thing . . . Well, if George is willing . . . I'll call him up and ask him. We haven't seen a show in two weeks. I'll call you back within the next half hour . . . No, I haven't done my marketing yet. . . . Yes, and have dinner downtown. Meet at seven.''

Into this orderly smooth-running mechanism was catapulted a bewildered old man. She no longer called him Pop. He never dreamed of squeezing the plump arm or pinching the smooth cheek. She called him Father. Sometimes George's Father. Sometimes, when she was telephoning, there came to him—''George's father's living with us now, you know. I can't.''

They were very kind to him, Nettie and George. ''Now just you sit right down here, Father. What do you want to go poking off into your own room for?''

He remembered that in the last year Nettie had said something about going back to work. There wasn't enough to do around the house to keep her busy. She was sick of afternoon parties. Sew and eat, that's all, and gossip, or play bridge. Besides, look at the money. Business was awful. The two old people had resented this idea as much as George had—more, in fact. They were scandalised.

''Young folks nowadays!'' shaking their heads. ''Young folks nowadays. What are they thinking of! In my days when you got married you had babies.''

George and Nettie had had no babies. At first Nettie had said, ''I'm so happy. I just want a chance to rest. I've been working since I was seventeen. I just want to rest, first.'' One year. Two years. Three. And now Pa Minick.

Ma Minick, in the old house on Ellis Avenue, had kept a loose sort of larder; not lavish, but plentiful. They both ate a great deal, as old people are likely to do. Old man Minick, especially, had liked to nibble. A handful of raisins from the box on the shelf. A couple of nuts from the dish on the sideboard. A bit of candy rolled beneath the tongue. At dinner (sometimes, toward the last, even at noon-time) a plate of steaming soup, hot, revivifying, stimulating. Plenty of this and plenty of that. ''What's the matter, Jo? You're not eating.'' But he was, amply. Ma Minick had liked to see him eat too much. She was wrong, of course.

But at Nettie's things were different. Hers was a sufficient but stern ménage. So many mouths to feed; just so many lamb chops. Nettie knew about calories and vitamins and mysterious things like that, and talked about them. So many calories in this. So many calories in that. He never was quite clear in his mind about these things said to be lurking in his food. He had always thought of spinach as spinach, chops as chops. But to Nettie they were calories. They lunched together, these two. George was, of course, downtown. For herself Nettie would have one of those feminine pick-up lunches; a dab of apple sauce, a cup of tea, and a slice of cold toast left from breakfast. This she would eat while old man Minick guiltily supped up his cup of warmed-over broth, or his coddled egg. She always pressed upon him any bit of cold meat that was left from the night before, or any remnants of vegetable or spaghetti. Often there was quite a little fleet of saucers and sauce plates grouped about his main plate. Into these he dipped and swooped uncomfortably, and yet with a relish. Sometimes, when he had finished, he would look about, furtively.

"What'll you have, Father? Can I get you something?"

"Nothing, Nettie, nothing. I'm doing fine." She had finished the last of her wooden toast and was waiting for him kindly.

Still, this balanced and scientific fare seemed to agree with him. As the winter went on he seemed actually to have regained most of his former hardiness and vigour. A handsome old boy he was, ruddy, hale, with the zest of a juicy old apple, slightly withered but still sappy. It should be mentioned that he had a dimple in his cheek which flashed unexpectedly when he smiled. It gave him a roguish—almost boyish—effect most appealing to the beholder. Especially the feminine beholder. Much of his spoiling at the hands of Ma Minick had doubtless been due to this mere depression of the skin.

Spring was to bring a new and welcome source of enrichment into his life. But these first six months of his residence with George and Nettie were hard. No spoiling there. He missed being made much of. He got kindness, but he needed love. Then, too, he was rather a gabby old man. He liked to hold forth. In the old house on Ellis there had been visiting back and forth between men and women of his own age, and Ma's. At these gatherings he had waxed oratorical or argumentative, and they had heard him, some in agreement, some in disagreement, but always respectfully, whether he prated of real estate or social depravity; prohibition or European exchange.

"Let me tell you, here and now, something's got to be done before you can get a country back on a sound financial basis. Why, take Russia alone, why . . . " Or: "Young people nowadays! They don't know what respect means. I tell you there's got to be a change and there will be, and it's the older generation that's got to bring it about. What do they know of hardship! What do they know about work—real work. Most of 'em's never done a real day's work in their life. All they think of is dancing and gambling and drinking. Look at the way they dress! Look at . . . "

Ad lib.

"That's so," the others would agree. "I was saying only yesterday . . . "

Then, too, until a year or two before, he had taken active part in business. He had retired only at the urging of Ma and the children. They said he ought to rest and play and enjoy himself.

Now, as his strength and good spirits gradually returned he began to go downtown, mornings. He would dress, carefully, though a little shakily. He had always shaved himself and he kept this up. All in all, during the day, he occupied the bathroom literally for hours, and this annoyed Nettie to the point of frenzy, through she said nothing. He liked the white cheerfulness of the little tiled room. He puddled about in the water endlessly. Snorted and splashed and puffed and snuffled and blew. He was one of those audible washers who emerge dripping and whose ablutions are distributed impartially over ceiling, walls, and floor.

Nettie, at the closed door: "Father, are you all right?"

Splash! Prrrf! "Yes. Sure. I'm all right."

"Well, I didn't know. You've been in there so long."

He was a neat old man, but there was likely to be a spot or so on his vest or his coat lapel, or his tie. Ma used to remove these, on or off him, as the occasion demanded, rubbing carefully and scolding a little, making a chiding sound between tongue and teeth indicative of great impatience of his carelessness. He had rather enjoyed these sounds, and this rubbing and scratching on the cloth with the fingernail and moistened rag. They indicated that some one cared. Cared about the way he looked. Had pride in him. Loved him. Nettie never removed spots. Though infrequently she said, "Father, just leave that suit out, will you? I'll send it to the cleaner's with George's. The man's coming to-morrow morning." He would look down at himself, hastily, and attack a spot here and there with a futile fingernail.

His morning toilette completed, he would make for the Fifty-first Street L. Seated in the train he would assume an air of importance and testy haste; glance out of the window; look at his watch. You got the impres-

sion of a handsome and well-preserved old gentleman on his way downtown to consummate a shrewd business deal. He had been familiar with
Chicago's downtown for fifty years and he could remember when State
Street was a tree-shaded cottage district. The noise and rush and clangour
of the Loop had long been familiar to him. But now he seemed to find the
downtown trip arduous, even hazardous. The roar of the elevated trains,
the hoarse hoots of the motor horns, the clang of the street cars, the bed-
lam that is Chicago's downtown district bewildered him, frightened him
almost. He would skip across the street like a harried hare, just missing a
motor truck's nose and all unconscious of the stream of invective directed
at him by its charioteer. "Heh! Whatcha! . . . Look!"— Sometimes a
policeman came to his aid, or attempted to, but he resented his proffered
help.

"Say, look here, my lad," he would say to the tall, tired, and not at
all burly (standing on one's feet directing traffic at Wabash and Madison
for eight hours a day does not make for burliness) policeman, "I've been
coming downtown since long before you were born. You don't need to
help me. I'm no jay from the country."

He visited the Stock Exchange. This depressed him. Stocks were lower than ever and still going down. His five hundred a year was safe, but the
rest seemed doomed for his lifetime, at least. He would drop in at George's
office. George's office was pleasantly filled with dapper, neat young men
and (surprisingly enough) dapper, slim young women, seated at desks in
the big light-flooded room. At one corner of each desk stood a polished
metal placard on a little standard and bearing the name of the desk's oc-
cupant. Mr. Owens. Mr. Satterlee. Mr. James. Miss Rauch. Mr. Minick.

"Hello, Father," Mr. Minick would say, looking annoyed. "What's
bringing you down?"

"Oh, nothing. Nothing. Just had a little business to tend to over at
the Exchange. Thought I'd drop in. How's business?"

"Rotten."

"I should think it was!" Old man Minick would agree. "I—should
—think it—was! Hm."

George wished he wouldn't. He couldn't have it, that's all. Old man
Minick would stroll over to the desk marked Satterlee, or Owens, or James.
These brisk young men would toss an upward glance at him and concentrate again on the sheets and files before them. Old man Minick would
stand, balancing from heel to toe and blowing out his breath a little. He
looked a bit yellow and granulated and wavering, there in the cruel morn-

ing light of the big plate glass windows. Or perhaps it was the contrast he presented with these slim, slick young salesmen.

"Well, h'are you to-day, Mr.—uh—Satterlee? What's the good word?"

Mr. Satterlee would not glance up this time. "I'm pretty well. Can't complain."

"Good. Good."

"Anything I can do for you?"

"No-o-o. No. Not a thing. Just dropped in to see my son a minute."

"I see." Not unkindly. Then, as old man Minick still stood there, balancing, Mr. Satterlee would glance up again, frowning a little. "Your son's desk is over there, I believe. Yes."

George and Nettie had a bedtime conference about these visits and Nettie told him gently, that the bond house head objected to friends and relatives dropping in. It was against office rules. It had been so when she was employed there. Strictly business. She herself had gone there only once since her marriage.

Well, that was all right. Business was like that nowadays. Rush and grab and no time for anything.

The winter was a hard one, with a record snowfall and intense cold. He stayed indoors for days together. A woman of his own age in like position could have occupied herself usefully and happily. She could have hemmed a sash-curtain; knitted or crocheted; tidied a room; taken a hand in the cooking or preparing of food; ripped an old gown; made over a new one; indulged in an occasional afternoon festivity with women of her own years. But for old man Minick there were no small tasks. There was nothing he could do to make his place in the household justifiable. He wasn't even particularly good at those small jobs of hammering, or painting, or general "fixing." Nettie could drive a nail more swiftly, more surely than he. "Now, Father, don't you bother. I'll do it. Just you go and sit down. Isn't it time for your afternoon nap?"

He waxed a little surly. "Nap! I just got up. I don't want to sleep my life away."

George and Nettie frequently had guests in the evening. They played bridge, or poker, or talked.

"Come in, Father," George would say. "Come in. You all know Dad, don't you, folks?" He would sit down, uncertainly. At first he had attempted to expound, as had been his wont in the old house on Ellis. "I want to say, here and now, that this country's got to . . . " But they went on, heedless of him. They interrupted or refused, politely, to listen. So he sat in the room, yet no part of it. The young people's talk swirled and eddied all about him. He was utterly lost in it. Now and then Nettie or George would turn to him and with raised voice (he was not at all deaf and prided himself on it) would shout, "It's about this or that, Father. He was saying . . ."

When the group roared with laughter at a sally from one of them he would smile uncertainly but amiably, glancing from one to the other in complete ignorance of what had passed, but not resenting it. He took to sitting more and more in his kitchen bedroom, smoking a comforting pipe and reading and re-reading the evening paper. During that winter he and Canary, the negro washwoman, became quite good friends. She washed down in the basement once a week but came up to the kitchen for her massive lunch. A walrus-waisted black woman, with a rich throaty voice, a rolling eye, and a kindly heart. He actually waited for her appearance above the laundry stairs.

"Weh, how's Mist' Minick to-day! Ah nev' did see a gemun spry's you ah fo' you' age. No, suh! Nev' did."

At this rare praise he would straighten his shoulders and waggle his head. "I'm worth any ten of these young sprats to-day." Canary would throw back her head in a loud and companionable guffaw.

Nettie would appear at the kitchen swinging door. "Canary's having her lunch, Father. Don't you want to come into the front room with me? We'll have our lunch in another half-hour."

He followed her obediently enough. Nettie thought of him as a troublesome and rather pathetic child—a child who would never grow up. If she attributed any thoughts to that fine old head they were ambling thoughts, bordering, perhaps, on senility. Little did she know how expertly this old one surveyed her and how ruthlessly he passed judgment. She never suspected the thoughts that formed in the active brain.

He knew about women. He had married a woman. He had had children by her. He looked at this woman—his son's wife—moving about her little five-room flat. She had theories about children. He had heard her expound them. You didn't have them except under such and such circumstances. It wasn't fair otherwise. Plenty of money for their education. Well. He and his wife had had three children. Paul, the second, had died at thirteen. A blow, that had been. They had not always planned for the coming of the three but they always had found a way, afterward. You managed, somehow, once the little wrinkled red ball had fought its way into the world. You managed. You managed. Look at George! Yet when he was born, thirty-nine years ago, Pa and Ma Minick had been hard put to it.

Sitting there, while Nettie dismissed him as negligible, he saw her clearly, grimly. He looked at her. She was plump, but not too short, with a generous width between the hips; a broad full bosom, but firm; round arms and quick slim legs; a fine sturdy throat. The curve between arm and breast made a graceful, gracious line . . . Working in a bond office . . . Working in a bond office . . . There was nothing in the Bible about working in a bond office. Here was a woman built for child-bearing.

She thought him senile, negligible.

In March Nettie had in a sewing woman for a week. She had her two or three times a year. A hawk-faced woman of about forty-nine, with a blue-bottle figure and a rapacious eye. She sewed in the dining room and there was a pleasant hum of machine and snip of scissors and murmur of conversation and rustle of silky stuff; and hot savoury dishes for lunch. She and old man Minick became great friends. She even let him take out bastings. This when Nettie had gone out from two to four, between fittings.

He chuckled and waggled his head. "I expect to be paid regular assistant's wages for this," he said.

"I guess you don't need any wages, Mr. Minick," the woman said. "I guess you're pretty well fixed."

"Oh, well, I can't complain." (Five hundred a year.)

"Complain! I should say not! If I was to complain it'd be different. Work all day to keep myself; and nobody to come home to at night."

"Widow, ma'am?"

"Since I was twenty. Work, work, that's all I've had. And lonesome! I suppose you don't know what lonesome is."

"Oh, don't I!" slipped from him. He had dropped the bastings.

The sewing woman flashed a look at him from the cold hard eye. "Well, maybe you do. I suppose living here like this, with sons and daughters, ain't so grand, for all your money. Now me, I've always managed to keep my own little place that I could call home, to come back to. It's only two rooms, and nothing to rave about, but it's home. Evenings I just cook and fuss around. Nobody to fuss for, but I fuss, anyway. Cooking, that's what I love to do. Plenty of good food, that's what folks need to keep their strength up." Nettie's lunch that day had been rather scant.

She was there a week. In Nettie's absence she talked against her. He protested, but weakly. Did she give him egg-noggs? Milk? Hot toddy? Soup? Plenty of good rich gravy and meat and puddings? Well! That's

what folks needed when they weren't so young any more. Not that he
looked old. My, no. Spryer than many young boys, and handsomer than
his own son if she did say so.

He fed on it, hungrily. The third day she was flashing meaning glances
at him across the luncheon table. The fourth she pressed his foot beneath
the table. The fifth, during Nettie's afternoon absence, she got up, ostensibly to look for a bit of cloth which she needed for sewing, and, passing
him, laid a caressing hand on his shoulder. Laid it there and pressed his
shoulder ever so little. He looked up, startled. The glances across the luncheon had largely passed over his head; the foot beneath the table might
have been an accident. But this—this was unmistakable. He stood up, a
little shakily. She caught his hand. The hawk-like face was close to his.

"You need somebody to love you," she said. "Somebody to do for
you, and love you." The hawk face came nearer. He leaned a little toward
it. But between it and his face was Ma Minick's face, plump, patient, quizzical, kindly. His head came back sharply. He threw the woman's hot
hand from him.

"Woman!" he cried. "Jezebel!"

The front door slammed. Nettie. The woman flew to her sewing.
Old man Minick, shaking, went into his kitchen bedroom.

"Well," said Nettie, depositing her bundles on the dining-room
table, "did you finish that faggoting? Why, you haven't done so very
much, have you!"

"I ain't feeling so good," said the woman. "That lunch didn't agree
with me."

"Why, it was a good plain lunch. I don't see—"

"Oh, it was plain enough, all right."

Next day she did not come to finish her work. Sick, she telephoned.
Nettie called it an outrage. She finished the sewing herself, though she
hated sewing. Pa Minick said nothing, but there was a light in his eye.
Now and then he chuckled, to Nettie's infinite annoyance, though she
said nothing.

"Wanted to marry me!" he said to himself, chuckling. "Wanted to
marry me! The old rip!"

At the end of April, Pa Minick discovered Washington Park, and the
Club, and his whole life was from that day transformed.

He had taken advantage of the early spring sunshine to take a walk,
at Nettie's suggestion.

"Why don't you go into the Park, Father? It's really warm out. And the sun's lovely. Do you good.''

He had put on his heaviest shirt, and a muffler, and George's old red sweater with the great white "C" on its front, emblem of George's athletic prowess at the University of Chicago; and over all, his greatcoat. He had taken warm mittens and his cane with the greyhound's-head handle, carved. So equipped he had ambled uninterestedly over to the Park across the way. And there he had found new life.

New life in old life. For the Park was full of old men. Old men like himself, with greyhound's-head canes, and mufflers and somebody's sweater worn beneath their greatcoats. They wore arctics, though the weather was fine. The skin of their hands and cheek-bones was glazed and had a tight look though it lay in fine little folds. There were splotches of brown on the backs of their hands, and on the temples and forehead. Their heavy grey or brown socks made comfortable folds above their ankles. From that April morning until winter drew on the Park saw old man Minick daily. Not only daily but by the day. Except for his meals, and a brief hour for his after-luncheon nap, he spent all his time there.

For in the Park old man Minick and all the old men gathered there found a Forum—a safety valve—a means of expression. It did not take him long to discover that the Park was divided into two distinct sets of old men. There were the old men who lived with their married sons and daughters-in-law or married daughters and sons-in-law. Then there were the old men who lived in the Grant Home for Aged Gentlemen. You saw its fine red-brick façade through the trees at the edge of the Park.

And the slogan of these first was:

"My son and my da'ter they wouldn't want me to live in any public Home. No, sirree! They want me right there with them. In their own home. That's the kind of son and daughter I've got!''

The slogan of the second was:

"I wouldn't live with any son or daughter. Independent. That's me. My own boss. Nobody to tell me what I can do and what I can't. Treat you like a child. I'm my own boss! Pay my own good money and get my keep for it.''

The first group, strangely enough, was likely to be spotted of vest and a little frayed as to collar. You saw them going on errands for their daughters-in-law. A loaf of bread. Spool of white No. 100. They took their small grandchildren to the duck pond and between the two toddlers hand in hand—the old and infirm and the infantile and infirm—it was hard to tell which led which.

The second group was shiny as to shoes, spotless as to linen, dapper as to clothes. They had no small errands. Theirs was a magnificent leisure. And theirs was magnificent conversation. The questions they discussed and settled there in the Park—these old men—were not international merely. They were cosmic in scope.

The War? Peace? Disarmament? China? Free love? Mere conversational bubbles to be tossed in the air and disposed of in a burst of foam. Strong meat for old man Minick who had so long been fed on pap. But he soon got used to it. Between four and five in the afternoon, in a spot known as Under The Willows, the meeting took the form of a club—an open forum. A certain group made up of Socialists, Free Thinkers, parlour anarchists, bolshevists, had for years drifted there for talk. Old man Minick learned high-sounding phrases. "The Masters . . . democracy . . . toil of the many for the good of the few . . . the ruling class . . . free speech . . . the People . . . ''

The strong-minded ones held forth. The weaker ones drifted about on the outskirts, sometimes clinging to the moist and sticky paw of a round-eyed grandchild. Earlier in the day—at eleven o'clock, say—the talk was not so general nor so inclusive. The old men were likely to drift into groups of two or three or four. They sat on sun-bathed benches and their conversation was likely to be rather smutty at times, for all they looked so mild and patriarchal and desiccated. They paid scant heed to the white-haired old women who, like themselves, were sunning in the park. They watched the young women switch by, with appreciative glances at their trim figures and slim ankles. The day of the short skirt was a grand time for them. They chuckled among themselves and made wicked comment. One saw only white-haired, placid, tremulous old men, but their minds still worked with belated masculinity like naughty small boys talking behind the barn.

Old man Minick early achieved a certain leadership in the common talk. He had always liked to hold forth. This last year had been one of almost unendurable bottling up. At first he had timidly sought the less assertive ones of his kind. Mild old men who sat in rockers in the pavilion waiting for lunch time. Their conversation irritated him. They remarked everything that passed before their eyes.

"There's a boat. Fella with a boat."

A silence. Then, heavily: "Yeh."

Five minutes.

"Look at those people laying on the grass. Shouldn't think it was warm enough for that . . . Now they're getting up."

A group of equestrians passed along the bridle path on the opposite side of the lagoon. They made a frieze against the delicate spring greenery. The coats of the women were scarlet, vivid green, arresting, stimulating.

"Riders."

"Yes."

"Good weather for riding."

A man was fishing near by. "Good weather for fishing."

"Yes."

"Wonder what time it is, anyway." From a pocket, deep-buried, came forth a great gold blob of a watch. "I've got one minute to eleven."

Old man Minick dragged forth a heavy globe. "Mm. I've got eleven."

"Little fast, I guess."

Old man Minick shook off this conversation impatiently. This wasn't conversation. This was oral death, though he did not put it thus. He joined the other men. They were discussing Spiritualism. He listened, ventured an opinion, was heard respectfully and then combated mercilessly. He rose to the verbal fight, and won it.

"Let's see," said one of the old men. "You're not living at the Grant Home, are you?"

"No," old man Minick made reply, proudly. "I live with my son and his wife. They wouldn't have it any other way."

"Hm. Like to be independent myself."

"Lonesome, ain't it? Over there?"

"Lonesome! Say, Mr.—what'd you say your name was? Minick? Mine's Hughes—I never was lonesome in my life 'cept for six months when I lived with my daughter and her husband and their five children. Yes, sir. That's what I call lonesome, in an eight-room flat."

George and Nettie said, "It's doing you good, Father, being out in the air so much." His eyes were brighter, his figure straighter, his colour better. It was that day he had held forth so eloquently on the emigration question. He had to read a lot—papers and magazines and one thing and another—to keep up. He devoured all the books and pamphlets about bond issues and national finances brought home by George. In the Park he was considered an authority on bonds and banking. He and a retired real estate man named Mowry sometimes debated a single question for weeks. George and Nettie, relieved, thought he ambled to the Park and spent senile hours with his drooling old friends discussing nothing amiably and witlessly. This while he was eating strong meat, drinking strong drink.

Summer sped. Was past. Autumn held a new dread for old man Minick. When winter came where should he go? Where should he go? Not back to the five-room flat all day, and the little back bedroom, and nothingness. In his mind there rang a childish old song they used to sing at school. A silly song:

> Where do all the birdies go?
> *I* know. *I* know.

But he didn't know. He was terror-stricken. October came and went. With the first of November the Park became impossible, even at noon, and with two overcoats and the sweater. The first frost was a black frost for him. He scanned the heavens daily for rain or snow. There was a cigar store and billiard room on the corner across the boulevard and there he sometimes went, with a few of his Park cronies, to stand behind the players' chairs and watch them at pinochle or rum. But this was a dull business. Besides, the Grant men never came there. They had card rooms of their own.

He turned away from his smoky little den on a drab November day, sick at heart. The winter. He tried to face it, and at what he saw he shrank and was afraid.

He reached the apartment and went around to the rear, dutifully. His rubbers were wet and muddy and Nettie's living-room carpet was a fashionable grey. The back door was unlocked. It was Canary's day downstairs, he remembered. He took off his rubbers in the kitchen and passed into the dining room. Voices. Nettie had company. Some friends, probably for tea. He turned to go to his room, but stopped at hearing his own name. Father Minick. Father Minick. Nettie's voice.

"Of course, if it weren't for Father Minick I would have. But how can we as long as he lives with us? There isn't room. And we can't afford a bigger place now, with rents what they are. This way it wouldn't be fair to the child. We've talked it over, George and I. Don't you suppose? But not as long as Father Minick is with us. I don't mean we'd use the maid's room for a—for the—if we had a baby. But I'd have to have some one in to help, then, and we'd have to have that extra room."

He stood there in the dining room, quiet. Quiet. His body felt queerly remote and numb, but his mind was working frenziedly. Clearly, too, in spite of the frenzy. Death. That was the first thought. Death. It would be easy. But he didn't want to die. Strange, but he didn't want to die. He liked Life. The Park, the trees, the Club, the talk, the whole show. . . . Nettie was a good girl . . . The old must make way for the young. They had the right to be born . . . Maybe it was just another excuse. Almost four years married. Why not three years ago? . . . The right to live. The right to live. . . .

He turned, stealthily, stealthily, and went back into the kitchen, put on his rubbers, stole out into the darkening November afternoon.

In an hour he was back. He entered at the front door this time, ringing the bell. He had never had a key. As if he were a child they would not trust him with one. Nettie's women friends were just leaving. In the air you smelled a mingling of perfume, and tea, and cakes, and powder. He sniffed it, sensitively.

"How do you do, Mr. Minick!" they said. "How are you! Well, you certainly look it. And how do you manage these gloomy days?"

He smiled genially, taking off his greatcoat and revealing the red sweater with the big white "C" on it. "I manage, I manage." He puffed out his cheeks. "I'm busy moving."

"Moving!" Nettie's startled eyes flew to his, held them. "Moving, Father?"

"Old folks must make way for the young," he said gaily. "That's the law of life. Yes, sir! New ones. New ones."

Nettie's face was scarlet. "Father, what in the world—"

"I signed over at the Grant Home to-day. Move in next week." The women looked at her, smiling. Old man Minick came over to her and patted her plump arm. Then he pinched her smooth cheek with a quizzical thumb and forefinger. Pinched it and shook it ever so little.

"I don't know what you mean," said Nettie, out of breath.

"Yes, you do," said old man Minick, and while his tone was light and jesting there was in his old face something stern, something menacing. "Yes, you do."

When he entered the Grant Home a group of them was seated about the fireplace in the main hall. A neat, ruddy, septuagenarian circle. They greeted him casually, with delicacy of feeling, as if he were merely approaching them at their bench in the Park.

"Say, Minick, look here. Mowry here says China ought to have been included in the four-power treaty. He says—"

Old man Minick cleared his throat. "You take China, now," he said, "with her vast and practically, you might say, virgin country, why—"

An apple-cheeked maid in a black dress and a white apron stopped before him. He paused.

"Housekeeper says for me to tell you your room's all ready, if you'd like to look at it now."

"Minute. Minute, my child." He waved her aside with the air of one who pays five hundred a year for independence and freedom. The girl turned to go. "Uh—young lady! Young lady!" She looked at him. "Tell the housekeeper two pillows, please. Two pillows on my bed. Be sure."

"Yes, sir. Two pillows. Yes, sir. I'll be sure."

2

THE FAMILY LIFE CYCLE

Our need to connect with other human beings, to establish intimate relationships, extends throughout the life span. One mechanism for creating nurturing interactions is through the primary social unit of the family. The family unit has a developmental cycle of its own, although the rhythm has changed somewhat over the last few generations. People today are marrying slightly later, having fewer children, and divorcing more often. In addition, alternative family styles are emerging; cohabitation, or living together, is more prevalent; and the roles of husband and wife, father and mother are undergoing considerable transformation.

The family context provides a stage where much of the drama of adulthood is carried out. Nearly all men and women in our culture are married at some point in their adult lives, and most couples become parents. Marriage and parenthood, usually occurring in young adulthood, set into motion the family cycle, with its own developmental tasks and role changes. When the youngest child begins school the family unit moves into a new stage of interrelating and role performance. Adults in early middle age must deal with guiding teenagers into adulthood while at the same time finding ways to accommodate their own changing goals. As children leave the family for school, work, or marriage, adults once again enter a transitional period. Without the presence of children to deflect their attention, spouses must sometimes learn to relate on a more direct basis. Adults in late middle age may also find themselves "parenting" their own aging parents. Finally, older adulthood is characterized by adapting to the roles of grandparent and widow(er). Other changes related to the family life cycle such as divorce, remarriage, or death of a child are generally unanticipated. Nevertheless, these unplanned, off-timed events will have a significant impact on the adult's life and may require adjustments that some will be unable to make.

MANY FACETS OF PARENTHOOD

Becoming a new parent is a developmental task that some adjust to positively, while for others it is a period of crisis. The adjustment to the new role with its constraints, its responsibilities, its rewards, is something one can only superficially prepare for. Parenthood is a life event that has to be experienced to be fully understood. In the selection from Anne Richardson Roiphe's novel *Up the Sandbox!* we as readers can feel the frustration and love, the emotional investment involved in being a parent. Even the adult-world thoughts of a new mother are continually brought into check by the demands that two small children make upon the parent in this story.

While the selection from *Up the Sandbox!* gives us a vivid sense of the adjustment to motherhood, there are other stories (not included here) that one might want to read that explore the vicissitudes of the long-term process of parenting. In Tillie Olsen's story "I Stand Here Ironing," for example, the mother traces the struggle of raising a daughter from an infant to a young adult. It has been a journey of pain and worry, accomplishment and joy. Herbert Gold's story "The Heart of the Artichoke" offers a poignant glimpse of parenting and intergenerational relationships from an adolescent's perspective.

A child's teenage years are often as difficult for the parents as they are for the child. For parents, marital instability peaks at this time; for teens it is a period of self-discovery and ambiguity — one is at once a child and an adult. Knox (1977) has noted that much of the conflict between parents and teens arises from three issues that trouble a youth's movement into adulthood and parents' acceptance of their offspring as adults. The first is the issue of limits: parents wonder "when to be firm and how to be permissive without implying lack of concern," while adolescents want to experiment outside boundaries set by parents. Secondly, there is a discrepancy between parents' and teens' expectations with regard to participation in family activities and household chores. Finally, communication problems center on parents' wondering how much to ask about their children's personal lives and how much to reveal of their own, while adolescents are uncertain about "how much to reveal, especially regarding controversial matters" (pp. 104–5).

Very often the greatest distance between parent and child occurs when teenagers move into young adulthood and leave the family unit. At this stage, the "child" is trying to forge an identity separate from that of the parent. Such a task may involve rejection of parental values and experimentation with new life-styles. Differences between generations at this point in the family cycle may be so great that communicating at any meaningful level is an impossible task. Such is the case in the story "Teddy, Where Are You?" by Stephen Minot. Stella tries desperately to understand and accept her college-age son and his live-in girlfriend. It becomes apparent, however, that mother and son no longer have enough in common to sustain them through even a short visit. Neither can accommodate the values and life-style of the other. It is a painful but perhaps necessary stage in the evolving parent-child relationship.

Because the family structure is the primary social unit in our society, the role of parent accompanies nearly everyone throughout adulthood. In a work not included in this anthology, the protagonist in John Updike's *A Month of Sundays* says,

> Society in its conventional wisdom sets a term to childhood; of parenthood there is no riddance. Though the child be a sleek Senator of seventy, and the parent a twisted husk mounted in a wheelchair, the wreck must still grapple with the ponderous sceptre of parenthood (p. 141).

Middle-aged adults, in fact, may find themselves in a dual parenting role — that of being parents to their own fathers and mothers as well as to their teenage offspring. As some elderly persons become less able to care for themselves, either economically or physically, middle-aged children find it necessary to provide the care once given to themselves. This takes the form of paying bills, making visits (if the parent is living elsewhere), or providing a place either in their home or in an institution if the parent is unable to function independently. In "Immortality," by Robert Henderson, middle-aged Martin Gaines returns from a business trip to great demands on his parenting role. His seventeen-year-old son has banged up the family car, his married daughter is battling with her aunt, Martin's sister, and a decision needs to be made about the residence and care of his ailing father. Being the middle one of three generations also brings into focus Martin's own aging. On the one hand, Martin has lost the youthful vigor that his son represents; on the other, he is not yet ready to face aging and death. Martin's family unit thus provides a context wherein he cannot avoid confronting the issues of aging and immortality.

DISRUPTION OF THE FAMILY UNIT

Both anticipated and unanticipated events of everyday life require changes and adjustments throughout adulthood. People differ in the resources, both personal and social, that they can bring to bear in coping with life events. Those events that occur in the arena of the family, such as learning to live with a marriage partner, becoming a parent, or dealing with aging parents, are surrounded by social norms and expectations that help to define appropriate responses. But sometimes it is not clear what constitutes an acceptable response, and sometimes adults do not have a wide range of resources to assist them in making transitions. This is particularly true of those happenings that are highly disruptive of one's pattern of life. The selections in this section deal with three events that can disrupt the family unit—widowhood, death of a child, and divorce.

In the short story "The Lost Phoebe," by Theodore Dreiser, Henry's wife Phoebe dies after forty-eight years of happy marriage. After five months of sitting alone with his grief, Henry sees an apparition of his dead Phoebe. That sets him on a search for her, not the old woman who has died but the young girl whom he had married. The story is a moving account of one man's adjustment, or perhaps lack of adjustment, to losing a lifelong companion. It is also a story of meager resources that are not enough to facilitate the resolution of grief. Instead Henry escapes into a dream world in search of his wife. Henry's few social contacts respond in various ways to his search, suggesting that there is little consensus as to how a person in his state should be handled. Loss of a spouse in old age might be anticipated—indeed, Henry "used to speculate at times as to what he would do if she were to die"—but that does not alleviate the pain of the loss.

Losing a child through death is perhaps even more painful because it is usually unexpected and one mourns for the life a child has not been allowed to live. The surviving parents are further burdened by feeling that they could have done more to prevent the death or that they should have died instead. In a famous short story, "Heartache," by Anton Chekhov (not included in this volume), the protagonist, a horse-and-buggy driver, cannot understand why his son died and not himself. None of his passengers can provide an answer or alleviate his grieving. He finally turns to his horse for solace. In a poem presented in this group, "February 11, 1977," by Frederick Morgan, another father mourns his son's death, but a lapse of nine years has brought about a melancholy acceptance of that which cannot be explained.

Separation or divorce is yet another source of disruption in the family life cycle. Even when the divorce is mutually desired, the dissolution of a marriage is almost always accompanied by stress and pain for both members. It is a time of transition, a time for reexamining one's identity, and a time for assuming new roles and patterns of social participation. "Jury Duty," by Robert Henderson, is the story of one person's continuing adjustment to a divorce that had occurred several years earlier. Owen Gilbert is called to be a juror in a divorce and child custody case. Listening to the testimony triggers a review of his childhood family life and a reanalysis of his own marriage and divorce. He discovers that neither the jury case nor his own situation can be judged on strictly rational grounds. The bonding of two adults by marriage, the breaking of the bond, and the nurturing of children as a result of a marriage are complex events in the family cycle requiring emotional as well as rational responses.

In summary, the family, of which nearly every person is a member, is a medium for establishing patterns of intimacy throughout the life span. Its many events, both anticipated and unexpected, require that adjustments be made, that changes and growth take place.

From UP THE SANDBOX!

Anne Richardson Roiphe

Elizabeth is playing with the blue-and-white ball I have just bought her at the five-and-ten on Broadway. It rolls away and I see her chase it and suddenly trip on a toy truck and fall on the cement ground. I am attentive, taut, ready to charge forward. I put down the notebook and in another second I hear her scream as if her universe were empty and her sound would never find a human listener. I run to her and as I get close, I feel her scream in my chest, ready at the edge of an explosion. I see blood pouring from her mouth, covering her chin and staining the pink-and-white flowered dress she's wearing. Quickly I take her in my arms. "Nothing to be frightened of, just a little blood, nothing to worry about—Mommy will fix it." The screaming subsides to a sobbing and my own heart is pounding—so much blood is coming—my arms and the front of my dress are also red. I'm certain it's just a superficial mouth cut, but still my legs are trembling as I carry her to the water fountain. A friend lends me a diaper to use as a towel.—"It's nothing, it's nothing," I say over and over. My life is not my own any more, it belongs in part to her. I have committed myself to taking care of her and I must not fail. She must be the better part of me. She must be the more beautiful, the more graceful, the more loving part of me. I am in and of myself no longer complete, I need her. I wipe with the diaper. I use cold water and press against her pale face and stained mouth, and in a matter of moments she is quiet, leaning on my shoulder. The blood has stopped. Her teeth are all there and I can't even see in her mouth where such a terrible cut could have been. That pink soft tissue opens, profusely bleeds and then closes, leaving no trace of a slash. Elizabeth wants to sit on her seat in the stroller, and now the baby who has watched the drama with open eyes wants to be held and smiled at. I give them both cookies and sit back on the bench, the baby on my lap. The heat again feels like a weight, like someone stuffing cotton down one's chest. Sometimes as I sit watching the children I suddenly think of Paul, of the smell and feel of him. I don't know if the images I have are lascivious or tender, I think perhaps they are both. In and out of my mind all during the day move thoughts of him.

Paul's sleeping now on our bed, breathing heavily, his hair wet across his forehead. Not tonight, tonight I'll be too tired, he won't be well enough, but certainly tomorrow or perhaps in the early morning he'll reach over and touch my breasts and I'll roll toward him and for a while nothing else will matter, not his cold, not our children, not the book on revolutions—it will all wait for us to finish, to separate again.

The baby is struggling to move around. I put him down off my lap and take from his hand a cigarette about to go into his mouth. I watch as he crawls to the next bench, and quickly I jump up and grab him before his fingers get caught beneath a carriage wheel. I put him back in the stroller and he cries in fury. His face turns red, his period of freedom was too short, too delicious, to be given up so quickly. But I'm tired, I cannot watch him, protect him with total vigilance, and one accident a day is enough. The other mothers are looking at me. Why is that child screaming, why doesn't she do something? She's probably one of those cold, indifferent types, the kind that breed damaged children; hasn't she read Bettelheim, Spock, Gesell? I give him a smile, I push the stroller back and forth. Elizabeth leans forward and tickles his cheek—which usually makes him laugh. Nothing works. Elizabeth pinches him too hard, the pinch of anger, at his tears, at his very existence. He cries louder. I am an interfering, spoiling mother and from the sound of his crying I am never to be forgiven. From the strength of her pinch I can tell she will never forgive me for having borne him. It's early but I'm going to leave this hot playground and go to the air-conditioned pizza place on 115th Street. The children will cover themselves with tomato sauce. I will sit in the dark booth, my elbows on the shiny Formica tabletop, and play the jukebox. And then at last it will be time to go home.

I was thinking about Paul's cold earlier today. I noticed how pale and mottled his face was and the sticky damp dark spots on the sheets, and the frail sound of his nasal voice humming Mozart melodies as he watched the afternoon's soap opera on television—What when he is really ill, what when he or I lie in bed dying? It is absolutely certain that one of us will die before the other, and the stronger one will tend the sick one, grow to loathe the illness and the patient, and then suddenly be left alone, like a statue without arms, legs or nose, be permanently undone. That thought can't be tolerated long and yet it can't be pushed entirely aside, because the moment will arrive and I want my perceptions and attitudes to be ready, I want to be prepared.

Once last March Elizabeth ran a fever of 104 and her breath came heavy, slow and painful. The doctor came, not very disturbed, and used penicillin. A sharp disposable needle, a cry from Elizabeth, a pat on my back, a prescription on the table, and he was gone. I stayed up all that night, bringing her cold washcloths, rubbing her chest with alcohol, watching the vaporizer and the strange shapes that appeared in the steam. I wasn't really frightened, but as I stared at her flushed face and the dilated pupils, I realized that I couldn't be without her—that I had fiercely and passionately involved myself in the limbs and brain, the body and soul of my child. Why? Why was I proud when she learned numbers early, pleased when she fitted together pieces of a puzzle, proving an intelligence expected and necessary for survival? Why was I embarrassed when she wet her pants in the playground and the urine streamed down her legs, settling in puddles in her socks—why was I so angry and hurt the day the little boy called her ''Cross-eyes'' and wouldn't play daddy in her game of house? Why did I nearly cry as I held her in my arms and explained that he was just a bad boy? Is it something perhaps in the secret sticky protoplasm out of which I molded her—myself now devoted to a replica of myself, now slave, now master, caught in a bind; not pleasant, certainly *nowhere* happy, predictably bound for clashing of wills, disappointments, expectations unmet, pride hurt—all that I know will happen between a mother and a daughter, between me and Elizabeth. What do I want from her when she grows up? Whatever it is, I am sure I won't get it. Whatever she will do will be less than what I have planned, because I can't help planning so much, asking so much of her. I always used to share the joke and point the finger at the ambitious stage mother, or the possessive Jewish mother whose son could not go to the bathroom without her following behind to wipe and admire his parts. And now I think those are visible caricatures of the even more sinister reality, the more ordinary poisonous ooze that flows between parent and child—Elizabeth is marred because she is mine and each waking hour I transmit in a thousand unconscious ways the necessary code for her to absorb my personality, to identify with my sex, and to catch, like a communicable plague, all my inadequacies and mimic them or convert them to massive ugly splotches on her own still young soul. For example, I have never told her in any kind of words that I am afraid of the dark, and yet she will not let me put out her bedside lamp and I don't insist, because I remember giants and witches, evil blobs of unknown menace, lying directly at the cover's edge when it's dark. I still sometimes feel an unseen presence behind my back, readying itself to leap and force me into some unspeakable violence. Sometimes I think perhaps it's wrong, morally wrong to have children, when I am so uncertain whether or not I am a good person, enough of a person to create another. I so badly want my children to grow strong and be meaningfully rebellious, to take some corner of the earth and claim it for their own. I look around me in the playground at all the other mothers and their children. We are united in our strong feelings of ambition for our children.

Elizabeth is sometimes afraid of dogs, large ones that pull on their leashes or little ones that bark too much. Sometimes she's afraid of the moon. She says it's like a ghost hand in the sky. Sometimes she curls up in my lap and says she wishes she were the tiny baby in the house, that growing up is a nasty thing. I point out all the wonders of maturity, but I still can't convince her. Sometimes she seems to want to contract until she's no more than a few cells, visible only through a microscope, nestling against the wall of my sealed-off uterus. I too sometimes would like to progress in reverse so my mother could brush my hair each morning and complain about my roller skates left out to rust in the backyard, so I could take my dolls to bed and draw pictures in my schoolbooks of a prince waiting to make me, Margaret Ferguson of Paramus, New Jersey, his bride.

How was I before Elizabeth was born? Even though it's only a few short years, I seem to have always listened for the sound of a child's crying or calling. When I think of losing her, and of illness, long nights in the hushed corridors of bleak hospitals, the sound of children crying for their mothers or their teddy bears, and nurses rustling by in the dark whispering bad news to each other, I think about how I would drink dark coffee out of paper cups, and wait. Sometimes I am frightened of a possible car crash, a fall, a pot of boiling water overturned, a bobbypin experimentally poked into an electric socket. And then, after the death, I would be a woman with a limb amputated—worse, perhaps, I would be a woman with a hole in the center, in the bowels, a great gaping hole from breast to genitals, for the wind to blow through, for trash to collect in, for everyone to know I am emptied of myself.

I must pick up Elizabeth from the dirt by the water fountain where she is sitting with another little girl, drawing in the mud. There is a leak at the base of the fountain and it has created a miniature river whose geography is being carefully studied by the children. She is dirty, and I like to see her that way. The dirt is from the feeling and the touching of all possible surfaces, and a certain lack of concern, a certain pleasure in doing things uninhibited by prissy thoughts and stuffy manners. The baby is sleeping on his back, his hands flung out on either side of the stroller. Too late for pizza, instead I will take them both home and stop at the drugstore and pick up some cough medicine for Paul. Maybe if I can find enough change hidden in the corners of my bag, I can bring him the *New American Review* to take his mind off his nasal congestion.

TEDDY, WHERE ARE YOU?

Stephen Minot

Of course he's my son. I'll admit it's a little silly having a snapshot like that in a silver frame, but I never could get him to Bachrach's. He's rather independent.

Oh, don't apologize. *Most* people are surprised. I don't mean just his appearance—he *is* a bit shaggy—but his being so *old*. He was a college sophomore last fall, you know. Who'd think that little me would have a boy in college?

No, he hasn't been around much. Some of my best friends have never seen him in person. Like Felicia. Of course, she knew I'd *had* a son somewhere along the line—I've never really concealed the fact—but she just never happened to be around when he was here. That's fantastic when you realize how long we've known each other. We met the year I was between marriages, and we see each other almost every week. She was absolutely astounded when she saw this snapshot. She simply gasped. And then she said, "Darling . . . " (you know that stagy way she has). "Darling," she said, "you must have conceived at *ten*!" She's delicious.

Well, I wasn't exactly ten, but I wasn't twenty either. We matured early in those days. Which is why I understand Teddy's world. People tell me, "My God, Stella, can't you get the boy shaved and scrubbed? We can't even *see* him." But that's his *world*, you know. I mean, it's like Samson—that's where he gets his *identity*. And that's *it*. I mean really *it*, these days. Identity is everything. I know a lot of parents who don't take that seriously, but they just don't listen to the kids. There no communication. Honestly, it's a crying shame.

Like last Christmas. For some reason he decided to take his vacation with me rather than his father. Usually he visits Theo—that's his father—in the winter break so he can get a little of that Florida sun, though how the poor boy puts up with all the criticism is beyond me. The two of them have an honest, open hatred for each other. Can you imagine a father telling his own son that he won't take the boy to the club because he looks like a hairy freak? But somehow Teddy manages to endure it. He just keeps quiet. God only knows what he's thinking. It's not very healthy if you ask me, but at least Teddy's got *one* parent who's sympathetic.

Well, it did surprise me a bit when Teddy said he was coming to see *me* in the December break, because he's always said New York just isn't a winter city. That's the way he puts it. He says New York is an autumn and spring city. Teddy's really rather poetic sometimes—which is lucky, because God knows he *looks* poetic. But anyway, this year he decided he wanted to be with his mother at Christmas, which was just lovely even though it's an appallingly busy time what with the usual parties and shopping, and it's even worse now that they've put me on the damn refugee board, which *of course* has to have its annual *thing* right at the height of the season. But I'm always glad to see my Teddy, busy or not, and that's more than I can say for a lot of mothers.

When he wrote me that he was taking the *train* all the way from Chicago, my heart bled. You see, his father won't pay a cent—not even for tuition—until the boy shaves off his beard and gets a crewcut. I know it's incredible, but stubbornness just runs in his genes, I guess. And Teddy won't let me go to court. He wants his father to live with his own moral decision. Isn't that beautiful? Well anyway, Teddy's *tremendously* conscientious with my money, and that's why he wouldn't fly.

He arrived around suppertime, exhausted and in his usual state of shaggy disrepair. He was absolutely famished. All he'd eaten since Chicago was a can of cold spaghetti. Obviously it was my job to revive him. I told him right away he needed a good drink and a decent meal and got him off to Henri's before he could protest. Thank God I'd thought to make reservations that morning, because in the Christmas season Henri really does more business than he deserves.

Now I've always been partial to Henri, bless his flighty little heart, but listen to this:

We walk in, Teddy and I, and I spot Caroline with that extraordinary Romanian—the one who's about to be deported to *Bolivia,* of all places—and we were catching up on things in the foyer when Henri glides in, puts his arm on my boy's shoulder and says, "Deliveries go out back." Honestly! That's exactly what he said.

"*Hilarious,*" I say to Henri, trying to cover as best I could—though Lord knows why I should cover for that kind of hairdresser snobbery. So I introduced them formally, last name and all with the emphasis on *Mister* and stressing my *son,* and you should have seen Henri blush right up to the glue line.

Then Caroline's oily Romanian said something about their planning to meet with friends—which was a typically Slavic lie because until his trial comes up he's about as popular as a case of radiation; and besides, later on I *saw* them eating alone. But me, I'm always trying to smooth things over, so I suggested that we all have a drink together at the bar and then each go our way as couples, and they agreed.

Now I'll admit that Teddy was not at his best. But how can you blame him? I mean, what can a *philosophy* major say to some damn *Romanian* anyway? And I realized that night that Caroline can talk all she wants about raising money for Korean children, but she just can't relate with *real* kids. I mean, she'd ask him where he went to college and what he was taking and whether he had any good teachers—just like some grandmother. I didn't blame him for mumbling answers. I mean, would you? It was about on the level of "Well, *haven't* you *grown?*" Honestly!

I told her this afterward, and she asked me what *should* she have talked about, and I told her about the *live* issues, things they really think and talk about. "You should have asked him about pot," I told her. He probably would have offered her a joint—that's a smoke—right there. "Or about the Black Caucus." After all, she knew he'd been in Chicago. "Or at least you could have asked him about the war," I told her. He would have given her a blast right between the eyes. That's the way these kids are. It's not that they're impolite, it's just that they're *very* direct. Honest, you might say. Yes, very honest. To a fault, sometimes. I tried to explain all this to Caroline, but I don't think she was even listening. She's one of those *terribly* well-meaning people who just never learn.

Well, I imagine Teddy and I made an interesting sight. I had on my white sheath—the Bergdorf thing with the high collar—and the spiky earrings Paxton had made for me in Mexico, and he had on the corduroy jacket he had slept in on the trip and no tie and of course that *incredible* hair and the beard. To me he's a big, frowzy bear who deep down is *terribly* vulnerable. Now I'll admit I did think of asking him to comb the snarls out of his beard just a bit—after all, I do have the instincts of a mother. But I kept my mouth shut. I mean, what right do I have? He's an adult. As they say, he has his bag and I have mine.

Oh, and the beads. I forgot that. They all wear these little colored beads. Very masculine, really—once you get used to them. They certainly make more sense than being choked by a tie.

So we didn't exactly blend in. And I discovered that people at Henri's are really not very sophisticated—money, but no breeding. I don't mean that they gawked, but they *peeked* at us out of the corners of their eyes. It put me off at first. I was asking him about his grades and his apartment (which, frankly, I'm glad I never saw), and I wasn't really listening to the answers partly because he spoke so low but mostly because of all this Peeping Tom stuff. You'd think we were on our honeymoon.

But after about the second drink I realized I was just being foolish. After all, hadn't I brought him up to be independent and on his own? I've always protected him against coercion. The few times Theo writes to me nowadays is to get me to put pressure on the boy and I'm glad I can say that I've never buckled under. "Can't you get Ted to quit these political organizations?" he'd write—as if Teddy's affiliations in Chicago would damage his father's lousy marina in Fort Lauderdale. So I'd write the boy the next day saying he had *my* approval to do whatever he damn well liked. And then his father would write about forcing Teddy to shave. He even suggested *I* cut off the tuition money, too. How's that? I just sent the letter right on to Chicago with "HA!" written at the bottom. We have a good understanding, Teddy and I.

But I'm not saying that we always see eye to eye. He has his dark streak just like his father. Theo and I used to be taken as lovers even after we'd been married two years—it was that good. But every so often something—or some*one*—would turn up and bang! we'd walk out on each other. No discussion. Just bang! It went on like that for several years, on and off. Thanks to Theo's black streak. That's what I called it. And sometimes I think I see it coming through in poor Teddy. Of course, he couldn't have been nicer at dinner and all, but you can't relax completely when you have the feeling that maybe at any moment something will go wrong and everything will fall to pieces. It's a matter of confidence. I mean, after two bad marriages you often get the feeling you're skating on thin ice, if you know what I mean.

But never mind that. By dessert—Henri has perfectly *fabulous* pastries—I was feeling marvelous and maybe it was the cognac, but anyway I suggested that we take in a few of the old spots for dancing. He gave me an odd look—not really a smile, but perhaps amused.

"You're not for real," he said. I decided to take it as a compliment, though you never know for sure. I assumed that he was also vetoing the dance plan. But then he said, "Like, why not? I mean, if you want to." That's about as much enthusiasm as he can muster for such low-level concerns. So off we went, me overtipping as I always do when I'm in a good mood.

As it turned out, we only got to one place. After a couple of dances it was me that suggested that we go home. Partly it was his dancing. I guess he just hadn't learned. I tried leading him through a fox trot and a samba, but it was a painful business—him with his ankle-high combat boots. And another thing: for the first time I realized what it would be like to go into some decent midtown place with a Negro date. I don't mean that as a crack about Teddy. It's the *society* that's sick. I've never been stared at like that in my life. Granted, Teddy didn't exactly match the decor—it cost me an extra five dollars to get him into the place at all—but the looks we got were more than that. They were *obscene*.

Well, at least he could tell that *I* wasn't one of *them*. I doubt if very many of his classmates have mothers who would put up with half of what I did that night.

And I guess he must have understood that because when we got back to the apartment he offered to mix me a drink. That may not seem like much, but it was a touch of the civilized boy we thought he had become in boarding school. You wouldn't know it, but there was a time when he wore decent tweeds and a tie and stood up when a woman came in the room. I know that's old stuff, and I wouldn't dream of asking him to go back to it, but somehow, seeing this bearded, woolly creature saying, "Would you care for a drink?" well, it made tears come to my eyes.

So I had another, even though I surely didn't need one. I mentioned the fact that his father had the knack of offering a drink in a way one couldn't refuse. I couldn't tell whether he smiled or not under all that shrubbery, but there was a little familiar flourish in the way he handed me the double Scotch that gave me a jolt.

That was nothing compared with the jolt he had in store for me. "Mother," he says with great solemnity, "about that apartment in Chicago. . . . " I held my breath. I guessed that he wanted something more expensive. I would have agreed to it, of course, though no one has unlimited income—even from alimony. But that wasn't it at all.

"I guess you know I have a roommate." I nodded. "But, like I guess you haven't met her."

"Her?" I asked.

"Her."

"I'd like to meet her very much," I said. I think it was the first real lie I'd told all evening. But then, he hadn't been too honest with me either. All this time I'd thought he'd been studying.

"Well, she's in town," he told me. I suggested that she drop by the next day—I'd had enough surprises for one evening. But he said she was fairly close, and could she join us that evening. What could I say?

As far as I can see, the girl must have been standing in a phone booth waiting for him to call. It took her about four minutes to ring the apartment bell. Teddy let her in, and they stood there looking at each other for a moment, not saying a word. No kiss, no greeting; just sort of a soul-search, you might say. And then he brushed the snow off her shoulders and from the top of her head. No hat, of course. She warmed her hands on the back of his neck. They were blue. All of this time I was standing behind them in the foyer, a nonperson, wondering if I should retreat until the welcoming ceremony was over.

Now I must be fair. I've had two mothers-in-law who were genuinely psychotic, so I know what it is to be misrepresented. This half-frozen little waif was not quite as grotesque as what I had been imagining for four minutes. True, she wore an old, full-length army coat that gave her a bit of the Bowery look, but she didn't have flowers in her hair or paint on her face or anything like that. Under that absurd army coat she was just another college freshman in sweater and skirt. She had the standard long hair, beautiful but oh-so-solemn eyes, and a complexion ruined by pockmarks. My first reaction was pity: even with money, she'd never be really beautiful.

Naturally I had to ask what her name was. Otherwise we'd go the whole evening saying "hey you." She said it was Paula, and I was about to ask for her last name when something told me that they might think I was groping for ethnic background or something like that, so to this day I don't know whether Paula is Smith or Kovoleski. No matter.

I took her coat—I suppose Teddy would have left her in it all evening —and as soon as I felt the weight of the sodden thing I realized that she must have been standing in the snow all evening like the little matchstick girl. It bent the wire hanger right down and slid to the floor, so I had to heave it up again, this time onto a wooden one. It must have weighed more than she did.

All the time, of course, I was chattering away about the snow, about how heavy the coat was, how chic I thought the new military uniforms were (my second lie, I'm afraid), how well Teddy was doing in college. It was a valiant job even if I do say so. You must realize that their end of this sparkling exchange consisted of unintelligible grunts. Honestly, I could have done better with a couple of Korean refugees.

But I know enough not to be offended. It's their world, and if I have to take the full burden of conversation until they think of some Major Issue to discuss, so be it. You have to make the effort.

As we started into the living room I couldn't help hearing the sound of her boots. They were cracked leather things with pointed toes—old cavalry boots for all I know—and they were caked with half-frozen slop and salt from the street. Clearly they were soaked through because at every step she sounded as if she were marching through the Okeechobee swamp. Now I *know* I shouldn't have cared one bit, but my rug is made of thirteen natural-white lamb fleeces that Paxton—he was my second husband— brought me back from Greece; and, well, I just couldn't *bear* the thought.

"Would you like to take off your boots?" I asked her.

"All right," she said. For a moment she seemed very manageable, and I felt things might go all right. And then she plunked herself right down on the floor like some Great Dane and pulled off the filthy things. When she stood up again I could see that we hadn't made much progress. Her bare feet—no socks, mind you—were as wet and as black as the boots.

"Are you hungry?" I asked her. "How about a sandwich?" It was a last-ditch maneuver—the kitchen has a lineoleum floor.

She nodded, thank God. I don't honestly know what I would have done otherwise. I mean there are limits.

So I saved the rug, but there was no way to save the rest of the evening. I'm not sure what led to what. For one thing, those dreadful feet put me off. To my mind, there's nothing very attractive about even a *clean* foot. And the way the two of them sat beside each other at the table, chairs up close, she rubbing his leg, I suppose, right there in front of me, in my kitchen.

I asked her what kind of sandwich she wanted, and she just shrugged. I mean, honestly, couldn't she have said "Do you have ham?" or "How about bologna?" But no, she just shrugged and started gnawing her thumbnail. It wasn't until then that I noticed that all her fingers were bitten down to the quick and were sooty black. That got me—those nails or what was left of them. I stood there waiting for her to find a word, and I saw this picture of her installed in my son's apartment, cooking on some rusty little hot plate, handing him food with those filthy fingers, reading the letters I'd written to him, using his toothbrush. The picture may not have been fair, but it was damn clear; art nouveau on the wall, beer cans and bottles on the floor, and instead of a bed, an old mattress on the floor. Honestly, it wasn't the morality that bothered me, it was the *filth*.

Well, it was clear that I wasn't going to get an English sentence out of her, so I did my best to gather together some bread and a jar of mayonnaise and a few tomatoes, all of which wasn't too easy because that last drink Teddy had mixed me was one I really didn't need.

Of course, it never occurred to this lovely child to offer to help. That would have been terribly "straight." So they behaved as if I were the maid, talking to each other in low tones and sometimes giggling—God knows what at. I could pick up a phrase here or there, but they must have been about bands I wasn't familiar with or people I didn't know because none of it made sense. I could have been a Puerto Rican cook trying to eavesdrop. I wanted to say to them, "Kids, I'm right here in the same room with you. I'm right *here*. Look at me. Say *something* to me for God's sake." But I held my tongue; I mean, I wasn't *that* drunk, thank heaven.

And then I cut my finger. The tomato must have been softer than I expected because the knife went right through and sliced my index finger at the joint. And would you believe it, neither of those sweet children even *noticed*. I said "damn" or something like that and sucked my finger and Teddy didn't so much as look up. You'd think she'd drugged him, and maybe she had. I mean, you never know these days.

Well, from then on it was like a dream. I was looking through the cabinets for a Band-Aid, and I heard my Teddy saying, "She'll never make it," just as if I didn't understand English. "Like, she'll freak out again," he said. "Every time."

And Paula said something like "It's only the exams. She's cool until exams. I've got her going to the clinic. I don't know, but when you're up tight like that, maybe the clinic makes sense."

I was trying to make something out of that when, right in the middle of a sentence, she reached out and took *my* drink. The one Teddy had mixed for me. Not even "please" or "may I?" She just *took* it.

When she set it down, I said very clearly, "I've *cut* my *finger*," which at least made them look at me. "I can't find an antiseptic." And while they were mulling that over I grabbed my drink back again and put my bleeding finger in it. Of course, it was just common sense to sterilize the cut, but maybe I was also making sure she wouldn't go on stealing my drink. I'll admit I wasn't crystal-clear rational at that point. So for a moment the three of us watched the blood spread out in the Scotch.

"Did the knife reach the bone?" she asked me.

"If it had," I told her sweetly, "I would have mentioned it."

"Our cat has a runny eye," she said.

"Teddy never told me he had a cat," I said.

Teddy cleared his voice like an orator and said, "We have a cat." There was a little pause and then he said, "I've always wanted a cat. So Paula found this one. In a used-car lot. But, like pus comes out of its eye."

"Get it to a doctor," I said.

"Doctors don't see cats," Teddy said.

"There are cat doctors," I said.

He opened his eyes very wide. "Crazy!" he said.

"Oh no!" I said "I mean *human* doctors who see *cats*. You know. Vets."

"Not in our neighborhood," he said.

"Of *course* there are," I said.

"In our neighborhood they *eat* cats."

I gasped and turned to Paula. If she had smiled it would have been a joke, but she was solemn as ever. She even nodded. "It started with the Haitian family down the hall," she said, "but then some of our friends—"

"*Enough*," I said. I didn't want to hear another word about eating cats or runny eyes or about Paula. It just seemed impossible to me that my Teddy had gotten himself into all this. He had *never* liked cats. I'm sure of it. I mean, if he had said anything at all about wanting a cat, we would have got him one. A healthy one. We never deprived him. It was as if somehow I didn't know him at all. My own son. In all his childhood he never even *mentioned* cats.

I suddenly felt very, very tired, and closed my eyes for a moment. And when I opened them I saw that this incredible girl had snatched up the half-made sandwich and was wolfing it down. The way she ate, it sounded the way she did walking in those wet boots.

"You seem very hungry," I said, holding on to the edge of the table, my other hand still submerged in my drink.

"Two days on this cold spaghetti," Teddy said. "That's a real down-trip. Two days on the road."

"Road?"

"Hitchhiking."

"You said you took the train."

"I said we *might*. That was to keep you from psyching out."

"But I sent you money."

She was quiet during this exchange—except for the slurping sound of her devouring the tomatoes one after another. I hadn't noticed it before, but she had unpleasantly sensual lips for one so young. I guess I was staring at her when she looked up, half a tomato still in her mouth, and said, "The money—it wasn't really ours."

"Of course not," I said. "But it was *his*."

"We share," he said. "Everything." He let the word hang there. I understood—for the first time, I guess—that from then on whatever I gave to Teddy, anything at all, would be shared by this girl. I felt dizzy—loss of blood maybe—and sat down. I took my finger out of the glass. It had stopped bleeding, but the skin had puckered. I started at the cut line wondering if it would leave a scar. I have a thing about disfigurement. For some reason it all seemed her fault.

"What on earth did you come here for?" I asked her suddenly. "I mean, Teddy's free to lead his own life, but. . . . " It was hard to find words. I turned to him. "Why did you have to bring her back here? It's just plain mean—"

"He's not mean," she said quickly. "Stella, believe me, we worked this out together." So now it was going to be Stella and Paula, woman to woman. I braced myself. "You've been sending this money," she said. "It's what we live on. Like, it's no good if we don't level with you. So here I am."

"That's the way it is," Teddy said.

There was something touching about that, I have to admit it. They got to me. Almost. I tried to pretend that she was one of the family already. I really tried.

"I suppose you help out with some kind of part-time work?" I said. I smiled, until she shook her head.

"Why not?"

"Why should I? I go to classes. I mean, we get along on what Teddy gets."

"You don't even *try* to get a job?"

Teddy threw up his hands. "Holy, holy, holy! What's so holy about work? Have *you* ever worked? We get along on what we get. Like you. Where's the super-sin in that?"

"I'm not talking about sin," I told them. "I'm not a *moralist*, for heaven's sake. But there are limits. I pay for my own son, but there's nothing in the books that says I have to pay for some coed who moves in on him." I looked her in the eye and said, "Can you give me one reason why *I* should pay for *your* living expenses?"

She looked me right back and said, very softly, "Love." And then she started biting her filthy thumbnail.

Can you imagine it? What on earth did she know about love? I mean, honestly, she was about the most unlovable creature on earth. Well, I really let them have it then.

"I don't know what on earth *you* know about love," I told them. "You've got no right to even *use* the word. But I'll tell you this. Love or no love, there's no law that says I have to support some cheapside bordello." Teddy was standing up, but he had it coming. "The rent's not all," I told him. "There's no law that makes me pay for next term's tuition." I took a long drink. "Why should I pay to let you lie in bed with some teenage prostitute?"

That was harsh. I'll admit that. In bad taste. I think I apologized, but Teddy just stared down at me wide-eyed as if I had just grown fangs.

"Wait a minute," Paula said suddenly, "do you want to see him in the army? Is that it? Or in jail?"

Well, I honestly hadn't thought of it that way. It was a jolt. But there was panic on her face. I wasn't thinking very fast, but it came to me finally that these were two places where she couldn't get at him. Maybe I smiled. I don't know. But she was saying—shouting almost, "She *does*. Oh Jesus, she *does*!"

Does what? I was wondering. What's she saying? But nothing really made sense then, and they were pushing by me to get out of the kitchen, and all I could think of saying was that no one could use profanity like that in *my* house, and there was a kind of scramble for coats at the door while I mixed myself a fresh drink with my back turned to them, waiting for an apology.

And all I heard was the click of the door. Not a "thanks" or even a "so long, Mom." Just the door closing and the two of them going out without anything decided.

I could hardly believe it. I stood there by the window for quite a time, watching. You get a long view from the fifteenth story. It was snowing heavily then, and the traffic along the avenue had almost stopped. They finally came into view and paused for a moment in the circle of white light from the streetlamp as if they didn't know where to go. Then I saw those two small forms, arms around each other, moving down the avenue to God knows where. I kept saying his name over and over like a chant, thinking that he would look up. But he didn't. The apartment suddenly seemed very cold.

Oh, I knew then that something terrible had happened. I'd been through it before though I don't know just when. But even now in the sobriety of days upon cold days, I wonder what I should have done. And what I should do now? He never re-registered. So now I don't have any idea where he is. Does he even *know* what he's done to me?

IMMORTALITY

Robert Henderson

On a Wednesday morning in February, a man by the name of Martin Gaines left his sprawling apartment on Murray Hill, stopped at his office on West Forty-fifth Street, and went on a business trip. Between then and the time he returned home on Friday evening, several things took place more or less at random, and settled down to lie in wait for him.

On Wednesday afternoon, Ellen, his wife—a composed, habitually smiling woman of fifty—picked up at her hairdresser's a magazine abandoned there by a girl who had bought it to read an article about Swedish glass. In it, Mrs. Gaines read an article about pernicious anemia. Her secret and baseless conviction had long been that her body, round and firm as it was, could never last out the natural term of a life as wonderful as hers. Compensation would surely set in. By nightfall, symptoms were at her, and by Friday, though still smiling, she was stiff with fear. On Wednesday night, Martin's son Steven quarrelled with his girl (who had just finished quarrelling with her sister) and stayed out in sorrow until four o'clock, cruising the city in the family car. In the morning, his mother forbade him the use of the car for a week. Being seventeen years old, he found his fate unacceptable, and, after lying elaborately about where he was going, took the car out again that night and banged it up. And on Friday afternoon Martin's married daughter, Leora—pregnant, and anxious for the sake of her child to have what belonged to her—called on an aunt, her father's sister, to claim a pair of candlesticks she believed her grandmother had left her. The aunt, who believed, or wished to believe, that they had been left to her, refused Leora, who grew angry, and promised to appeal to her father for justice that very night.

Of course, Martin Gaines knew of none of these matters when, returning, he reached his office toward dark on Friday. Even so, he was reluctant to go home; what he did know was that his father would be there overnight. His father was lame from a broken knee suffered the year before, his blood pressure was a standing cause of family alarm, and he had no business on earth living alone in his old house in New Jersey. This Martin was going to have to say to him, as he had said it before, being duty bound. He would have to insist that his father sell the house and move to the city, where his children could keep an eye on him. There would be an argument.

So Martin stayed longer in his office than he need have. He telephoned his wife, and was struck by the dull tone of a voice that habitually welcomed him home from a two-day trip with the gladness owed to someone back from war. When he questioned her, she told him only about Steven and about Leora. Martin shook his head, knowing that that was not all that was the trouble. He washed, still delaying, but accepting the whole responsibility for putting things in order when he did go home. It had never in his adult life occurred to him that he was not answerable for everything that came to his attention. He was a tall, lumbering, sombre man, lit by occasional gleams of hopeful humor, and he lived, in a way, a little apart from his wife and children, whom he cared for deeply. He longed for them to be reasonable, honest, fair, and, above all, safe. To these ends, he was somewhat of a justice of the peace with them; if he had not been, he would have indulged them wildly.

He waited a few minutes more, staring out the window at the sky turning purple as night came. It was an effect of clouds and city that he loved. Then he saw that the rain that had been falling earlier had stopped. He rolled his umbrella into a neat foil. He emptied his briefcase and put into it papers he would not read that evening because he would be explaining to his father the hazards of age. And, having delayed that long, he reached the sidewalk outside his building in time to see a man, who had just been struck by a car, lying out in the middle of Forty-fifth Street.

The man lay on his side on the wet, glistening pavement, near the cover of a steaming manhole. A policeman bent over him. A doorman directed passing cars to the far side of the street. People had begun to gather. The man's hat and glasses had fallen off, and his overcoat lay bunched across his hips like a lifted skirt. His hair was short, neat, and lightly gray. A foot in a polished shoe was thrown out crookedly. One trouser leg was pulled up, showing a few inches of white skin. In the distorted moment, this seemed distressing to Martin; he was immensely sorry for the man who was helpless to correct it. The man was of indeterminable age—forty, fifty, no age in particular—a commuter sort of man, in tweed jacket and dark slacks, on his way to his train, going home. Blood was spreading out slowly from underneath him. The policeman took his wallet from his jacket and dug through it. One of the onlookers picked up the man's briefcase and umbrella and stood holding them uncertainly. An ambulance siren screamed far away, and then screamed nearer. Steam from the manhole blew across the man's face. Martin, who had already seen more than he wanted to see, walked away.

He put the thought and sight of the man out of his mind as well as he could, but the man persisted in returning. His briefcase had become Martin's briefcase, and his umbrella Martin's also—or perhaps it was the other way around. Martin crossed Fifth Avenue among swarms of people, thinking it incredible that all of them should be unaware that half a block away from them a man lay alone—absolutely alone, for all the gathering crowd—in the wet street. He tried to rehearse what he would say to his father, but he could not find cheerful words. He wanted to paint the picture of a small, bright, safe apartment in the city, with the old man in it, safe from vertigo and falls. But though the picture had come to him often and clearly in the past, he could see nothing now but the man there in the street and his quiet face—the face, he thought, of an established, educated man, well groomed, a husband and father—and the steam, and the shining pavement. The man was the sort of man to whom, surely, such things are expected not to happen. Death (and Martin was sure this was death) comes to such people in prescribed and manageable ways. It comes dishevelled in the street only to the faceless, bodiless ones, the people whose paths one has never imaginably crossed, whose addresses are on strange avenues of their own, where one has never walked—not to men just leaving the office, as on all Friday evenings of their lives, dressed like oneself and on their way to dinner.

He walked another block among commuters funnelling into Grand Central. A tall, red-faced man, topcoat flying, clutching under one arm a package merry with valentine hearts, drove himself zigzag toward some train; clearly he would be ruined if he missed it. (The man lying in the street had been tall, too, or had seemed so: this man's height, perhaps—

Martin's height.) Who was waiting for the man in the open topcoat at the far end of his train ride? Probably—and Martin now found the idea both astonishing and heart-rending—it had not even dawned on him that he could conceivably not get there. And the whole station, Martin knew, was at that moment full of breakable people who were not thinking of themselves as such. Breakable people were in the stories in the newspapers they were carrying. They themselves were only going home.

Martin turned south toward his own home, as aware as he had been only once or twice in his life that he was mortal. The fact, as a simple fact, was an old, unquestioned one; mortality had always been lurking, out there at the far end. But it had seldom quietly stood by in the near distance.

Steven Gaines was in his room—a fort where he immured himself much of the time. He was making pencil sketches of his left hand when he heard his father open the front door. Steven selected two of the sketches and threw the rest away, first tearing them into minute pieces, then stirring them in among the other trash in his wastebasket. He dated and initialled the two, and put them in a folder of drawings that had a title page reading, "The Sketchbooks of Steven Gaines, Museum of Modern Art, New York, New York, 1967." He put the book in his suitcase, which he kept, locked, in a padlocked compartment under a window seat. Then he set out to see his father and get it over with.

His father, too, was anxious to have it over with. He had kissed his wife, and had gone into the living room—a room that had not changed very much in twenty-five years, and one that Martin had never imagined looking otherwise than as it always did. But it occurred sharply to him now that the pictures were sure sometime to come down from the walls and not go up again, the windowpanes would sometime, somehow, be broken and not replaced. Steven came in, braced for judgment, and Martin wondered for a moment what to say—what was important enough to say. Then his mind reliably supplied the answers: It was not so much the damaged car that mattered as the lying. The car called for a penalty—a curtailed allowance. Deceit called for discussion. Martin began to discuss. The required words came, but they struck him as being almost entirely weightless.

They struck him, in fact, as being quite stupid and irrelevant, though the idea that they could be so was preposterous. He had never doubted the importance of honesty, and he did not doubt it now. What he was saying was only what was expected of him—by Steven and by himself—but that was the very trouble. He did not want to say it. He felt as if he were speaking ponderously to an inconsequential misdeed, not talking to his son. He wanted to reassure himself on the point, but he did not know exactly how to go about it. Still discussing, he put his left hand on Steven's shoulder, striking a pose that he recognized at once as condescending, though he had by no means meant it so. He had not considered at all what Steven would think; he had merely wanted to touch him, here, in their room that would sometime cease to exist. A dozen seconds went by, and then there was a tiny movement of the shoulder. Martin dropped his hand, and went on listening to his own words justly deploring falsehood.

When the lecture was finished ("We'll say no more about it," Martin said, in conclusion), Steven went to clean up, and Martin stayed where he was. He thought that Steven was a distant boy, a secret boy, who kept things to himself. Then the telephone rang, like a portent, and as Martin went down the hall to answer it, he thought again of the man lying in the street. Would the man's wife be setting the table, or would she know by now that he was dead? If she did not, was a telephone ringing, this minute, in the dark, high up in some echoing office (an office with a desk in it exactly like Martin's desk, chairs like his chairs)—ringing and stopping, and almost at once beginning to ring again? Martin picked up his own telephone. His angry daughter was calling. He said yes, of course she could come and talk to him in an hour or so.

And in her apartment in Cooper Village, Leora Gaines Downey (by her married name) hung up the phone and went back to the table where she and her husband were finishing an early dinner; it was early because her husband studied at night. She was a slight, graceful girl, with glasses that enhanced the seriousness of her small face. While she ate her cheese and fruit, she marshalled arguments in favor of her child, who would need a few modest heirlooms, and against her aunt, who had everything a lone woman could want, including candlesticks that did not belong to her, and—now that Leora thought of it—a seashore cottage she never used and certainly never lent. To Leora, justice was far from blind; it saw clearly through her eyes. When dinner was over, she stacked the dishes, and told her husband, to his relief, that he must not think of going with her to see her father. She put on coat and boots and a red stocking cap, and, before she left, saw that her husband was comfortably arranged with books and pencils and pipe at the cleared dining table. She kissed his bald spot, which she regarded as a foreshadowing of eminence, and went out.

So now it was Martin's daughter who was talking earnestly about affairs that three hours before would have been of weight, and he who was listening silently. And again the whole familiar process of establishing what was right and what was wrong seemed to have gone off balance, and words were being spent on trivialities. Leora had come as the family were having coffee, and while she filed her brief for the candlesticks, Martin looked around at them all—his discursive (and, he thought, rather greedy) daughter, his distant son, his troubled wife (*something* was troubling her), his stubborn father—seeing them in a strange double perspective, as if he were at the same time there in his chair and somewhere outside the room or beyond the window.

Then Leora paused and took off her glasses, and put them on again and looked at him, and in that instant Martin saw her as she had once stood looking at him when she was seven—tiny and owlish and dubious, but severe—showing him her first glasses. The glimpse vanished, but it left Martin filled with love for her, and with pity for her shortcomings, which did not seem to matter as much tonight as they often did. He ached at the thought that people besides himself might be aware of them, and he wanted her to have the candlesticks. But what he said to her, as if by rote, was that he would discuss the whole question with her aunt, and sort out what the case was. Whoever was fairly entitled to the candlesticks should have them. And as he said this, a queer thought ran into his head —that not only had Leora always needed him, if only to settle her disputes, but he had always needed her to bring them to him.

Ellen Gaines, her hands steady, her smile serene and fixed, cleared the dinner table, walking with the light stateliness she had early learned to walk with. But she felt as if she were in a tight case—an invisible garment that cramped and suffocated her, and shut out all but the mere sight of her surroundings. Through it neither love for nor pride in her silver and her Wedgwood managed to seep. Out of it, when she smiled at her father-in-law, she was sure her smile emerged a ghastly grin. From inside it, she absently waved Leora home to her husband, though Leora's husband signified little to Ellen at the moment. Inside, with her, were thoughts of hospitals and pain, and bills—enormous bills for her husband to spend his good years paying. And, to be sure, the tips of her fingers were cold, and tingling constantly, and the base of her spine felt hollow. She looked in a mirror for ravages, or at least for the bedragglement of the sick, and saw, mocking her, her clear skin, her clear eyes, the soft, perfect waves of her gray hair. She told herself brusquely that her fears were imagination, and then, weakly and ruefully, she laughed at herself for the folly of trying to pretend that she was well. And all the time she was dreading, and longing for, the moment when she would tell her husband of her fears, as she always did. He would be scornful, and would talk about hobgoblins. He would tell her to be reasonable. He would point out that she had been examined only lately and found to be blooming. He would restrain his evident impatience, though giving her selected glimpses of it, while explaining that her symptoms were pure nerves. And at last, whether because he had said and done these things or merely because she had come out into the open with her fear and talked about it, the fear would begin to ebb, and she would feel abashed and relieved, and life and her silver would look lovely to her again.

Meanwhile, Martin had lit a cigarette and gone into his study. It was time for a television roundup of the news, and he turned it on, then turned it off. It was foolish to wonder if any notice would be taken of one man killed by a car. That was a commonplace, not a piece of news. And yet the man's life had ended there, by the steaming manhole; it had all been bound for that spot. It seemed to Martin that the block might have been shut off for a while—kept quiet—but of course such a thing was ridiculous. People were swarming along it this very minute—noisy, bound for theatres. But he hoped it would not occur to the man's wife, wherever she was, to think how quickly his death could vanish from the street. Then Martin, putting out his cigarette, went to the kitchen to help his own wife, whom he did not want to leave by herself any longer.

He walked through the swinging door into the bright kitchen, and took a towel from a rack, and for a short while, in the warm kitchen world, his own world looked like itself again. True, he had a peculiar, a senseless moment when he saw his wife visibly there beside the sink and in the same second was stormed by a longing for her, as if she were far away. But then she told him about her tingling fingertips, and he recognized, and climbed onto, what he thought was solid ground. He spoke about morbid spells and fancies, and not giving way. She mentioned vague, terrible diseases of the blood. He went on with his curative discussion. But presently, looking tired, she dropped her work and sat on a stool, her hands folded in her lap, like a large but wholly biddable child waiting to be told what to think, and at once his sound common sense and his balance collapsed again, and he was not sure of himself. He heard himself reminding her of all the good things the doctors had said, but the indulgent, scoffing note he tried to strike was missing. She nodded with no conviction whatever, and alarm grew up in him. He told himself that there was not a chance in a thousand that she was right, and then that there was indeed just that.

So the hobgoblins crossed over into Martin, and the man in Forty-fifth Street, who had reduced the importance of other things tonight, had now reduced that of reason and common sense. It seemed to Martin that he and Ellen were standing there alone in a small pocket of light and comfort encircled and crowded by loss—not his loss of her, or hers of him (though he was appalled at the thought of ever being out of reach of her if she should need him), but all loss, all ending. And there was no time, in a mortal moment, to be reasonable. He said dutifully, hopefully, that her symptoms were pure nerves, but still he could not bring the necessary—the unanswerable—impatience into his voice. She listened, and nodded again, and went back to the sink, and Martin was sure that he had failed her.

Perhaps he had failed them all, he thought a little later, but he could not say in what way, or why he thought so. He felt perplexed and thwarted. Right was right, fairness was fairness, honesty was honesty, sense was sense, and yet all these old, dependable companions seemed to be standing guard between him and his family tonight. They would not let him go close, which was all he wanted, and he guessed with a shock that perhaps they seldom had. Now it was nearly nine of this queer evening. The dishes were done. His father was in the study watching television and waiting. There were not many places for Martin to go, many things to do—many excuses for delay—in even a large apartment.

He went into the living room and tried to think of his father's house, and his father endangered in it. Nowadays, the old man forgot things, and this exasperated him, and when he found he had forgotten something, he would stamp away intemperately, upstairs or down, to do or get whatever he had forgotten. He had set up a workshop in the basement, and he was repairing half the furniture in the house. The basement stairs were steep and dim. The furniture he dragged down was cumbersome.

The house was too big; the house was too old. But the more persistently Martin tried to reason against it, the more persistently a memory kept pressing to be recalled. In front of the house was a tree that one night long ago had been sheathed in ice and had bewitched him. It had, in fact, caused him to feel a good deal as he felt now, and when he let the memory come, he did so reluctantly, not wanting it to make him compound the evening's heresies.

He and Ellen had come back from their honeymoon that night. Their apartment was not finished. They were staying in Martin's old room, and Ellen was already asleep when, past the edge of the drawn blind, Martin caught a glimpse of the tree sparkling in the light of the street lamp under it. And he did something foreign to a nature that did little on impulse and was designed, on the whole, to see icy trees as merely trees in danger of cracking. He got up and raised the blind, and the tree blazed in at him, glittering and still, and more beautiful than any tree— or anything else—had seemed to him before. He went back to bed and lay a long time looking at it, while it entangled itself in his life. Ellen beside him, and his parents in the next room, and his childhood and his hopes, and the old house and the tree became part of one another, and all of them were suddenly, for the first time, capable of ending. The past was already gone, and the future—bright though it was, and varicolored and lovely as the tree—now also had a treasonable look of brevity. But in spite of transience and loss, the spell of a moment of light that would never come again enclosed and gently, sweetly exalted him. The tree would lose its enchantment, and presently grow green again, and later storms would ice it, but he knew that that night would be unique among the nights of his life.

Now Martin went into the study and saw that, though the set was on, his father was not looking at television. He was gazing blankly down the length of his legs, stretched out in front of him. When he heard Martin come in, he heaved himself up and limped to the set and turned it off. He sat down and smiled hesitantly at Martin, who realized that it might not be necessary to argue, after all. The realization undid him. He knew—he allowed himself to know, though he had spent a year keeping the demoralizing knowledge at arm's length—that his father wanted beyond anything else in the world to spend the rest of his life in his own house. And Martin suddenly wanted overwhelmingly to stop trying to do the prim, trifling things he would have done on any ordinary night, and to give a gift, however foolish, however risky, to one of the people he loved.

"Well, Papa," he said. "I think we ought to have a talk about the house."

"I know how you feel about it," his father said. "I suppose you're right."

"I don't think you'd be happy in an apartment, or in the city," Martin said, while his mind, in its rectitude, protested and retreated and protested. "I don't think I'd consider it, if I were you."

"What's that?" his father asked.

"You want to stay at home," Martin said, "so why don't you?"

"I would like that," his father said slowly. "I think I will. You're positive you don't mind?"

"No," Martin said, already dismayed. "You stay at home."

Steven Gaines, leaving the dinner table, had seen his father look at his sister with an expression that brought into relief a wonderfully fluent line of forehead, nose, and jaw. He went to his room, and, after a few tries, jubilantly decided that he had caught it. He put the sketch in his folder, and set out to visit his girl. He considered asking her to marry him. He yearned to take the sketch along, but he did not; it was something to be revealed only when the time came.

Ellen Gaines, in her kitchen, had finished the dishes in panic. It seemed plain enough to her that Martin knew how ill she was; she had heard it in his voice. Then she watched his back as he went out the door, and abruptly she knew that he knew nothing—nothing at all. He was only afraid. He was afraid, without reason, for her. The panic lifted. What became plain to her now was that he needed her solace, and she felt glad and guilty. The fear of the last three days began to drain away. She wanted only to reassure him, to protect him. She resolved that she would not be so foolish again—so childish. She thought fondly that she must take better care of her husband.

Steven came hurrying through the kitchen on his way out. He kissed his mother as he passed, astonishing her; it was not exactly a thing he did every day. Heartened, she decided that she would save Martin a chore. She went into their room and called her sister-in-law. The sister-in-law laughed, and said that of course she would gladly give the candlesticks to Leora. The trouble was only that Leora had insisted that they belonged to her.

The goodness of Ellen Gaines' life flowed over and through her once more. She called Leora and told her that she could have the candlesticks at the price of a small retreat. Seeing her child already passing the candlesticks on, with grace, to new generations, Leora planned a handsome retreat, intended so to propitiate her aunt that when summer came she would offer her the beach house. Then, looking ahead as her habit was, Leora saw herself inheriting it.

Martin's father was, by this time, on his way to bed. He reflected that if Martin had not changed his mind, he would have had to give in. Later, secretly, in the dark, he confessed to the darkness that he was not certain how long he could keep the house up. Still, he was excited—too excited to sleep. He thought that one minute you could be about to live your life out in a place you'd rather be dead than live in, and the next you could be on your way home, where you belonged. Silently, he promised Martin that he would be careful on the stairs. One had to slow down a little as one grew older. But, by and large, it seemed to him that now he had all he was prepared to ask of life. He could not make out what had got into Martin, but whatever it was, he would always be grateful that it had.

It was now just past eleven. On a short, winding county road leading from Route 22 a few miles north of Armonk, there were three houses, well apart. In the one nearest the highway, a single bedroom light was shining, back of slanted Venetian blinds. In the second, there were no lights. In the third—a half-timbered house set on a knoll and surrounded by rhododendron and small firs—all the lights were burning. At eleven-ten, an enclosed black car—a small hearse—turned off Route 22, wound along the short road, and turned in at the driveway of the third house.

THE LOST PHOEBE

Theodore Dreiser

They lived together in a part of the country which was not so prosperous as it had once been, about three miles from one of those small towns that, instead of increasing in population, is steadily decreasing. The territory was not very thickly settled; perhaps a house every other mile or so, with large areas of corn- and wheat-land and fallow fields that at odd seasons had been sown to timothy and clover. Their particular house was part log and part frame, the log portion being the old original home of Henry's grandfather. The new portion, of now rain-beaten, time-worn slabs, through which the wind squeaked in the chinks at times, and which several overshadowing elms and a butternut-tree made picturesque and reminiscently pathetic, but a little damp, was erected by Henry when he was twenty-one and just married.

That was forty-eight years before. The furniture inside, like the house outside, was old and mildewy and reminiscent of an earlier day. You have seen the what-not of cherry wood, perhaps, with spiral legs and fluted top. It was there. The old-fashioned four poster bed, with its ball-like protuberances and deep curving incisions, was there also, a sadly alienated descendant of an early Jacobean ancestor. The bureau of cherry was also high and wide and solidly built, but faded-looking, and with a musty odor. The rag carpet that underlay all these sturdy examples of enduring furniture was a weak, faded, lead-and-pink-colored affair woven by Phoebe Ann's own hands, when she was fifteen years younger than she was when she died. The creaky wooden loom on which it had been done now stood like a dusty, bony skeleton, along with a broken rocking-chair, a worm-eaten clothes-press—Heaven knows how old—a lime-stained bench that had once been used to keep flowers on outside the door, and other decrepit factors of household utility, in an east room that was a lean-to against this so-called main portion. All sorts of other broken-down furniture were about this place; an antiquated clothes-horse, cracked in two of its ribs; a broken mirror in an old cherry frame, which had fallen from a nail and cracked itself three days before their youngest son, Jerry, died; an extension hat-rack, which once had had porcelain knobs on the ends of its pegs; and a sewing-machine, long since outdone in its clumsy mechanism by rivals of a newer generation.

The orchard to the east of the house was full of gnarled old apple-trees, worm-eaten as to trunks and branches, and fully ornamented with green and white lichens, so that it had a sad, greenish-white, silvery effect in moonlight. The low outhouses, which had once housed chickens, a horse or two, a cow, and several pigs, were covered with patches of moss as to their roof, and the sides had been free of paint for so long that they were blackish gray as to color, and a little spongy. The picket-fence in front, with its gate squeaky and askew, and the side fences of the stake-and-rider type were in an equally run-down condition. As a matter of fact, they had aged synchronously with the persons who lived here, old Henry Reifsneider and his wife Phoebe Ann.

They had lived here, these two, ever since their marriage, forty-eight years before, and Henry had lived here before that from his childhood up. His father and mother, well along in years when he was a boy, had invited him to bring his wife here when he had first fallen in love and decided to marry; and he had done so. His father and mother were the companions of himself and his wife for ten years after they were married, when both died; and then Henry and Phoebe were left with their five children growing lustily apace. But all sorts of things had happened since then. Of the seven children, all told, that had been born to them, three had died; one girl had gone to Kansas; one boy had gone to Sioux Falls, never even to be heard of after; another boy had gone to Washington; and the last girl lived five counties away in the same State, but was so burdened with cares of her own that she rarely gave them a thought. Time and a commonplace home life that had never been attractive had weaned them thoroughly, so that, wherever they were, they gave little thought as to how it might be with their father and mother.

Old Henry Reifsneider and his wife Phoebe were a loving couple. You perhaps know how it is with simple natures that fasten themselves like lichens on the stones of circumstance and weather their days to a crumbling conclusion. The great world sounds widely, but it has no call for them. They have no soaring intellect. The orchard, the meadow, the corn-field, the pig-pen, and the chicken-lot measure the range of their human activities. When the wheat is headed it is reaped and threshed; when the corn is browned and frosted it is cut and shocked; when the tim-othy is in full head it is cut, and the hay-cock erected. After that comes winter, with the hauling of grain to market, the sawing and splitting of wood, the simple chores of fire-building, meal-getting, occasional repair-ing, and visiting. Beyond these and the changes of weather—the snows, the rains, and the fair days—there are no immediate, significant things. All the rest of life is a far-off, clamorous phantasmagoria, flickering like Northern lights in the night, and sounding as faintly as cow-bells tinkling in the distance.

Old Henry and his wife Phoebe were as fond of each other as it is pos-sible for two old people to be who have nothing else in this life to be fond of. He was a thin old man, seventy when she died, a queer, crotchety per-son with coarse gray-black hair and beard, quite straggly and unkempt. He looked at you out of dull, fishy, watery eyes that had deep-brown crow's-feet at the sides. His clothes, like the clothes of many farmers, were aged and angular and baggy, standing out at the pockets, not fitting about the neck, protuberant and worn at elbow and knee. Phoebe Ann was thin and shapeless, a very umbrella of a woman, clad in shabby black, and with a black bonnet for her best wear. As time had passed, and they had only themselves to look after, their movements had become slower and slower, their activities fewer and fewer. The annual keep of pigs had been reduced from five to one grunting porker, and the single horse which Henry now retained was a sleepy animal, not overnourished and not very clean. The chickens, of which formerly there was a large flock, had almost disappeared, owing to ferrets, foxes, and the lack of proper care, which produces disease. The former healthy garden was now a straggling mem-ory of itself, and the vines and flower-beds that formerly ornamented the windows and dooryard had now become choking thickets. A will had been made which divided the small tax-eaten property equally among the re-maining four, so that it was really of no interest to any of them. Yet these two lived together in peace and sympathy, only that now and then old Henry would become unduly cranky, complaining almost invariably that something had been neglected or mislaid which was of no importance at all.

"Phoebe, where's my corn-knife? You ain't never minded to let my things alone no more."

"Now you hush, Henry," his wife would caution him in a cracked and squeaky voice. "If you don't, I'll leave yuh. I'll git up and walk out of here some day, and then where would y' be? Y' ain't got anybody but me to look after yuh, so yuh just behave yourself. Your corn-knife's on the mantel where it's allus been unless you've gone an' put it summers else."

Old Henry, who knew his wife would never leave him in any circumstances, used to speculate at times as to what he would do if she were to die. That was the one leaving that he really feared. As he climbed on the chair at night to wind the old, long-pendulumed, double-weighted clock, or went finally to the front and the back door to see that they were safely shut in, it was a comfort to know that Phoebe was there, properly ensconced on her side of the bed, and that if he stirred restlessly in the night, she would be there to ask what he wanted.

"Now, Henry, do lie still! You're as restless as a chicken."

"Well, I can't sleep, Phoebe."

"Well, yuh needn't roll so, anyhow. Yuh kin let me sleep."

This usually reduced him to a state of somnolent ease. If she wanted a pail of water, it was a grumbling pleasure for him to get it; and if she did rise first to build the fires, he saw that the wood was cut and placed within easy reach. They divided this simple world nicely between them.

As the years had gone on, however, fewer and fewer people had called. They were well-known for a distance of as much as ten square miles as old Mr. and Mrs. Reifsneider, honest, moderately Christian, but too old to be really interesting any longer. The writing of letters had become an almost impossible burden too difficult to continue or even negotiate via others, although an occasional letter still did arrive from the daughter in Pemberton County. Now and then some old friend stopped with a pie or cake or a roasted chicken or duck, or merely to see that they were well; but even these kindly minded visits were no longer frequent.

One day in the early spring of her sixty-fourth year Mrs. Reifsneider took sick, and from a low fever passed into some indefinable ailment which, because of her age, was no longer curable. Old Henry drove to Swinnerton, the neighboring town, and procured a doctor. Some friends called, and the immediate care of her was taken off his hands. Then one chill spring night she died, and old Henry, in a fog of sorrow and uncer-

tainty, followed her body to the nearest graveyard, an unattractive space
with a few pines growing in it. Although he might have gone to the
daughter in Pemberton or sent for her, it was really too much trouble and
he was too weary and fixed. It was suggested to him at once by one friend
and another that he come to stay with them awhile, but he did not see fit.
He was so old and so fixed in his notions and so accustomed to the exact
surroundings he had known all his days, that he could not think of leaving. He wanted to remain near where they had put his Phoebe; and the
fact that he would have to live alone did not trouble him in the least. The
living children were notified and the care of him offered if he would leave,
but he would not.

"I kin make a shift for myself," he continually announced to old Dr.
Morrow, who had attended his wife in this case. "I kin cook a little, and,
besides, it don't take much more'n coffee an' bread in the mornin's to
satisfy me. I'll get along now well enough. Yuh just let me be." And after
many pleadings and proffers of advice, with supplies of coffee and bacon
and baked bread duly offered and accepted, he was left to himself. For a
while he sat idly outside his door brooding in the spring sun. He tried to
revive his interest in farming, and to keep himself busy and free from
thought by looking after the fields, which of late had been much neglected. It was a gloomy thing to come in of an evening, however, or in the afternoon and find no shadow of Phoebe where everything suggested her.
By degrees he put a few of her things away. At night he sat beside his lamp
and read in the papers that were left him occasionally or in a Bible that he
had neglected for years, but he could get little solace from these things.
Mostly he held his hand over his mouth and looked at the floor as he sat
and thought of what had become of her, and how soon he himself would
die. He made a great business of making his coffee in the morning and frying himself a little bacon at night; but his appetite was gone. The shell in
which he had been housed so long seemed vacant, and its shadows were
suggestive of immedicable griefs. So he lived quite dolefully for five long
months, and then a change began.

It was one night, after he had looked after the front and the back
door, wound the clock, blown out the light, and gone through all the self-
same motions that he had indulged in for years, that he went to bed not so
much to sleep as to think. It was a moonlight night. The green-lichen-
covered orchard just outside and to be seen from his bed where he now lay
was a silvery affair, sweetly spectral. The moon shone through the east
windows, throwing the pattern of the panes on the wooden floor, and

making the old furniture, to which he was accustomed, stand out dimly in the room. As usual he had been thinking of Phoebe and the years when they had been young together, and of the children who had gone, and the poor shift he was making of his present days. The house was coming to be in a very bad state indeed. The bed-clothes were in disorder and not clean, for he made a wretched shift of washing. It was a terror to him. The roof leaked, causing things, some of them, to remain damp for weeks at a time, but he was getting into that brooding state where he would accept anything rather than exert himself. He preferred to pace slowly to and fro or to sit and think.

By twelve o'clock of this particular night he was asleep, however, and by two had waked again. The moon by this time had shifted to a position on the western side of the house, and it now shone in through the windows of the living-room and those of the kitchen beyond. A certain combination of furniture—a chair near a table, with his coat on it, the half-open kitchen door casting a shadow, and the position of a lamp near a paper—gave him an exact representation of Phoebe leaning over the table as he had often seen her do in life. It gave him a great start. Could it be she —or her ghost? He had scarcely ever believed in spirits; and still—He looked at her fixedly in the feeble half-light, his old hair tingling oddly at the roots, and then sat up. The figure did not move. He put his thin legs out of the bed and sat looking at her, wondering if this could really be Phoebe. They had talked of ghosts often in their lifetime, of apparitions and omens; but they had never agreed that such things could be. It had never been a part of his wife's creed that she could have a spirit that could return to walk the earth. Her after-world was quite a different affair, a vague heaven, no less, from which the righteous did not trouble to return. Yet here she was now, bending over the table in her black skirt and gray shawl, her pale profile outlined against the moonlight.

"Phoebe," he called, thrilling from head to toe and putting out one bony hand, "have yuh come back?"

The figure did not stir, and he arose and walked uncertainly to the door, looking at it fixedly the while. As he drew near, however, the apparition resolved itself into its primal content—his old coat over the high-backed chair, the lamp by the paper, the half-open door.

"Well," he said to himself, his mouth open, "I thought shore I saw her." And he ran his hand strangely and vaguely through his hair, the while his nervous tension relaxed. Vanished as it had, it gave him the idea that she might return.

Another night, because of this first illusion, and because his mind was now constantly on her and he was old, he looked out of the window that was nearest his bed and commanded a hen-coop and pig-pen and a part of the wagon-shed, and there, a faint mist exuding from the damp of the ground, he thought he saw her again. It was one of those little wisps of mist, one of those faint exhalations of the earth that rise in a cool night after a warm day, and flicker like small white cypresses of fog before they disappear. In life it had been a custom of hers to cross this lot from her kitchen door to the pig-pen to throw in any scrap that was left from her cooking, and here she was again. He sat up and watched it strangely, doubtfully, because of his previous experience, but inclined, because of the nervous titillation that passed over his body, to believe that spirits really were, and that Phoebe, who would be concerned because of his lonely state, must be thinking about him, and hence returning. What other way would she have? How otherwise could she express herself? It would be within the province of her charity so to do, and like her loving interest in him. He quivered and watched it eagerly; but, a faint breath of air stirring, it wound away toward the fence and disappeared.

A third night, as he was actually dreaming, some ten days later, she came to his bedside and put her hand on his head.

"Poor Henry!" she said. "It's too bad."

He roused out of his sleep, actually to see her, he thought, moving from his bed-room into the one living-room, her figure a shadowy mass of black. The weak straining of his eyes caused little points of light to flicker about the outlines of her form. He arose, greatly astonished, walked the floor in the cool room, convinced that Phoebe was coming back to him. If he only thought sufficiently, if he made it perfectly clear by his feeling that he needed her greatly, she would come back, this kindly wife, and tell him what to do. She would perhaps be with him much of the time, in the night, anyhow; and that would make him less lonely, this state more endurable.

In age and with the feeble it is not such a far cry from the subtleties of illusion to actual hallucination, and in due time this transition was made for Henry. Night after night he waited, expecting her return. Once in his weird mood he thought he saw a pale light moving about the room, and another time he thought he saw her walking in the orchard after dark. It was one morning when the details of his lonely state were virtually unendurable that he woke with the thought that she was not dead. How he had arrived at this conclusion it is hard to say. His mind had gone. In its place was a fixed illusion. He and Phoebe had had a senseless quarrel. He had reproached her for not leaving his pipe where he was accustomed to find it, and she had left. It was an aberrated fulfillment of her old jesting threat that if he did not behave himself she would leave him.

"I guess I could find yuh ag'in," he had always said. But her cackling threat had always been.

"Yuh'll not find me if I ever leave yuh. I guess I kin git some place where yuh can't find me."

This morning when he arose he did not think to build the fire in the customary way or to grind his coffee and cut his bread, as was his wont, but solely to meditate as to where he should search for her and how he should induce her to come back. Recently the one horse had been dispensed with because he found it cumbersome and beyond his needs. He took down his soft crush hat after he had dressed himself, a new glint of interest and determination in his eye, and taking his black crook cane from behind the door, where he had always placed it, started out briskly to look for her among the nearest neighbors. His old shoes clumped soundly in the dust as he walked, and his gray-black locks, now grown rather long, straggled out in a dramatic fringe or halo from under his hat. His short coat stirred busily as he walked, and his hands and face were peaked and pale.

"Why, hello, Henry! Where're yuh goin' this mornin'?" inquired Farmer Dodge, who, hauling a load of wheat to market, encountered him on the public road. He had not seen the aged farmer in months, not since his wife's death, and he wondered now, seeing him looking so spry.

"Yuh ain't seen Phoebe, have yuh?" inquired the old man, looking up quizzically.

"Phoebe who?" inquired Farmer Dodge, not for the moment connecting the name with Henry's dead wife.

"Why, my wife Phoebe, o' course. Who do yuh s'pose I mean?" He stared up with a pathetic sharpness of glance from under his shaggy, gray eyebrows.

"Wall, I'll swan, Henry, yuh ain't jokin', are yuh?" said the solid Dodge, a pursy man, with a smooth, hard, red face. "It can't be your wife yuh're talkin' about. She's dead."

"Dead! Shucks!" retorted the demented Reifsneider. "She left me early this mornin', while I was sleepin'. She allus got up to build the fire, but she's gone now. We had a little spat last night, an' I guess that's the reason. But I guess I kin find her. She's gone over to Matilda Race's; that's where she's gone.''

He started briskly up the road, leaving the amazed Dodge to stare in wonder after him.

"Well, I'll be switched!" he said aloud to himself. "He's clean out'n his head. That poor old feller's been livin' down there till he's gone outen his mind. I'll have to notify the authorities." And he flicked his whip with great enthusiasm. "Geddap!" he said, and was off.

Reifsneider met no one else in this poorly populated region until he reached the whitewashed fence of Matilda Race and her husband three miles away. He had passed several other houses en route, but these not being within the range of his illusion were not considered. His wife, who had known Matilda well, must be here. He opened the picket-gate which guarded the walk, and stamped briskly up to the door.

"Why, Mr. Reifsneider," exclaimed old Matilda herself, a stout woman, looking out of the door in answer to his knock, "what brings yuh here this mornin'?"

"Is Phoebe here?" he demanded eagerly.

"Phoebe who? What Phoebe?" replied Mrs. Race, curious as to this sudden development of energy on his part.

"Why, my Phoebe, o' course. My wife Phoebe. Who do yuh s'pose? Ain't she here now?"

"Lawsy me!" exclaimed Mrs. Race, opening her mouth. "Yuh pore man! So you're clean out'n your mind now. Yuh come right in and sit down. I'll git yuh a cup o' coffee. O' course your wife ain't here; but yuh come in an' sit down. I'll find her fer yuh after a while. I know where she is."

The old farmer's eyes softened, and he entered. He was so thin and pale a specimen, pantalooned and patriarchal, that he aroused Mrs. Race's extremest sympathy as he took off his hat and laid it on his knees quite softly and mildly.

"We had a quarrel last night, an' she left me," he volunteered.

"Laws! laws!" sighed Mrs. Race, there being no one present with whom to share her astonishment as she went to her kitchen. "The pore man! Now somebody's just got to look after him. He can't be allowed to run around the country this way lookin' for his dead wife. It's turrible."

She boiled him a pot of coffee and brought in some of her new-baked bread and fresh butter. She set out some of her best jam and put a couple of eggs to boil, lying whole-heartedly the while.

"Now yuh stay right there, Uncle Henry, till Jake comes in, an' I'll send him to look for Phoebe. I think it's more'n likely she's over to Swinnerton with some o' her friends. Anyhow, we'll find out. Now yuh just drink this coffee an' eat this bread. Yuh must be tired. Yuh've had a long walk this mornin'." Her idea was to take counsel with Jake, "her man," and perhaps have him notify the authorities.

She bustled about, meditating on the uncertainties of life, while old Reifsneider thrummed on the rim of his hat with his pale fingers and later ate abstractedly of what she offered. His mind was on his wife, however, and since she was not here, or did not appear, it wandered vaguely away to a family by the name of Murray, miles away in another direction. He decided after a time that he would not wait for Jake Race to hunt his wife but would seek her for himself. He must be on, and urge her to come back.

"Well, I'll be goin'," he said, getting up and looking strangely about him. "I guess she didn't come here after all. She went over to the Murrays', I guess. I'll not wait any longer, Mis' Race. There's a lot to do over to the house to-day." And out he marched in the face of her protests taking to the dusty road again in the warm spring sun, his cane striking the earth as he went.

It was two hours later that this pale figure of a man appeared in the Murrays' doorway, dusty, perspiring, eager. He had tramped all of five miles, and it was noon. An amazed husband and wife of sixty heard his strange query, and realized also that he was mad. They begged him to stay to dinner, intending to notify the authorities later and see what could be done; but though he stayed to partake of a little something, he did not stay long, and was off again to another distant farmhouse, his idea of many things to do and his need of Phoebe impelling him. So it went for that day and the next and the next, the circle of his inquiry ever widening.

The process by which a character assumes the significance of being peculiar, his antics weird, yet harmless, in such a community is often involute and pathetic. This day, as has been said, saw Reifsneider at other doors, eagerly asking his unnatural question, and leaving a trail of amazement, sympathy, and pity in his wake. Although the authorities were informed—the county sheriff, no less—it was not deemed advisable to take him into custody; for when those who knew old Henry, and had for so long, reflected on the condition of the county insane asylum, a place which, because of the poverty of the district, was of staggering aberration and sickening environment, it was decided to let him remain at large; for, strange to relate, it was found on investigation that at night he returned peaceably enough to his lonesome domicile there to discover whether his wife had returned, and to brood in loneliness until the morning. Who would lock up a thin, eager, seeking old man with iron-gray hair and an attitude of kindly, innocent inquiry, particularly when he was well known for a past of only kindly servitude and reliability? Those who had known him best rather agreed that he should be allowed to roam at large. He could do no harm. There were many who were willing to help him as to food, old clothes, the odds and ends of his daily life—at least at first. His figure after a time became not so much a common-place as an accepted curiosity, and the replies, ''Why, no, Henry; I ain't see her,'' or ''No, Henry; she ain't been here to-day,'' more customary.

For several years thereafter then he was an odd figure in the sun and rain, on dusty roads and muddy ones, encountered occasionally in strange and unexpected places, pursuing his endless search. Undernourishment, after a time, although the neighbors and those who knew his history gladly contributed from their store, affected his body; for he walked much and ate little. The longer he roamed the public highway in this manner, the deeper became his strange hallucination; and finding it harder and harder to return from his more and more distant pilgrimages, he finally began taking a few utensils with him from his home, making a small package of them, in order that he might not be compelled to return. In an old tin coffee-pot of large size he placed a small tin cup, a knife, fork, and spoon, some salt and pepper, and to the outside of it, by a string forced through a pierced hole, he fastened a plate, which could be released, and which was his woodland table. It was no trouble for him to secure the little food that he needed, and with a strange, almost religious dignity, he had no hesitation in asking for that much. By degrees his hair became longer and longer, his once black hat became an earthen brown, and his clothes threadbare and dusty.

For all of three years he walked, and none knew how wide were his perambulations, nor how he survived the storms and cold. They could not see him, with homely rural understanding and forethought, sheltering himself in hay-cocks, or by the sides of cattle, whose warm bodies protected him from the cold, and whose dull understandings were not opposed to his harmless presence. Overhanging rocks and trees kept him at times from the rain, and a friendly hay-loft or corn-crib was not above his humble consideration.

The involute progression of hallucination is strange. From asking at doors and being constantly rebuffed or denied, he finally came to the conclusion that although his Phoebe might not be in any of the houses at the doors of which he inquired, she might nevertheless be within the sound of his voice. And so, from patient inquiry, he began to call sad, occasional cries, that ever and anon waked the quiet landscapes and ragged hill regions, and set to echoing his thin ''O-o-o Phoebe! O-o-o Phoebe!'' It had a pathetic, albeit insane, ring, and many a farmer or plowboy came to know it even from afar and say, ''There goes old Reifsneider.''

Another thing that puzzled him greatly after a time and after many hundreds of inquiries was, when he no longer had any particular dooryard in view and no special inquiry to make, which way to go. These crossroads, which occasionally led in four or even six directions, came after a time to puzzle him. But to solve this knotty problem, which became more and more of a puzzle, there came to his aid another hallucination. Phoebe's spirit or some power of the air or wind or nature would tell him. If he stood at the center of the parting of the ways, closed his eyes, turned thrice about, and called ''O-o-o Phoebe!'' twice, and then threw his cane straight before him, that would surely indicate which way to go for Phoebe, or one of these mystic powers would surely govern its direction and fall! In whichever direction it went, even though, as was not infrequently the case, it took him back along the path he had already come, or across fields, he was no so far gone in his mind but that he gave himself ample time to search before he called again. Also the hallucination seemed to persist that at some time he would surely find her. There were hours when his feet were sore, and his limbs weary, when he would stop in the heat to wipe his seamed brow, or in the cold to beat his arms. Sometimes, after throwing away his cane, and finding it indicating the direction from which he had just come, he would shake his head wearily and philosophically, as if contemplating the unbelievable or an untoward fate, and then start briskly off. His strange figure came finally to be known in the farthest reaches of three or four counties. Old Reifsneider was a pathetic character. His fame was wide.

Near a little town called Watersville, in Green County, perhaps four miles from that minor center of human activity, there was a place or precipice locally known as the Red Cliff, a sheer wall of red sandstone, perhaps a hundred feet high, which raised its sharp face for half a mile or more above the fruitful cornfields and orchards that lay beneath, and which was surmounted by a thick grove of trees. The slope that slowly led up to it from the opposite side was covered by a rank growth of beech, hickory, and ash, through which threaded a number of wagontracks crossing at various angles. In fair weather it had become old Reifsneider's habit, so inured was he by now to the open, to make his bed in some such patch of trees as this to fry his bacon or boil his eggs at the foot of some tree before laying himself down for the night. Occasionally, so light and inconsequential was his sleep, he would walk at night. More often, the moonlight or some sudden wind stirring in the trees or a reconnoitering animal arousing him, he would sit up and think, or pursue his quest in the moonlight or the dark, a strange, unnatural, half wild, half savage-looking but utterly harmless creature, calling at lonely road crossings, staring at dark and shuttered houses, and wondering where, where Phoebe could really be.

That particular lull that comes in the systole-diastole of this earthly ball at two o'clock in the morning invariably aroused him, and though he might not go any farther he would sit up and contemplate the darkness or the stars, wondering. Sometimes in the strange processs of his mind he would fancy that he saw moving among the trees the figure of his lost wife, and then he would get up to follow, taking his utensils, always on a string, and his cane. If she seemed to evade him too easily he would run, or plead, or, suddenly losing track of the fancied figure, stand awed or disappointed, grieving for the moment over the almost insurmountable difficulties of his search.

It was in the seventh year of these hopeless peregrinations, in the dawn of a similar springtime to that in which his wife had died, that he came at last one night to the vicinity of this self-same patch that crowned the rise to the Red Cliff. His far-flung cane, used as a divining-rod at the last cross-roads, had brought him hither. He had walked many, many miles. It was after ten o'clock at night, and he was very weary. Long wandering and little eating had left him but a shadow of his former self. It was a question now not so much of physical strength but of spiritual endurance which kept him up. He had scarcely eaten this day, and now exhausted he set himself down in the dark to rest and possibly to sleep.

Curiously on this occasion a strange suggestion of the presence of his wife surrounded him. It would not be long now, he counseled with himself, although the long months had brought him nothing, until he should see her, talk to her. He fell asleep after a time, his head on his knees. At midnight the moon began to rise, and at two in the morning, his wakeful hour, was a large silver disk shining through the trees to the east. He opened his eyes when the radiance became strong, making a silver pattern at his feet and lighting the woods with strange lusters and silvery, shadowy forms. As usual, his old notion that his wife must be near occurred to him on this occasion, and he looked about him with a speculative, anticipatory eye. What was it that moved in the distant shadows along the path by which he had entered—a pale, flickering will-o'-the-wisp that bobbed gracefully among the trees and riveted his expectant gaze? Moonlight and shadows combined to give it a strange form and a stranger reality, this fluttering of bogfire or dancing of wandering fireflies. Was it truly his lost Phoebe? By a circuitous route it passed about him, and in his fevered state he fancied that he could see the very eyes of her, not as she was when he last saw her in the black dress and shawl but now a strangely younger Phoebe, gayer, sweeter, the one whom he had known years before as a girl. Old Reifsneider got up. He had been expecting and dreaming of this hour all these years, and now as he saw the feeble light dancing lightly before him he peered at it questioningly, one thin hand in his gray hair.

Of a sudden there came to him now for the first time in many years the full charm of her girlish figure as he had known it in boyhood, the pleasing, sympathetic smile, the brown hair, the blue sash she had once worn about her waist at a picnic, her gay, graceful movements. He walked around the base of the tree, straining with his eyes, forgetting for once his cane and utensils, and following eagerly after. On she moved before him, a will-o'-the-wisp of the spring, a little flame above her head, and it seemed as though among the small saplings of ash and beech and the thick trunks of hickory and elm that she signaled with a young, a lightsome hand.

"O Phoebe! Phoebe!" he called. "Have yuh really come? Have yuh really answered me?" And hurrying faster, he fell once, scrambling lamely to his feet, only to see the light in the distance dancing illusively on. On and on he hurried until he was fairly running, brushing his ragged arms against the trees, striking his hands and face against impeding twigs. His hat was gone, his lungs were breathless, his reason quite astray, when coming to the edge of the cliff he saw her below among a silvery bed of apple-trees now blooming in the spring.

"O Phoebe!" he called. "O Phoebe! Oh, no, don't leave me!" And feeling the lure of a world where love was young and Phoebe as this vision presented her, a delightful epitome of their quondam youth, he gave a gay cry of "Oh, wait, Phoebe!" and leaped.

Some farmer-boys, reconnoitering this region of bounty and prospect some few days afterward, found first the tin utensils tied together under the tree where he had left them, and then later at the foot of the cliff, pale, broken, but elate, a molded smile of peace and delight upon his lips, his body. His old hat was discovered lying under some low-growing saplings the twigs of which had held it back. No one of all the simple population knew how eagerly and joyously he had found his lost mate.

FEBRUARY 11, 1977

Frederick Morgan

to my son John

You died nine years ago today.
I see you still sometimes in dreams
in white track-shirt and shorts, running,
against a drop of tropic green.

It seems to be a meadow, lying
open to early morning sun:
no other person is in view,
a quiet forest waits beyond.

Why do you hurry? What's the need?
Poor eager boy, why can't you see
once and for all you've lost this race
though you run for all eternity?

Your youngest brother's passed you by
at last: he's older now than you—
and all our lives have ramified
in meanings which you never knew.

And yet, your eyes still burn with joy,
your body's splendor never fades—
sometimes I seek to follow you
across the greenness, into the shade

of that great forest in whose depths
houses await and lives are lived,
where you haste in gleeful search of me
bearing a message I must have—

but I, before I change, must bide
the "days of my appointed time,"
and so I age from self to self
while you await me, always young.

JURY DUTY

Robert Henderson

It is a winter morning. Snow of the night before still lies on the walks of the streets that lead to Foley Square, or, where the walks are cleared, forms banks alongside them. A gray-haired man named Owen Gilbert scoops a handful of snow, makes a ball of it, and pitches it into the street, recalling the winter pastimes of his boyhood. He lives a good deal in his past, often gently amending it in his favor. He is on his way to serve as a juror—a duty he has never before performed and which he is eager to try. Once (in the eighth grade), he read the story of Abraham Lincoln's early years in Springfield, and decided that he himself was ineluctably called to the bar. This purpose held firm until he reached Columbia and was lured into becoming a mathematics major by a professor whose idol was Euclid. The professor contended that in mathematics Owen would find a haven more tranquil than the law. In the end, this view prevailed. Owen then meant to take an advanced degree and teach, but he married early and became instead a certified public accountant—also a peaceful calling, in which he has thrived.

So now he goes up the courthouse steps and finds his way to a huge, smoky room, where he sits waiting with scores of other prospective jurors. After a long while, his name is called by a clerk, and the panel of which he is part is taken by a bailiff to a courtroom. There the questioning—the weeding out—of the panel by attorneys and judge begins. To pass the time, Owen imagines himself firing off far more penetrating questions than those he is hearing. And then his own turn comes. He goes to sit in the jury box and is told (as he has heard each previous candidate told) that this is a child-custody case. It will introduce testimony regarding adultery and divorce. I have had experience of both, Owen thinks. I should be able to judge.

The child in question—a boy—is not present. The mother is. She is young, blond, primly dressed, haggard-looking. She and the child's father have recently been divorced. Her lawyer is an intense man with a large, shaggy head and bulging eyes. The father is also present—full, it seems to Owen, of youthful aplomb. He sits between his parents, both themselves lawyers, as Owen is to learn. The man representing the young father is sleek, understated, but in questioning he has a tendency to pace thoughtfully, then pounce. (He has borrowed the manner from some courtroom drama, Owen thinks. A *television* courtroom drama.)

The mother's lawyer begins to ask questions of Owen. Does he know anyone connected with the case? The principals? Either attorney? The judge? Owen does not. The queries run on. They are easily answered. Then, "Have you ever been involved in a divorce action?" Owen hesitates. He has long since been divorced. But if he says so, he will very likely be dismissed, and this he certainly does not want. But "involved in"? surely one could hedge a bit. His wife had divorced him for an adultery he did not commit, but he had in no way been *involved* in the *action*. He had told her lawyer simply that he would not stand in the way. He had washed his hands of the action. The lawyer had answered that in New York these matters could be arranged. They were arranged daily. Everyone knew it. Witnesses were easily come by. The lawyer would take care of it. So Owen says, "No," and the questions drone on predictably, and he is accepted as a juror.

There is a recess for lunch. Owen finds a crowded, congenial restaurant and has a double Martini before ordering his food. The judge is also there, with two other men. Have I lied in court, Owen wonders—troubled now. Watching the judge. I have *been* divorced, and in the course of it I condoned a fraud. Is that involvement?

The question lurks in the back of his mind through the afternoon. The jury is finally selected late in the day, and the principals leave, the young mother taking a circuitous route, avoiding her former husband and his parents. Her name, the jury has learned, is Lucy Conrad; the father's is Russell. The judge tells the jury that when the case opens in the morning they must consider the evidence presented and *only* the evidence. They are not to discuss the case with anyone outside or with each other. Then he dismisses them.

Around a turn in the dim courthouse corridor, Owen comes suddenly face to face with Lucy Conrad, who is standing there with her lawyer. She spins away from Owen, but he has seen that she is tense and trembling. She seems about to put her head on her lawyer's shoulder, but instead she covers her face with both hands and a small sound—a voiced sigh—escapes her. Owen hurries on.

He dines alone in a place near his rambling old apartment off lower Fifth Avenue. He has few friends, but, having many books and records, seldom feels a need for them. He is sixty. His three best friends are the other members of an amateur string quartet in which Owen plays the cello. They meet at his apartment most Thursday evenings. It is now only Monday, and Owen finds himself wishing that he could advance time by a couple of days.

All evening, he is unaccountably restless. It is hard for him to concentrate on reading or music. He gives up both, roams the apartment, and eventually makes himself a nightcap and goes to bed. And lies awake. He keeps seeing Lucy Conrad in the courtroom and then in the hallway. It is far too early to think of judging, but at least he can wonder what sort of mother she would make. He thinks of his own wife, of his divorce. He had not minded it too much. He had protested, argued with her, but—he thinks in retrospect—it had in fact seemed harder for her than for him. He had cursed and choked, with tears held back, but only once—only when, weeping, she had refused to reconsider and he had felt humiliated. He realizes this now, though at the time he thought he had raged for grief. And he recognizes Lucy's gesture and her sigh; in one of their quieter talks, his wife had done just that. To his surprise, the recollection gives him a small pang—owed to Lucy as much as to his wife. But as a man who had once intended to be a lawyer, as a juryman who fully means to consider only the evidence presented in the case, he must dismiss all feeling, all involvement.

In the morning, the lawyers make their opening statements. Both come close to the jury box and lean over the rail, each as he tells what he expects to prove trying to fix the eyes of individual jurors. It is a tactic before which Owen shrinks; it is both a challenge and an unwarranted intimacy. Russell Conrad's lawyer proposes to show that Lucy is not a fit mother. Her lawyer plans to refute this. The first witness called is a house-maid. She testifies that in Russell's absence Lucy twice entertained other men at dinner. This seems less than damning to Owen. The maid mentions the couple's divorce trial, at which she had given the same testimony. The judge sustains an objection and tells the jury to disregard the remark. How much, Owen wonders, of what he is going to hear can he put out of his mind when ordered to? And why may he not know all that goes on—what happens in those head-together whisperings at the bench? Was this divorce, like his, founded on false testimony? No, not necessarily. The law in New York long ago accepted other grounds. Still, he would like to know everything that is relevant to this case, and it seems he is not going to. The law is not going to let him.

That night, Owen, wakeful again, thinks once more of his marriage. His wife was impulsive, vulnerable, darkly pretty, and deeply immersed in any cause that struck her conscience, as a succession of causes did. Owen was hardly one for causes. The earnestness, the striving, made him uneasy, but all the same he was deeply flattered by her attention. Her name was Jean. They met in their senior year in college. Around graduation time, Jean seemed to believe, or hope, that they would marry, and soon they did, with Owen abandoning advanced study, getting a series of ill-paying jobs, and working at night toward his C.P.A. certificate. Once he had it, their lot improved. Within a year, he joined an architectural firm as one of several accountants, and in time became the chief one. He and Jean took the apartment near lower Fifth Avenue, and Jean rearranged the furniture and pictures on a seasonal basis and sometimes oftener. Owen found this distracting; he liked his surroundings to remain reassuringly stable winter and summer. But he wanted also to indulge Jean and contrived to believe that he did so successfully—believed, even, that he was a model husband. And so it came as a shock when she told him she wanted to divorce him.

She wanted to marry a man Owen had met a time or two and rather enjoyed, though the man, like Jean, was restless and full of causes. He was not well off; there would have to be a New York divorce, since Owen, though refusing to stand in the way, did not feel obliged to finance a trip to Reno by his wife. And, feeling mildly treasonable, he found that when the first jolt had worn off he was looking toward the future almost with relief. Jean was the one who took the whole thing badly, though she was determined to go through with it. And when the divorce was out of the way she enrolled in a secretarial school and later got a job in a dean's office back at Columbia. She never married the man she said she wanted to marry.

The actual trial is in its third day. It is Thursday. Now the jury waits in a room down a little hall from the court. The judge is—again—hearing an argument to which the jury may not be privy. The jurors talk and smoke, drink water, desultorily play cards. Two of them are women who, against the judge's instructions, are already discussing the case in low voices in a corner. Two of the men are black. One is a full juror, the other an alternate. They habitually stay together, though they are immensely amiable —jovial—toward their colleagues. The rest are an assortment—a grocer, a clerk in a department store, and so on.

Owen stands beside a window alone. He is thinking of Lucy Conrad, who that morning, for the third time, had interrupted a witness. The points had all been small ones and she could only harm her case by unseemly behavior. The judge had reprimanded her sternly twice. The third time, he had threatened to hold her in contempt. She had not broken in again, but later she had run from the courtroom weeping. Overwrought, Owen thinks—unhappily, for he likes her. Lucy Conrad is unstable. But he cannot believe in the adultery Russell's lawyer is trying to establish. Owen has listened carefully to the testimony, and he is not at all convinced. Besides, she seems so simple, so isolated. She has not yet testified, nor has her former husband. But her misery is plain in her face, in her shrinking body, and in her hands that twist constantly. She seems far from venturesome enough for secret affairs. She seems weak and pitiable, rather.

It appears to Owen that Russell is quite the opposite. He looks to be the son of his parents. All three of them—especially the parents—have all along looked determined, looked sure. And Owen wonders if Russell's parents themselves may want the virtual custody of the child.

Then, inexplicably, Owen finds his thoughts veering once more to his own wife. He wonders why she did not, after all, marry. He wonders— now, after nearly thirty years—what had really gone on in Jean's mind; she had, in fact, revealed so little. Had she ever truly intended to marry? If not, why *had* she wanted the divorce? In what way had he been lacking? In failing to share her shifting social ardors? Their sexual life had been good, if rather tranquil. *Too* tranquil? They had seldom quarrelled. Peace had always come quickly. Too quickly? Leaving her a residue, a resentment? Had she simply had second thoughts about her plan to marry? Why, then, had she not come back to him? Too much pride? He would, of course, have welcomed her. Or would he? Questions that are in no way germane to the present or the trial, though, obscurely, they persist in seeming so to him.

There is a lunch break. The jury will go back to court afterward. The taller of the black men—a Mr. Travis, a retired mailman with large, humorous eyes and a sprinkling of white in his close-cut hair—comes up to Mr. Owen as the jurors are leaving. Mr. Travis says that he and his friend have found a good and inexpensive place to eat not far away. Good soup, good omelettes, real good veal cacciatore. He invites Owen to join them. Owen thanks Mr. Travis profusely, but refuses. He says that he knows the proprietor of the place he goes to regularly and that the proprietor expects him—even makes the prices right for him. Owen *has* a passing acquaintance with the proprietor of the restaurant he favors, but the rest is polite evasion. Mr. Travis nods, smiles, and he and his friend saunter out. Very slowly, Owen notices.

In the restaurant, lunching at the rates given on the menu, Owen worries. He is sure that the slow saunter was deliberate. He believes that he has offended Mr. Travis, whom he has come to like. Mr. Travis will think that Owen did not go along because the two men are black, and this is simply not so. The second violinist in Owen's quartet is black—a Jamaican—and a friend. Owen refused Mr. Travis because he prefers to be alone, because he does not want to experiment with a new restaurant, and because he does know both the proprietor and a waitress who has begun to make something of a pet of him. Still, Owen is distressed. He wishes the matter had never come up.

The jurors return to their room to wait for the bailiff who will take them back to court. Mr. Travis and his companion arrive. Mr. Travis comes over to Owen and says, "Ole buddy, you missed out on a good lunch, but I expect yours was just as fine." Then, after a pause, he peers at Owen and says, "You the quiet one here, you know? Quietest little juror I ever did see," and with a shout of laughter, he gives Owen a hug and a pat on the shoulder, ending his distress, if momentarily.

Now the jurors file into court and take their places. A surprise witness —a handsome woman of indefinite age—is called to the stand by Lucy's lawyer. She is plainly wretched. Russell Conrad for the first time looks upset. The witness is only a few feet from where Owen sits, and, watching her, he is embarrassed and stares down at his lap. The lawyer is pressing his questions rapidly, pausing now and then for a glance at the jury. The witness agrees that she is married. She has been married for ten years. She knows Mr. Conrad. Yes—in a whisper—she has had an affair with him.

The lawyer waits. Owen looks up. The witness has begun to weep. The affair took place three years ago, over a period of six months. Owen is miserable for her, for what he considers a shocking intrusion into her life. Unproven adultery is being countered by an earlier, real adultery. Russell Conrad's parents are visibly disconcerted. His lawyer will not cross-examine. Presumably the facts have been stated and to prolong the ordeal would merely create sympathy for Lucy, who seems not to realize that this is a fortunate turn in her case. She gazes aghast at the witness. The woman leaves. Owen wonders why she was willing to testify. Perhaps she was subpoenaed and had no choice. Or perhaps she came forward out of revenge. To get even for a slight, for having been dropped. Then Owen recalls an episode of his own.

There were few affairs after Owen's divorce from Jean, but the first was with a married woman, an old and pleasant friend. Her name was Alice. The affair was largely sexual, or so he thought at the time. An accommodation. Its emotional intensity was small. But now, at the end of the day, Owen leaves still thinking of the crying witness and then of that long-past time. "I did it to get even, to show Jean," he tells himself for the first time and with some astonishment. "That was all. Nothing more. Of course, she never even knew of it. But I did. *That* was the reason. What Alice's may have been I have no idea."

It is Thursday evening. The members of the string quartet gather in Owen's living room under the high ceiling, which makes for excellent sound. Sherry is served. Drinks will come afterward, and sandwiches brought in from an old and always reliable neighborhood restaurant. Owen is still thinking about the trial. He cannot seem to get himself away from it, but the music is certain to help, to free him. They are to work on a Haydn quartet. Its serene order, its mathematical precision are already taking hold of his mind, carrying him into themselves and away from the confusions of the day—of every day. Away from himself.

The sherry and the accompanying small talk are finished and the playing begins. It goes easily, smoothly, until the second violinist makes a slip. It is ignored. A little later, he makes another, and, apologizing, asks if they may start again. He knows now that the problem was the fingering he was using. During that small pause, looking at the Jamaican violinist, Owen thinks suddenly of Mr. Travis. He hears himself politely refusing to go to lunch. He would rather not be remembering this, but the spell of the Haydn has been broken. Why *did* he refuse? *Why?* There is no reason for his thinking of Mr. Travis now, for asking himself such questions.

Travis and the Jamaican are in no way similar. What sets them apart may be merely the violinist's accent—British-tinged and therefore somewhat lofty. Also, of course, he is a capable musician. Still, if he were a new acquaintance, Owen would probably decline an invitation to lunch with him. And—Owen is sure—for all the original reasons, which he now perfectly recalls.

The playing starts again. This time it is Owen who is embarrassed by small mistakes in his playing. It is the trial, always the trial, burrowing in his mind that upsets him. He apologizes, and the group moves into the Haydn for the third time.

On Friday morning Russell Conrad testifies. He wants the custody of his child for reasons already brought forth. (Custody, Owen thinks. I guess you could say I was in custody from my tenth year on. Custody of Mother's family after she and Father were killed.) Russell has recovered his poise. He speaks of his comfortable circumstances, and, accordingly, his ability to raise the child in comfort. Everything he says implies a solid background, and opportunities for the child, which—he implies—Lucy would not be able to supply. His parents, with whom he conferred intensely and at length before he was called, lean forward, chins on hands, appearing to prompt him with their eyes. A pair of gargoyles, Owen thinks, but solid, well-to-do. He is prepared to feel some dislike of Russell, but instead he feels a kind of kinship. This sense of—alliance—puzzles him. No matter. His duty is to listen to the testimony. One thing, though, is becoming more than evident: the young Conrads' marriage was never at any time a good one. The two had almost nothing in common. Then, did Russell go into it hastily? To escape, perhaps? To escape from his stony gargoyle parents?

Now it is lunchtime. Owen goes to his restaurant and to his friendly waitress. I know now what it was I felt for Russell, he thinks. *I* escaped into marriage. I see that at last. I had to escape that family—disciplinarians all. They wanted to keep me in leash even after I was grown. I *had* to break away. Poor Jean.

When Lucy Conrad comes to the stand in the afternoon, Russell's lawyer presses the question of negligence, perhaps because his adultery balloon has been largely deflated. Lucy denies neglect of any sort. Owen wonders, unsure. Her answers are alternately defiant and sad. She does not weep but stares in a blank way out over the courtroom, over the heads of the spectators. At the end of her testimony, the lawyers briefly sum up their cases, and the trial is recessed for the weekend.

But Owen cannot get away from the trial. After dinner, he goes to a foreign film to try. The picture is dense and cryptic. It requires concentration if one is to get much out of it, and that is why Owen has chosen it. But, in his seat, he finds himself thinking instead of his mother, and of how, not long before her death in the auto accident, an aunt, speaking in the privacy of her own family, had accused his mother of neglecting him. He had never felt at all neglected. His mother was young and exciting, that was all. He has thought of her the rest of his life as beautiful. But now he recalls her misery when, inevitably, the story of the accusation reached her. He thinks of her tears. He thinks of Lucy. The movie is meaningless. He walks home trying once more to put the trial from his mind and not for a moment succeeding.

On Saturday afternoon, Owen goes to a concert in Carnegie Hall. Now, for a time, he does seem to escape his obsession with the trial in the formality of the music. But afterward he begins to feel an undefined alarm. It stays with him through dinner and accompanies him home.

Never mind. I must review the evidence, he thinks. In the apartment, he stands for a while in his half-dark living room, looking down at the street. The snow of the first of the week has melted, leaving small glittering pennants of ice on the pavement, and new snow, light and powdery, is swirling across them. Occasionally—rarely enough to make the street seem bleak—a single car goes by, and Owen grows lonely. There is a cheerful ancient bar in the neighborhood. He will go there.

As always on Saturday night, the place is busy. Owen finds himself a corner that he can back into comfortably at the far end of the bar. He reflects that here he can be quite as alone as in his own apartment and yet not lonely. Still, just for the moment, he wishes he were one of the crowd, wishes he were the sort that could pick up easy talk with one or another of the chattering groups or couples. I guess I'm just the quiet type, he tells himself, then—*quietest little juror I ever*—and Mr. Travis seems to loom, a friendly black bear, beside him. I wouldn't feel out of place with him here, Owen assures himself. I wouldn't feel self-conscious. It wouldn't be the same as going to lunch.

But—the evidence. Owen then goes back beyond it all to the first day, to the lawyer's question about involvement in divorce. True, I didn't want to be dismissed, he thinks, but there was something more than that. He sees the lawyers leaning across the rail, fixing him with their eyes. I didn't want—I *never* want—anything private to me to be made public. All along, back even when I was a boy, I have tried to keep my thoughts and doings to myself. I have been bound to reticence. Also to order. They go together. Twin havens. Disorder has always been at least a venial sin. Well, I have arranged my life as carefully as I could. But now I know I was escaping that family—fleeing into privacy—long before I married Jean. I don't know why I am thinking all this. I have always felt that introspection itself is disorderly.

The evidence, then. But—escape? If marriage was an escape for me, so was the divorce. I had that solitary outburst because of some sort of chagrin. But now I believe it was also because my orderly life was shaken. Afterward, I could see that, alone, I could make it still more tidy. Did Jean want the divorce to get *away* from order?

Owen wakens late on Sunday morning feeling that his nameless fear has grown. Or, rather, it now takes the form of a kind of paralysis, an emptiness, a deeply physical craving not to rise at all. Still, one must rise as always.

The sun is high, making the night's snow sparkle. After a noontime breakfast, he rides a bus uptown and gets off at Central Park to walk and breathe the cold air, hoping to exorcise his misgivings. Passing the lightly frozen pond, he thinks of Lucy Conrad and wonders once more why she would take the risk of calling out against witnesses. He thinks of Jean and all the reasons he has conjured up (or failed to conjure) for her wanting the divorce. He thinks of Travis and is again uncertain of his own impulses. Why? Why? Why did mismatched Lucy and Russell ever marry? And suddenly his alarm takes shape for just a moment before he firmly puts it by. He cannot possibly accept the notion that there are no final answers to all the haunting questions the trial has brought him. Security. Safety. Unquestioning, undoubting order. Answers that come readily. These are needed things. Without them, one walks in a wilderness. So it is best to turn back to the trial itself. By all means, now, sift the evidence, find the outcome he will vote for. He is sorry for Lucy. She is a waif. But, though nothing was really proved against her, she does seem quite unstable. Overemotional. Adultery was testified against Russell, but that is no great matter when set against protection for the child. Lucy, if the case should go her way, will doubtless be awarded child support, but Russell can provide support in depth. Backed by his parents, gargoyles or no, he can give the child whatever he may need, on and on into the future. Owen can see that he has no choice but to decide for security and order. He is not completely happy with his verdict. The snow on the slopes seems to have lost a good bit of its glitter. But that can be laid to the waning of the day, and Owen, if rather grimly, clings to his safe choice.

On Monday morning, Owen goes to court, still resolutely of the same mind. But, as the jury files down the hall to its deliberations, he is aware that in some none too welcome way he is a little changed. Now whenever he takes the reasonable course, always before so clearly marked for him, he is likely to have doubts. He does not relish this.

In the jury room, he sits next to the foreman at the end of a long polished table. The foreman suggests that no vote be taken so soon. They are to talk for a while, raise peripheral questions, avoid commitments that would tend to harden their views. Owen sits silent, paying small attention; his mind, after all, is made up.

But a person he has never seen intrudes upon his thoughts. Lucy's child. Owen does his best to see it growing up well cared for, going to the better schools, hovered over by grandparents whom he now tries to envision in a warmer light. Doting elders, themselves surrogate parents. He rejects the image of Lucy deprived of her child; he refuses to remember her misery when things went badly for her in court. Still, he cannot help wondering what she will do when the verdict goes as it must—how she will behave. He wishes he could not be present. Indeed, he wishes now that he had never been chosen for this jury—perhaps for any jury. It is nonsense to be told not to become involved in the lives of the people one is required by law to judge. Who could have judged *him* at any given time? Who could ever have known why he did what he did? Not always himself, it would seem.

So, eventually, the foreman calls for a vote. He nods to Owen, by his side. Owen draws himself up. His lips part, but he freezes. For a moment he simply cannot speak. There is no way he can vote to give that unseen child to Russell and his parents. The other jurors wait. Owen is bewildered, almost hurt. Hurt with himself, betrayed by himself. And then he hears himself, as if from somewhere beyond the far end of the long table, saying that he votes to give the child's custody to its mother.

He sits appalled at what he has done while the others vote. He is dimly aware that most of them have joined him. Only two are for Russell. Owen cannot believe it, and for a moment he thinks he must cry out, protest. But he does not. He listens to the others arguing with the minority of two. Mr. Travis is highly vocal, insisting over and over that no clear case has been made against Lucy Conrad. Someone else, agreeing, says that in such circumstances it is usual, almost routine, to give the child to its mother. It is at least a comfort to Owen to know that he is with the majority—is part, as he thinks wryly, of the establishment. One of the holdouts mentions Lucy's instability. A whole chorus points out that she has been under great stress. And in time the verdict is unanimous.

They are doing just what I have done, Owen thinks, with a slowly rising exhilaration. They are arguing from their feelings. The evidence is inconclusive and forgotten. They are all as involved as I am, and I have been involved—deeply involved—from the beginning.

Half an hour later, leaving the courtroom, Owen's exhilaration, his sense of self-assertion, almost of discovery, still grows in him. For the first time in a week, or even longer—far, far longer, it seems to him—he feels lighthearted. He is almost giddy. He tells himself that if he were at home he would get his cello out this minute and play it.

Then, at the courthouse door, he feels a hand drop on his shoulder. The hand belongs to Mr. Travis. "Well, ole buddy, we won, didn't we?" says Mr. Travis.

Owen smiles and nods. "Why, yes," he says. "Why, yes, in a way, we did."

3

IDENTITY

Developing an identity, a sense of the self, is a lifelong process. As a very young child, one does not differentiate him or herself from the people who are central to one's life. Parents, teachers, and, increasingly, friends do, however, have a significant influence in the formation of identity that takes place in adolescence. Erikson (1950) has theorized that achieving a sense of identity is the major developmental task of late adolescence. A teenager who accomplishes this task becomes definite about who he or she is, has a sense of belonging, and performs in social roles appropriate to that stage in life. One who does not achieve a sense of identity at this time will suffer from role or identity diffusion—that is, will feel awkward in social situations, will not have a clear sense of the self as separate from others, and may act in socially inappropriate, perhaps delinquent ways. Erikson feels that this dilemma must be resolved satisfactorily in late adolescence if a person is to relate meaningfully to others in adulthood.

YOUNG ADULTHOOD

The formation of a sense of identity rarely occurs without notice. It often involves bitter conflicts with parents, rejection of parental mores, experimentation with new and seemingly contradictory modes of behavior, and radical mood changes. This stormy period of development with all of its problems has received considerable attention from social scientists and writers. As a young person leaves the family for college, marriage, or a job, conflicts may diminish, but the "new" adult person continues to develop. The roles he or she has chosen to play, the values adopted, the self projected, all become more or less solidified as they are tested in the arena of adult social situations and work settings.

Leaving the family of one's youth is an important first step in the formation of identity. Occasionally a young person can remain at home physically while separating him or herself emotionally from parental influence. Sometimes the process is considerably delayed, and in rare cases the child never leaves, either emotionally or physically, forever thwarting the emergence of a separate identity. More commonly, however, young people move out on their own and relish the independence of their new "adult" status. The mixture of emotions felt at the moment of leaving is captured in the poem "Young Man Leaving Home," by Sydney Lea. During the parting, the young man catches poignant glimpses of familiar places and senses his parents' sorrow and their "benedictions." This rite of passage is ultimately a positive experience, though, as the "hero" hails "The Future, that unimaginable lode of riches."

In the second selection in this section, "My Brother Is a Cowboy," by Carolyn Osborn, we watch as a brother and sister find their way into the adult world. The efforts of their parents to get Kenyon and his sister to adopt adult life-styles compatible with the parents' values ultimately fail. Kenyon goes from flunking out of college to rodeo riding, to paratrooping, to being a cowboy, which is what he wanted to do in the first place. Juxtaposed to Kenyon, who has more freedom to experiment, is his sister, whose identity formation is smothered by her parents and by her overly protective brother. She finally realizes, at the age of twenty-six, that she must leave home if she is ever to make a life of her own. At the end of the story we see two very independent adults, each living a life satisfying to themselves.

MID-LIFE ASSESSMENT

One's sense of self continues to evolve in middle age. Whereas a young adult is engrossed in the question of who he or she is becoming, a middle-aged person evaluates who he or she has become and whether or not the results are satisfying. This mid-life assessment is prompted by the psychological and physical changes characteristic of this stage in life. For a young adult, life stretches ahead almost indefinitely. The middle-aged person begins to realize that life is finite, that aging is an irreversible process leaving one with a limited number of years. One's time perspective shifts to measuring how many years there are left to accomplish the goals set down in youth. The distress that results from this realization is further exacerbated by the physical evidence of aging — hairlines recede, fat accumulates, and muscle tone changes.

All areas of one's life come into question in middle age. Career and family as well as self are sectioned out and scrutinized like the pieces of a jigsaw puzzle. At best it is an uncomfortable period of transition; at worst it becomes a full-blown crisis in which one is incapacitated. Some adults find coping with mid-life assessment to be relatively easy; for others it is a devastating experience. In order for growth to continue, fragmentation must give way to a restructuring or reintegration of the many aspects of one's life.

Taking stock of oneself at mid-life can lead to forging a new self by setting new goals and reforming or discarding old relationships and customary vocational roles. Such is the case with Nora in Ibsen's play A Doll's House. Nora realizes that she has no identity of her own, that she has merely absorbed first her father's and then her husband's values and opinions. To achieve a sense of self, she leaves her family. This play also illustrates sex differences in adult developmental patterns. Psychologists have observed that women in the traditional family role seldom have the opportunity men have had to achieve a separate sense of identity in young adulthood. For many such women this task is postponed until middle age.

Part of the mid-life reassessment of the self involves relinquishing or putting into proper perspective the accomplishments of young adulthood. One cannot dwell in the past but must move on to the tasks that the next stage of life presents. In Irwin Shaw's short story "The Eighty-Yard Run," the protagonist, Darling, cannot in mid-life repeat the feats of young adulthood. He had been a great football player, but as we meet him fifteen years later it becomes apparent that he has been unable to adjust to his own aging. Set against his own thwarted growth is the continued development of his wife Louise. As he clings to the past and becomes more and more ineffectual, Louise meets the challenges of her stage in life with vigor and enthusiasm.

Mid-life, like other phases of adulthood, has its periods of stability as well as upheaval. It is, after all, probably the most powerful period of life because one is often in a position to exert great influence over the next generation and the society in which one lives. The ability to cope with responsibility and change also varies from individual to individual. What may bring about a crisis for one person may not be significant to another. In the poem "The Fisherman," by Michael Van Walleghen, we see a man in crisis. He is no longer sure who he is nor what is real or imagined. It is not until the end of the poem that we learn what has jolted him into his troubled state.

The mid-life search for the self is a common theme in twentieth-century literature. Full-length works such as Miller's *Death of a Salesman*, Hesse's *Steppenwolf*, Kazan's *The Arrangement*, Updike's *Rabbit, Run*, Connell's *Mr. Bridge*, Bellow's *Herzog*, Fitzgerald's *Tender Is the Night*, and Malamud's *Dubin's Lives* offer portraits of men and women in their middle years. For the most part the anchors of family, career, and self no longer seem relevant. The urgent questioning of all things that had formerly given meaning to existence precipitates a critical state or transitional period that in most cases leads to a new sense of identity and purpose. Failure to negotiate this period of adult development can have disastrous results, as in the case of Willy Loman's suicide or Dick Diver's alcoholism.

THE LIFE REVIEW

In middle age, one evaluates the person one has become. If one is dissatisfied with this person, there usually is still time to modify or even significantly change those aspects of our lives that define who we are. Changes in interpersonal relationships such as a divorce or extramarital affairs, or in work such as a mid-career change, are common occurrences in mid-life. Old age also has its own developmental task, in which one must answer the question of who one has been.

According to several writers, the imminence of death in old age precipitates a need on the part of older persons to review and evaluate their life experiences. If one can accept "one's one and only life cycle as something that had to be and that by necessity permitted of no substitute" (Erikson, 1950, p. 268), then one feels a sense of integrity in later life rather than despair. Gerontologist Robert Butler (1963) has labeled this process the *life review*. In carrying out the life review, one consciously reminisces about his or her past life with the intention of accepting and integrating unresolved conflicts and past experiences, both pleasant and painful. In this way the sense of the self, or one's identity, continues to evolve in later life.

Katherine Anne Porter's story "The Jilting of Granny Weatherall" is a good example of an older person's efforts to deal with an unresolved conflict that has been buried within. With death approaching she must at last grapple with the anger she feels at having been rejected on her wedding day some sixty years before.

Successfully coming to terms with one's life is a task that can be accomplished late in life. In fact, it is perhaps easier to do so at this stage than earlier in adulthood when responsibilities and worries may occupy most of our time and thoughts. "Ilyás," a short story by Tolstoy, makes this very point. Ilyás and his wife have lost much of their wealth, but they do not dwell on their losses and finish their lives in despair. Instead they enjoy the contentment and the time for reflection they have found in the simpler life. There is no time left to change their circumstances. They have accepted their lives and in doing so find the peace that eludes younger people.

Samuel Beckett's drama *Krapp's Last Tape* (not included in this collection) and Shakespeare's *King Lear* (partial selection included) are two well-known representations of men struggling with the task of preserving ego integrity in old age. In *Krapp's Last Tape*, a weary old man symbolically tries to put his life in order by arranging and listening to tapes made some thirty years earlier. At one point he tapes his reaction to hearing himself as he was years ago. The unwinding tapes reflect both the evolving identity of Krapp from youth to old age and the unraveling of his own sense of self as he realizes death is near. Krapp's last years are full of despair rather than integrity. While Lear "retires" from his kingly role, he demands status and respect in his role as parent. When two of his daughters, Goneril and Regan, flout his parental authority and reduce him to playing the part of an obedient child, Lear loses touch with reality. What ensues is a confrontation with himself, a coming to terms with what he has been. In act 3, scene 4, Lear begins to see himself without the protective trappings of his kingly role. Lear's reunion with Cordelia in act 4, scene 7, reveals that he, unlike Krapp, has achieved a sense of wholeness, of integrity and contentment, that allows him to face death courageously.

The formation of an individual identity is a lifelong process. It begins with a sense of a self that is distinguishable from all other selves. The formation of identity in late adolescence allows adults to establish meaningful intimate relationships with others throughout the rest of adulthood. A young adult is in the process of becoming someone. By the time one has lived half of his or her life, the self is well formed. Whether one is satisfied with his or her identity is a crucial question in mid-life. There is usually still time to alter and modify. Old age has its own task — that of reviewing and, one hopes, coming to terms with the person one has been and making sense of the life one has led.

YOUNG MAN LEAVING HOME

Sydney Lea

Over the dropped eggs and hash, his elders
poured unaccustomed benedictions.

The morning broke fair, but they
insisted on sensing rain.

That last spring, after so many,
the tree with the rope swing blossomed,

random plum blooms dropping groundward
where the playhouse leaned.

Later, the tracks with their switchbacks among
the shanties outside the station

had a somewhat surprising Protestant look
of a hopeless proposition.

Adieu: to the father who fobbed and fondled
his watch, at the end of his chain,

whose simple grief no halting final
declaration seemed to soften;

to the mother feigning impatience
with the lateness of the train.

They. Tree. House. Yard.
All had called for his valediction,

but now was already the hour prior
to greeting whatever it is that this is,

hour of assembly, of public instead
of certain longed-for private kisses,

hour of livered grandmothers, aunts,
whose cheeks the plain tears stained. . . .

It passed in the fashion of dreams, at once
chaotic and sluggish.

En route: in silence, he hailed The Future,
that unimaginable lode of riches,

this hero, composed of a dozen young rebels
out of thin novels, groaning with luggage.

MY BROTHER IS A COWBOY

Carolyn Osborn

My daddy used to advise my brother and me, "Don't tell everything you know." This was his golden rule. I keep it in mind as I constantly disregard it. I've been busy most of my life telling everything I know. My brother Kenyon took it to heart. He tells nothing, not even the most ordinary answers to questions about his everyday existence. If my mother asks when he'll be home for supper, he says, "I don't know." The nearest he'll come to giving the hour for when he'll come in or go out is "Early" or "Late." His common movements, the smallest events of his day, are secret.

Mother follows these like a female detective. "Kenyon left the bread out this morning and the pimento cheese. I wonder if he had pimento cheese for breakfast, or took sandwiches for lunch, or both?" If, after she counts the remaining bread slices, sandwiches seem a possibility, she wonders where he has to go that's so distant he needs to take lunch with him. The names of surrounding towns come to her mind. "He won't be going anywhere near Lampasas because they have good barbeque there and he wouldn't take pimento cheese if he could get barbeque." She has advantage over Daddy; at least she's observed Kenyon's eating habits through the years and can spend hours happily trying to guess what he's going to do about lunch and whether or not he's going to turn up for supper.

Daddy doesn't care about where Kenyon eats lunch. What he wants to know is how many ranches Kenyon is leasing, how his sheep, goats, and cattle are doing, if he's making money or not.

We all want to know if he's ever going to get married. Does he have a girl? Does he want to marry? He is almost thirty, taller than my father's six feet, though how much we don't know for he won't stand and be measured. He has dark hair that curls when he forgets to get it cut, which is most of the time. The curls come over his forehead and disgust him so much he is forever jamming his hat down low to cover his hair. When we were children he made me cut the front curls off. I was spanked for doing it. His nose is long and straight. There is a small slanting scar just missing his eye running over his left eyebrow. His eyes are brown. His mouth is wide and generally closed.

When we ask if he's ever going to marry, and nothing will stop us from asking, he says, "Find me a girl who'll live out in the country, cook beans, and wash all day." He runs his hands over the creases in his clean blue jeans, sticks the shirttail of his clean shirt in, and laughs. Mother gets angry then. She's responsible for all his clean clothes and feels sometimes this is the only reason he shows up at the house. Often she says, "He doesn't need a wife! He needs a washerwoman!" Not once, however, has she ever said this to him, fearing he'll put on his boots and walk out the door to some unknown cafe one last time.

She isn't curious about where I'm going to eat. Everybody in town knows I eat lunch every day at the Leon High School cafeteria. I'm the singing teacher. Wouldn't you know it! Since I've already told you Kenyon's almost thirty, you might as well know I'm almost twenty-six. At least nobody asks me when I'm going to get married, not to my face anyway. Being related and having practically no heart at all, Kenyon has the gall to wonder out loud if I'm ever going to catch a man. When he does this, I tell him I have as much right to uphold the long tradition of old-maidhood as he has to represent the last of the old west. My brother is a cowboy.

I tell him, "You're the last of a vanishing breed, the tail end of the roundup of the longhorn steers, the last great auk alive, a prairie rooster without a hen!"

All he replies to this is, "Sister, there ain't no substitute for beef on the hoof." He gets out real quick before I can go on about helicopters substituting for horses and feed lots replacing the open range.

Since the wires have been cut between Kenyon and his family, we have to depend on other sources of information, the weekly newspaper for instance. That's where we found out he'd been riding bulls in rodeos the summer after he flunked out of college. He got his picture on the front page for falling off a Brahma bull headfirst. The photographer caught the bull still doubled up and Kenyon in midair, his hands out in front of him right before he hit the dirt. My daddy strictly forbade any more bull-riding on the grounds he wasn't going to have his son associating with a bunch of rodeo bums.

Kenyon said, ''These bums are the best friends I got and I'll associate with whoever I want.''

''You are going to kill yourself and me too.'' Daddy put his hand over his heart like he was going to have an attack that minute. ''And, further-more, I'm going to cut you out of my will if you keep up this fool riding.'' Then he laid down on the bed and made me take his blood pressure. I was home on vacation from nursing school in Galveston.

Kenyon smiled, showing he still had all his teeth, and the next thing we read in the newspaper was he'd gone off and joined the paratroopers, joined of his own free will, mind you, for three years. Daddy, who'd been in the infantry in WW II, was half proud and half wild. ''He doesn't have enough sense to keep his feet on the ground! If he isn't being thrown from a bull, he's throwing himself out of airplanes!'' He wrote an old army buddy of his who'd retired, like he did, near his last post—except the post was up in Tennessee where Kenyon was stationed instead of Texas where we are. This old buddy wrote back saying:

Dear Willie,
   Your boy is doing fine. I talked to his C.O. yesterday. He told me Pvt. Kenyon K. Lane is making a good soldier.

Yours truly,

Henry C. Worth, Lt. Col., Ret.
P.S. He told me Kenyon inspires good morale because he jumps out of planes with a wad of tobacco in his mouth and spits all the way down.

Your friend,

Lt. Col. Henry C. Worth, Ret.

I think Daddy was happy for a while. He showed the letter to me be-fore he went downtown to show it to some of his friends at the drugstore where they all meet for coffee. By the time he came home, Mother was back from the grocery.

"William, how can you go around showing everybody that letter when I haven't read it!" She read it and was crying before she finished. "Who taught him how to chew tobacco? He'll ruin his teeth. He was such a nice clean boy."

"Ruin his teeth!" Daddy shouted. "You've got to worry about his teeth when he's falling out of airplanes every day!"

"He's not falling," I said. "He's jumping and he's doing it of his own free will."

"Free will nothing!" Daddy turned on me. "Don't you be telling me about free will in the U.S. Army. I know about the army. I spent twenty years in the army."

I had to take his blood pressure after that. He spent the next three years writing to his army buddies near whatever post my brother happened to be on, and getting news of Kenyon from them. All his letters were signed Col. William K. Lane, Ret.

I spent those years finishing my education, they thought. In the daytime I was. I wore a white uniform and low white shoes and went to nursing school in Galveston. Friday and Saturday nights I put on a red sequined dress and a pair of red high heels and went to sing at one of the nightclubs. My stage name was Gabriella and I wore so much makeup nobody from Leon would have known it was me. I had learned something from Kenyon, not to tell everything I knew and to follow my own free will. It worked too. When I was home I took Daddy's blood pressure and Mother's temperature; when I was in Galveston I was singing two nights a week.

Don't get any ideas either—singing and wearing a red dress was all I was doing. The men in the combo I sang with were more strict with me than they would have been with their own daughters if they had had any. I could drink soda pop only, and I had to sit with one of them while I was drinking. Except for the sequins I might as well have been in a convent. I sang songs like "I Can't Say No" without ever having a chance to not say it. Still, I was satisfied. Singing was what I wanted. I thought if I could support myself by nursing, I could gradually work my way into show biz and up to New York. So I was down in Galveston nursing and singing while my brother was on some army post jumping out of airplanes, I supposed.

One Friday night I was giving out with "Zip-Pah-De-Do-Dah" trying to cheer up a few barflies when in walks Kenyon. He knows me right away, red sequins, makeup, and all. He is wearing a tight-fitting paratrooper's uniform, his pants tied up in his boots, which laced to the knee practically. Very spiffy and clean. Mother would have been happy to see him.

"My, oh, my, what a wonderful day!" I finish. The barflies applaud. My brother just stands quietly while I slink off the platform. It's time for the break, so Tiny the drummer, who is actually a big fat man, married with a wife and baby he calls every night in Dallas, takes me by the arm to a table. Kenyon comes right over. I can see immediately he has gotten himself all shined up for one reason—to get roaring drunk—to the disgrace of family and country. He's just off the reservation and ready to howl. Obviously, I'm in his way.

I smile at him and say, "Hi. What are doing down here? Are you AWOL?"

"No," he grins, "I'm on leave. You're the one that's AWOL."

Tiny says, "Scram, soldier boy."

"It's my brother, Tiny. He's in the paratroopers. He jumps out of airplanes."

"Gay Baby, don't pull the brother bit on me."

"But he is," I insist. "Show him your birthmark or something, Kenyon."

"Jump on out of here, fly boy," says Tiny.

"If I go, you go too, Gay Baby," says Kenyon with a merciless smirk.

"I'm not going anywhere till I finish here tonight. You sit down and behave yourself. Have a beer."

"You're leaving right now. My sister isn't going to hang around no honky-tonk." With this he grabs me by the arm and I scream at him, "Let go!" But he doesn't and by this time I'm furious. "You auk! You dodo! You idiot!"

Tiny rises like a giant blimp slowly filling with air. Before he can signal to the other fellows though, Kenyon pulls me to my feet. The other four members of the combo—Louie, the piano player; Max, the bass; Joe, the sax; and Evans, the trumpet—run to assist us.

Kenyon turns the table on its side. "She's going with me," he says.

I peek between the fingers of my free hand to see if he's got a six-shooter in his free hand. He's got nothing, nothing but swagger. Pretty soon he has a cut over his left eye—Tiny did it with a chair—and I have not one red cent left of all my savings from singing nights. My going-to-New York money has gone to bail Dangerous Dan Kenyon McGrew out of the Galveston jail.

"Listen, Kenyon," I tell him, "this is not Leon and this is not the nineteenth century. It's the second half of the twentieth in case you haven't noticed it from your airplane riding! There is nothing wrong with me singing in a quiet respectable bar."

"No sister of mine—"

"You just pretend I'm not any sister of yours. We're so different one of us must have been left on the doorstep."

"You think I'm a bastard?"

"Well, you're the one calling the cards," I said and flounced out of the jail. I was mad and in a hurry to get home to bed. All I cared about right then was sleep. That particular Saturday I had to work the 7:00 A.M. shift at the hospital. Kenyon being such a zipper-lip type, I certainly wasn't worrying about him telling anybody I was working in a nightclub and him spending some time in jail. I should have let him stay in jail. He got in his car that very same night and drove straight to Leon. And, when he got there early the next morning, he told. He told everything he knew.

They didn't give me any warning, not a phone call—nothing. Daddy appeared in full uniform, the old army pinks and greens with eagles flapping on both shoulders. He had been getting ready to leave for a battalion reunion at Ft. Sam Houston when Kenyon showed up, and he didn't waste time changing clothes. He should have. His stomach had expanded some since WW II so his trousers were lifted an inch too high over his socks.

The first thing I said when I saw him was, "Daddy, what on earth are you doing down here in your uniform? It's non-reg. They don't wear that kind anymore."

"Sister, don't you tell me about the U.S. Army regulations. I gave twenty years of my life to them."

"Well, they are likely to slap you in the loony bin here for walking around dressed up like that."

"If I was you, I wouldn't be talking about how other people are dressed."

"Daddy, there is nothing wrong with my uniform," I said. I'd been wearing it for eight hours and hadn't spilt a thing on it. There was nothing wrong with the way I looked at all except for the circles under my eyes from staying up till 2:00 A.M. getting a certain person out of jail. I was just about dead from exhaustion.

"I hear you've got another dress, a red one."

We were talking in the lobby of the hospital and when he said that I wanted to call for a stretcher.

"No daughter of mine is going to hang around with gangsters at nightclubs."

I don't know where he got the gangsters, probably from the last time he was in a nightclub.

"This isn't 1920 and I don't know any gangsters. The fellows Kenyon got in a fight with are musicians. They were trying to protect me." He wasn't listening. He didn't want to hear my side. His mind was already made up.

"You go and get your things," he told me. "No daughter of mine is going to be corrupted by jazz and booze."

What could I do? I'd spent all my savings getting Kenyon out of jail. I went with Daddy back to Leon thinking it would all blow over after a while. Mother, at least, would be on my side since she knew what it was to live with a husband who still thought he was in the first half of the twentieth century and a son who hadn't progressed past 1900. When we got to Leon though, I found out different. The very first thing Mother did was to show me mine and Kenyon's birth certificates.

"Look here, young lady, neither you nor your brother was left on anybody's doorstep. I hope this is proof enough for you." She shoved the yellowed pages with their loopy-de-loop handwriting in my face and started crying before I could say I never really meant it.

I stayed home that weekend and the rest of that semester. Goodbye nursing. I wasn't so crazy about it anyway. I guess what happened to me could happen to anybody, but I wonder how many girls end up teaching a bunch of high school kids to sing "Sweet Adeline" after they started out with a great career in show biz. Daddy took me completely out of school. In January he let me enroll in a Baptist church college only forty miles from Leon. I got my teacher's certificate there in music education and that's all I got. They had a short rope on me.

When I finished I was twenty-three, due to the interruption in my education. Daddy had a heart attack that year and I went home to help Mother nurse him and to teach singing in Leon High School.

My brother, when he was through with the paratroopers, came home too. He started working on ranches and slowly saved enough to lease places of his own. He hadn't paid me back the bail money yet. I hadn't paid him back either, but I was planning on how I was going to. Someday, I thought, he is going to find some girl who wants to quit riding the barrel races in rodeos and get married. When he brings this cutie home in her embroidered blouse and her buckskin fringes, I am going to tell everything I know, not about him being in jail. The fact he spent a few hours in the Galveston jail wouldn't bother her. Galveston's a long way from Leon.

I wasn't going to tell this rodeo queen Kenyon was bound to drag home about his past; I was going to predict her future. I was going to let this little girl know she might as well throw away her western breeches and get into a skirt that hit the floor. And, I was going to tell her she'd better wave goodbye forever to the bright lights, the crowd, the band, and the Grand Entry Parade because all that was in store for her was a pot of beans to stir and blue jeans to wash at home on the range. She wasn't to expect any modern appliances to help her out either, because I knew Kenyon. He wouldn't buy her a single machine, not even a radio. If she wanted to hear any music she'd have to invite me out to sit on the front porch and sing ''Zip-Pah-De-Do-Dah'' as the sun sank slowly in the west.

I had it all planned out, a feeble sort of revenge, but at least I'd have my say—me, the Cassandra of Leon, prophesying a terrible future for a fun-loving cowboy's sweetheart. Of course, like a lot of too well planned revenges, it didn't turn out that way. I got restless sitting around in the teacher's lounge, going to the movie every Saturday night with a man I'd known since we were both in high school, Alvin Neeley, the band director. We weren't anything to each other but companions in boredom, chained together by what everyone thought was our common interest, music. We were supposed to be a perfect couple because we could both read notes. Everyone imagined we were sitting on the piano bench warbling duets, but we weren't.

Alvin was a marcher. He kept in step even when we were walking a few blocks down the street, and believe me, he wasn't marching to the sound of any distant drum. Alvin had his own drum in his head, and when he puckered his lips, I knew he wasn't puckering up for me; he was puckering up for Sousa. Sometimes, just for diversion, I'd refuse to march in step with him. If he put his left foot forward, I'd start out on my right, but he'd always notice and with a quick little skip in the air, he'd be in step with me. Off we'd go marching to the movie to the tune of ''The Stars and Stripes Forever'' every Saturday. And all this time Kenyon was stomping in and out of the house bird-free, intent on his own secret purposes.

Mother would come and sit on the foot of my bed after I got home from a date with Alvin. ''Did you have a good time?'' she'd say.

''All right.'' I wasn't going to tell her I'd had a bad time. She had enough troubles as it was. Since his heart attack my daddy spent most of his time sitting around the house with his right hand on the left side of his chest the way actors used to indicate great pain in the old silent films.

She'd ask me what movie we saw and I'd tell her, *Monsters of the Slimy Green Deep* or whatever it was. Nothing but Grade B movies ever made it to Leon, and Alvin and I went regularly no matter what was showing—like taking a pill on schedule.

"Well, how is Alvin getting along?"

She wasn't interested in Alvin's health. What she wanted to know was how Alvin and I were getting along. I'd say all right to that too. I kept on saying the same thing till one night she said, "I sure would like to have some grandchildren."

"Mother, you better get Kenyon to work on that because you're not going to get any grandchildren out of me and Alvin Neeley."

"Why not?"

"I'd have to marry him—that's why, and I'm not going to even if he asks, and he's not going to ask. He can barely hold a conversation anyway. All he can do is whistle—and march." I was sitting across the room from her rubbing my aching legs.

"Why do you keep on going out with him then?"

"I don't see anybody else bashing the door down to ask me to a movie. I go out with Alvin because he takes me. It's one way of getting away from this house, a way of getting out of Leon even if it's to go to the *Slimy Green Deep*."

"You worry me," said Mother.

"I worry myself," I told her and I did. I was stuck with Alvin Neeley in Leon. I'd done what they all wanted me to do and now they were stuck with me. They had me on their hands.

Mother evidently spoke to Kenyon about my miserable unwed existence and insisted he find somebody for me. I say Mother did it, put the idea in Kenyon's head that he find somebody for me, because, left to himself, Kenyon was not at all bothered by an old-maid sister. He thought he'd saved me from the gutter. From there on I was supposed to be continually thankful and permanently respectable.

When I got home early one Saturday night I was told, before I had time to say anything, that he'd "fixed up" a date for me the following Saturday.

"Who with?"

"Fellow named Frank Harwell from Lampasas. He ranches out west of town. He's going to take you dancing."

"He's from a big family. I know some of them. Harwells are spread all over Lampasas," Mother said happily.

"He served in Korea, in the infantry," said Daddy as if he'd just pinned the Distinguished Conduct Medal on somebody.

They all knew what they wanted to know about Frank Harwell and I didn't know a thing. "How old is he? Is he short or tall, skinny or fat, intelligent or ignorant, handsome or ugly?" I could have gone on all night throwing questions at them, but I quit. They were all sitting there looking so smug.

"He's the best I could do," said Kenyon. "You'll like him. All the girls do."

"Where are we going dancing?" Since Leon's in a dry county there's not a real nightclub within twenty miles.

"We'll go out to the VFW Club," Kenyon said.

"We? Are you going too? Who do you have a date with?"

"Nobody. I'm just going along for the ride."

"Kenyon, I'm twenty-five years old going on twenty-six, and I'll be damned if you're going anywhere as my chaperone."

"Sister, watch your language," said Daddy. "Is he a good dancer, Kenyon?"

"Daddy, what do you care if he's a good dancer or not? You're not the one who's going to be dancing with him."

"I don't want my daughter marrying some Valentino. Good dancers make bad husbands."

"Daddy! You are hopelessly behind times! If you'd turn on your TV set you'd see people dancing without even touching each other. The Valentinos are all gone. Anyway, I'm not going to my wedding Saturday night. I'm going to the VFW Club!"

They had me. I was trapped into having a date with Frank Harwell just to prove to Daddy he wasn't a Valentino. I didn't mind so much. After all, I'd endured a long dry march in the desert with Alvin Neeley. And, I wanted to know what Kenyon did with himself when he wasn't riding the range.

On Saturday night I pranced into the living room in my best and fullest skirt. You have to have plenty of leg room for country dances. Kenyon was standing talking to Frank Harwell, who looked like a cowboy straight out of a cigarette advertisement, lean, tanned, and terribly sure of himself. He was every young girl's dream, and old girl's too. My knees were shaking a little when he looked me over. For a minute I wished I hadn't worn a sensible dress. I wished I was all togged out in my red sequins and red high heels again.

We all three got in Frank's pickup. He and Kenyon did most of the talking. We hadn't gone two blocks before Kenyon insisted he had to stop and look at some stock at the auction barn on the way to the VFW.

"Fine," said Frank in a grand, easy-going way. He was the most totally relaxed man I'd ever seen. He drove his pickup through town with one hand on the wheel, guiding it to the right and left as if he were reining a horse.

When we got to the auction barn Kenyon shot out of the truck, leaving the door open behind him.

"Always in a hurry," said Frank and leaned over me to pull the door shut. I felt like a huge old cat had fallen in my lap.

"You don't seem to be."

"Naw." He eased himself up, pulled out a package of cigarettes, lit one, then leaned back and blew smoke out. I kept expecting to hear an announcer's voice saying something about how good cigarettes were so I waited a minute before saying anything myself. Finally, I asked him about his ranch. He told me about his spring round-up, how much mohair had been clipped from his goats, how many cows had calved, the number of rattlesnakes he'd killed, how much a good rain would help, and other interesting things like that. We sat there, with Frank worrying about his wells running dry and the miles of fence he needed to repair; I was worrying about whether we'd ever get to the dance. The VFW Club was on top of a hill behind the auction barn. We could have walked up there, but it could have been in the next county as far as Frank was concerned. He got a bottle of bourbon out of the glove compartment and took a long swallow from it. When Kenyon came back he passed the bottle to him. Neither one of them offered me a swallow and I knew I'd have to be seventy and taking whiskey for medicinal purposes before either one of those two would dream of offering a girl a drink.

Kenyon was excited about a bull he'd seen. "He's the same old Brahma that throwed me. I'd know him anywhere. Gentle as he can be outside the ring, but let somebody get on his back and he goes wild. Wonder why they're selling him. He's a good rodeo bull."

"Getting old maybe," Frank drawled. They both laughed as if he'd said the most hilarious thing in the world. Then they both took another drink so *they* were in a good mood when we got to the VFW at 9:30 P.M. The hall was an old WW II army surplus barracks the veterans had bought and painted white. Judging from the noise coming out of the place, the men standing around cars outside talking and sneaking drinks, and the two cops at the doorway, it was wilder than any Galveston club on a Saturday night. The cops nodded at us as we went in. The girl who was selling tickets to the dance warned Frank and Kenyon to hold on to them because nobody was allowed to come back in without one.

Frank swung me out on the dance floor and that was the last I saw of Kenyon for a while except for a glimpse of him out of the corner of my eye. He was dancing with one of my ex-students, a not so bright one, who'd somehow managed to graduate the year before. Every once in a while Frank would excuse himself to go out and take a swig from his bottle. I sat at a table by myself drinking soda pop and thinking about my Galveston days when I at least had the company of some grown men when I was drinking. The musicians at the VFW that night, by the way, hardly deserved the name. They sawed and wheezed through their whole repertory which consisted of about fifteen songs, all sounding alike. It's fashionable now to like what everyone calls "country music," but if you had to sit out in the VFW and listen to it, you'd get pretty tired of the music and the country.

After a while I caught sight of Frank strolling in the front door. He stopped by another table for a minute to pat a girl on the top of her frizzy blonde head, then he ambled on over to me.

"Where's Kenyon?" I was tired of listening to the whining songs, tired of being flung around the dance floor. The new dances I'd told Daddy about hadn't gotten to Leon yet—they probably never will get to Frank Harwell. The more he drank the harder he danced, not on my toes, but stomping hard on the floor taking great wide steps and swinging me around in circles. It was 1:00 A.M., time to go home. Nobody else seemed to think so though. The hall was even more packed than when we first came in.

"Last time I saw him Kenyon was outside arguing with the cops. He's lost his ticket and they won't let him back in."

"Why doesn't he buy another one?"

"He thinks they ought to take his word he already bought one. You know he's got high principles and—"

"I know about his principles all right. He's got high principles and no scruples!!"

"Aw, don't be too hard on your brother."

I was getting ready to tell him that Kenyon had been hard on me when we both turned our heads to see what was causing all the shouting down by the door. It was my brother leading that gentle old Brahma bull by a rope around his neck. The crowd was parting before him. Some of them were jumping out the windows and everybody else was headed for the back door. The blonde Frank had patted on the head was standing on top of a table screaming, "Help! Somebody do something!" Nobody was doing anything but getting out. Kenyon staggered through the hall with a mean grin on his face, drunk as the lord of the wild frontier and cool as a walking ice cube. Behind the bandstand the musicians were crawling out the windows. The bass fiddler tried to throw his fiddle out first, but it got stuck. He left it there, half in, half out, and wriggled through another window. A man following him didn't watch where he was going and caught his foot in the middle of a drum.

Behind Kenyon the bull, uncertain of his footing on the slippery floor, was trying to adjust himself. He slid along, his tail lashing frantically, his hooves skidding in all directions. When Kenyon slowed down a little to get past some tables the Brahma snorted and jumped—like Alvin Neeley doing his little skip in mid-air to keep in step.

"Come on. We can't stand here gawking. Somebody's going to get hurt if Kenyon lets that old bull go." Frank grabbed my hand and we headed for the back door. By the time we got out Kenyon and the bull had the VFW Club to themselves.

We waited out back. The cops waited too. Kenyon appeared in the doorway. The bull nudged up behind him. He turned and scratched the bull's head.

"I told you," Kenyon hollered at the cops, "I already bought one ticket." Then he walked down the steps carefully leading the bull, talking to him all the way. "Watch your step, old buddy. That's right. Easy now."

The cops let Kenyon put the bull back in the auction pen, and when he was finished, they put him in their car. He was laughing so hard he couldn't fight very well, but he tried.

"Oh Lord!" Frank sighed lazily from the safety of his pickup. "If he wouldn't fight, they'd let him go. Those boys were ready for that dance to break up anyway."

"Aren't you going to help him?"

"Naw. He took this on hisself. You want us both in jail?"

"In jail?"

"Yeah," Frank drawled and hoisted his big handsome self across the seat toward me.

"Shouldn't we follow them?"

"Look at that moon."

There wasn't a moon in sight, not a sliver of one. Gorgeous Frank Harwell was so sleepy drunk he mistook somebody's headlights for the moon. All the excitement on top of all the dancing we'd done was too much for him I guess, because the next thing I knew he'd passed out. I lifted his head off my shoulder, propped it up against the window, and climbed into the driver's seat.

I got to the jail in time to hear them book Kenyon for being drunk and disorderly and disturbing the peace. He paid his own way out this time, but the only reason they didn't lock him up for the night was I was there to take him home. Of course, I couldn't take him home in his condition. Daddy would have had an attack and Mother would have probably fainted at the sight of him. Her clean-cut, hard-working, tight-lipped boy was a living mess. He looked like he'd been riding the bull rather than leading him. I managed to brush most of the dust off of him. The cops gave him back his hat. We stopped at Leon's one open-all-night cafe, where I went in and got a quart of black coffee. When he'd finished this he was sober enough to go in the men's room and wash his face. Frank slept through the whole rehabilitation.

Kenyon wanted to park the pickup on the square across from the jail and walk home, leaving Frank there snoring. "Maybe the cops will come out and get him," he said.

"It's not any use to get mad at Frank. It was your idea to bring that animal into the dance hall."

"You taking up for him?"

"I got you out of jail, didn't I?"

Kenyon nodded. I went in the cafe to get some more coffee for Frank. When I came back out Kenyon started shaking him, but before he got him awake he turned to me and said, "Sister, don't tell everything you know."

"Why not? Mother and Daddy are going to find out anyway. By church time tomorrow everybody in town will be talking—"

"I'd rather they get it second-hand."

By this time I was so mad I jabbed Frank with my elbow, handed him the coffee, and lit into Kenyon. "You'd rather everybody get everything second-hand. Nobody is supposed to do anything but you."

"What are you talking about?"

"Never mind! You wouldn't understand if I kept talking till sunup, but I'll tell you this, Kenyon—I'm not going to devote the rest of my life to keeping you out of jail. From now on you are on your own."

"Sister, I've always been on my own."

How contrary can a person be? Here I'd just saved him from a night in the Leon County jail, not to mention the time I got him out of the Galveston jail. I didn't argue with him though. I knew if I told him he wasn't on his own till he left home, he wouldn't wait a minute before telling me the same thing—with Frank Harwell sitting right next to me taking in every word.

"You want me to drive?" Kenyon asked him.

"Naw, you have got in enough trouble tonight, you and that dancing bull. I'll make it."

They both laughed. Frank even tried to slap my knee, but I dodged him.

"I want to go home," I said.

"Gal, that's where we're going."

It was 2:30 A.M. I could imagine Daddy sitting on the front porch wrapped in his overcoat with his M-1 stretched across his knees. For once, we were lucky. Mother and Daddy were both in bed asleep. Kenyon and I tiptoed to our rooms without waking either one of them. When they asked us the next morning where we'd been so late, Kenyon said, "Dancing." Since they were used to short answers from him he didn't have to say anything else. Of course Mother came and sat on the foot of my bed and asked me all about Frank Harwell.

"Mother, Frank is a very handsome man and no doubt all the other girls like him, but he is a cowboy and I think one cowboy is enough in the family."

Then I told her. "In June I'm going down to San Antonio and look for a job in one of the schools there."

"You can't—"

"Yes, I can. If I don't leave home now, I'll be right here the rest of my days."

"She might as well," Kenyon said. He was leaning in the doorway, eavesdropping to see whether I was going to tell on him. "She's too uppity for anybody in Leon." With that he turned around and left. He didn't know it, but it was the best thing he could have said. Daddy blamed himself for giving me too much education and Mother was so anxious to be a grandmother I think she'd have been happy to see me off to New York.

In June I went to San Antonio and found a job at one of the high schools. I found a husband, too, a fine doctor who sings in the chorus during opera season. That's where I met him—in the chorus. We were rehearsing for *La Traviata*. His name is Edward Greenlee. Dr. Edward Greenlee.

"Can he rope?" Kenyon asked.

"Can you tie a suture?"

"What branch of the army was he in?"

"He was in the navy, Daddy."

"Is he from a large family?"

"Mother, there are Greenlees all over San Antonio."

We had a June wedding in the First Methodist in Leon. Daddy gave me away. Kenyon was an usher. He looked handsome in his white tux jacket, the only one he'd ever worn in his life. I told him so when I got to the church in my bridal finery. He said thanks and grinned his tight-lipped grin. I looked down. The black pants covered all of the stitching decorating the tops, but I could plainly see, and so could everybody else at my wedding, that Kenyon had his boots on.

I guess he'll go on being true to the code and die with them on. He's living out on one of his ranches now, fifteen miles from the nearest town and ninety miles from San Antonio. Sometimes on Sunday afternoons Edward and I take the children and drive up to see him. There's no way of letting him know we're coming because he doesn't have a telephone. We don't have to worry about inconveniencing anybody though; Kenyon lives by himself.

The last time we were there we missed him. My five-year-old boy, William, walked around on the bare floors and said, "Doesn't he have any rugs?"

When we were checking the cupboards in the almost bare kitchen Cynthia, our three-year-old, wailed, "Doesn't he have any cookies?"

"No, he doesn't have any rugs and he doesn't have any cookies. But he does have a bathtub, hot and cold running water, a bed, a fire, three cans of chili, a sack of flour, two horses, a sheep dog, and a whole lot of sheep, goats, and cattle."

"Why doesn't he have any cookies?"

"This sure is a lumpy old chair," said William. He should have known. He was sitting in the only one in the room. "Is Uncle Kenyon poor?"

"All of your Uncle Kenyon's money is tied up in stock, the sheep, and goats and cattle," said Edward, who always tries to explain things.

"Uncle Kenyon is a cowboy," I said, which was really the only explanation.

From A DOLL'S HOUSE

Henrik Ibsen

ACT III

NORA: We have been married now eight years. Does it not occur to you that this is the first time we two, you and I, husband and wife, have had a serious conversation?

HELMER: What do you mean by serious?

NORA: In all these eight years—longer than that—from the very beginning of our acquaintance, we have never exchanged a word on any serious subject.

HELMER: Was it likely that I would be continually and for ever telling you about worries that you could not help me to bear?

NORA: I am not speaking about business matters. I say that we have never sat down in earnest together to try and get at the bottom of anything.

HELMER: But, dearest Nora, would it have been any good to you?

NORA: That is just it; you have never understood me. I have been greatly wronged, Torvald—first by papa and then by you.

HELMER: What! By us two—by us two, who have loved you better than any one else in the world?

NORA: (*shaking her head*) You have never loved me. You have only thought it pleasant to be in love with me.

HELMER: Nora, what do I hear you saying?

NORA: It is perfectly true, Torvald. When I was at home with papa, he told me his opinion about everything, and so I had the same opinions;

Reprinted, with permission, from Henrik Isben's *A Doll's House*, translated by R. Farquharson Sharp in the Everyman's Library Series. London: J. M. Dent & Sons, 1958.

and if I differed from him I concealed the fact, because he would not
have liked it. He called me his doll-child, and he played with me just as
I used to play with my dolls. And when I came to live with you—

HELMER: What sort of an expression is that to use about our marriage?

NORA: (*undisturbed*) I mean that I was simply transferred from papa's
hands into yours. You arranged everything according to your own taste,
and so I got the same tastes as you—or else I pretended to, I am really
not quite sure which—I think sometimes the one and sometimes the
other. When I look back on it, it seems to me as if I had been living here
like a poor woman—just from hand to mouth. I have existed merely to
perform tricks for you, Torvald. But you would have it so. You and
papa have committed a great sin against me. It is your fault that I have
made nothing of my life.

HELMER: How unreasonable and how ungrateful you are, Nora. Have you
not been happy here?

NORA: No, I have never been happy. I thought I was, but it has never really been so.

HELMER: Not—not happy!

NORA: No, only merry. And you have always been so kind to me. But our
home has been nothing but a playroom. I have been your doll-wife,
just as at home I was papa's doll-child; and here the children have been
my dolls. I thought it great fun when you played with me, just as they
thought it great fun when I played with them. That is what our marriage has been, Torvald.

HELMER: There is some truth in what you say—exaggerated and strained
as your view of it is. But for the future it shall be different. Playtime
shall be over, and lesson-time shall begin.

NORA: Whose lessons? Mine, or the children's?

HELMER: Both yours and the children's, my darling Nora.

NORA: Alas, Torvald, you are not the man to educate me into being a
proper wife for you.

HELMER: And you can say that!

NORA: And I—how am I fitted to bring up the children?

HELMER: Nora!

NORA: Didn't you say so yourself a little while ago—that you dare not
trust me to bring them up?

HELMER: In a moment of anger! Why do you pay any heed to that?

NORA: Indeed, you were perfectly right. I am not fit for the task. There is
another task I must undertake first. I must try and educate myself—you

are not the man to help me in that. I must do that for myself. And that is why I am going to leave you now.

HELMER: (*springing up*) What do you say?

NORA: I must stand quite alone, if I am to understand myself and every-thing about me. It is for that reason that I cannot remain with you any longer.

HELMER: Nora, Nora!

NORA: I am going away from here now, at once. I am sure Christine will take me in for the night—

HELMER: You are out of your mind! I won't allow it! I forbid you!

NORA: It is no use forbidding me anything any longer. I will take with me what belongs to myself. I will take nothing from you, either now or later.

HELMER: What sort of madness is this!

NORA: Tomorrow I shall go home—I mean, to my old home. It will be easiest for me to find something to do there.

HELMER: You blind, foolish woman!

NORA: I must try and get some sense, Torvald.

HELMER: To desert your home, your husband and your children! And you don't consider what people will say!

NORA: I cannot consider that at all. I only know that it is necessary for me.

HELMER: It's shocking. This is how you would neglect your most sacred duties.

NORA: What do you consider my most sacred duties?

HELMER: Do I need to tell you that? Are they not your duties to your hus-band and your children?

NORA: I have other duties just as sacred.

HELMER: That you have not. What duties could those be?

NORA: Duties to myself.

HELMER: Before all else, you are a wife and a mother.

NORA: I don't believe that any longer. I believe that before all else I am a reasonable human being, just as you are—or, at all events, that I must try and become one. I know quite well, Torvald, that most people would think you right, and that views of that kind are to be found in books; but I can no longer content myself with what most people say, or with what is found in books. I must think over things for myself and get to understand them.

HELMER: Can you not understand your place in your own home? Have you not a reliable guide in such matters as that?—have you no religion?

NORA: I am afraid, Torvald, I do not exactly know what religion is.

HELMER: What are you saying?

NORA: I know nothing but what the clergyman said, when I went to be confirmed. He told us that religion was this, and that, and the other. When I am away from all this, and am alone, I will look into that matter too. I will see if what the clergyman said is true, or at all events if it is true for me.

HELMER: This is unheard of in a girl of your age! But if religion cannot lead you aright, let me try and awaken your conscience. I suppose you have some moral sense? Or—answer me—am I to think you have none?

NORA: I assure you, Torvald, that is not an easy question to answer. I really don't know. The thing perplexes me altogether. I only know that you and I look at it in quite a different light. I am learning, too, that the law is quite another thing from what I supposed; but I find it impossible to convince myself that the law is right. According to it a woman has no right to spare her old dying father, or to save her husband's life. I can't believe that.

HELMER: You talk like a child. You don't understand the conditions of the world in which you live.

NORA: No, I don't. But now I am going to try. I am going to see if I can make out who is right, the world or I.

HELMER: You are ill, Nora; you are delirious; I almost think you are out of your mind.

NORA: I have never felt my mind so clear and certain as tonight.

HELMER: And is it with a clear and certain mind that you forsake your husband and your children?

NORA: Yes, it is.

HELMER: Then there is only one possible explanation.

NORA: What is that?

HELMER: You do not love me any more.

NORA: No, that is just it.

HELMER: Nora!—and you can say that?

NORA: It gives me great pain, Torvald, for you have always been so kind to me, but I cannot help it. I do not love you any more.

HELMER: (*regaining his composure*) Is that a clear and certain conviction too?

NORA: Yes, absolutely clear and certain. That is the reason why I will not stay here any longer.

HELMER: And can you tell me what I have done to forfeit your love?

NORA: Yes, indeed I can. It was tonight, when the wonderful thing did not happen; then I saw you were not the man I had thought you.

HELMER: Explain yourself better—I don't understand you.

NORA: I have waited so patiently for eight years; for, goodness knows, I knew very well that wonderful things don't happen every day. Then this horrible misfortune came upon me; and then I felt quite certain that the wonderful thing was going to happen at last. When Krogstad's letter was lying out there, never for a moment did I imagine that you would consent to accept this man's conditions. I was so absolutely certain that you would say to him: Publish the thing to the whole world. And when that was done—

HELMER: Yes, what then?—when I had exposed my wife to shame and disgrace?

NORA: When that was done, I was so absolutely certain you would come forward and take everything upon yourself, and say: I am the guilty one.

HELMER: Nora—!

NORA: You mean that I would never have accepted such a sacrifice on your part? No, of course not. But what would my assurances have been worth against yours? That was the wonderful thing which I hoped for and feared; and it was to prevent that, that I wanted to kill myself.

HELMER: I would gladly work night and day for you, Nora—bear sorrow and want for your sake. But no man would sacrifice his honor for the one he loves.

NORA: It is a thing hundreds of women have done.

HELMER: Oh, you think and talk like a heedless child.

NORA: Maybe. But you neither think nor talk like the man I could bind myself to. As soon as your fear was over—and it was not fear for what threatened me, but for what might happen to you—when the whole thing was past, as far as you were concerned it was exactly as if nothing at all had happened. Exactly as before, I was your little skylark, your doll, which you would in future treat with doubly gentle care, because it was so brittle and fragile. (*Getting up.*) Torvald—it was then it dawned upon me that for eight years I had been living here with a strange man, and had borne him three children—Oh, I can't bear to think of it! I could tear myself into little bits!

HELMER: (*sadly*) I see, I see. An abyss has opened between us—there is no denying it. But, Nora, would it not be possible to fill it up?

NORA: As I am now, I am no wife for you.

HELMER: I have it in me to become a different man.

NORA: Perhaps—if your doll is taken away from you.

HELMER: But to part!—to part from you! No, no, Nora, I can't understand that idea.

NORA: (*going out to the right*) That makes it all the more certain that it must be done. (*She comes back with her cloak and hat and a small bag which she puts on a chair by the table.*)

HELMER: Nora, Nora, not now! Wait till tomorrow.

NORA: (*putting on her cloak*) I cannot spend the night in a strange man's room.

HELMER: But can't we live here like brother and sister—?

NORA: (*putting on her hat*) You know very well that would not last long. (*Puts the shawl round her.*) Good-by, Torvald. I won't see the little ones. I know they are in better hands than mine. As I am now, I can be of no use to them.

HELMER: But some day, Nora—some day?

NORA: How can I tell? I have no idea what is going to become of me.

HELMER: But you are my wife, whatever becomes of you.

NORA: Listen, Torvald. I have heard that when a wife deserts her husband's house, as I am doing now, he is legally freed from all obligations towards her. In any case I set you free from all your obligations. You are not to feel yourself bound in the slightest way, any more than I shall. There must be perfect freedom on both sides. See, here is your ring back. Give me mine.

HELMER: That too?

NORA: That too.

HELMER: Here it is.

NORA: That's right. Now it is all over. I have put the keys here. The maids know all about everything in the house—better than I do. Tomorrow, after I have left her, Christine will come here and pack up my own things that I brought with me from home. I will have them sent after me.

HELMER: All over! All over!—Nora, shall you never think of me again?

NORA: I know I shall often think of you and the children and this house.

HELMER: May I write to you, Nora?

NORA: No—never. You must not do that.

HELMER: But at least let me send you—

NORA: Nothing—nothing—

HELMER: Let me help you if you are in want.

NORA: No. I can receive nothing from a stranger.

HELMER: Nora—can I never be anything more than a stranger to you?

NORA: (*taking her bag*) Ah, Torvald, the most wonderful thing of all would have to happen.

HELMER: Tell me what that would be!

NORA: Both you and I would have to be so changed that—Oh, Torvald, I don't believe any longer in wonderful things happening.

HELMER: But I will believe in it. Tell me? So changed that—?

NORA: That our life together would be a real wedlock. Good-by. (*She goes out through the hall.*)

HELMER: (*sinks down on a chair at the door and buries his face in his hands*) Nora! Nora! (*Looks round, and rises.*) Empty. She is gone. (*A hope flashes across his mind.*) The most wonderful thing of all—? (*The sound of a door shutting is heard from below.*)

THE EIGHTY-YARD RUN

Irwin Shaw

The pass was high and wide and he jumped for it, feeling it slap flatly against his hands, as he shook his hips to throw off the halfback who was diving at him. The center floated by, his hands desperately brushing Darling's knee as Darling picked his feet up high and delicately ran over a blocker and an opposing linesman in a jumble on the ground near the scrimmage line. He had ten yards in the clear and picked up speed, breathing easily, feeling his thigh pads rising and falling against his legs, listening to the sound of cleats behind him, pulling away from them, watching the other backs heading him off toward the sideline, the whole picture, the men closing in on him, the blockers fighting for position, the ground he had to cross, all suddenly clear in his head, for the first time in his life not a meaningless confusion of men, sounds, speed. He smiled a little to himself as he ran, holding the ball lightly in front of him with his two hands, his knees pumping high, his hips twisting in the almost girlish run of a back in a broken field. The first halfback came at him and he fed him his leg, then swung at the last moment, took the shock of the man's shoulder without breaking stride, ran right through him, his cleats biting securely into the turf. There was only the safety man now, coming warily at him, his arms crooked, hands spread. Darling tucked the ball in, spurted at him, driving hard, hurling himself along, all two hundred pounds bunched into controlled attack. He was sure he was going to get past the safety man. Without thought, his arms and legs working beautifully together, he headed right for the safety man, stiff-armed him, feeling blood

"The Eighty-Yard Run," by Irwin Shaw, reprinted, with permission of the author, from *Short Story Masterpieces*, edited by Robert Penn Warren and Albert Erskine. New York: Dell, 1954.

spurt instantaneously from the man's nose onto his hand, seeing his face go awry, head turned, mouth pulled to one side. He pivoted away, keeping the arm locked, dropping the safety man as he ran easily toward the goal line, with the drumming of cleats diminishing behind him.

How long ago? It was autumn then, and the ground was getting hard because the nights were cold and leaves from the maples around the stadium blew across the practice fields in gusts of wind, and the girls were beginning to put polo coats over their sweaters when they came to watch practice in the afternoons. . . . Fifteen years. Darling walked slowly over the same ground in the spring twilight, in his neat shoes, a man of thirty-five dressed in a double-breasted suit, ten pounds heavier in the fifteen years, but not fat, with the years between 1925 and 1940 showing in his face.

The coach was smiling quietly to himself and the assistant coaches were looking at each other with pleasure the way they always did when one of the second stringers suddenly did something fine, bringing credit to them, making their two thousand dollars a year a tiny bit more secure.

Darling trotted back, smiling, breathing deeply but easily, feeling wonderful, not tired, though this was the tail end of practice and he'd run eighty yards. The sweat poured off his face and soaked his jersey and he liked the feeling, the warm moistness lubricating his skin like oil. Off in a corner of the field some players were punting and the smack of leather against the ball came pleasantly through the afternoon air. The freshmen were running signals on the next field and the quarterback's sharp voice, the pound of the eleven pairs of cleats, the "Dig, now *dig!*" of the coaches, the laughter of the players all somehow made him feel happy as he trotted back to midfield, listening to the applause and shouts of the students along the sidelines, knowing that after that run the coach would have to start him Saturday against Illinois.

Fifteen years, Darling thought, remembering the shower after the workout, the hot water steaming off his skin and the deep soapsuds and all the young voices singing with the water streaming down and towels going and managers running in and out and the sharp sweet smell of oil of wintergreen and everybody clapping him on the back as he dressed and Packard, the captain, who took being captain very seriously, coming over to him and shaking his hand and saying, "Darling, you're going to go places in the next two years."

The assistant manager fussed over him, wiping a cut on his leg with alcohol and iodine, the little sting making him realize suddenly how fresh and whole and solid his body felt. The manager slapped a piece of adhesive tape over the cut, and Darling noticed the sharp clean white of the tape against the ruddiness of the skin, fresh from the shower.

He dressed slowly, the softness of his shirt and the soft warmth of his wool socks and his flannel trousers a reward against his skin after the harsh pressure of the shoulder harness and thigh and hip pads. He drank three glasses of cold water, the liquid reaching down coldly inside of him, soothing the harsh dry places in his throat and belly left by the sweat and running and shouting of practice.

Fifteen years.

The sun had gone down and the sky was green behind the stadium and he laughed quietly to himself as he looked at the stadium, rearing above the trees, and knew that on Saturday when the seventy thousand voices roared as the team came running out onto the field, part of that enormous salute would be for him. He walked slowly, listening to the gravel crunch satisfactorily under his shoes in the still twilight, feeling his clothes swing lightly against his skin, breathing the thin evening air, feeling the wind more softly in his damp hair, wonderfully cool behind his ears and at the nape of his neck.

Louise was waiting for him at the road, in her car. The top was down and he noticed all over again, as he always did when he saw her, how pretty she was, the rough blonde hair and the large, inquiring eyes and the bright mouth, smiling now.

She threw the door open. "Were you good today?" she asked.

"Pretty good," he said. He climbed in, sank luxuriously into the soft leather, stretched his legs far out. He smiled, thinking of the eighty yards. "Pretty damn good."

She looked at him seriously for a moment, then scrambled around, like a little girl, kneeling on the seat next to him, grabbed him, her hands along his ears, and kissed him as he sprawled, head back, on the seat cushion. She let go of him, but kept her head close to his, over his. Darling reached up slowly and rubbed the back of his hand against her cheek, lit softly by a street lamp a hundred feet away. They looked at each other, smiling.

Louise drove down to the lake and they sat there silently, watching the moon rise behind the hills on the other side. Finally he reached over, pulled her gently to him, kissed her. Her lips grew soft, her body sank into his, tears formed slowly in her eyes. He knew, for the first time, that he could do whatever he wanted with her.

"Tonight," he said. "I'll call for you at seven-thirty. Can you get out?"

She looked at him. She was smiling, but the tears were still full in her eyes. "All right," she said, "I'll get out. How about you? Won't the coach raise hell?"

Darling grinned. "I got the coach in the palm of my hand," he said. "Can you wait till seven-thirty?"

She grinned back at him. "No," she said.

They kissed and she started the car and they went back to town for dinner. He sang on the way home.

Christian Darling, thirty-five years old, sat on the frail spring grass, greener now than it ever would be again on the practice field, looked thoughtfully up at the stadium, a deserted ruin in the twilight. He had started on the first team that Saturday and every Saturday after that for the next two years, but it had never been as satisfactory as it should have been. He never had broken away, the longest run he'd ever made was thirty-five yards, and that in a game that was already won, and then that kid had come up from the third team, Diederich, a blank-faced German kid from Wisconsin, who ran like a bull, ripping lines to pieces Saturday after Saturday, plowing through, never getting hurt, never changing his expression, scoring more points, gaining more ground than all the rest of the team put together, making everybody's All-American, carrying the ball three times out of four, keeping everybody else out of the headlines. Darling was a good blocker and he spent his Saturday afternoons working on the big Swedes and Polacks who played tackle and end for Michigan, Illinois, Purdue, hurling into huge pile-ups, bobbing his head wildly to elude the great raw hands swinging like meat-cleavers at him as he went charging in to open up holes for Diederich coming through like a locomotive behind him. Still, it wasn't so bad. Everybody liked him and he did his job and he was pointed out on the campus and boys always felt important when they introduced their girls to him at their proms, and Louise loved him and watched him faithfully in the games, even in the mud, when your own mother wouldn't know you, and drove him around in her car keeping the top down because she was proud of him and wanted to show everybody that she was Christian Darling's girl. She bought him crazy presents because her father was rich, watches, pipes, humidors, an icebox for beer for his room, curtains, wallets, a fifty-dollar dictionary.

"You'll spend every cent your old man owns," Darling protested once when she showed up at his rooms with seven different packages in her arms and tossed them onto the couch.

"Kiss me," Louise said, "and shut up."

"Do you want to break your poor old man?"

"I don't mind. I want to buy you presents."

"Why?"

"It makes me feel good. Kiss me. I don't know why. Did you know that you're an important figure?"

"Yes," Darling said gravely.

"When I was waiting for you at the library yesterday two girls saw you coming and one of them said to the other, 'That's Christian Darling. He's an important figure.'"

"You're a liar."

"I'm in love with an important figure."

"Still, why the hell did you have to give me a forty-pound dictionary?"

"I wanted to make sure," Louise said, "that you had a token of my esteem. I want to smother you in tokens of my esteem."

Fifteen years ago.

They'd married when they got out of college. There'd been other women for him, but all casual and secret, more for curiosity's sake, and vanity, women who'd thrown themselves at him and flattered him, a pretty mother at a summer camp for boys, an old girl from his home town who'd suddenly blossomed into a coquette, a friend of Louise's who had dogged him grimly for six months and had taken advantage of the two weeks that Louise went home when her mother died. Perhaps Louise had known, but she'd kept quiet, loving him completely, filling his rooms with presents, religiously watching him battling with the big Swedes and Polacks on the line of scrimmage on Saturday afternoons, making plans for marrying him and living with him in New York and going with him there to the night clubs, the theaters, the good restaurants, being proud of him in advance, tall, white-teethed, smiling, large, yet moving lightly, with an athlete's grace, dressed in evening clothes, approvingly eyed by magnificently dressed and famous women in theater lobbies, with Louise adoringly at his side.

Her father, who manufactured inks, set up a New York office for Darling to manage and presented him with three hundred accounts, and they lived on Beekman Place with a view of the river with fifteen thousand dollars a year between them, because everybody was buying everything in those days, including ink. They saw all the shows and went to all the speakeasies and spent their fifteen thousand dollars a year and in the afternoons

Louise went to the art galleries and the matinees of the more serious plays that Darling didn't like to sit through and Darling slept with a girl who danced in the chorus of *Rosalie* and with the wife of a man who owned three copper mines. Darling played squash three times a week and remained as solid as a stone barn and Louise never took her eyes off him when they were in the same room together, watching him with a secret, miser's smile, with a trick of coming over to him in the middle of a crowded room and saying gravely, in a low voice, "You're the handsomest man I've ever seen in my whole life. Want a drink?"

Nineteen twenty-nine came to Darling and to his wife and father-in-law, the maker of inks, just as it came to everyone else. The father-in-law waited until 1933 and then blew his brains out and when Darling went to Chicago to see what the books of the firm looked like he found out all that was left were debts and three or four gallons of unbought ink.

"Please, Christian," Louise said, sitting in their neat Beekman Place apartment, with a view of the river and prints of paintings by Dufy and Braque and Picasso on the wall, "please, why do you want to start drinking at two o'clock in the afternoon?"

"I have nothing else to do," Darling said, putting down his glass, emptied of its fourth drink. "Please pass the whisky."

Louise filled his glass. "Come take a walk with me," she said. "We'll walk along the river."

"I don't want to walk along the river," Darling said, squinting intensely at the prints of paintings by Dufy, Braque and Picasso.

"We'll walk along Fifth Avenue."

"I don't want to walk along Fifth Avenue."

"Maybe," Louise said gently, "you'd like to come with me to some art galleries. There's an exhibition by a man named Klee. . . ."

"I don't want to go to any art galleries. I want to sit here and drink Scotch whisky," Darling said. "Who the hell hung these goddam pictures up on the wall?"

"I did," Louise said.

"I hate them."

"I'll take them down," Louise said.

"Leave them there. It gives me something to do in the afternoon. I can hate them." Darling took a long swallow. "Is that the way people paint these days?"

"Yes, Christian. Please don't drink any more."

"Do you like painting like that?"

"Yes, dear."

"Really?"

"Really."

Darling looked carefully at the prints once more. "Little Louise Tucker. The middle-western beauty. I like pictures with horses in them. Why should you like pictures like that?"

"I just happen to have gone to a lot of galleries in the last few years . . ."

"Is that what you do in the afternoon?"

"That's what I do in the afternoon," Louise said.

"I drink in the afternoon."

Louise kissed him lightly on the top of his head as he sat there squinting at the pictures on the wall, the glass of whisky held firmly in his hand. She put on her coat and went out without saying another word. When she came back in the early evening, she had a job on a woman's fashion magazine.

They moved downtown and Louise went out to work every morning and Darling sat home and drank and Louise paid the bills as they came up. She made believe she was going to quit work as soon as Darling found a job, even though she was taking over more responsibility day by day at the magazine, interviewing authors, picking painters for the illustrations and covers, getting actresses to pose for pictures, going out for drinks with the right people, making a thousand new friends whom she loyally introduced to Darling.

"I don't like your hat," Darling said, once, when she came in in the evening and kissed him, her breath rich with Martinis.

"What's the matter with my hat, Baby?" she asked, running her fingers through his hair. "Everybody says it's very smart."

"It's too damned smart," he said. "It's not for you. It's for a rich, sophisticated woman of thirty-five with admirers."

Louise laughed. "I'm practicing to be a rich, sophisticated woman of thirty-five with admirers," she said. He stared soberly at her. "Now, don't look so grim, Baby. It's still the same simple little wife under the hat." She took the hat off, threw it into a corner, sat on his lap. "See? Homebody Number One."

"Your breath could run a train," Darling said, not wanting to be mean, but talking out of boredom, and sudden shock at seeing his wife curiously a stranger in a new hat, with a new expression in her eyes under the little brim, secret, confident, knowing.

Louise tucked her head under his chin so he couldn't smell her breath.

"I had to take an author out for cocktails," she said. "He's a boy from the Ozark Mountains and he drinks like a fish. He's a Communist."

"What the hell is a Communist from the Ozarks doing writing for a woman's fashion magazine?"

Louise chuckled. "The magazine business is getting all mixed up these days. The publishers want to have a foot in every camp. And anyway, you can't find an author under seventy these days who isn't a Communist."

"I don't think I like you to associate with all those people, Louise," Darling said. "Drinking with them."

"He's a very nice, gentle boy," Louise said. "He reads Ernest Dowson."

"Who's Ernest Dowson?"

Louise patted his arm, stood up, fixed her hair. "He's an English poet."

Darling felt that somehow he had disappointed her. "Am I supposed to know who Ernest Dowson is?"

"No, dear. I'd better go in and take a bath."

After she had gone, Darling went over to the corner where the hat was lying and picked it up. It was nothing, a scrap of straw, a red flower, a veil, meaningless on his big hand, but on his wife's head a signal of something . . . big city, smart and knowing women drinking and dining with men other than their husbands, conversation about things a normal man wouldn't know much about, Frenchmen who painted as though they used their elbows instead of brushes, composers who wrote whole symphonies without a single melody in them, writers who knew all about politics and women who knew all about writers, the movement of the proletariat, Marx, somehow mixed up with five-dollar dinners and the best-looking women in America and fairies who made them laugh and half-sentences immediately understood and secretly hilarious and wives who called their husbands "Baby." He put the hat down, a scrap of straw and a red flower, and a little veil. He drank some whisky straight and went into the bathroom where his wife was lying deep in her bath, singing to herself and smiling from time to time like a little girl, paddling the water gently with her hands, sending up a slight spicy fragrance from the bath salts she used.

He stood over her, looking down at her. She smiled up at him, her eyes half closed, her body pink and shimmering in the warm, scented water. All over again, with all the old suddenness, he was hit deep inside him with the knowledge of how beautiful she was, how much he needed her.

"I came in here," he said, "to tell you I wish you wouldn't call me 'Baby'."

She looked up at him from the bath, her eyes quickly full of sorrow, half understanding what he meant. He knelt and put his arms around her, his sleeves plunged heedlessly in the water, his shirt and jacket soaking wet as he clutched her wordlessly, holding her crazily tight, crushing her breath from her, kissing her desperately, searchingly, regretfully.

He got jobs after that, selling real estate and automobiles, but somehow, although he had a desk with his name on a wooden wedge on it, and he went to the office religiously at nine each morning, he never managed to sell anything and he never made any money.

Louise was made assistant editor, and the house was always full of strange men and women who talked fast and got angry on abstract subjects like mural painting, novelists, labor unions. Negro short-story writers drank Louise's liquor, and a lot of Jews, and big solemn men with scarred faces and knotted hands who talked slowly but clearly about picket lines and battles with guns and leadpipe at mine-shaft-heads and in front of factory gates. And Louise moved among them all, confidently, knowing what they were talking about, with opinions that they listened to and argued about just as though she were a man. She knew everybody, condescended to no one, devoured books that Darling had never heard of, walked along the streets of the city, excited, at home, soaking in all the million tides of New York without fear, with constant wonder.

Her friends liked Darling and sometimes he found a man who wanted to get off in the corner and talk about the new boy who played fullback for Princeton, and the decline of the double wing-back, or even the state of the stock market, but for the most part he sat on the edge of things, solid and quiet in the high storm of words. "The dialectics of the situation . . . The theater has been given over to expert jugglers . . . Picasso? What man has a right to paint old bones and collect ten thousand dollars for them? . . . I stand firmly behind Trotsky . . . Poe was the last American critic. When he died they put lilies on the grave of American criticism. I don't say this because they panned my last book, but . . . "

Once in a while he caught Louise looking soberly and consideringly at him through the cigarette smoke and the noise and he avoided her eyes and found an excuse to get up and go into the kitchen for more ice or to open another bottle.

"Come on," Cathal Flaherty was saying, standing at the door with a girl, "you've got to come down and see this. It's down on Fourteenth Street, in the old Civic Repertory, and you can only see it on Sunday nights and I guarantee you'll come out of the theater singing.'' Flaherty was a big young Irishman with a broken nose who was the lawyer for a long-shoreman's union, and he had been hanging around the house for six months on and off, roaring and shutting everybody else up when he got in an argument. "It's a new play, *Waiting for Lefty*; it's about taxi-drivers.''

"Odets,'' the girl with Flaherty said. "It's by a guy named Odets.''

"I never heard of him,'' Darling said.

"He's a new one,'' the girl said.

"It's like watching a bombardment,'' Flaherty said. "I saw it last Sunday night. You've got to see it.''

"Come on, Baby,'' Louise said to Darling, excitement in her eyes already. "We've been sitting in the Sunday *Times* all day, this'll be a great change.''

"I see enough taxi-drivers every day,'' Darling said, not because he meant that, but because he didn't like to be around Flaherty, who said things that made Louise laugh a lot and whose judgment she accepted on almost every subject. "Let's go to the movies.''

"You've never seen anything like this before,'' Flaherty said. "He wrote this play with a baseball bat.''

"Come on,'' Louise coaxed, "I bet it's wonderful.''

"He has long hair,'' the girl with Flaherty said. "Odets. I met him at a party. He's an actor. He didn't say a goddam thing all night.''

"I don't feel like going down to Fourteenth Street,'' Darling said, wishing Flaherty and his girl would get out. "It's gloomy.''

"Oh, hell!'' Louise said loudly. She looked coolly at Darling, as though she'd just been introduced to him and was making up her mind about him, and not very favorably. He saw her looking at him, knowing there was something new and dangerous in her face and he wanted to say something, but Flaherty was there and his damned girl, and anyway, he didn't know what to say.

"I'm going,'' Louise said, getting her coat. "I don't think Four-teenth Street is gloomy.''

"I'm telling you,'' Flaherty was saying, helping her on with her coat, "it's the Battle of Gettysburg, in Brooklynese.''

"Nobody could get a word out of him,'' Flaherty's girl was saying as they went through the door. "He just sat there all night.''

The door closed. Louise hadn't said good night to him. Darling walked around the room four times, then sprawled out on the sofa, on top of the Sunday *Times*. He lay there for five minutes looking at the ceiling, thinking of Flaherty walking down the street talking in that booming voice, between the girls, holding their arms.

Louise had looked wonderful. She'd washed her hair in the afternoon and it had been very soft and light and clung close to her head as she stood there angrily putting her coat on. Louise was getting prettier every year, partly because she knew by now how pretty she was, and made the most of it.

"Nuts," Darling said, standing up. "Oh, nuts."

He put on his coat and went down to the nearest bar and had five drinks off by himself in a corner before his money ran out.

The years since then had been foggy and downhill. Louise had been nice to him, and in a way, loving and kind, and they'd fought only once, when he said he was going to vote for Landon. ("Oh, Christ," she'd said, "doesn't *anything* happen inside your head? Don't you read the papers? The penniless Republican!") She'd been sorry later and apologized for hurting him, but apologized as she might to a child. He'd tried hard, had gone grimly to the art galleries, the concert halls, the bookshops, trying to gain on the trail of his wife, but it was no use. He was bored, and none of what he saw or heard or dutifully read made much sense to him and finally he gave it up. He had thought, many nights as he ate dinner alone, knowing that Louise would come home late and drop silently into bed without explanation, of getting a divorce, but he knew the loneliness, the hopelessness, of not seeing her again would be too much to take. So he was good, completely devoted, ready at all times to go any place with her, do anything she wanted. He even got a small job, in a broker's office and paid his own way, bought his own liquor.

Then he'd been offered the job of going from college to college as a tailor's representative. "We want a man," Mr. Rosenberg had said, "who as soon as you look at him, you say, 'There's a university man.'" Rosenberg had looked approvingly at Darling's broad shoulders and well-kept waist, at his carefully brushed hair and his honest, wrinkleless face. "Frankly, Mr. Darling, I am willing to make you a proposition. I have inquired about you, you are favorably known on your old campus, I understand you were in the backfield with Alfred Diederich."

Darling nodded. "Whatever happened to him?"

"He is walking around in a cast for seven years now. An iron brace. He played professional football and they broke his neck for him."

Darling smiled. That, at least, had turned out well.

"Our suits are an easy product to sell, Mr. Darling," Rosenberg said. "We have a handsome, custom-made garment. What has Brooks Brothers got that we haven't got? A name. No more."

"I can make fifty-sixty dollars a week," Darling said to Louise that night. "And expenses. I can save some money and then come back to New York and really get started here."

"Yes, Baby," Louise said.

"As it is," Darling said carefully, "I can make it back here once a month, and holidays and the summer. We can see each other often."

"Yes, Baby." He looked at her face, lovelier now at thirty-five than it had ever been before, but fogged over now as it had been for five years with a kind of patient, kindly, remote boredom.

"What do you say?" he asked. "Should I take it?" Deep within him he hoped fiercely, longingly, for her to say, "No, Baby, you stay right here," but she said, as he knew she'd say, "I think you'd better take it."

He nodded. He had to get up and stand with his back to her, looking out the window, because there were things plain on his face that she had never seen in the fifteen years she'd known him. "Fifty dollars is a lot of money," he said. "I never thought I'd ever see fifty dollars again." He laughed. Louise laughed, too.

Christian Darling sat on the frail green grass of the practice field. The shadow of the stadium had reached out and covered him. In the distance the lights of the university shone a little mistily in the light haze of evening. Fifteen years. Flaherty even now was calling for his wife, buying her a drink, filling whatever bar they were in with that voice of his and that easy laugh. Darling half-closed his eyes, almost saw the boy fifteen years ago reach for the pass, slip the halfback, go skittering lightly down the field, his knees high and fast and graceful, smiling to himself because he knew he was going to get past the safety man. That was the high point, Darling thought, fifteen years ago, on an autumn afternoon, twenty years old and far from death, with the air coming easily into his lungs, and a deep feeling inside him that he could do anything, knock over anybody, outrun whatever had to be outrun. And the shower after and the three glasses of water and the cool night air on his damp head and Louise sitting hatless in the open car with a smile and the first kiss she ever really meant. The high point, an eighty-yard run in the practice, and a girl's kiss and everything after that a decline. Darling laughed. He had practiced the wrong thing, perhaps. He hadn't practiced for 1929 and New York City and a girl who would turn into a woman. Somewhere, he thought, there must have been a point where she moved up to me, was even with me for a moment, when I could have held her hand, if I'd known, held tight, gone with her. Well, he'd never known. Here he was on a playing field that was fifteen years away and his wife was in another city having dinner with another and better man, speaking with him a different, new language, a language nobody had ever taught him.

Darling stood up, smiled a little, because if he didn't smile he knew the tears would come. He looked around him. This was the spot. O'Connor's pass had come sliding out just to here . . . the high point. Darling put up his hands, felt all over again the flat slap of the ball. He shook his hips to throw off the halfback, cut back inside the center, picked his knees high as he ran gracefully over two men jumbled on the ground at the line of scrimmage, ran easily, gaining speed, for ten yards, holding the ball lightly in his two hands, swung away from the halfback diving at him, ran, swinging his hips in the almost girlish manner of a back in a broken field, tore into the safety man, his shoes drumming heavily on the turf, stiff-armed, elbow locked, pivoted, raced lightly and exultantly for the goal line.

It was only after he had sped over the goal line and slowed to a trot that he saw the boy and girl sitting together on the turf, looking at him wonderingly.

He stopped short, dropping his arms. "I . . . " he said, gasping a little, though his condition was fine and the run hadn't winded him. "I—once I played here."

The boy and the girl said nothing. Darling laughed embarrassedly, looked hard at them sitting there, close to each other, shrugged, turned and went toward his hotel, the sweat breaking out on his face and running down into his collar.

THE FISHERMAN

Michael Van Walleghen

For nearly a month he had been having dreams in which he appeared to himself as someone he didn't like, someone he couldn't trust—and waking up he felt hysterical, dull, dishonest and ashamed. But his wife thought that perhaps he had been working too hard and that maybe he ought to go fishing. He didn't particularly want to go fishing—he knew things were more serious than that—but the next morning before five o'clock he was dressed and driving to the river.

He had been awake all night, and now, in his exhaustion, the river appeared a little too familiar, the hard clay path down to the water too predictably slick and dangerous. He was sure he had dreamt about this place. Perhaps he would sink into quicksand and miss his step and be swept away by the current. He can't remember now how it finally goes . . . but the path, certainly, seems something he remembers—also, the glittering cave of trees and the greasy, treacherous look of water bulging over stones.

Now he remembers he must throw a little wooden minnow along the edge of some fallen trees. The minnow is painted silver with terrified yellow eyes and he must throw it out over and over again, watching it return from deep water like something really alive, wounded, frantic and pursued. He has dreamt this dream so often—himself pursued, himself the fisherman —he can hardly breathe. And then, when the fish hits, it's like waking up to a phone call he thought he'd answered already in his sleep.

The startled, headlong heaviness of the thing! But there's no question of ever landing it . . . only the heavy instant pulling him toward the dark before the line breaks—and afterwards, the whole forest humming implacably as a dial tone after someone loved has just hung up. He sits down and can't believe it. He sits down like a man overwhelmed with mortgages, cracked foundations and fallen gutters. And he can't believe the bluejay either, hopping toward him down the muddy bank like a mechanical toy —or that his wife is really seeing someone else.

THE JILTING
OF GRANNY WEATHERALL

Katherine Anne Porter

She flicked her wrist neatly out of Doctor Harry's pudgy careful fingers and pulled the sheet up to her chin. The brat ought to be in knee breeches. Doctoring around the country with spectacles on his nose! "Get along now, take your schoolbooks and go. There's nothing wrong with me."

Doctor Harry spread a warm paw like a cushion on her forehead where the forked green vein danced and made her eyelids twitch. "Now, now, be a good girl, and we'll have you up in no time."

"That's no way to speak to a woman nearly eighty years old just because she's down. I'd have you respect your elders, young man."

"Well, Missy, excuse me." Doctor Harry patted her cheek. "But I've got to warn you, haven't I? You're a marvel, but you must be careful or you're going to be good and sorry."

"Don't tell me what I'm going to be. I'm on my feet now, morally speaking. It's Cornelia. I had to go to bed to get rid of her."

Her bones felt loose, and floated around in her skin, and Doctor Harry floated like a balloon around the foot of the bed. He floated and pulled down his waistcoat and swung his glasses on a cord. "Well, stay where you are, it certainly can't hurt you."

"Get along and doctor your sick," said Granny Weatherall. "Leave a well woman alone. I'll call for you when I want you. . . . Where were you forty years ago when I pulled through milk-leg and double pneumonia? You weren't even born. Don't let Cornelia lead you on," she shouted, because Doctor Harry appeared to float up to the ceiling and out. "I pay my own bills, and I don't throw my money away on nonsense!"

She meant to wave good-by, but it was too much trouble. Her eyes closed of themselves, it was like a dark curtain drawn around the bed. The pillow rose and floated under her, pleasant as a hammock in a light wind. She listened to the leaves rustling outside the window. No, somebody was swishing newspapers: no, Cornelia and Doctor Harry were whispering together. She leaped broad awake, thinking they whispered in her ear.

"She was never like this, *never* like this!" "Well, what can we expect?" "Yes, eighty years old. . . . "

Well, and what if she was? She still had ears. It was like Cornelia to whisper around doors. She always kept things secret in such a public way. She was always being tactful and kind. Cornelia was dutiful; that was the trouble with her. Dutiful and good: "So good and dutiful," said Granny, "that I'd like to spank her." She saw herself spanking Cornelia and making a fine job of it.

"What'd you say, Mother?"

Granny felt her face tying up in hard knots.

"Can't a body think, I'd like to know?"

"I thought you might want something."

"I do. I want a lot of things. First off, go away and don't whisper."

She lay and drowsed, hoping in her sleep that the children would keep out and let her rest a minute. It had been a long day. Not that she was tired. It was always pleasant to snatch a minute now and then. There was always so much to be done, let me see: tomorrow.

Tomorrow was far away and there was nothing to trouble about. Things were finished somehow when the time came; thank God there was always a little margin over for peace: then a person could spread out the plan of life and tuck in the edges orderly. It was good to have everything clean and folded away, with the hair brushes and tonic bottles sitting straight on the white embroidered linen: the day started without fuss and the pantry shelves laid out with rows of jelly glasses and brown jugs and white stone-china jars with blue whirligigs and words painted on them: coffee, tea, sugar, ginger, cinnamon, allspice: and the bronze clock with the lion on top nicely dusted off. The dust that lion could collect in twenty-four hours! The box in the attic with all those letters tied up, well, she'd have to go through that tomorrow. All those letters—George's letters and

John's letters and her letters to them both—lying around for the children to find afterwards made her uneasy. Yes, that would be tomorrow's business. No use to let them know how silly she had been once.

While she was rummaging around she found death in her mind and it felt clammy and unfamiliar. She had spent so much time preparing for death there was no need for bringing it up again. Let it take care of itself now. When she was sixty she had felt very old, finished, and went around making farewell trips to see her children and grandchildren, with a secret in her mind: This is the very last of your mother, children! Then she made her will and came down with a long fever. That was all just a notion like a lot of other things, but it was lucky too, for she had once for all got over the idea of dying for a long time. Now she couldn't be worried. She hoped she had better sense now. Her father had lived to be one hundred and two years old and had drunk a noggin of strong hot toddy on his last birthday. He told the reporters it was his daily habit, and he owed his long life to that. He had made quite a scandal and was very pleased about it. She believed she'd just plague Cornelia a little.

"Cornelia! Cornelia!" No footsteps, but a sudden hand on her cheek. "Bless you, where have you been?"

"Here, mother."

"Well, Cornelia, I want a noggin of hot toddy."

"Are you cold, darling?"

"I'm chilly, Cornelia. Lying in bed stops the circulation. I must have told you that a thousand times."

Well, she could just hear Cornelia telling her husband that Mother was getting a little childish and they'd have to humor her. The thing that most annoyed her was that Cornelia thought she was deaf, dumb, and blind. Little hasty glances and tiny gestures tossed around her and over her head saying, "Don't cross her, let her have her way, she's eighty years old," and she sitting there as if she lived in a thin glass cage. Sometimes Granny almost made up her mind to pack up and move back to her own house where nobody could remind her every minute that she was old. Wait, wait, Cornelia, till your own children whisper behind your back!

In her day she had kept a better house and had got more work done. She wasn't too old yet for Lydia to be driving eighty miles for advice when one of the children jumped the track, and Jimmy still dropped in and talked things over: "Now, Mammy, you've a good business head, I want to know what you think of this? . . . " Old. Cornelia couldn't change the furniture around without asking. Little things, little things! They had been so sweet when they were little. Granny wished the old days were back again with the children young and everything to be done over. It had been a hard pull, but not too much for her. When she thought of all the food she had cooked, and all the clothes she had cut and sewed, and all the gardens she had made—well, the children showed it. There they were, made out of her, and they couldn't get away from that. Sometimes she wanted to see John again and point to them and say, Well, I didn't do so badly, did I? But that would have to wait. That was for tomorrow. She used to think of him as a man, but now all the children were older than their father, and he would be a child beside her if she saw him now. It seemed strange and there was something wrong in the idea. Why, he couldn't possibly recognize her. She had fenced in a hundred acres once, digging the post holes herself and clamping the wires with just a negro boy to help. That changed a woman. John would be looking for a young woman with the peaked Spanish comb in her hair and the painted fan. Digging post holes changed a woman. Riding country roads in the winter when women had their babies was another thing: sitting up nights with sick horses and sick negroes and sick children and hardly ever losing one. John, I hardly ever lost one of them! John would see that in a minute, that would be something he could understand, she wouldn't have to explain anything!

It made her feel like rolling up her sleeves and putting the whole place to rights again. No matter if Cornelia was determined to be everywhere at once, there were a great many things left undone on this place. She would start tomorrow and do them. It was good to be strong enough for everything, even if all you made melted and changed and slipped under your hands, so that by the time you finished you almost forgot what you were working for. What was it I set out to do? she asked herself intently, but she could not remember. A fog rose over the valley, she saw it marching across the creek swallowing the trees and moving up the hill like an army of ghosts. Soon it would be at the near edge of the orchard, and then it was time to go in and light the lamps. Come in, children, don't stay out in the night air.

Lighting the lamps had been beautiful. The children huddled up to her and breathed like little calves waiting at the bars in the twilight. Their eyes followed the match and watched the flame rise and settle in a blue curve, then they moved away from her. The lamp was lit, they didn't have to be scared and hang on to mother any more. Never, never, never more. God, for all my life I thank Thee. Without Thee, my God, I could never have done it. Hail, Mary, full of grace.

I want you to pick all the fruit this year and see that nothing is wasted.

There's always someone who can use it. Don't let good things rot for want of using. You waste life when you waste good food. Don't let things get lost. It's bitter to lose things. Now, don't let me get to thinking, not when I am tired and taking a little nap before supper. . . .

The pillow rose about her shoulders and pressed against her heart and the memory was being squeezed out of it: oh, push down the pillow, somebody: it would smother her if she tried to hold it. Such a fresh breeze blowing and such a green day with no threats in it. But he had not come, just the same. What does a woman do when she has put on the white veil and set out the white cake for a man and he doesn't come? She tried to remember. No, I swear he never harmed me but in that. He never harmed me but in that . . . and what if he did? There was the day, the day, but a whirl of dark smoke rose and covered it, crept up and over into the bright field where everything was planted so carefully in orderly rows. That was hell, she knew hell when she saw it. For sixty years she had prayed against remembering him and against losing her soul in the deep pit of hell, and now the two things were mingled in one and the thought of him was a smoky cloud from hell that moved and crept in her head when she had just got rid of Doctor Harry and was trying to rest a minute. Wounded vanity, Ellen, said a sharp voice in the top of her mind. Don't let your wounded vanity get the upper hand of you. Plenty of girls get jilted. You were jilted, weren't you? Then stand up to it. Her eyelids wavered and let in streamers of blue-gray light like tissue paper over her eyes. She must get up and pull the shades down or she'd never sleep. She was in bed again and the shades were not down. How could that happen? Better turn over, hide from the light, sleeping in the light gave you nightmares. "Mother, how do you feel now?" and a stinging wetness on her forehead. But I don't like having my face washed in cold water!

Hapsy? George? Lydia? Jimmy? No, Cornelia, and her features were swollen and full of little puddles. "They're coming, darling, they'll all be here soon." Go wash your face, child, you look funny.

Instead of obeying, Cornelia knelt down and put her head on the pillow. She seemed to be talking but there was no sound. "Well, are you tongue-tied? Whose birthday is it? Are you going to give a party?"

Cornelia's mouth moved urgently in strange shapes. "Don't do that, you bother me, daughter."

"Oh, no, Mother. Oh, no. . . . "

Nonsense. It was strange about children. They disputed your every word. "No what, Cornelia?"

"Here's Doctor Harry."

"I won't see that boy again. He just left five minutes ago."

"That was this morning, Mother. It's night now. Here's the nurse."

"This is Doctor Harry, Mrs. Weatherall. I never saw you look so young and happy!"

"Ah, I'll never be young again—but I'd be happy if they'd let me lie in peace and get rested."

She thought she spoke up loudly, but no one answered. A warm weight on her forehead, a warm bracelet on her wrist, and a breeze went on whispering, trying to tell her something. A shuffle of leaves in the everlasting hand of God, He blew on them and they danced and rattled. "Mother, don't mind, we're going to give you a little hypodermic." "Look here, daughter, how do ants get in this bed? I saw sugar ants yesterday." Did you send for Hapsy too?

It was Hapsy she really wanted. She had to go a long way back through a great many rooms to find Hapsy standing with a baby on her arm. She seemed to herself to be Hapsy also, and the baby on Hapsy's arm was Hapsy and himself and herself, all at once, and there was no surprise in the meeting. Then Hapsy melted from within and turned flimsy as gray gauze and the baby was a gauzy shadow, and Hapsy came up close and said, "I thought you'd never come," and looked at her very searchingly and said, "You haven't changed a bit!" They leaned forward to kiss, when Cornelia began whispering from a long way off, "Oh, is there anything you want to tell me? Is there anything I can do for you?"

Yes, she had changed her mind after sixty years and she would like to see George. I want you to find George. Find him and be sure to tell him I forgot him. I want him to know I had my husband just the same and my children and my house like any other woman. A good house too and a good husband that I loved and fine children out of him. Better than I hoped for even. Tell him I was given back everything he took away and more. Oh, no, oh, God, no, there was something else besides the house and the man and the children. Oh, surely they were not all? What was it? Something not given back. . . . Her breath crowded down under her ribs and grew into a monstrous frightening shape with cutting edges; it bored up into her head, and the agony was unbelievable: Yes, John, get the Doctor now, no more talk, my time has come.

When this one was born it should be the last. The last. It should have been born first, for it was the one she had truly wanted. Everything came in good time. Nothing left out, left over. She was strong, in three days she would be as well as ever. Better. A woman needed milk in her to have her full health.

"Mother, do you hear me?"

"I've been telling you—"

"Mother, Father Connolly's here."

"I went to Holy Communion only last week. Tell him I'm not so sinful as all that."

"Father just wants to speak to you."

He could speak as much as he pleased. It was like him to drop in and inquire about her soul as if it were a teething baby, and then stay on for a cup of tea and a round of cards and gossip. He always had a funny story of some sort, usually about an Irishman who made his little mistakes and confessed them, and the point lay in some absurd thing he would blurt out in the confessional showing his struggles between native piety and original sin. Granny felt easy about her soul. Cornelia, where are your manners? Give Father Connolly a chair. She had her secret comfortable understanding with a few favorite saints who cleared a straight road to God for her. All as surely signed and sealed as the papers for the new Forty Acres. Forever . . . heirs and assigns forever. Since the day the wedding cake was not cut, but thrown out and wasted. The whole bottom dropped out of the world, and there she was blind and sweating with nothing under her feet and the walls falling away. His hand had caught her under the breast, she had not fallen, there was the freshly polished floor with the green rug on it, just as before. He had cursed like a sailor's parrot and said, "I'll kill him for you." Don't lay a hand on him, for my sake leave something to God. "Now, Ellen, you must believe what I tell you. . . . "

So there was nothing, nothing to worry about any more, except sometimes in the night one of the children screamed in a nightmare, and they both hustled out shaking and hunting for the matches and calling, "There, wait a minute, here we are!" John, get the doctor now, Hapsy's time has come. But there was Hapsy standing by the bed in a white cap. "Cornelia, tell Hapsy to take off her cap. I can't see her plain."

Her eyes opened very wide and the room stood out like a picture she had seen somewhere. Dark colors with the shadows rising towards the ceiling in long angles. The tall black dresser gleamed with nothing on it but John's picture, enlarged from a little one, with John's eyes very black when they should have been blue. You never saw him, so how do you know how he looked? But the man insisted the copy was perfect, it was very rich and handsome. For a picture, yes, but it's not my husband. The table by the bed had a linen cover and a candle and a crucifix. The light was blue from Cornelia's silk lampshades. No sort of light at all, just frippery. You had to live forty years with kerosene lamps to appreciate honest electricity. She felt very strong and she saw Doctor Harry with a rosy nimbus around him.

"You look like a saint, Doctor Harry, and I vow that's as near as you'll ever come to it."

"She's saying something."

"I heard you, Cornelia. What's all this carrying-on?"

"Father Connolly's saying—"

Cornelia's voice staggered and bumped like a cart in a bad road. It rounded corners and turned back again and arrived nowhere. Granny stepped up in the cart very lightly and reached for the reins, but a man sat beside her and she knew him by his hands, driving the cart. She did not look in his face, for she knew without seeing, but looked instead down the road where the trees leaned over and bowed to each other and a thousand birds were singing a Mass. She felt like singing too, but she put her hand in the bosom of her dress and pulled out a rosary, and Father Connolly murmured Latin in a very solemn voice and tickled her feet. My God, will you stop that nonsense? I'm a married woman. What if he did run away and leave me to face the priest by myself? I found another a whole world better. I wouldn't have exchanged my husband for anybody except St. Michael himself, and you may tell him that for me with a thank you in the bargain.

Light flashed on her closed eyelids, and a deep roaring shook her. Cornelia, is that lightning? I hear thunder. There's going to be a storm. Close all the windows. Call the children in. . . . "Mother, here we are, all of us." "Is that you, Hapsy?" "Oh, no, I'm Lydia. We drove as fast as we could." Their faces drifted above her, drifted away. The rosary fell out of her hands and Lydia put it back. Jimmy tried to help, their hands fumbled together, and Granny closed two fingers around Jimmy's thumb. Beads wouldn't do, it must be something alive. She was so amazed her thoughts ran round and round. So, my dear Lord, this is my death and I wasn't even thinking about it. My children have come to see me die. But I can't, it's not time. Oh, I always hated surprises. I wanted to give Cornelia the amethyst set—Cornelia, you're to have the amethyst set, but Hapsy's to wear it when she wants, and, Doctor Harry, do shut up. Nobody sent for you. Oh, my dear Lord, do wait a minute. I meant to do something about the Forty Acres, Jimmy doesn't need it and Lydia will later on, with that worthless husband of hers. I meant to finish the altar cloth and send six bottles of wine to Sister Borgia for her dyspepsia. I want to send six bottles of wine to Sister Borgia, Father Connolly, now don't let me forget.

Cornelia's voice made short turns and tilted over and crashed. "Oh, Mother, oh, Mother, oh, Mother. . . . ''

"I'm not going, Cornelia. I'm taken by surprise. I can't go.''

You'll see Hapsy again. What about her? "I thought you'd never come.'' Granny made a long journey outward, looking for Hapsy. What if I don't find her? What then? Her heart sank down and down, there was no bottom to death, she couldn't come to the end of it. The blue light from Cornelia's lampshade drew into a tiny point in the center of her brain, it flickered and winked like an eye, quietly it fluttered and dwindled. Granny lay curled down within herself, amazed and watchful, staring at the point of light that was herself; her body was now only a deeper mass of shadow in an endless darkness and this darkness would curl around the light and swallow it up. God, give a sign!

For the second time there was no sign. Again no bridegroom and the priest in the house. She could not remember any other sorrow because this grief wiped them all away. Oh, no, there's nothing more cruel than this— I'll never forgive it. She stretched herself with a deep breath and blew out the light.

ILYÁS

Leo Tolstoy

In the Government of Ufá there lived a Bashkir, Ilyás. His father had left him no wealth. His father had died a year after he had got his son married. At that time Ilyás had seven mares, two cows, and a score of sheep; but Ilyás was a good master and began to increase his possessions; he worked with his wife from morning until night, got up earlier than anybody, and went to bed later, and grew richer from year to year. Thus Ilyás passed thirty-five years at work, and came to have a vast fortune.

Ilyás finally had two hundred head of horses, 150 head of cattle, and twelve hundred sheep. Men herded Ilyás's herds and flocks, and women milked the mares and cows, and made kumys, butter, and cheese. Ilyás had plenty of everything, and in the district everybody envied him his life. People said:

"Ilyás is a lucky fellow. He has plenty of everything,—he does not need to die."

Good people made Ilyás's friendship and became his friends. And guests came to him from a distance. He received them all, and fed them, and gave them to drink. No matter who came, he received kumys, and tea, and sherbet, and mutton. If guests came to see him, a sheep or two were killed, and if many guests arrived, he had them kill a mare.

Ilyás had two sons and a daughter. He had got all of them married. When Ilyás had been poor, his sons had worked with him and had herded the horses and the cattle and the sheep; but when they grew rich, the sons

Reprinted from *The Complete Works of Count Tolstoy,* copyright 1904 by Dana Estes & Co. Translated by Nathan Haskell Dole.

became spoiled, and one of them even began to drink. One of them, the eldest, was killed in a fight, and the other, the younger, had a proud wife, and did not obey his father, and his father had to give him a separate maintenance.

Ilyás gave him a house and cattle, and his own wealth was diminished. Soon after a plague fell on Ilyás's sheep, and many of them died. Then there was a famine year, the hay crop was a failure, and in the winter many head of cattle died. Then the Kirgizes drove off the best herd of horses. And thus Ilyás's estate grew less, and he fell lower and lower, and his strength began to wane.

When he was seventy years old, he began to sell off his furs, rugs, saddles, and tents, and soon had to sell his last head of cattle, so that he was left without anything. Before he knew it, all was gone, and in his old age he had to go with his wife to live among strangers. All that Ilyás had left of his fortune was what garments he had on his body, a fur coat, a cap, and his morocco slippers and shoes, and his wife, Sham-shemagi, who was now an old woman. The son to whom he had given the property had left for a distant country, and his daughter had died. And so there was nobody to help the old people.

Their neighbour, Muhamedshah, took pity on them. Muhamedshah was neither rich nor poor, and he lived an even life, and was a good man. He remembered Ilyás's hospitality, and so pitied him, and said to Ilyás:

"Come to live with me, Ilyás, and bring your wife with you! In the summer work according to your strength in my truck-garden, and in the winter feed the cattle, and let Sham-shemagi milk the mares and make kumys. I will feed and clothe you and will let you have whatever you may need."

Ilyás thanked his neighbour, and went to live with his wife as Muhamedshah's labourers. At first it was hard for them, but soon they got used to the work, and the old people worked according to their strength.

It was profitable for the master to keep these people, for they had been masters themselves and knew all the order and were not lazy, but worked according to their strength; but it pained Muhamedshah to see the well-to-do people brought down so low.

One day distant guests, match-makers, happened to call on Muhamedshah; and the mulla, too, came. Muhamedshah ordered his men to catch a sheep and kill it. Ilyás flayed the sheep and cooked it and sent it in to the guests. They ate the mutton, drank tea, and then started to drink kumys. The guests and the master were sitting on down cushions on the rugs, drinking kumys out of bowls, and talking; but Ilyás got through with his work and walked past the door. When Muhamedshah saw him, he said to a guest:

"Did you see the old man who just went past the door?"

"I did," said the guest; "but what is there remarkable about him?"

"What is remarkable is that he used to be our richest man. Ilyás is his name; maybe you have heard of him?"

"Of course I have," said the guest. "I have never seen him, but his fame has gone far abroad."

"Now he has nothing left, and he lives with me as a labourer, and his wife is with him,—she milks the cows."

The guest was surprised. He clicked with his tongue, shook his head, and said:

"Evidently fortune flies around like a wheel: one it lifts up, another it takes down. Well, does the old man pine?"

"Who knows? He lives quietly and peaceably, and works well."

Then the guest said:

"May I speak with him? I should like to ask him about his life."

"Of course you may," said the master, and he called out of the tent: "Babay!" (This means "grandfather" in the Bashkia language.) "Come in and drink some kumys, and bring your wife with you!"

Ilyás came in with his wife. He exchanged greetings with the guests and with the master, said a prayer, and knelt down at the door; but his wife went back of a curtain and sat down with the mistress.

A bowl of kumys was handed to Ilyás. Ilyás saluted the guests and the master, made a bow, drank a little, and put down the bowl.

"Grandfather," the guest said to him, "I suppose it makes you feel bad to look at us and think of your former life, considering what fortune you had and how hard your life is now."

But Ilyás smiled and said:

"If I should tell you about my happiness and unhappiness, you would not believe me,—you had better ask my wife. She is a woman, and what is in her heart is on her tongue: she will tell you all the truth about this matter."

And the guest spoke to her beind the curtain:

"Well, granny, tell us how you judge about your former happiness and present sorrow."

And Sham-shemagi spoke from behind the curtain:

"I judge like this: My husband and I lived for fifty years trying to find happiness, and we did not find it; but now it is the second year that we have nothing left and that we live as labourers, and we have found that happiness and need no other.''

The guests were surprised and the master marvelled, and he even got up to throw aside the curtain and to look at the old woman. But the old woman was standing with folded hands, smiling and looking at her husband, and the old man was smiling, too. The old woman said once more:

''I am telling you the truth, without any jest: for half a century we tried to find happiness, and so long as we were rich, we did not find it; now nothing is left, and we are working out,—and we have come to have such happiness that we wish for no other.''

''Wherein does your happiness lie?''

''In this: when we were rich, my husband and I did not have an hour's rest: we had no time to talk together, to think of our souls, or to pray. We had so many cares! Now guests called on us,—and there were the cares about what to treat them to and what presents to make so that they should not misjudge us. When the guests left, we had to look after the labourers: they thought only of resting and having something good to eat, but we cared only about having our property attended to,—and so sinned. Now we were afraid that a wolf would kill a colt or a calf, and now that thieves might drive off a herd. When we lay down to sleep, we could not fall asleep, fearing lest the sheep might crush the lambs. We would get up in the night and walk around; no sooner would we be quieted than we would have a new care,—how to get fodder for the winter. And, worse than that, there was not much agreement between my husband and me. He would say that this had to be done so and so, and I would say differently, and so we began to quarrel, and sin. Thus we lived from one care to another, from one sin to another, and saw no happy life.''

''Well, and now?''

''Now my husband and I get up, speak together peaceably, in agreement, for we have nothing to quarrel about, nothing to worry about,—all the care we have is to serve our master. We work according to our strength, and we work willingly so that our master shall have no loss, but profit. When we come back, dinner is ready, and supper, and kumys. If it is cold, there are dung chips to make a fire with and a fur coat to warm ourselves. For fifty years we looked for happiness, but only now have we found it.''

The guests laughed.

And Ilyás said:

''Do not laugh, brothers! This is not a joke, but a matter of human life. My wife and I were foolish and wept because we had lost our fortune, but now God has revealed the truth to us, and we reveal this to you, not for our amusement but for your good.''

And the mulla said:

''That was a wise speech, and Ilyás has told the precise truth,—it says so, too, in Holy Writ.''

And the guests stopped laughing and fell to musing.

From KING LEAR

William Shakespeare

ACT III, Scene IV.

The heath, near a hovel. Enter Lear, Kent, and Fool

KENT.   Here is the place, my lord; good my lord, enter;
   The tyranny of the open night's too rough
   For nature to endure.   [*Storm still*]
LEAR.   Let me alone.
KENT.   Good my lord, enter here.
LEAR.   Wilt break my heart?
KENT.   I had rather break mine own. Good my lord, enter.
LEAR.   Thou think'st 't is much that this contentious storm
   Invades us to the skin: so 't is to thee;
   But where the greater malady is fix'd,
   The lesser is scarce felt. Thou'dst shun a bear;
   But if thy flight lay toward the roaring sea,
   Thou'dst meet the bear i' th' mouth. When the mind's free,
   The body's delicate; the tempest in my mind
   Doth from my senses take all feeling else
   Save what beats there. Filial ingratitude!
   Is it not as this mouth should tear this hand
   For lifting food to 't? But I will punish home.

Reprinted from *The New Hudson Shakespeare*. © 1911 by Ginn and Company. Boston, Mass.: Athenaeum Press.

No, I will weep no more. In such a night
To shut me out! Pour on; I will endure.
In such a night as this! O Regan, Goneril!
Your old kind father, whose frank heart gave all,—
O, that way madness lies; let me shun that;
No more of that.

KENT.   Good my lord, enter here.

LEAR.   Prithee, go in thyself; seek thine own ease.
This tempest will not give me leave to ponder
On things would hurt me more. But I'll go in.
In, boy; go first. You houseless poverty,—
Nay, get thee in. I'll pray, and then I'll sleep.   [*Fool goes in*]
Poor naked wretches, wheresoe'er you are,
That bide the pelting of this pitiless storm,
How shall your houseless heads and unfed sides,
Your loop'd and window'd raggedness, defend you
From seasons such as these? O, I have ta'en
Too little care of this! Take physic, pomp;
Expose thyself to feel what wretches feel,
That thou mayst shake the superflux to them,
And show the heavens more just.

EDGAR. [*Within*] Fathom and half, fathom and half!
Poor Tom!   [*The Fool runs out from the hovel*]

FOOL.   Come not in here, nuncle, here's a spirit. Help me, help me!

KENT.   Give me thy hand. Who's there?

FOOL.   A spirit, a spirit! he says his name's poor Tom.

KENT.   What art thou that dost grumble there i' th' straw? Come forth.

Enter Edgar, disguised as a madman

EDGAR. Away! the foul fiend follows me!

Through the sharp hawthorn blows the cold wind.

Hum! go to thy cold bed, and warm thee.

LEAR.   Didst thou give all to thy daughters? And art thou come to this?

EDGAR. Who gives any thing to poor Tom? whom the foul fiend hath led
through fire and through flame, through ford and whirlpool, over bog
and quagmire; that hath laid knives under his pillow, and halters in his
pew; set ratsbane by his porridge; made him proud of heart, to ride on a

bay trotting-horse over four-inch'd bridges, to course his own shadow for a traitor. Bless thy five wits! Tom's a-cold. O, do de, do de, do de. Bless thee from whirlwinds, starblasting, and taking! Do poor Tom some charity, whom the foul fiend vexes. There could I have him now, and there, and there again, and there.   [*Storm still*]

LEAR.   Has his daughters brought him to this pass?
Couldst thou save nothing? Wouldst thou give 'em all?

FOOL.   Nay, he reserv'd a blanket, else we had been all sham'd.

LEAR.   Now, all the plagues that in the pendulous air
Hang fated o'er men's faults light on thy daughters!

KENT.   He hath no daughters, sir.

LEAR.   Death, traitor! nothing could have subdu'd nature
To such a lowness but his unkind daughters.
Is it the fashion that discarded fathers
Should have thus little mercy on their flesh?
Judicious punishment! 't was this flesh begot
Those pelican daughters.

EDGAR.

Pillicock sat on Pillicock-hill.

Halloo, halloo, loo, loo!

FOOL.   This cold night will turn us all to fools and madmen.

EDGAR.   Take heed o' th' foul fiend: obey thy parents; keep thy word justly; swear not; set not thy sweet heart on proud array. Tom 's a-cold.

LEAR.   What hast thou been?

EDGAR.   A serving-man, proud in heart and mind; that curl'd my hair, wore gloves in my cap, swore as many oaths as I spake words, and broke them in the sweet face of heaven. Wine lov'd I deeply, dice dearly, and in woman out-paramour'd the Turk; false of heart, light of ear, bloody of hand; hog in sloth, fox in stealth, wolf in greediness, dog in madness, lion in prey. Let not the creaking of shoes nor the rustling of silks betray thy poor heart to woman. Keep thy pen from lender's books, and defy the foul fiend.

Still through the hawthorn blows the cold wind.

Says suum, mun, ha, no, nonny. Dolphin my boy, boy, sessa! let him trot by.   [*Storm still*]

LEAR.   Why, thou wert better in thy grave than to answer with thy uncover'd body this extremity of the skies. Is man no more than this? Consider him well. Thou ow'st the worm no silk, the beast no hide, the sheep no wool, the cat no perfume. Ha! here's three on's are sophisticated! Thou are the thing itself; unaccommodated man is no more but such a poor, bare, fork'd animal as thou are. Off, off, you lendings! come, unbutton here.   [*Tearing off his clothes*]

FOOL.   Prithee, nuncle, be contented; 't is a naughty night to swim in. Now a little fire in a wide field were like an old lecher's heart, a small spark, all the rest on's body cold. Look, here comes a walking fire.

ACT IV, Scene VII.

A tent in the French camp. Enter Cordelia, Kent, and Doctor

CORDELIA.   O thou good Kent, how shall I live and work,
To match thy goodness? My life will be too short,
And every measure fail me.

KENT.   To be acknowledg'd, madam, is o'erpaid.
All my reports go with the modest truth;
Nor more nor clipp'd, but so.

CORDELIA.   Be better suited;
These weeds are memories of those worser hours;
I prithee, put them off.

KENT.   Pardon, dear madam;
Yet to be known shortens my made intent.
My boon I make it, that you know me not
Till time and I think meet.

CORDELIA.   Then be 't so, my good lord.   [*To the Doctor*]
How does the king?

DOCTOR.   Madam, sleeps still.

CORDELIA.   O you kind gods,
Cure this great breach in his abused nature!
Th' untun'd and jarring senses, O, wind up
Of this child-changed father!

DOCTOR.   So please your majesty
That we may wake the king? he hath slept long.

CORDELIA. Be govern'd by your knowledge, and proceed
  I' th' sway of your own will. Is he array'd?

Enter Lear in a chair carried by Servants. Gentleman in attendance

GENTLEMAN. Ay, madam; in the heaviness of sleep
  We put fresh garments on him.
DOCTOR. Be by, good madam, when we do awake him;
  I doubt not of his temperance.
CORDELIA.   Very well.
DOCTOR. Please you, draw near. Louder the music there.
CORDELIA. O my dear father, restoration hang
  Thy medicine on my lips; and let this kiss
  Repair those violent harms that my two sisters
  Have in thy reverence made!
KENT.   Kind and dear princess!
CORDELIA. Had you not been their father, these white flakes
  Had challeng'd pity of them. Was this a face
  To be oppos'd against the warring winds?
  To stand against the deep dread-bolted thunder?
  In the most terrible and nimble stroke
  Of quick, cross lightning? to watch—poor perdu!—
  With this thin helm? Mine enemy's dog,
  Though he had bit me, should have stood that night
  Against my fire; and wast thou fain, poor father,
  To hovel thee with swine and rogues forlorn,
  In short and musty straw? Alack, alack!
  'T is wonder that thy life and wits at once
  Had not concluded all. He wakes; speak to him.
DOCTOR. Madam, do you; 't is fittest.
CORDELIA. How does my royal lord? how fares your majesty?
LEAR. You do me wrong to take me out o' th' grave.
  Thou are a soul in bliss; but I am bound
  Upon a wheel of fire, that mine own tears
  Do scald like molten lead.
CORDELIA.   Sir, do you know me?
LEAR. You are a spirit, I know; when did you die?
CORDELIA. Still, still, far wide!
DOCTOR. He's scarce awake; let him alone a while.
LEAR. Where have I been? where am I? Fair daylight?

I am mightily abus'd. I should e'en die with pity,
To see another thus. I know not what to say.
I will not swear these are my hands: let's see;
I feel this pin prick. Would I were assur'd
Of my condition!

CORDELIA.   O, look upon me, sir,
And hold your hands in benediction o'er me.
No, sir, you must not kneel.

LEAR.   Pray, do not mock me.
I am a very foolish fond old man,
Fourscore and upward, not an hour more nor less;
And, to deal plainly,
I fear I am not in my perfect mind.
Methinks I should know you, and know this man;
Yet I am doubtful: for I am mainly ignorant
What place this is; and all the skill I have
Remembers not these garments; nor I know not
Where I did lodge last night. Do not laugh at me;
For, as I am a man, I think this lady
To be my child Cordelia.

CORDELIA.   And so I am, I am.

LEAR.   Be your tears wet? yes, faith. I pray, weep not.
If you have poison for me, I will drink it.
I know you do not love me; for your sisters
Have, as I do remember, done me wrong;
You have some cause, they have not.

CORDELIA.   No cause, no cause.

LEAR.   Am I in France?

KENT.   In your own kingdom, sir.

LEAR.   Do not abuse me.

DOCTOR.   Be comforted, good madam: the great rage,
You see, is kill'd in him; and yet 't is danger
To make him even o'er the time he has lost.
Desire him to go in; trouble him no more
Till further settling.

CORDELIA.   Will 't please your highness walk?

LEAR.   You must bear with me.
Pray you now, forget and forgive; I am old and foolish.

[*Exeunt all but Kent and Gentleman*]

4

THE WORLD OF WORK

The work we do as adults organizes our lives and determines our socio-economic standard of living. Work is what adolescents spend years preparing for and what allows men and women to be contributing members of society. In addition, work significantly shapes each person's self-concept. One's work may even be *the* primary factor in answering the question, Who am I?

Most men and more than half of all women in our society are either working or looking for work. Work means different things to different people. For some it is merely a means of making a living and financing leisure hours. For others, work is a source of self-esteem, power, or prestige. Still others use work to be of service to people, for companionship, or as an outlet for creative self-expression.

A developmental perspective on the world of work involves delineating the changes that occur in work patterns as workers get older. From private studies and government statistics, the following age-related generalizations about the work force can be made:

- Job mobility declines with age, while unemployment increases after late middle age.
- Job satisfaction increases with age.
- Work-related accidents decline with age.
- Illness-related absences from work decline with age, while length of absences of older workers due to illness increases.

• Peak performances or outstanding achievements tend to occur in younger adulthood, although there is some variability depending upon the field
(Knox, 1977; Troll, 1975).

Changes with age in an individual's work pattern are largely determined by the nature of the employment. Many writers make a distinction
between having a job and having a career. To the extent that a job is related to earlier formal preparation and to past and future employment, it can
be considered part of a career. "Career" usually implies that one has had
special training and that all work experiences are interrelated. Movement
from one job to another is usually horizontal, that is, no new skills or formal education (other than on-the-job training) are needed, while movement
in a career is vertical, each step "up" requiring the accumulation and use
of new knowledge or skills. Typically, occupations requiring professional
training, such as law, medicine, teaching, engineering, or social work, follow career patterns, whereas occupations involving little formal training,
such as clerical work, manual labor, and semiskilled employment, reflect
"job" characteristics (Knox, 1977).

Whether one has a job or a career, most adults follow a relatively predictable pattern of work experience. In adolescence one becomes aware
of the options available and the preparation needed for various occupations. Young adulthood is traditionally a time of extended training or settling into a particular job or career. In the first years on the job one explores
the possibilities within the chosen setting or finds that the work is unsuit-
able and makes a change. The thirties and early forties are characterized
by a settling into a particular work pattern. Mid-life, however, may bring
with it an assessment of work achievements. Some set new directions, even
undertake mid-career change; others resign themselves to more realistic
goals; still others feel satisfied with their accomplishments. Finally, retirement is the significant work-related event of late life. Again, there are numerous adjustments to this developmental task ranging from refusing to
retire to gracefully withdrawing from the work role.

Of the six literary selections chosen to illustrate work experience, two
are representative of early career, two deal with mid-career assessments,
and two illuminate the concerns of later work life.

EARLY CAREER AND WORK EXPERIENCE

In two stories illustrative of work life in young adulthood, we meet
four adults—two women, in O. Henry's "The Trimmed Lamp," and two
men in Andrew Fetler's "Longface." Each one views work from a slightly

different perspective, while learning to adjust to the demands of being an economically independent adult.

Nancy, in "The Trimmed Lamp," is a salesgirl in a department store. She earns half of what Lou makes as an ironer in a laundry. Work, for Nancy, is an opportunity to learn and grow. For her the department store is an "educational institution" with a "curriculum." Her "teachers" are the customers and the other salesgirls. Lou, on the other hand, views work as merely a means to an end. She lives for the time away from work: "In the steaming laundry there was nothing but work, work and her thoughts of the evening pleasures to come."

In the short story "Longface," we meet two young men whose work lives have followed very different paths. Bradley Walker is an advertising man and is financially well off. The reader senses, however, that Bradley has traded loftier ambitions for economic security. He also appears personally insecure, not quite certain where he fits into the adult world. Mark, an old college friend, refuses to compromise his artistic goals and thus remains an unemployed cellist. Bradley must suppress his creative talent in order to work (ironically he writes for "Kellogg's Complete Creative Service"), while Mark is not able to find work because he refuses to settle for less than his dream. Each protagonist has yet to establish a personally satisfying work situation.

MID-LIFE ASSESSMENT

While young adulthood can be viewed as a period of career establishment, middle age is a time when one senses a plateau has been reached. Work-related accomplishments are reviewed, and goals are reevaluated. Each individual subjectively determines whether he or she is on time or behind time in career development. Many question the extent to which they are responsible for their success or lack of it. Even for those who judge themselves as successful, a mid-life career malaise may diminish feelings of fulfillment. Some become bored with their jobs, some become so preoccupied coping with age-related problems that they are unable to function. Still others may feel trapped, too old to make a career change.

In the selection from Joseph Heller's novel *Something Happened*, Bob Slocum is a very successful businessman. In mid-life, though, he no longer finds satisfaction in his work. Near the top of his company, he asks, "Is this *all* there is for me to do? Is this really the *most* I can get from the few years left in this one life of mine?" He is intensely bored: "I am bored with my work very often now. Everything routine that comes in I pass along to somebody else. This makes my boredom worse." To pass the time, Slocum devises "happiness charts" in which he ranks employees on the basis of such unhappy traits as envy, fear, ambition, frustration. The people who rank highest on these charts are those with little commitment to their jobs and who could leave at any time. He, however, feels trapped, too old to make a change: "I am making no plans to leave. I have the feeling now that there is no place left for me to go."

Unlike Slocum, who is still able to function, Willy Loman in Arthur Miller's *Death of a Salesman* becomes unable to perform his job-related responsibilities. He believes in his worth as a salesman but cannot overcome the inertia brought on by his aging. In act 1, scene 1, Willy returns early, never having made the intended sales call. "I just couldn't make it," he tells his wife. It becomes obvious that Willy can no longer make it at all. His sense of futility — "Work a lifetime to pay off a house . . . and there's nobody to live in it" — and his loss of physical stamina have paralyzed him. For both Slocum and Loman, the mid-life and late mid-life changes in attitudes toward work must be acknowledged and dealt with if either is to move on to the challenges of later life.

LATE-LIFE ADJUSTMENT

Retirement is the culminating event in the work cycle. It can be viewed as one of life's developmental tasks, as a position in the work cycle, or as a process involving adjustments at each step of the way. Atchley (1975) has delineated a seven-step model in the retirement process that provides helpful insights into what adults might go through as they deal with this task. The seven stages are

1. Early preretirement: one becomes aware that retirement will eventually occur, but it is still remote.
2. Near preretirement: a period when employer and worker begin a mutual disengagement. The end of this period is marked by a retirement ceremony.
3. Honeymoon period: retired workers feel freed from daily responsibility and phantasize about what they will do with their time.
4. Disenchantment: a period of letdown, depression.
5. Reorientation: the realization that retirement is not a honeymoon and that assistance might be needed in planning time or financial affairs.
6. Stability: a realistic pattern of everyday living emerges.
7. Termination of retired role: this occurs by death, debilitating illness, or the assumption of a new job or other involvement (pp. 63–71).

The protagonist in the story "Loose Ends," by Anthony E. Stockanes, is in stage 2, "near preretirement," of Atchley's model. He is in late midlife, and the company is transferring him to New Mexico. The transfer is clearly the beginning of his disengagement from the world of work: "The company's announcement was so blandly chilling; he is being transferred —not promoted, transferred. . . . No one advances from New Mexico at his level. He will replace Abramson who is retiring." Adjusting to the change in his work is further compounded by depressing signs of physical aging and by a less than vital relationship with his wife of twenty-seven years.

The final selection in this section, "A Village Singer," by Mary Wilkins Freeman, is about the forced retirement of Candace Whitcomb, church soloist. Her reaction is to fight back by drowning out the new soloist, by using the retirement gift of a photograph album as a footstool, and by being feisty with the minister. She cannot adjust to her retired status. It becomes apparent that her worth as a person has been largely defined by her role as church soloist. Stripped of that role, her life is no longer worth living.

There is, then, a developmental sequence characteristic of most people's work life. The changes that take place as one moves from exploration of work in young adulthood to reassessment in mid-life to retirement in later life offer opportunities for growth but also require adjustments. Some men and women are able to find fulfillment and meaning in their work and to make the necessary changes that age and situation demand. Others use work as a vehicle for finding satisfaction elsewhere. Whatever the case, the centrality of work in an adult's life is equal only to establishing meaningful relationships with others. "Reduced to the simplest level, both work and love are governed by the search for the same goal: more lasting, realistic, and socially responsible pleasure" (Hale, 1980, p. 30).

THE TRIMMED LAMP

O. Henry

Of course there are two sides to the question. Let us look at the other. We often hear "shop-girls" spoken of. No such persons exist. There are girls who work in shops. They make their living that way. But why turn their occupation into an adjective? Let us be fair. We do not refer to the girls who live on Fifth Avenue as "marriage-girls."

Lou and Nancy were chums. They came to the big city to find work because there was not enough to eat at their homes to go around. Nancy was nineteen; Lou was twenty. Both were pretty, active country girls who had no ambition to go on the stage.

The little cherub that sits up aloft guided them to a cheap and respectable boarding-house. Both found positions and became wage-earners. They remained chums. It is at the end of six months that I would beg you to step forward and be introduced to them. Meddlesome Reader: My Lady Friends, Miss Nancy and Miss Lou. While you are shaking hands please take notice—cautiously—of their attire. Yes, cautiously; for they are as quick to resent a stare as a lady in a box at the horse show is.

Lou is a piece-work ironer in a hand laundry. She is clothed in a badly fitting purple dress, and her hat plume is four inches too long; but her ermine muff and scarf cost $25, and its fellow beasts will be ticketed in the windows at $7.98 before the season is over. Her cheeks are pink, and her light blue eyes bright. Contentment radiates from her.

Nancy you would call a shop-girl—because you have the habit. There

Reprinted from *The Trimmed Lamp*, by O. Henry, copyright 1907 by Doubleday & Company, Inc.

is no type; but a perverse generation is always seeking a type; so this is what the type should be. She has the high-ratted pompadour and the exaggerated straight-front. Her skirt is shoddy, but has the correct flare. No furs protect her against the bitter spring air, but she wears her short broadcloth jacket as jauntily as though it were Persian lamb! On her face and in her eyes, remorseless type-seeker, is the typical shop-girl expression. It is a look of silent but contemptuous revolt against cheated womanhood; of sad prophecy of the vengeance to come. When she laughs her loudest the look is still there. The same look can be seen in the eyes of Russian peasants; and those of us left will see it some day on Gabriel's face when he comes to blow us up. It is a look that should wither and abash man; but he has been known to smirk at it and offer flowers—with a string tied to them.

Now lift your hat and come away, while you receive Lou's cheery "See you again," and the sardonic, sweet smile of Nancy that seems, somehow, to miss you and go fluttering like a white moth up over the housetops to the stars.

The two waited on the corner for Dan. Dan was Lou's steady company. Faithful? Well, he was on hand when Mary would have had to hire a dozen subpoena servers to find her lamb.

"Ain't you cold, Nancy?" said Lou. "Say, what a chump you are for working in that old store for $8 a week! I made $18.50 last week. Of course ironing ain't as swell work as selling lace behind a counter, but it pays. None of us ironers make less than $10. And I don't know that it's any less respectful work, either."

"You can have it," said Nancy, with uplifted nose. "I'll take my eight a week and hall bedroom. I like to be among nice things and swell people. And look what a chance I've got! Why, one of our glove girls married a Pittsburgh—a steel maker, or blacksmith or something—the other day worth a million dollars. I'll catch a swell myself some time. I ain't bragging on my looks or anything; but I'll take my chances where there's big prizes offered. What show would a girl have in a laundry?"

"Why, that's where I met Dan," said Lou, triumphantly. "He came in for his Sunday shirt and collars and saw me at the first board, ironing. We all try to get to work at the first board. Ella Maginnis was sick that day, and I had her place. He said he noticed my arms first, how round and white they was. I had my sleeves rolled up. Some nice fellows come into laundries. You can tell 'em by their bringing their clothes in suit cases, and turning in the door sharp and sudden."

"How can you wear a waist like that, Lou?" said Nancy, gazing down at the offending article with sweet scorn in her heavy-lidded eyes. "It shows fierce taste."

"This waist?" said Lou, with wide-eyed indignation. "Why, I paid $16 for this waist. It's worth twenty-five. A woman left it to be laundered, and never called for it. The boss sold it to me. It's got yards and yards of hand embroidery on it. Better talk about that ugly, plain thing you've got on."

"This ugly, plain thing," said Nancy, calmly, "was copied from one that Mrs. Van Alstyne Fisher was wearing. The girls say her bill in the store last year was $12,000. I made mine, myself. It cost me $1.50. Ten feet away you couldn't tell it from hers."

"Oh, well," said Lou, good-naturedly, "if you want to starve and put on airs, go ahead. But I'll take my job and good wages; and after hours give me something as fancy and attractive to wear as I am able to buy."

But just then Dan came—a serious young man with a ready-made necktie, who had escaped the city's brand of frivolity—an electrician earning $30 per week who looked upon Lou with the sad eyes of Romeo, and thought her embroidered waist a web in which any fly should delight to be caught.

"My friend, Mr. Owens—shake hands with Miss Danforth," said Lou.

"I'm mighty glad to know you, Miss Danforth," said Dan, with outstretched hand. "I've heard Lou speak of you so often."

"Thanks," said Nancy, touching his fingers with the tips of her cool ones, "I've heard her mention you—a few times."

Lou giggled.

"Did you get that handshake from Mrs. Van Alstyne Fisher, Nance?" she asked.

"If I did, you can feel safe in copying it," said Nancy.

"Oh, I couldn't use it at all. It's too stylish for me. It's intended to set off diamond rings, that high shake is. Wait till I get a few and then I'll try it."

"Learn it first," said Nancy, wisely, "and you'll be more likely to get the rings."

"Now, to settle this argument," said Dan, with his ready, cheerful smile, "let me make a proposition. As I can't take both of you up to Tiffany's and do the right thing, what do you say to a little vaudeville? I've got the tickets. How about looking at stage diamonds since we can't shake hands with the real sparklers?''

The faithful squire took his place close to the curb; Lou next, a little peacocky in her bright and pretty clothes; Nancy on the inside, slender, and soberly clothed as the sparrow, but with the true Van Alstyne Fisher walk—thus they set out for their evening's moderate diversion.

I do not suppose that many look upon a great department store as an educational institution. But the one in which Nancy worked was something like that to her. She was surrounded by beautiful things that breathed of caste and refinement. If you live in an atmosphere of luxury, luxury is yours whether your money pays for it, or another's.

The people she served were mostly women whose dress, manners, and position in the social world were quoted as criterions. From them Nancy began to take toll—the best from each according to her view.

From one she would copy and practice a gesture, from another an eloquent lifting of an eyebrow, from others, a manner of walking, of carrying a purse, of smiling, of greeting a friend, of addressing ''inferiors in station.'' From her best beloved model, Mrs. Van Alstyne Fisher, she made requisition for that excellent thing, a soft, low voice as clear as silver and as perfect in articulation as the notes of a thrush. Suffused in the aura of this high social refinement and good breeding, it was impossible for her to escape a deeper effect of it. As good habits are said to be better than good principles, so, perhaps, good manners are better than good habits. The teachings of your parents may not keep alive your New England conscience; but if you sit on a straight-back chair and repeat the words ''prisms and pilgrims'' forty times the devil will flee from you. And when Nancy spoke in the Van Alstyne Fisher tones she felt the thrill of *noblesse oblige* to her very bones.

There was another source of learning in the great departmental school. Whenever you see three or four shop-girls gather in a bunch and jingle their wire bracelets as an accompaniment to apparently frivolous conversation, do not think that they are there for the purpose of criticizing the way Ethel does her back hair. The meeting may lack the dignity of the deliberative bodies of man; but it has all the importance of the occasion on which Eve and her first daughter first put their heads together to make Adam understand his proper place in the household. It is Woman's Conference for Common Defense and Exchange of Strategical Theories of Attack and Repulse upon and against the World, which is a Stage, and Man, its Audience who Persists in Throwing Bouquets Thereupon. Woman, the most helpless of the young of any animal—with the fawn's grace but without its fleetness; with the bird's beauty but without its power of flight; with the honey-bee's burden of sweetness but without its—Oh, let's drop that simile—some of us may have been stung.

During this council of war they pass weapons one to another, and exchange stratagems that each has devised and formulated out of the tactics of life.

"I says to 'im," says Sadie, "ain't you the fresh thing! Who do you suppose I am, to be addressing such a remark to me? And what do you think he says to me?"

The heads, brown, black, flaxen, red, and yellow bob together; the answer is given; and the parry to the thrust is decided upon, to be used by each thereafter in passages-at-arms with the common enemy, man.

Thus Nancy learned the art of defense; and to women successful defense means victory.

The curriculum of a department store is a wide one. Perhaps no other college could have fitted her as well for her life's ambition—the drawing of a matrimonial prize.

Her station in the store was a favored one. The music room was near enough for her to hear and become familiar with the works of the best composers—at least to acquire the familiarity that passed for appreciation in the social world in which she was vaguely trying to set a tentative and aspiring foot. She absorbed the educating influence of art wares, of costly and dainty fabrics, of adornments that are almost culture to women.

The other girls soon became aware of Nancy's ambition. "Here comes your millionaire, Nancy," they would call to her whenever any man who looked the role approached her counter. It got to be a habit of men, who were hanging about while their women folk were shopping, to stroll over to the handkerchief counter and dawdle over the cambric squares. Nancy's imitation high-bred air and genuine dainty beauty was what attracted. Many men thus came to display their graces before her. Some of them may have been millionaires; others were certainly no more than their sedulous apes. Nancy learned to discriminate. There was a window at the end of the handkerchief counter; and she could see the rows of vehicles waiting for the shoppers in the street below. She looked and perceived that automobiles differ as well as do their owners.

Once a fascinating gentleman bought four dozen handkerchiefs, and wooed her across the counter with a King Cophetua air. When he had gone one of the girls said:

"What's wrong, Nance, that you didn't warm up to that fellow? He looks the swell article, all right, to me."

"Him?" said Nancy, with her coolest, sweetest, most impersonal, Van Alstyne Fisher smile; "not for mine. I saw him drive up outside. A 12 H.P. machine and an Irish chauffeur! And you saw what kind of handkerchiefs he bought—silk! And he's got dactylis on him. Give me the real thing or nothing, if you please."

Two of the most "refined" women in the store—a forelady and a cashier—had a few "swell gentlemen friends" with whom they now and then dined. Once they included Nancy in an invitation. The dinner took place in a spectacular café whose tables are engaged for New Year's Eve a year in advance. There were two "gentlemen friends"—one without any hair on his head—high living ungrew it; and we can prove it—the other a young man whose worth and sophistication he impressed upon you in two convincing ways—he swore that all the wine was corked; and he wore diamond cuff buttons. This young man perceived irresistible excellencies in Nancy. His taste ran to shop-girls; and here was one that added the voice and manners of his high social world to the franker charms of her own caste. So, on the following day, he appeared in the store and made her a serious proposal of marriage over a box of hemstitched, grass-bleached Irish linens. Nancy declined. A brown pompadour ten feet away had been using her eyes and ears. When the rejected suitor had gone she heaped carboys of upbraidings and horror upon Nancy's head.

"What a terrible little fool you are! That fellow's a millionaire—he's a nephew of old Van Skittles himself. And he was talking on the level, too. Have you gone crazy, Nance?"

"Have I?" said Nancy. "I didn't take him, did I? He isn't a millionaire so hard that you could notice it, anyhow. His family only allows him $20,000 a year to spend. The baldheaded fellow was guying him about it the other night at supper."

The brown pompadour came near and narrowed her eyes.

"Say, what do you want?" she inquired, in a voice hoarse for lack of chewing-gum. "Ain't that enough for you? Do you want to be a Mormon, and marry Rockefeller and Gladstone Dowie and the King of Spain and the whole bunch? Ain't $20,000 a year good enough for you?"

Nancy flushed a little under the level gaze of the black, shallow eyes.

"It wasn't altogether the money, Carrie," she explained. "His friend caught him in a rank lie the other night at dinner. It was about some girl he said he hadn't been to the theater with. Well, I can't stand a liar. Put everything together—I don't like him; and that settles it. When I sell out it's not going to be on any bargain day. I've got to have something that sits up in a chair like a man, anyhow. Yes. I'm looking out for a catch; but it's got to be able to do something more than make a noise like a toy bank."

"The physiopathic ward for yours!" said the brown pompadour, walking away.

These high ideas, if not ideals—Nancy continued to cultivate on $8 per week. She bivouacked on the trail of the great unknown "catch" eating her dry bread and tightening her belt day by day. On her face was the faint, soldierly, sweet, grim smile of the preordained man-hunter. The store was her forest; and many times she raised her rifle at game that seemed broad-antlered and big; but always some deep unerring instinct—perhaps of the huntress, perhaps of the woman—made her hold her fire and take up the trail again.

Lou flourished in the laundry. Out of her $18.50 per week she paid $6 for her room and board. The rest went mainly for clothes. Her opportunities for bettering her taste and manners were few compared with Nancy's. In the steaming laundry there was nothing but work, work and her thoughts of the evening pleasures to come. Many costly and showy fabrics passed under her iron; and it may be that her growing fondness for dress was thus transmitted to her through the conducting metal.

When the day's work was over Dan awaited her outside, her faithful shadow in whatever light she stood.

Sometimes he cast an honest and troubled glance at Lou's clothes that increased in conspicuity rather than in style; but this was no disloyalty; he deprecated the attention they called to her in the streets.

And Lou was no less faithful to her chum. There was a law that Nancy should go with them on whatever outings they might take. Dan bore the extra burden heartily and in good cheer. It might be said that Lou furnished the color, Nancy the tone, and Dan the weight of the distraction-seeking trio. The escort, in his neat but obviously ready-made suit, his ready-made tie and unfailing, genial, ready-made wit never startled or clashed. He was of that good kind that you are likely to forget while they are present, but remember distinctly after they are gone.

To Nancy's superior taste the flavor of these ready-made pleasures was sometimes a little bitter: but she was young, and youth is a gourmand, when it cannot be a gourmet.

"Dan is always wanting me to marry him right away," Lou told her once. "But why should I? I'm independent. I can do as I please with the money I earn; and he never would agree for me to keep on working afterward. And say, Nance, what do you want to stick to that old store for, and half starve and half dress yourself? I could get you a place in the laundry right now if you'd come. It seems to me that you could afford to be a little less stuck-up if you could make a good deal more money."

"I don't think I'm stuck-up, Lou," said Nancy, "but I'd rather live on half rations and stay where I am. I suppose I've got the habit. It's the chance that I want. I don't expect to be always behind a counter. I'm learning something new every day. I'm right up against refined and rich people all the time—even if I do only wait on them; and I'm not missing any pointers that I see passing around."

"Caught your millionaire yet?" asked Lou with her teasing laugh.

"I haven't selected one yet," answered Nancy. "I've been looking them over."

"Goodness! the idea of picking over 'em! Don't you ever let one get by you, Nance—even if he's a few dollars shy. But of course you're joking—millionaires don't think about working girls like us."

"It might be better for them if they did," said Nancy, with cool wisdom. "Some of us could teach them how to take care of their money."

"If one was to speak to me," laughed Lou, "I know I'd have a duck-fit."

"That's because you don't know any. The only difference between swells and other people is you have to watch 'em closer. Don't you think that red silk lining is just a little bit too bright for that coat, Lou?"

Lou looked at the plain, dull olive jacket of her friend.

"Well, no, I don't—but it may seem so beside that faded-looking thing you've got on."

"This jacket," said Nancy, complacently, "has exactly the cut and fit of one that Mrs. Van Alstyne Fisher was wearing the other day. The material cost me $3.98. I suppose hers cost about $100 more."

"Oh, well," said Lou, lightly, "it don't strike me as millionaire bait. Shouldn't wonder if I catch one before you do, anyway."

Truly it would have taken a philosopher to decide upon the values of the theories held by the two friends. Lou, lacking that certain pride and fastidiousness that keeps stores and desks filled with girls working for the barest living, thumped away gaily with her iron in the noisy and stifling laundry. Her wages supported her even beyond the point of comfort; so that her dress profited until sometimes she cast a sidelong glance of impatience at the neat but inelegant apparel of Dan—Dan the constant, the immutable, the undeviating.

As for Nancy, her case was one of tens of thousands. Silk and jewels and laces and ornaments and the perfume and music of the fine world of good-breeding and taste—these were made for woman; they are her equitable portion. Let her keep near them if they are a part of life to her, and if she will. She is no traitor to herself, as Esau was; for she keeps her birthright and the pottage she earns is often very scant.

In this atmosphere Nancy belonged; and she throve in it and ate her frugal meals and schemed over her cheap dresses with a determined and contented mind. She already knew woman; and she was studying man, the animal, both as to his habits and eligibility. Some day she would bring down the game that she wanted; but she promised herself it would be what seemed to her the biggest and the best, and nothing smaller.

Thus she kept her lamp trimmed and burning to receive the bridegroom when he should come.

But another lesson she learned, perhaps unconsciously. Her standard of values began to shift and change. Sometimes the dollar-mark grew blurred in her mind's eye, and shaped itself into letters that spelled such words as "truth" and "honor" and now and then just "kindness." Let us make a likeness of one who hunts the moose or elk in some mighty wood. He sees a little dell, mossy and embowered, where a rill trickles, babbling to him of rest and comfort. At these times the spear of Nimrod himself grows blunt.

So Nancy wondered sometimes if Persian lamb was always quoted at its market value by the hearts that it covered.

One Thursday evening Nancy left the store and turned across Sixth Avenue westward to the laundry. She was expected to go with Lou and Dan to a musical comedy.

Dan was just coming out of the laundry when she arrived. There was a queer, strained look on his face.

"I thought I would drop around to see if they heard from her," he said.

"Heard from who?" asked Nancy. "Isn't Lou there?"

"I thought you knew," said Dan. "She hasn't been here or at the house where she lived since Monday. She moved all her things from there.

She told one of the girls in the laundry she might be going to Europe.''

"Hasn't anybody seen her anywhere?'' asked Nancy.

Dan looked at her with his jaws set grimly, and a steely gleam in his steady gray eyes.

"They told me in the laundry,'' he said, harshly, "that they saw her pass yesterday—in an automobile. With one of the millionaires, I suppose, that you and Lou were forever busying your brains about.''

For the first time Nancy quailed before a man. She laid her hand that trembled slightly on Dan's sleeve.

"You've no right to say such a thing to me, Dan—as if I had anything to do with it!''

"I didn't mean it that way,'' said Dan, softening. He fumbled in his vest pocket.

"I've got the tickets for the show to-night,'' he said, with a gallant show of lightness. "If you—''

Nancy admired pluck whenever she saw it.

"I'll go with you, Dan,'' she said.

Three months went by before Nancy saw Lou again.

At twilight one evening the shop-girl was hurrying home along the border of a little quiet park. She heard her name called, and wheeled about in time to catch Lou rushing into her arms.

After the first embrace they drew their heads back as serpents do, ready to attack or to charm, with a thousand questions trembling on their swift tongues. And then Nancy noticed that prosperity had descended upon Lou, manifesting itself in costly furs, flashing gems, and creations of the tailor's art.

"You little fool!'' cried Lou, loudly and affectionately. "I see you are still working in that store, and as shabby as ever. And how about that big catch you were going to make—nothing doing yet, I suppose?''

And then Lou looked, and saw that something better than prosperity had descended upon Nancy—something that shone brighter than gems in her eyes and redder than a rose in her cheeks, and that danced like electricity anxious to be loosed from the tip of her tongue.

"Yes, I'm still in the store,'' said Nancy, "but I'm going to leave it next week. I've made my catch—the biggest catch in the world. You won't mind now Lou, will you?—I'm going to be married to Dan—to Dan!—he's my Dan now—why, Lou!''

Around the corner of the park strolled one of those new-crop, smooth-faced young policemen that are making the force more endurable—at least to the eye. He saw a woman with an expensive fur coat and diamond-ringed hands crouching down against the iron fence of the park sobbing turbulently, while a slender, plainly dressed working girl leaned close, trying to console her. But the Gibsonian cop, being of the new order, passed on, pretending not to notice, for he was wise enough to know that these matters are beyond help so far as the power he represents is concerned, though he rap the pavement with his nightstick till the sound goes up to the furthermost stars.

LONGFACE

Andrew Fetler

A car drove by in the rain and splashed his feet. He touched the wet
cello case for the bow. It was there.

On the far side of the street another young man came out of a novelty
shop, recognized Mark, and ran over. It was Bradley Walker, Mark saw
with annoyance. Not since college, Bradley said, and four long years.
They had not been close friends in college, but to Bradley Walker the passing of four years meant being in a far country, and he was hugging a fellow
tourist.

Could they get out of the rain? Had Mark eaten? Bradley's car stood
parked around the corner. What was he doing with a fiddle? Bradley himself had turned professional. Did he remember Bradley's column, "File
13," in *The Shaft*? Well, Bradley was writing copy for Sylvester Kellogg
—Kellogg's Complete Creative Service. Kellogg knew technique when he
saw it and paid very good money, by the way. Mark used to make witty
jingles, Bradley remembered. Did he still make them?

"No."

Bradley laughed. "You haven't changed a bit. You're not playing in
Orchestra Hall?"

"No."

Mark turned to see if the bus was coming. Rain. Bradley pulled at his
arm. He did not have to go home yet, did he? A reunion, after all. After
dinner at Le Bistro, Bradley would give him a ride home.

"You're not married?" Bradley asked.

Mark shook his head.

They turned the corner to Bradley's car, a new model that looked like a fish. Bradley flicked on the radio as they drove off. Pardon, but Mark did look run-down. Was he working or having a good time? Bradley was working and even thinking of getting married. Can't fool around all your life.

Mark enjoyed the car. He sat feeling the rain in his left shoe. His girl, Cathy, waited for him in his basement. She was cooking meat dumplings. There would also be cake and hot chocolate, she had promised, and green paper napkins to celebrate the start of a new life.

They drove to Le Bistro. As they went in, Bradley Walker clapped the doorman on the back. In the cloakroom he patted the cheek of a rouged woman who held her head like a camel. Under his coat Bradley wore the adman's uniform for that season, beige trousers and jacket buttoned very high. Could Mark eat a steak? A drink first? He led him to the bar.

"Can't they serve at a table?" Mark asked.

"Sure." But Bradley, touching his tie, saw a face at the bar and excused himself for a moment.

A hidden mechanical system in the dining room cooled in the cold autumn, and another system hummed music for everybody's dining pleasure. Mark felt a hot spasm in his stomach. He sat down to a table in an icy draft and clasped his hands. He looked up. Bradley stood leaning over a man at the bar, his hand on the man's shoulder.

Cathy would be sitting on his bed now, watching the dinner go cold. A new day, she had hugged him. Regular practice now, and sleep. No more nights abed looking at the ceiling. She believed he would be seated in the orchestra. His wet feet felt numb.

Bradley was sorry he had kept him waiting. Some business was too important for the office. Had he ordered? He must try a nice big juicy steak—what did he say? He was Bradley's guest, of course. Not like school days, Bradley said, looking about for other faces and smiling. They'd had a good time, though. Were women still chasing him?

"What's brandy like?" Mark asked.

"Haven't you ever had brandy?"

"I'd like a little brandy, please," Mark said to the waiter. "And coffee."

Bradley ordered the steaks bloody. "Well done for you? That's ruining it." He sat back in his chair. "But tell me about yourself. What have you been doing?"

"You work for Kellogg, do you?"

Bradley talked. He had an idea what Mark thought of places like Kellogg's Complete Creative Service. He used to think so himself in college. But let's face it: it does keep our economy going.

Mark sat turning the water glass as Bradley talked. He had caught a chill. He crossed his arms and held himself tightly. The waiter served the brandy and coffee and salad. The brandy had a revolting taste, bitter and sticky. Mark drank it all. Then he bit into a shred of lettuce, cold and tasteless like ice.

"Don't you want salad oil?"

"Thank you."

Bradley watched him. "Getting any kicks lately?"

"You should know more about kicks. Kicks and tricks."

Bradley wiped his lips. Mark had cocked his head to one side. An unpleasant smile wrung his mouth.

Bradley said, "You had a very serious ambition once, didn't you? In college?"

"Was it your ambition to work for Sylvester Kellogg?"

Bradley looked over his shoulder to see where the waiter was. "Some more brandy for you?"

"No, thank you."

Bradley leaned forward, smiling. "Say, remember the time we picketed the president's house?"

Mark rubbed his eyes. He was cold. But he did not want to see Cathy yet. She had said he would save money and move out of that miserable basement to a room above ground. A window to the sun. In time he would see how good it is to be normal, sleep nights and work days, cut his hair, squander an hour bathing, and put on a laundered shirt with cuff links. You don't know how good you look when you take care of yourself, she said.

He clawed at the salad with his fork. Bradley talked. The waiter brought the steak, a slab of meat with small mouths oozing and bubbling hot blood. Mark put down his fork.

"Doesn't that look good? You can't beat this joint for steaks. I've tried them all."

"I'm not hungry."

"Well—would you like something else? How about a nice lobster tail?"

"No, nothing. Thank you."

The steak was very good, really, Bradley said, chewing. Wouldn't he try just a little piece? Hate to waste a perfectly good steak, and it would do him good. He looked underfed. He did it very well—Bradley winked—that lean look. Women went for it.

Four years had been one moment of waiting. Nothing had happened in four years. Bradley's jaw looked heavier, and he was beginning to have a belly. Mark remembered stopping at North Hall and looking out over the empty quadrangle. Nothing was changed and everything was gone.

"I know you never liked me," Bradley said suddenly.

"Can I have a cigarette?"

Bradley offered his pack and fumbled with his lighter. Mark lit the cigarette with his own match.

"It used to bother me in college," Bradley said. "I thought you were very smart, one of those people who have something on everybody. Would you like a hamburger? Another coffee?"

"Was it also your ambition to be everybody's friend?"

"I try to like everybody. I think it's a sign of maturity."

Mark felt the air conditioning on his wet feet. There was plenty of air in this windowless cave of plastic upholstery and indirect lighting, but it was cold and stale, as in a morgue.

"How do you like Le Bistro?" Bradley asked politely.

"Fine."

Bradley laughed again, jabbing at his mutilated steak. "Excuse me, I don't really know why I'm laughing. I guess it's your hair."

Mark disliked barbers, and let it grow. He had combed today, but the rain had curled his hair. Cathy had pleaded with him to get a haircut, but he had gone off to Orchestra Hall knowing he would fail and refused a haircut out of spite. After months of erratic practice he had wanted to fail brazenly. Nobody had noticed, of course. In Le Bistro his style was out of place, but in the music hall the heads of ten of thirty cellists were overgrown, all competing for one vacancy in the city's orchestra. His disgrace was not unique, but it was delicious to toss about such a bushy crown and be dismissed after sixteen bars of the allegro. Miserable hair, and the conductor yelling "Thank you!" to stop him.

"How about some dessert?"

"No, thank you."

Bradley called for more coffee. He was in no hurry to get the reunion over with. Mark accepted another cup and another cigarette. This time Bradley did not offer his Ronson Varaflame.

"You never told me what you're doing these days. What *are* you doing these days?"

"Nothing."

"Aren't you playing?"

"Just an audition. I didn't make it."

"I'm sorry. For the Symphony Orchestra? Kind of steep, isn't it?"

"Yes."

"Any other place you can try? I mean, something with less competition?"

"No. Shall we go?"

Bradley passed a finger over the bill to verify the sum cost. Mark went to the men's room. His legs were still and cold. Washing his hands, he avoided the mirror. He stood undecided for a moment, his hands dripping, his face turned to the cold white tile. There were no towels in the washroom, only a machine with a nozzle that blew air, a Dri-O-Matic for his sanitary comfort. The electric wire within was shot, and the air, blown out with a whine, was icy.

Bradley drove him home in the rain. Night had come and the rain fell heavier. Streams washed over the sidewalks under the lighted lamps, and Bradley drove slowly, his eyes peering through the running windshield.

"Turn left next corner." Mark said.

The houses became squalid after a while. Small taverns appeared, then an expanse of darkness, a park, and a brick clubhouse with smashed windows. Then miles of tenement houses. They turned into a narrow street and came out on one of those obscure broad thoroughfares that are used mostly by commercial vehicles. Dirty small shops, their windows showing auto tires and used office machines, had been abandoned years ago, it seemed. They passed an old movie house, scratched and defaced; the ticket box was fashioned to resemble a clown's head, and in the grinning mouth sat an old woman nodding over a newspaper. A drugstore shone yellow in the rain, its window cluttered with dusty bottles, empty toothpaste cartons, and plastic bow ties.

Mark never left this hinterland unless he had to. The direction of life was reversed here, and he watched it with satisfaction. An oil burner set fire to a house and firemen controlled the blaze and let the house burn to the ground. A roof collapsed and a grandmother was carried out and the walls were razed. The rubble was not cleared, but patted down and left.

He liked to see Blacks of a winter dawn, picks in their paws, crawling over a smoking ruin like maggots.

So there were gaps in the street past which the trucks took marvelous speed to the shining downtown. In some blocks no more than three or four houses remained. From ashes and debris sprang grass, and sometimes flowers. The city was crumbling and the prairie was coming back.

"You can always reach me at Kellogg's," Bradley said. "If you ever need anything."

"Thanks." Mark got out of the car and walked to the house in the rain.

"Don't hesitate," Bradley called.

Mark ducked down a passage between two houses and emerged in the backyard. He turned down the steps to the basement door. In the glass of the door was Cathy's face.

"You promised you'd come right home."

She was a small girl with narrow shoulders and thin arms, pretty as a child.

"The finals dragged," he said.

"You made the finals? Have they decided?"

"Next week," he lied.

"Oh, Longface!"

"No, no. There was an old cellist, some refugee. Very good. Wish you'd have heard him. Close the door."

"I bet he thinks the same of you."

They stood in the laundry room under a bare light bulb. Her brown hair touched her shoulders. She concealed her small breasts by stooping slightly. She had put on a blue wool dress. He liked her in this dress, a Peter Pan collar and satin belt. He moved to close the door.

She held him. "You see what you can do when you try! You won't knock yourself down again, will you, Longface?"

"I haven't got the job."

"Even if you don't get it, you won't lie down again. It doesn't matter, baby. You tried and I love you. If you don't make it this time, you'll make it next time. But you've got to keep trying, and I love you."

"I'm tired. Damn bus."

"Poor baby. I'll heat the dinner. Do you love me?"

"Yes, darling."

From the dark passage between the houses came the voice of Bradley Walker: "Hello!"

Bradley came in the rain carrying the cello wrong side up.

"You forgot your fiddle. God, it's like the Casbah," Bradley said, coming carefully down the steps. "You should put a light in that tunnel."

Mark introduced Bradley as an old school friend.

"I'm very pleased to meet you," Bradley said to Cathy, showing his teeth. He shook her small hand vigorously.

"Are you also a cellist?" Cathy asked.

"God, no. Kellogg's Complete Creative Service. A lot of plain hard work, that's all."

"It must be interesting work," Cathy said. She closed the door.

"*He* doesn't think so," Bradly said, smiling. "But everybody can't be a genius. Somebody has to do the dirty work and keep things going." Neither Mark nor Cathy made answer, and Bradley said, "Well, I hope we can have dinner again soon—both of you. Maybe next time he'll have a better appetite. He wouldn't touch the steak."

Cathy looked at Mark. Then she nodded to Bradley and walked out of the laundry room into the basement.

Bradley looked around. "Wonderful tubs. My mother wore herself to death over a sink like that. You don't live here?"

"My room's up front."

Mark turned to the window. The glass was dirty and he could not see through. It was raining hard and steady.

Bradley tried to see where Cathy had disappeared. Beyond the laundry room the basement fell into darkness. Wash lines were strung within, heavy with wet sheets, and the air smelled humid and sour.

"Brad, would you mind taking her home? The bus runs only on the hour."

Bradley said, "Glad to. Where does she live?"

"Elmview. Can you wait a second? . . . No, come in."

Mark took the cello and slipped in ahead. Bradley followed slowly. They bent low to clear the wash lines, ducked between sheets, and stepped around ashcans. At the boiler Mark halted and listened. They moved on past a row of stalls in which tenants kept their rubbish under lock. A light showed in the cracks of a partition at the far end, next to a coal bin. Mark opened a small door and they went in.

Cathy sat on a narrow steel bed. She had pulled a blanket over her shoulders and held the ends in her small fists. A pot of coffee steamed on a two-burner gas range, a bridge table was laid prettily for two. The glasses sparkled. A line of books and some stacks of music were arranged neatly on a large desk under the window. Tacked to the wall was a print cut from a magazine. The sound of rain beat on the window.

"Cathy," Mark said. He stood the cello in its corner and sat beside her.

The girl showed no surprise at seeing Bradley again. Her eyes turned to the window and there they held.

Mark reached for her hand, but she pulled it away. "Later," he said. "Brad will take you home now."

Bradley fidgeted with his car keys. Mark fetched her coat. As he held the coat for her she let go of the blanket and rose on unsteady feet. He brought her handbag and white gloves.

"Lucky thing, Brad driving you home. You won't need your boots after all. But wear them next time."

"My car's double-parked," Bradley said. "I hope it's all right."

"They don't bother you here."

Cathy ran out of the room. She knocked into something, and ran on. The yard door opened and she was out.

Mark opened the window. As Cathy passed on the sidewalk he called her name. She did not stop.

He closed the window and stood listening to the rain. A kitchen clock on the dresser showed twenty minutes past nine. The bus would not come for forty minutes.

"Nothing, don't worry," Mark said. "She'll be standing three blocks down, where the bus stops. Will you pick her up there? I'll appreciate it."

Bradley stood looking at him.

Mark tossed his hand. "She may not want to come at first. Will you do that?"

"Aren't you coming?"

"No."

Bradley left.

Mark uncased the cello and began to dry it with a rag. The cello was not wet, only its back was damp. He rubbed it all over, and said aloud to himself, "Won't be in a hurry this year."

From SOMETHING HAPPENED

Joseph Heller

The people in the company who are least afraid are the few in our small Market Research Department, who believe in nothing and are concerned with collecting, organizing, interpreting, and reorganizing statistical information about the public, the market, the country, and the world. For one thing, their salaries are small, and they know they will not have much trouble finding jobs paying just as little in other companies if they lose their jobs here. Their budget, too, is small, for they are no longer permitted to undertake large projects.

Most of the information we use now is obtained free from trade associations, the U.S. Census Bureau, the Department of Commerce, the U.S. Chamber of Commerce, the National Association of Manufacturers, and the Pentagon, and there is no way of knowing anymore whether the information on which we base our own information for distribution is true or false. But that doesn't seem to matter; all that does matter is that the information come from a reputable source. People in the Market Research Department are never held to blame for conditions they discover outside the company that place us at a competitive disadvantage. What is, is— and they are not expected to change reality, but merely to find it if they can and suggest ingenious ways of disguising it. To a great extent, that is the nature of my own work, and all of us under Green work closely with the Sales Department and the Public Relations Department in converting whole truths into half truths and half truths into whole ones.

I am very good with these techniques of deception, although I am not always able anymore to deceive myself (if I were, I would not know that, would I? Ha, ha). In fact, I am continually astonished by people in the company who do fall victim to their own (our own) propaganda. There are so many now who actually believe that what we do is really important. This happens not only to salesmen, who repeat their various sales pitches aloud so often they acquire the logic and authority of a mumbo-jumbo creed, but to the shrewd, capable executives in top management, who have access to all data ought to know better. It happens to people on my own level and lower. It happens to just about everybody in the company who graduated from a good business school with honors: these are uniformly the most competent and conscientious people in the company, and also the most gullible and naïve. Every time we launch a new advertising campaign, for example, people inside the company are the first ones to be taken in by it. Every time we introduce a new product, or an old product with a different cover, color, and name that we present as new, people inside the company are the first to rush to buy it—even when it's no good.

When salesmen and company spokesmen begin believing their own arguments, the result is not always bad, for they develop an outlook of loyalty, zeal, and conviction that is often remarkably persuasive in itself. It produces that kind of dedication and fanaticism that makes good citizens and good employees. When it happens to a person in my own department, however, the result can be disastrous, for he begins relying too heavily on what he now thinks is the truth and loses his talent for devising good lies. He is no longer convincing. It's exactly what happened to Holloway, the man in my own department who broke down (and is probably going to break down again soon).

"But it's true, don't you see?" he would argue softly to the salesmen, the secretaries, and even to me, with a knowing and indulgent smile, as though what he was saying ought to have been as obvious to everyone as it was to him. "We *are* the best." (The point he missed is that it didn't matter whether it was true or not; what mattered was what people *thought* was true.)

He is beginning to smile and argue that way again and to spend more time talking to us than we want to spend listening to him. My own wish when he is buttonholing me or bending the ear of someone else in my department is that he would hurry up and have his nervous breakdown already, if he is going to have one anyway, and get it—and himself—out of the way. He is the only one who talks to Martha, our typist who is going crazy, and she is the only one who listens to him without restlessness and irritation. She listens to him with great intensity because she is paying no attention to him at all.

Everyone grew impatient with him. And he lost his power to understand (as he is losing this power again) why the salesmen, who would come to him for solid proof to support their exaggerations and misrepresentations, turned skeptical, began to avoid him, and refused to depend on him any longer or even take him to lunch. He actually expected them to get by with only the "truth."

It's a wise person, I guess, who knows he's dumb, and an honest person who knows he's a liar. And it's a dumb person, I guess, who's convinced he is wise, I conclude to myself (wisely), as we wise grownups here at the company go gliding in and out all day long, scaring each other at our desks and cubicles and water coolers and trying to evade the people who frighten us. We come to work, have lunch, and go home. We goose-step in and goose-step out, change our partners and wander all about, sashay around for a pat on the head, and promenade home till we all drop dead. Really, I ask myself every now and then, depending on how well or poorly things are going with Green at the office or at home with my wife, or with my retarded son, or with my other son, or my daughter, or the colored maid, or the nurse for my retarded son, is this *all* there is for me to do? Is this really the *most* I can get from the few years left in this one life of mine?

And the answer I get, of course, is always . . . *Yes!*

Because I have my job, draw my pay, get my laughs, and seem to be able to get one girl or another to go to bed with me just about every time I want; because I am envied and looked up to by neighbors and coworkers with smaller salaries, less personality, drab wives; and because I really do seem to have everything I want, although I often wish I were working for someone other than Green, who likes me and likes my work but wouldn't let me make a speech at the company convention in Puerto Rico last year, or at the company convention in Florida the year before—and who knows I hate him for that and will probably never forgive him or ever forget it.

(I have dreams, unpleasant dreams, that relate, I think, to my wanting to speak at a company convention, and they are always dreams that involve bitter frustration and humiliation and insurmountable difficulty in getting from one location to another.)

Green now thinks I am conspiring to undermine him. He is wrong.

For one thing, I don't have the initiative; for another, I don't have the nerve; and for still another thing, I guess I really like and admire Green in many respects (even though I also hate and resent him in many others), and I know I am probably safer working for him than I would be working for anyone else—even for Andy Kagle in the Sales Department if they did decide to move me and my department from Green's department to Kagle's department.

In many ways and on many occasions Green and I are friends and allies and do helpful, sometimes considerate things for each other. Often, I protect and defend him when he is late or forgetful with work of his own, and I frequently give him credit for good work from my department that he does not deserve. But I never tell him I do this; and I never let him know when I hear anything favorable about him. I enjoy seeing Green apprehensive. I'm pleased he distrusts me (it does wonders for my self-esteem), and I do no more than necessary to reassure him.

And I am the best friend he has here.

So I scare Green, and Green scares White, and White scares Black, and Black scares Brown and Green, and Brown scares me and Green and Andy Kagle, and all of this is absolutely true, because Horace White really is afraid of conversation with Jack Green, and Johnny Brown, who bulldozes everyone around him with his strong shoulders, practical mind, and tough, outspoken mouth, is afraid of Lester Black, who protects him.

I know it's true, because I worked this whole color wheel out one dull, wet afternoon on one of those organizational charts I am always constructing when I grow bored with my work. I am currently occupied (as one of my private projects) with trying to organize a self-sufficient community out of people in the company whose names are the same as occupations, tools, or natural resources, for we have many Millers, Bakers, Taylors, Carpenters, Fields, Farmers, Hammers, Nichols (puns are permitted in my Utopia, else how could we get by?), and Butchers listed in the internal telephone directory; possibly we'd be a much better organization if all of us were doing the kind of work our names suggest, although I'm not sure where I'd fit in snugly there, either, because my name means nothing that I know of and I don't know where it came from.

Digging out valuable information of no importance distracts and amuses me. There are eleven Greens in the company (counting Greenes), eight Whites, four Browns, and four Blacks. There is one Slocum . . . me. For a while, there were two Slocums; there was a Mary Slocum in our Chi-

cago office, a short, sexy piece just out of secretarial school with a wiggling
ass and a nice big bust, but she quit to get married and was soon pregnant
and disappeared. Here and there in the company colored men, Negroes,
in immaculate white or blue shirts and very firmly knotted ties are starting
to appear; none are important yet, and nobody knows positively why they
have come here or what they really want. All of us (almost all of us) are
ostentatiously polite to them and pretend to see no difference. In private,
the salesmen make jokes about them.

("Know what they said about the first Negro astronaut?"
"What?"
"The jig is up.")

I am bored with my work very often now. Everything routine that
comes in I pass along to somebody else. This makes my boredom worse.
It's a real problem to decide whether it's more boring to do something
boring than to pass along everything boring that comes in to somebody
else and then have nothing to do at all.

Actually, I enjoy my work when the assignments are large and urgent
and somewhat frightening and will come to the attention of many people.
I get scared, and am unable to sleep at night, but I usually perform at my
best under this stimulating kind of pressure and enjoy my job the most. I
handle all of these important projects myself, and I rejoice with tremendous pride and vanity in the compliments I receive when I do them well
(as I always do). But between such peaks of challenge and elation there is
monotony and despair. (And I find, too, that once I've succeeded in impressing somebody, I'm not much excited about impressing that same
person again; there is a large, emotional letdown after I survive each crisis,
a kind of empty, tragic disappointment, and last year's threat, opportunity, and inspiration are often this year's inescapable tedium. I frequently
feel I'm being taken advantage of merely because I'm asked to do the
work I'm paid to do.)

On days when I'm especially melancholy, I begin constructing tables
of organization from standpoints of plain malevolence, dividing, subdi-
viding, and classifying people in the company on the basis of envy, hope,
fear, ambition, frustration, rivalry, hatred, or disappointment. I call
these charts my Happiness Charts. These exercises in malice never fail to
boost my spirits—but only for a while. I rank pretty high when the
company is analyzed this way, because I'm not envious or disappointed,
and I have no expectations. At the very top, of course, are those people,
mostly young and without dependents, to whom the company is not yet

an institution of any sacred merit (or even an institution especially worth preserving) but still only a place to work, and who regard their present association with it as something temporary. To them, it's all just a job, from president to porter, and pretty much the same job at that. I put these people at the top because if you asked any one of them if he would choose to spend the rest of his life working for the company, he would give you a resounding *No!*, regardless of what inducements were offered. I was that high once. If you asked me that same question today, I would also give you a resounding *No!* and add:

"I think I'd rather die now."

But I am making no plans to leave.

I have the feeling now that there is no place left for me to go.

Near the very bottom of my Happiness Charts I put those people who are striving so hard to get to the top. I am better off (or think I am) than they because, first, I have no enemies or rivals (that I know of) and am almost convinced I can hold my job here for as long as I want to and, second, because there is no other job in the company I want that I can realistically hope to get. I wouldn't want Green's job; I couldn't handle it if I had it and would be afraid to take it if it were offered. There is too much to do. I'm glad it won't be (I'm sure it won't be).

I am one of those many people, therefore, most of whom are much older than I, who are without ambition already and have no hope, although I do want to continue receiving my raise in salary each year, and a good cash bonus at Christmastime, and I do want very much to be allowed to take my place on the rostrum at the next company convention in Puerto Rico (if it will be Puerto Rico again this year), along with the rest of the managers in Green's department and make my three-minute report to the company of the work we have done in my department and the projects we are planning for the year ahead.

From DEATH OF A SALESMAN

Arthur Miller

From **ACT I**

From the right, Willy Loman, the Salesman, enters, carrying two large sample cases. The flute plays on. He hears but is not aware of it. He is past sixty years of age, dressed quietly. Even as he crosses the stage to the doorway of the house, his exhaustion is apparent. He unlocks the door, comes into the kitchen, and thankfully lets his burden down, feeling the soreness of his palms. A word-sigh escapes his lips—it might be "Oh, boy, oh, boy." He closes the door, then carries his cases out into the living-room, through the draped kitchen doorway.

Linda, his wife, has stirred in her bed at the right. She gets out and puts on a robe, listening. Most often jovial, she has developed an iron repression of her exceptions to Willy's behavior—she more than loves him, she admires him, as though his mercurial nature, his temper, his massive dreams and little cruelties, served her only as sharp reminders of the turbulent longings within him, longings which she shares but lacks the temperament to utter and follow to their end.

LINDA, *hearing Willy outside the bedroom, calls with some trepidation:* Willy!

WILLY: It's all right. I came back.

LINDA: Why? What happened? *Slight pause.* Did something happen, Willy?

WILLY: No, nothing happened.

LINDA: You didn't smash the car, did you?

WILLY, *with casual irritation:*   I said nothing happened. Didn't you hear me?

LINDA: Don't you feel well?

WILLY: I'm tired to the death. *The flute has faded away. He sits on the bed beside her, a little numb.* I couldn't make it. I just couldn't make it, Linda.

LINDA, *very carefully, delicately:*   Where were you all day? You look terrible.

WILLY: I got as far as a little above Yonkers. I stopped for a cup of coffee. Maybe it was the coffee.

LINDA: What?

WILLY, *after a pause:*   I suddenly couldn't drive any more. The car kept going off onto the shoulder, y'know?

LINDA, *helpfully:*   Oh. Maybe it was the steering again. I don't think Angelo knows the Studebaker.

WILLY: No, it's me, it's me. Suddenly I realize I'm goin' sixty miles an hour and I don't remember the last five minutes. I'm—I can't seem to—keep my mind to it.

LINDA: Maybe it's your glasses. You never went for your new glasses.

WILLY: No, I see everything. I came back ten miles an hour. It took me nearly four hours from Yonkers.

LINDA, *resigned:*   Well, you'll just have to take a rest, Willy, you can't continue this way.

WILLY: I just got back from Florida.

LINDA: But you didn't rest your mind. Your mind is overactive, and the mind is what counts, dear.

WILLY: I'll start out in the morning. Maybe I'll feel better in the morning. *She is taking off his shoes.* These goddam arch supports are killing me.

LINDA: Take an aspirin. Should I get you an aspirin? It'll soothe you.

WILLY, *with wonder:*   I was driving along, you understand? And I was fine. I was even observing the scenery. You can imagine, me looking at scenery, on the road every week of my life. But it's so beautiful up there, Linda, the trees are so thick, and the sun is warm. I opened the windshield and just let the warm air bathe over me. And then all of a sudden I'm goin' off the road! I'm tellin' ya, I absolutely forgot I was driving. If I'd've gone the other way over the white line I might've killed somebody. So I went on again—and five minutes later I'm dreamin' again, and I nearly—*He presses two fingers against his eyes.* I have such thoughts. I have such strange thoughts.

LINDA: Willy, dear. Talk to them again. There's no reason why you can't work in New York.

WILLY: They don't need me in New York. I'm the New England man. I'm vital in New England.

LINDA: But you're sixty years old. They can't expect you to keep traveling every week.

WILLY: I'll have to send a wire to Portland. I'm supposed to see Brown and Morrison tomorrow morning at ten o'clock to show the line. Goddammit, I could sell them! *He starts putting on his jacket.*

LINDA, *taking the jacket from him:*   Why don't you go down to the place tomorrow and tell Howard you've simply got to work in New York? You're too accommodating, dear.

WILLY: If old man Wagner was alive I'd a been in charge of New York now! That man was a prince, he was a masterful man. But that boy of his, that Howard, he don't appreciate. When I went north the first time, the Wagner Company didn't know where New England was!

LINDA: Why don't you tell those things to Howard, dear?

WILLY, *encouraged:*   I will, I definitely will. Is there any cheese?

LINDA: I'll make you a sandwich.

WILLY: No, go to sleep, I'll take some milk. I'll be up right away. The boys in?

LINDA: They're sleeping. Happy took Biff on a date tonight.

WILLY, *interested:*   That so?

LINDA: It was so nice to see them shaving together, one behind the other, in the bathroom. And going out together. You notice? The whole house smells of shaving lotion.

WILLY: Figure it out. Work a lifetime to pay off a house. You finally own it, and there's nobody to live in it.

LINDA: Well, dear, life is a casting off. It's always that way.

WILLY: No, no, some people—some people accomplish something.

LOOSE ENDS

Anthony E. Stockanes

He is pacing a slow shadowless foot-scuffling hands-in-pockets circuit of the yard, pausing to pluck a weed, squatting to prod the soft com-
posted earth beneath one of the mezereons. When he straightens he
gingerly presses his fingers to his kidneys because (he is prey to multiple
"becauses") there is a nagging tightness, not pain exactly but the gentle
threat of pain, crawling above the beltline in the spongy pads he has developed in the last few years, and because he hopes Denise is watching
him from the sunroom window and he wants her eyes to touch him with
sympathy, and because the gesture is habitual, one of the automatic actions gradually accumulated: hands on chair arms when he sits or rises, a
squint and a kneading of his temples when he takes off his glasses, a hesitation while he carefully arranges his joints before he stoops, a bunching
of shoulders and a twist of his neck when he has been driving for a while.
They are an expanding repertoire of the body's separate surrenders to
time. None too worrisome. By itself.

Shoulder-high on the flanks, waist level in the rear, a fence of wide
redwood slats rims the yard. The yard slopes slightly. In one corner he has
constructed a semicircle of large, smooth stones inconspicuously joined
with cement, furred with moss. Completing the circle is a fan of washed
pea gravel within a sunken brick border. In the center of the gravel a stone
birdbath mushrooms out of loops of ivy; swaying from an iron bracket on
the fence behind the birdbath, a redwood bird feeder, a miniature barn

exact in detail down to a tiny trotting-horse weathervane of black plastic. In the opposite corner of the yard is a duplicate gravel and stone circle. A sundial with grayish green bronze gnomon, its patina freckled with minute pits, replaces the birdbath.

This area behind the house is his province, as are the garage and basement where he fussily arranges his tools, each outlined on enameled pegboard. In the basement, neatly rolled, are the yard plans, carefully scaled India ink diagrams on white posterboard showing the placement of each tree and shrub, the planned location of a trio of deutzias with their projected shadow patterns lightly penciled, the dotted straightedge dissections giving sight lines from all the rear windows. The drawings are something more than his hobby, as the scrupulous tending of the yard is something more than relaxation.

The house itself is Denise's.

The front yard is mutual neutral territory. The six-foot hedge screening the street is a barrier he trims and shapes twice a month, the twin sugar maples merging above the driveway are his choice. The wide flower beds, sporadically weeded, are Denise's. The seemingly unplanned array of perennials annoys him. He would prefer flowers of uniform height and bulk, bands of unobtrusive complementing colors, the beds themselves edged with brick. Better yet would be the removal of the flowers and their replacement with drawable shrubs, something with tiny dark green leaves and tight, organized branches, set in raked gravel.

This division of space within space is not planned. It simply evolved as they smoothed concentric circles of silence between them. There is nothing formal about it, but he cannot suggest changes in her territory—any more than she can alter his—without opening a sealed explosion. He thinks that if he trespasses, if she encroaches on his area, they will be unable to control themselves and everything will crumble. He is not sure what "everything" is.

Beyond the back fence the yard's curve flows down across fifty yards of open field to the shallow basin of Oat Lake. Lowell Parmenter's wry, "Damned puddle looks like the ocean after taxes," was passed quickly through the Willow Ridge parties they always seemed to be having then, was reduced by someone (Greg Rose? Probably. Greg was good at that sort of thing) to O.A.T. Lake and became fixed until now it was printed on maps of the county and was assumed, vaguely, to be based on wild oats that grew in the region. Only he and a few others remember its origin.

When he mentions it, new arrivals say, "Oh, really?" in that bemused way that indicates it is a dull anecdote and his little chuckle ebbs away. Three or four times a year he tells Denise he is going to get in touch with Lowell, finally respond to the postcard from Oregon, but he never does. Once he looked for the card, sure he knew exactly where it was, but he couldn't find it.

He pensively traces a knot in the fencing. Again he thinks those were good times, those early years when they—the original Willow Ridgers— sat on plastic-and-aluminum chairs, slapping at mosquitoes in the long lavender summer evenings, smearing themselves with insect repellant, sipping drinks from straw-sheathed glasses, heatedly debating the importance of Quemoy and Matsu, exchanging the rueful comments (that were a kind of communal pride) on the stretches of brown viscous earth years away from lawns, traded tools and recipes and stories of their jobs. There was no fence then, nothing between the few houses except a scattering of heavily fertilized, pitifully small leafless trees, and they moved back and forth easily between the glaringly bright kitchens and the gamerooms that smelled of fresh varnish.

He leans on the fence and watches a quick rush of wind fracture pale sunlight on the water into pearl-tipped wavelets. Across the lake, where yet another new house—a Lincolnshire mock-Tudor from the skeletal shape of it—is a child's toy of new lumber, carpenters' hammers bounce dull echoes over the water. Between the pale yellow frame and the lake, the refrigerator-shaped silliness of a Midwest Pottyhouse is a white lump. Again, he thinks he should have taken pictures when they first came, before it was crowded, when their own house was an openwork design rising out of the clay-streaked mud and he and Denise drove over in the evening to prowl through the shell, their footsteps loud on the plywood sheets; now it's difficult to remember exactly how the area looked when only the Parmenters and Greg, the Norbetts, Bill and Sarah Peterson, the Watseckis and—what was their name? (The thin couple with the psychotic Dalmatian? Wilson? Watson? Winslow? Something like that. Always squabbling over something, the proper mix for a martini or whether shag rugs were practical. He—Wilson? What-man?—always wore a cardigan sweater, buttoned up, and she—odd he could recall them, their quarrels, so completely, but couldn't remember their names) formed the nucleus of Willow Ridge.

He turns away from the fence and sucks his lips. Acacia leaves the color and shape of wood shavings soak in the birdbath, dyeing the water a deep red. He flicks a few of the leaves out. The water is disturbing, seems like diluted blood. Why didn't yellow leaves stain the water yellow?

He squats down suddenly. His heels smudge irremovable horseshoes into his trousers and (he knows) if Denise is at the window her mouth is puckered in a tight oval.

If she is watching (he knows) she is conscious of, but no longer admires, the narrowness of his hips, the angular line of his shoulders. Long ago they ceased caring, in any positive way, about their bodies, just as long ago she stopped, not abruptly but with a quiet, resigned cessation, complaining of his wearing slacks and good shirts and expensive sweaters when he did yardwork. She no longer says anything directly; it has become one of the little jokes dipped into informal gatherings: " . . . and I looked out and he was wearing his tan . . . " She says it with a four-note trill of laughter so it seems one of the exasperatedly affectionate jibes couples exchange and he always grins foolishly, lifts his shoulders in a shrug, never defends himself. But later in the evening, apparently a separate comment, he will point out, with equally affectionate tolerance, some small, slightly embarrassing trait of hers, punctuating it with a squeeze of her waist that stops (just) short of pain.

In twenty-seven years they have never publicly argued; for more than ten years there have been no private arguments, at least nothing with heat. Once, long ago, when there were such arguments, hoarse with shouting, long after midnight in the kitchen of another, smaller house they came close to separation, talked around the core of decision, but by then the effort of readjusting their lives, explaining to friends, dividing chairs and lamps, was too great an effort. And neither had someone else to replace the other, so they left the core untouched, stayed together without reconciliation or change. They simply agreed, tacitly, without consciously agreeing, to stop arguing and began to focus on their separate territories.

If she is watching from the sunroom window she may wonder, without real curiosity, why he is poking around the base of the fence by the birdfeeder.

Eyes narrowed, he studies the scattered piles of brown pellets. With a twig he nudges them, smooth chocolate-colored miniature cannon balls. The twig's tip is lightly smeared with a slick paste and his nose wrinkles. He traces the shallow furrow worn under the fence.

"Telephone!"

He hears without answering, imagining the plow of the belly grooving this trough through his yard. She steps out of the house, arms rolled in the hem of her sweater and crossed at her waist, shoulders hunched, skirt wind-pasted against her lean thighs.

"Telephone!"

She sounds impatient, her voice high-pitched. He knows the cool gray matte colors of late autumn depress her and she looks forward to New Mexico's brochured promise of sun and skies bare of charcoaled clouds.

Moving toward her, he says, "We've got rats."

"Merle's on the phone."

The phone in his hand, he stands beside the low petit-point chair, nods occasionally and moves his arms as though Merle can see him.

"Right, sure. Monday morning, first thing." He is seeing the polished sliding beneath the fence. "What? No, I hear you. I found out just now I've got rats in the backyard. Going after the birdseed, I guess."

Merle consoles him with the reminder that the house is sold, the problem someone else's now. He is not consoled, cuts off the conversation abruptly, irritated at Merle's failure to understand. It *is* his problem.

He is with Denise in the kitchen, standing with fists jammed in his pockets, shoulders pulled high, a defensive pose he has developed. "We've got rats in the backyard."

Her shudder is only a gesture. She is doing something with her hands in the cutlery drawer. "Well, we're getting out just in time. I know the water heater isn't going to last much longer. I'm just going to get rid of all these little plastic spoons. We never use them."

"We've got to do something about it." He frowns, wondering why he uses "we."

"Where *do* all these things come from?" She is shaking her head over a cupped palm of plastic bottle stoppers.

He wanders to the basement, stares blankly at the boxes of tools, each with its typewritten sheet of contents taped to the side. He is thinking of the rat defecating in his yard, a deliberate act of outrage.

He runs his thumb absently along the scarred edge of the workbench, traces the mark of the vise. There have been other houses—seven since the first, a flimsy draft-haunted one-bedroom box in Terre Haute that resisted all attempts he and Denise made to improve it, that ravenously absorbed fertilizer and grass seed in earth as hard and ugly as kiln-baked clay and pushed up small patches of spiky, fibrous weeds, limber and strong as piano wire, a house with walls that turned Denise's carefully chosen paints into uniformly drab purples through some mysterious and malevolent alchemy and yet, despite the problems, remains in the memory as a pleasant place—and other problems, porous septic tanks, leaking roofs, awkwardly shaped rooms, balky furnaces, weeping plumbing. But the problems were, somehow, minor, small disruptions of the moment, solved (with pleasure in the solving) by money and planning.

Perhaps, he thinks, it is the passage of time, nothing more than the accumulation of petty difficulties, the prospect of yet another house with its quirks. The weight of days. The shortness of breath from too little exercise and too many cigarettes is not a sudden affliction. Perhaps it is only the passage of time—and the move, this move, that makes the rat so unsettling.

The new owner admired the workbench. Perhaps he will spend much time down here.

He doesn't know why he is dissatisfied, could not say, exactly, what he thinks is wrong, what he would change—in Denise, in himself—to correct it.

His life, the pattern of habits that has become their life, has been such a smooth parabola with frequent moves during the early years and then a gradual, almost unnoticed leveling off, the slow realization (and, later and more slowly, the acceptance) that promotions are not inevitable, embarrassingly hairless shins will not be furred with a new season, the expanding and softening flesh around the middle is not a temporary encumbrance to be "someday" exercised away when he takes up tennis again "as soon as he has time," this yard is not the last and permanent square that will magically grow into the distance and will not be sculpted into an estate of solemnly beautiful trees and flagged walks curling away into a beautiful haze. He will not (he knows and—almost—admits) astonish Denise and himself with . . . with something.

He has three weeks (twenty-three days) before the movers load his neatly packed boxes and he and Denise, separated by an expanse of car seat, leave Willow Ridge.

This move is so—frightening. There is no other word for it. He is no longer (and he does not know when it happened or when he realized it) ascending. Something has happened to the arc. New Mexico is off the curve, a step sideways and therefore backward, remote in more than space. The company's announcement was so blandly chilling; he is being transferred —not promoted, transferred. The congratulations offered this time are subtly different. People do not say anything about his work; they pretend to be envious of the locale, tell him he is lucky to be going to New Mexico, joke that he can start wearing cowboy boots to the office.

No one advances from New Mexico at his level. He will replace Abramson who is retiring. No one seems to know who Abramson is.

Other houses, a few of them, had mice. One was infested with spiders. This is the first rat.

After dinner he turns on the patio light. It does not quite illuminate the birdfeeder. He peers into the shadows, wondering if the movement he thinks he sees is the rat or a bit of shubbery tugged by the wind, the ivy shifting.

In the morning he goes out to find more pellets. The groove beneath the fence seems deeper.

"Oh, forget it," Denise says. But he notes she will not go into the backyard now and when the wind combs the roof with a maple branch, her head tilts sharply; she listens, leaving a sentence unfinished.

He places two huge wooden traps on either side of the hole beneath the fence and lies awake listening. At three in the morning, shivering in his bathrobe, he goes out with a flashlight. There are fresh pellets. The traps are unsprung.

Two days later he replaces the wooden traps with an elaborate wire cage the man at the hardware store assures him is effective.

In the first snow he finds the scraped path leading under the fence. He follows it to a hole disappearing in a low mound of grass clippings dumped before he built the compost heap. He squats and listens, wondering what is happening deep inside. When he goes back into the yard he sees the snow lightly covers the bait in the trap.

There is no going-away party at the office. The Petersons have a small gathering. People he barely knows leave early. He insists on talking about the rat.

"If you see one, there's ten. If you see ten, you've got a hundred," he says. He notices that Bill Peterson now wears a cardigan most of the time.

Lisa Norbett rolls her eyes and says that's terrible, that she hopes rats can't swim since their house is directly across the lake, but her husband says it's an old wives' tale, the one-to-ten ratio.

Denise is swirling the diluted remains of her third drink. "Oh, he's such a pessimist, a regular Gloomy Gus," she says with a smile that seems indulgent. It is a criticism she makes more and more at these gatherings (when did Bill start wearing the sweater all the time?), a predictable comment. He always protests and then she says, oh no? and recites a string of events he was sure would turn out badly but didn't. He always smiles

when she does this and the conversation invariably slides away into re-
membrances of prophecies unfulfilled as it does when someone mentions
a dream and each interrupts with a particularly significant dream of his
own. Once he said, "In responsibilities begin dreams," and the Petersons
laughed knowingly and Lisa Norbett told him that was absolutely *ter*rible.
Denise blinked, knowing it was one of the inverted quotations he used
because, later, he could casually bring up the correct words. She used to
show an interest in what he said. That too stopped, but again not suddenly. Between the interest and the lack of it there must have been a period
when she merely pretended. He wondered how long that was.

Tonight he is not garbling quotations. He is worried about the rat.
He is not pessimistic, he denies that automatically and hides behind his
smile as Denise begins her familiar litany. He is thinking he is *not* really
pessimistic, that the predictions are talismans he uses as small payments
against a threat of large pain so that, if the worst does happen, he won't
find the bill overwhelming.

Denise is talking of the time he was absolutely sure the car's transmission was wearing out and it turned out to be a worn gasket, a minor repair. He would like to leave the party—no one has asked him what he will
do in New Mexico—and go home to his kitchen, to sit at the table telling
Denise, who listens with interest, what he has discovered about himself,
about the small payments and the large pain. It has been years since they
shared coffee and space in the kitchen and talked about unanswerable and
exciting questions.

He dreads the drive to New Mexico, the distance between them in
the car and in restaurant booths. For weeks he has been thinking about a
picture in a weekly magazine, a black-and-white shot of William Holden
and Stephanie Powers sitting in plain straight chairs, photographed against
a window. They lean forward, in comfortable isolation from the photographer and whatever else the room holds, and the space between them is in-
visibly filled. He can see himself in Holden's chair, but he cannot imagine
Denise in the other chair.

Denise has a fresh drink and there are circles of color like abrasions in
her cheeks. She is saying how much she misses Bing Crosby. Denise mourns
the deaths of strangers; Picasso's death depresses her, Lady Churchill's
demise warps the corners of her mouth, brings tears. It is the one fact from
the newspapers she calls to his attention, these deaths of people they don't
know.

He closes his eyes and sees the rat crouched motionless, staring at the house, and, superimposed, he sees himself leaning forward, elbows on knees, explaining to a girl with lovely cheekbones and large, interested eyes that the rat is a loose end, that it must be eliminated before he can leave, and the girl, her eyes wide and solemn on his face, nods, understanding.

"What are you going to do with that?"

This morning he saw the rat for the first time and it is exactly as he imagined it would be, a bold mud-colored menace. When he rapped sharply on the window the rat slid away under the fence with incredible speed.

The air pistol is much heavier than he thought it would be. "I can't put out poison, the birds will get it." He moves a chair by the window and balances the gun barrel on the sill, aiming at the dark tunnel under the fence. He tries to ignore Denise's complaints. He has explained it is not really a gun, that it fires little marbles, not bullets.

"You're going to hurt yourself."

He knows it is silly, but he feels younger, stronger, a romantic figure from the movies facing peril. A junco, perfectly adapted to the coming winter with dark top and white underbelly, bobs on a branch of the acacia and, startled, he squeezes the trigger, flinching tardily at the explosion that doesn't come. The pellet pings on the bracket holding the feeder and the junco is gone.

Denise crowds against his shoulder. "Was that it?"

"No, I was practicing, zeroing it in."

"It sounded like it hit something metal."

He says he was aiming at the bracket and Denise asks why he didn't aim at the hole.

When he turns back to the window, the rat is hunched over the seed scattered around the feeder, but it vanishes when he shifts the pistol.

For two hours he sits patiently. His eyes water and he closes them tightly. Through a film he sees the rat again. Before he can aim it is gone. The pellet ticks the snow six inches from the hole.

Denise says she is freezing with the window open. He says it is only open a crack, but he closes it. His fingers are numb. The rat reappears, scrambles in the seeds, scuttles back through its hole. He believes he can see the furrow deepen each time, become a permanent scar, its sides slick and polished.

"Why don't you forget it? In three days we'll be out of here."

He says that with the coming of really cold weather the rat will move into the house seeking warmth. He can't leave it like that. He tells her he doesn't like loose ends. He can't really explain it more concretely, even to himself.

She sniffs. "Why don't you put out some poison?"

"I told you why. The birds will get it."

"No, they won't. When I was filling up the car Ben told me birds won't touch rat poison."

He says that is stupid. How does a bird know if grain is poisoned? Almost before he is finished, as though she wants to trap him, she says, irrelevantly, devastatingly, Ben knew what he was talking about when he said the transmission didn't need work.

Unexpectedly, one day of mild weather melts the snow, but the temperature drops severely during the night and the ground is frozen. On the lake a few children, balloon figures in blue and red coats, are tentatively venturing out on the ice, squealing and racing back when it cracks under their feet.

He is squatting by the hole beyond the fence, a piece of cardboard, rolled and taped in a tube, thrust into the hole. Carefully, he sifts poison into the hole, using the tube as a funnel. He brushes a few grains away with his hands, worried about the birds.

The house seems strange and already empty, boxes in each room, the movable furniture shoved together to facilitate loading. He feels out of place. He sits by the window watching the hole.

"Look!" He does not hear Denise approach. Her fingers clutch at his shoulder. The rat is in the yard, but it does not pause by the seed. It races halfway up the yard along the fence, turns, runs a few feet, whirls again toward the house. He can no longer see it.

"What's it doing? Is it coming in here?" Her fingers knead his shoulder.

"It's looking for water. Because of the poison."

"Why?"

"I don't *know* why. That's the way it works. They go crazy for water."

"Oh, the poor thing."

"It's a rat," he says savagely and pushes her fingers away. The rat erupts into the yard, spins dizzily, a cartoon figure, is a brownish streak flowing through the hole.

He is prodding the hole with a stick. He has scraped away layers of spongy rotting grass and is amazed at the depth of the tunnel, its graceful protective curves, the laborious construction. He goes back to the house.

"The movers are here!"

He pushes the stiff slabs back into place, patting the frozen top sections with muddy fingers, trying to make it exactly as it was.

"Did you hear me?" Her voice is a brittle screech.

"I heard you." He flings the empty water can and watches it tumble in the air.

A VILLAGE SINGER

Mary Wilkins Freeman

The trees were in full leaf, a heavy south wind was blowing, and there was a loud murmur among the new leaves. The people noticed it, for it was the first time that year that the trees had so murmured in the wind. The spring had come with a rush during the last few days.

The murmur of the trees sounded loud in the village church, where the people sat waiting for the service to begin. The windows were open; it was a very warm Sunday for May.

The church was already filled with this soft sylvan music—the tender harmony of the leaves and the south wind, and the sweet, desultory whistles of birds—when the choir arose and began to sing.

In the centre of the row of women singers stood Alma Way. All the people stared at her, and turned their ears critically. She was the new leading soprano. Candace Whitcomb, the old one, who had sung in the choir for forty years, had lately been given her dismissal. The audience considered that her voice had grown too cracked and uncertain on the upper notes. There had been much complaint, and after long deliberation the church-officers had made known their decision as mildly as possible to the old singer. She had sung for the last time the Sunday before, and Alma Way had been engaged to take her place. With the exception of the organist, the leading soprano was the only paid musician in the large choir. The salary was very modest, still the village people considered it large for a young woman. Alma was from the adjoining village of East Derby: she had quite a local reputation as a singer.

Reprinted from *Great American Short Stories*, edited by Wallace Stegner and Mary Stegner, Dell, New York, 1954.

Now she fixed her large solemn blue eyes; her long, delicate face, which had been pretty, turned paler; the blue flowers on her bonnet trembled; her little thin gloved hands, clutching the singing-book, shook perceptibly; but she sang out bravely. That most formidable mountain-height of the world, self-distrust and timidity, arose before her, but her nerves were braced for its ascent. In the midst of the hymn she had a solo; her voice rang out piercingly sweet; the people nodded admiringly at each other; but suddenly there was a stir; all the faces turned toward the windows on the south side of the church. Above the din of the wind and the birds, above Alma Way's sweetly straining tones, arose another female voice, singing another hymn to another tune.

"It's her," the women whispered to each other; they were half aghast, half smiling.

Candace Whitcomb's cottage stood close to the south side of the church. She was playing on her parlor organ, and singing, to drown out the voice of her rival.

Alma caught her breath; she almost stopped; the hymn-book waved like a fan; then she went on. But the long husky drone of the parlor organ and the shrill clamor of the other voice seemed louder than anything else.

When the hymn was finished, Alma sat down. She felt faint; the woman next to her slipped a peppermint into her hand. "It ain't worth minding," she whispered, vigorously. Alma tried to smile; down in the audience a young man was watching her with a kind of fierce pity.

In the last hymn Alma had another solo. Again the parlor organ droned above the carefully delicate accompaniment of the church organ, and again Candace Whitcomb's voice clamored forth in another tune.

After the benediction, the other singers pressed around Alma. She did not say much in return for their expressions of indignation and sympathy. She wiped her eyes furtively once or twice, and tried to smile. William Emmons, the choir leader, elderly, stout, and smooth-faced, stood over her, and raised his voice. He was the old musical dignitary of the village, the leader of the choral club and the singing-schools. "A most outrageous proceeding," he said. People had coupled his name with Candace Whitcomb's. The old bachelor tenor and old maiden soprano had been wont to walk together to her home next door after the Saturday night rehearsals, and they had sung duets to the parlor organ. People had watched sharply her old face, on which the blushes of youth sat pitifully, when William Emmons entered the singing-seats. They wondered if he would ever ask her to marry him.

And now he said further to Alma Way that Candace Whitcomb's voice had failed utterly of late, that she sang shockingly, and ought to have had sense enough to know it.

When Alma went down into the audience-room, in the midst of the chattering singers, who seemed to have descended, like birds, from song flights to chirps, the minister approached her. He had been waiting to speak to her. He was a steady-faced, fleshy old man, who had preached from that one pulpit over forty years. He told Alma, in his slow way, how much he regretted the annoyance to which she had been subjected, and intimated that he would endeavor to prevent a recurrence of it. "Miss Whitcomb—must be—reasoned with," said he; he had a slight hesitation of speech, not an impediment. It was as if his thoughts did not slide readily into his words, although both were present. He walked down the aisle with Alma, and bade her good-morning when he saw Wilson Ford waiting for her in the doorway. Everybody knew that Wilson Ford and Alma were lovers; they had been for the last ten years.

Alma colored softly, and made a little imperceptible motion with her head; her silk dress and the lace on her mantle fluttered, but she did not speak. Neither did Wilson, although they had not met before that day. They did not look at each other's faces—they seemed to see each other without that—and they walked along side to side.

They reached the gate before Candace Whitcomb's little house. Wilson looked past the front yard, full of pink and white spikes on flowering bushes, at the lace-curtained windows; a thin white profile, stiffly inclined, apparently over a book, was visible at one of them. Wilson gave his head a shake. He was a stout man, with features so strong that they overcame his flesh. "I'm going up home with you, Alma," said he; "and then—I'm coming back, to give Aunt Candace one blowing up."

"Oh, don't, Wilson."

"Yes, I shall. If you want to stand this kind of a thing you may; I sha'n't."

"There's no need of your talking to her. Mr. Pollard's going to."

"Did he say he was?"

"Yes. I think he's going in before the afternoon meeting, from what he said."

"Well, there's one thing about it, if she does that thing again this afternoon, I'll go in there and break that old organ up into kindling wood." Wilson set his mouth hard, and shook his head again.

Alma gave little side glances up at him, her tone was deprecatory, but her face was full of soft smiles. "I suppose she does feel dreadfully about it," said she. "I can't help feeling kind of guilty, taking her place."

"I don't see how you're to blame. It's outrageous, her acting so."

"The choir gave her a photograph album last week, didn't they?"

"Yes. They went there last Thursday night, and gave her an album and a surprise-party. She ought to behave herself."

"Well, she's sung there so long, I suppose it must be dreadful hard for her to give it up."

Other people going home from church were very near Wilson and Alma. She spoke softly that they might not hear; he did not lower his voice in the least. Presently Alma stopped before a gate.

"What are you stopping here for?" asked Wilson.

"Minnie Lansing wanted me to come and stay with her this noon."

"You're going home with me."

"I'm afraid I'll put your mother out."

"Put mother out! I told her you were coming, this morning. She's got all ready for you. Come along; don't stand here."

He did not tell Alma of the pugnacious spirit with which his mother had received the announcement of her coming, and how she had stayed at home to prepare the dinner, and make a parade of her hard work and her injury.

Wilson's mother was the reason why he did not marry Alma. He would not take his wife home to live with her, and was unable to support separate establishments. Alma was willing enough to be married and put up with Wilson's mother, but she did not complain of his decision. Her delicate blond features grew sharper, and her blue eyes more hollow. She had had a certain fine prettiness, but now she was losing it, and beginning to look old, and there was a prim, angular, old maiden carriage about her narrow shoulders.

Wilson never noticed it, and never thought of Alma as not possessed of eternal youth, or capable of losing or regretting it.

"Come along, Alma," said he; and she followed meekly after him down the street.

Soon after they passed Candace Whitcomb's house, the minister went up the front walk and rang the bell. The pale profile at the window had never stirred as he opened the gate and came up the walk. However, the door was promptly opened, in response to his ring. "Good-morning, Miss Whitcomb," said the minister.

"*Good*-morning." Candace gave a sweeping toss of her head as she spoke. There was a fierce upward curl to her thin nostrils and her lips, as if she scented an adversary. Her black eyes had two tiny cold sparks of fury in them, like an enraged bird's. She did not ask the minister to enter, but he stepped lumberingly into the entry, and she retreated rather than led the way into her little parlor. He settled into the great rocking-chair and wiped his face. Candace sat down again in her old place by the window. She was a tall woman, but very slender and full of pliable motions, like a blade of grass.

"It's a—very pleasant day," said the minister.

Candace made no reply. She sat still, with her head drooping. The wind stirred the looped lace-curtains; a tall rose-tree outside the window waved; soft shadows floated through the room. Candace's parlor organ stood in front of an open window that faced the church; on the corner was a pitcher with a bunch of white lilacs. The whole room was scented with them. Presently the minister looked over at them and sniffed pleasantly.

"You have—some beautiful—lilacs there."

Candace did not speak. Every line of her slender figure looked flexible, but it was a flexibility more resistant than rigor.

The minister looked at her. He filled up the great rocking-chair; his arms in his shiny black coat-sleeves rested squarely and comfortably upon the hair-cloth arms of the chair.

"Well, Miss Whitcomb, I suppose I—may as well come to—the point. There was—a little—matter I wished to speak to you about. I don't suppose you were—at least I can't suppose you were—aware of it, but—this morning, during the singing by the choir, you played and—sung a little too—loud. That is, with—the windows open. It—disturbed us—a little. I hope you won't feel hurt—my dear Miss Candace, but I knew you would rather I would speak of it, for I knew—you would be more disturbed than anybody else at the idea of such a thing."

Candace did not raise her eyes; she looked as if his words might sway her through the window. "I ain't disturbed at it," said she. "I did it on purpose; I meant to."

The minister looked at her.

"You needn't look at me. I know jest what I'm about. I sung the way I did on purpose, an' I'm goin' to do it again, an' I'd like to see you stop me. I guess I've got a right to set down to my own organ, an' sing a psalm tune on a Sabbath day, 'f I want to; an' there ain't no amount of talkin' an' palaverin' a-goin' to stop me. See there!" Candace swung aside her skirts a little. "Look at that!"

The minister looked. Candace's feet were resting on a large red-plush photograph album.

"Makes a nice footstool, don't it?" said she.

The minister looked at the album, then at her; there was a slowly gathering alarm in his face; he began to think she was losing her reason.

Candace had her eyes full upon him now, and her head up. She laughed, and her laugh was almost a snarl. "Yes; I thought it would make a beautiful footstool," said she. "I've been wantin' one for some time." Her tone was full of vicious irony.

"Why, miss—" began the minister; but she interrupted him:

"I know what you're a-goin' to say, Mr. Pollard, an' now I'm goin' to have my say; I'm a-goin' to speak. I want to know what you think of folks that pretend to be Christians treatin' anybody the way they've treated me? Here I've sung in those singin'-seats forty year. I ain't never missed a Sunday, except when I've been sick, an' I've gone an' sung a good many times when I'd better been in bed, an' now I'm turned out without a word of warnin'. My voice is jest as good as ever 'twas; there can't anybody say it ain't. It wa'n't ever quite so high-pitched as that Way girl's, mebbe; but she flats the whole durin' time. My voice is as good an' high today as it was twenty years ago; an' if it wa'n't, I'd like to know where the Christianity comes in. I'd like to know if it wouldn't be more to the credit of folks in a church to keep an old singer an' an old minister, if they didn't sing an' hold forth quite so smart as they used to, ruther than turn 'em off an' hurt their feelin's. I guess it would be full as much to the glory of God. S'pose the singin' an' the preachin' wa'n't quite so good, what difference would it make? Salvation don't hang on anybody's hittin' a high note, that I ever heard of. Folks are gettin' as high-steppin' an' fussy in a meetin'-house as they are in a tavern, nowadays. S'pose they should turn you off, Mr. Pollard, come an' give you a photograph album, an' tell you to clear out, how'd you like it? I ain't findin' any fault with your preachin'; it was always good enough to suit me; but it don't stand to reason folks'll be as took up with your sermons as when you was a young man. You can't expect it. S'pose they should turn you out in your old age, an' call in some young bob squirt, how'd you feel? There's William Emmons, too; he's three years older'n I am, if he does lead the choir an' run all the singin' in town. If my voice has gi'en out, it stan's to reason his has. It ain't, though. William Emmons sings jest as well as he ever did. Why don't they turn him out the way they have me, an' give him a photograph album? I dun know but it would be a good idea to send everybody, as soon as they get a little old an' gone by, an' young folks begin to push, onto some desert island, an' give 'em each a photograph album. Then they can sit down an' look at pictures the rest of their days. Mebbe government'll take it up.

"There they come here last week Thursday, all the choir, jest about eight o'clock in the evenin', and pretended they'd come to give me a nice little surprise. Surprise! h'm! Brought cake an' oranges, an' was jest as nice as they could be, an' I was real tickled. I never had a surprise-party before in my life. Jenny Carr she played, an' they wanted me to sing alone, an' I never suspected a thing. I've been mad ever since to think what a fool I was, an' how they must have laughed in their sleeves.

"When they'd gone I found this photograph album on the table, all done up as nice as you please, an' directed to Miss Candace Whitcomb from her many friends, an' I opened it, an' there was the letter inside givin' me notice to quit.

"If they'd gone about it any decent way, told me right out honest that they'd got tired of me, an' wanted Alma Way to sing instead of me, I wouldn't minded so much; I should have been hurt 'nough, for I'd felt as if some that had pretended to be my friends wa'n't; but it wouldn't have been as bad as this. They said in the letter that they'd always set great value on my services, an' it wa'n't from any lack of appreciation that they turned me off, but they thought the duty was gettin' a little too arduous for me. H'm! I hadn't complained. If they'd turned me right out fair an' square, showed me the door, an' said, 'Here, you get out,' but to go an' spill molasses, as it were, all over the threshold, tryin' to make me think it's all nice an' sweet—

"I'd sent that photograph album back quick's I could pack it, but I didn't know who started it, so I've used it for a footstool. It's all it's good for, 'cordin' to my way of thinkin'. An' I ain't been particular to get the dust off my shoes before I used it neither."

Mr. Pollard, the minister, sat staring. He did not look at Candace; his eyes were fastened upon a point straight head. He had a look of helpless solidity, like a block of granite. This country minister, with his steady, even temperament, treading with heavy precision his one track for over forty years, having nothing new in his life except the new sameness of the seasons, and desiring nothing new, was incapable of understanding a woman like this, who had lived as quietly as he, and all the time held within herself the elements of revolution. He could not account for such violence, such extremes, except in a loss of reason. He had a conviction that Candace was getting beyond herself. He himself was not a typical New

Englander; the national elements of character were not pronounced in him. He was aghast and bewildered at this outbreak, which was tropical, and more than tropical, for a New England nature has a floodgate, and the power which it releases is an accumulation. Candace Whitcomb had been a quiet woman, so delicately resolute that the quality had been scarcely noticed in her, and her ambition had been unsuspected. Now the resolution and the ambition appeared raging over her whole self.

She began to talk again. "I've made up my mind that I'm goin' to sing Sundays the way I did this mornin', an' I don't care what folks say," said she. "I've made up my mind that I'm goin' to take matters into my own hands. I'm goin' to let folks see that I ain't trod down quite flat, that there's a little rise left in me. I ain't goin' to give up beat yet a while; an' I'd like to see anybody stop me. If I ain't got a right to play a psalm tune on my organ an' sing, I'd like to know. If you don't like it, you can move the meetin'-house."

Candace had had an inborn reverence for clergymen. She had always treated Mr. Pollard with the utmost deference. Indeed, her manner toward all men had been marked by a certain delicate stiffness and dignity. Now she was talking to the old minister with the homely freedom with which she might have addressed a female gossip over the back fence. He could not say much in return. He did not feel competent to make headway against any such tide of passion; all he could do was to let it beat against him. He made a few expostulations, which increased Candace's vehemence; he expressed his regret over the whole affair, and suggested that they should kneel and ask the guidance of the Lord in the matter, that she might be led to see it all in a different light.

Candace refused flatly. "I don't see any use prayin' about it," said she. "I don't think the Lord's got much to do with it, anyhow."

It was almost time for the afternoon service when the minister left. He had missed his comfortable noontide rest, through this encounter with his revolutionary parishioner. After the minister had gone, Candace sat by the window and waited. The bell rang, and she watched the people file past. When her nephew Wilson Ford with Alma appeared, she grunted to herself. "She's thin as a rail," said she; "guess there won't be much left of her by the time Wilson gets her. Little softspoken nippin' thing, she wouldn't make him no kind of a wife, anyway. Guess it's jest as well."

When the bell had stopped tolling, and all the people entered the church, Candace went over to her organ and seated herself. She arranged a singing-book before her, and sat still, waiting. Her thin, colorless neck and temples were full of beating pulses; her black eyes were bright and eager; she leaned stiffly over toward the music-rack, to hear better. When the church organ sounded out she straightened herself; her long skinny fingers pressed her own organ-keys with nervous energy. She worked the pedals with all her strength; all her slender body was in motion. When the first notes of Alma's solo began, Candace sang. She had really possessed a fine voice, and it was wonderful how little she had lost it. Straining her throat with jealous fury, her notes were still for the main part true. Her voice filled the whole room; she sang with wonderful fire and expression. That, at least, mild little Alma Way could never emulate. She was full of steadfastness and unquestioning constancy, but there were in her no smouldering fires of ambition and resolution. Music was not to her what it had been to her older rival. To this obscure woman, kept relentlessly by circumstances in a narrow track, singing in the village choir had been as much as Italy was to Napoleon—and now on her island of exile she was still showing fight.

After the church service was done, Candace left the organ and went over to her old chair by the window. Her knees felt weak, and shook under her. She sat down, and leaned back her head. There were red spots on her cheeks. Pretty soon she heard a quick slam of her gate, and an impetuous tread on the gravel-walk. She looked up, and there was her nephew Wilson Ford hurrying up to the door. She cringed a little, then she settled herself more firmly in her chair.

Wilson came into the room with a rush. He left the door open, and the wind slammed it to after him.

"Aunt Candace, where are you?" he called out, in a loud voice.

She made no reply. He looked around fiercely, and his eyes seemed to pounce upon her.

"Look here, Aunt Candace," said he, "are you crazy?" Candace said nothing. "Aunt Candace!" She did not seem to see him. "If you don't answer me," said Wilson, "I'll just go over there and pitch that old organ out of the window!"

"Wilson Ford!" said Candace, in a voice that was almost a scream.

"Well, what say! What have you got to say for yourself, acting the way you have? I tell you what 'tis. Aunt Candace, I won't stand it."

"I'd like to see you help yourself."

"I will help myself. I'll pitch that old organ out of the window, and then I'll board up the window on that side of your house. Then we'll see."

"It ain't your house, and it won't never be."

"Who said it was my house? You're my aunt, and I've got a little lookout for the credit of the family. Aunt Candace, what are you doing this way for?"

"It don't made no odds what I'm doin' so for. I ain't bound to give my reasons to a young fellar like you, if you do act so mighty toppin'. But I'll tell you one thing, Wilson Ford, after the way you've spoke today, you sha'n't never have one cent of my money, an' you can't never marry that Way girl if you don't have it. You can't never take her home to live with your mother, an' this house would have been might nice an' convenient for you some day. Now you won't get it. I'm goin' to make another will. I'd made one, if you did but know it. Now you won't get a cent of my money, you nor your mother neither. An' I ain't goin' to live a dreadful while longer, neither. Now I wish you'd go home; I want to lay down. I'm 'bout sick."

Wilson could not get another word from his aunt. His indignation had not in the least cooled. Her threat of disinheriting him did not cow him at all; he had too much rough independence, and indeed his aunt Candace's house had always been too much of an air-castle for him to contemplate seriously. Wilson, with his burly frame and his headlong common-sense, could have little to do with air-castles, had he been hard enough to build them over graves. Still, he had not admitted that he never could marry Alma. All his hopes were based upon a rise in his own fortunes, not by some sudden convulsion, but by his own long and steady labor. Some time, he thought, he should have saved enough for the two homes.

He went out of his aunt's house still storming. She arose after the door had shut behind him, and got out into the kitchen. She thought that she would start a fire and make a cup of tea. She had not eaten anything all day. She put some kindling-wood into the stove and touched a match to it; then she went back to the sitting-room, and settled down again into the chair by the window. The fire in the kitchen-stove roared, and the light wood was soon burned out. She thought no more about it. She had not put on the teakettle. Her head ached, and once in a while she shivered. She sat at the window while the afternoon waned and the dusk came on. At seven o'clock the meeting bell rang again, and the people flocked by. This time she did not stir. She had shut her parlor organ. She did not need to out-sing her rival this evening; there was only congregational singing at the Sunday-night prayer-meeting.

She sat still until it was nearly time for meeting to be done; her head ached harder and harder, and she shivered more. Finally she arose. "Guess

I'll go to bed,'' she muttered. She went about the house, bent over and shaking, to lock the doors. She stood a minute in the back door, looking over the fields to the woods. There was a red light over there. ''The woods are on fire,'' said Candace. She watched with a dull interest the flames roll up, withering and destroying the tender green spring foliage. The air was full of smoke, although the fire was half a mile away.

Candace locked the door and went in. The trees with their delicate garlands of new leaves, with the new nests of song birds, might fall, she was in the roar of an intenser fire; the growths of all her springs and the delicate wontedness of her whole life were going down in it. Candace went to bed in her little room off the parlor, but she could not sleep. She lay awake all night. In the morning she crawled to the door and hailed a little boy who was passing. She bade him go for the doctor as quickly as he could, then to Mrs. Ford's, and ask her to come over. She held on to the door while she was talking. The boy stood staring wonderingly at her. The spring wind fanned her face. She had drawn on a dress skirt and put her shawl over her shoulders, and her gray hair was blowing over her red cheeks.

She shut the door and went back to her bed. She never arose from it again. The doctor and Mrs. Ford came and looked after her, and she lived a week. Nobody but herself thought until the very last that she would die; the doctor called her illness merely a light run of fever; she had her senses fully.

But Candace gave up at the first. ''It's my last sickness,'' she said to Mrs. Ford that morning when she first entered; and Mrs. Ford had laughed at the notion; but the sick woman held to it. She did not seem to suffer much physical pain; she only grew weaker and weaker, but she was distressed mentally. She did not talk much, but her eyes followed everybody with an agonized expression.

On Wednesday William Emmons came to inquire for her. Candace heard him out in the parlor. She tried to raise herself on one elbow that she might listen better to his voice.

''William Emmons come in to ask how you was,'' Mrs. Ford said, after he was gone.

''I—heard him,'' replied Candace. Presently she spoke again. ''Nancy,'' said she, ''where's that photograph album?''

''On the table,'' replied her sister, hesitatingly.

''Mebbe—you'd better—brush it up a little.''

''Well.''

Sunday morning Candace wished that the minister should be asked to come in at the noon intermission. She had refused to see him before. He came and prayed with her, and she asked his forgiveness for the way she had spoken the Sunday before. "I—hadn't ought to—spoke so," said she. "I was—dreadful wrought up."

"Perhaps it was your sickness coming on," said the minister smoothingly.

Candace shook her head. "No—it wa'n't. I hope the Lord will—forgive me."

After the minister had gone, Candace still appeared unhappy. Her pitiful eyes followed her sister everywhere with the mechanical persistency of a portrait.

"What is it you want, Candace?" Mrs. Ford said at last. She had nursed her sister faithfully, but once in a while her impatience showed itself.

"Nancy!"

"What say?"

"I wish—you'd go out when—meetin's done, an'—head off Alma an' Wilson, an'—ask 'em to come in. I feel as if—I'd like to—hear her sing."

Mrs. Ford stared. "Well," said she.

The meeting was now in session. The windows were all open, for it was another warm Sunday. Candace lay listening to the music when it began, and a look of peace came over her face. Her sister had smoothed her hair back, and put on a clean cap. The white curtain in the bedroom window waved in the wind like a white sail. Candace almost felt as if she were better, but the thought of death seemed easy.

Mrs. Ford at the parlor window watched for the meeting to be out. When the people appeared, she ran down the walk and waited for Alma and Wilson. When they came she told them what Candace wanted, and they all went in together.

"Here's Alma an' Wilson, Candace," said Mrs. Ford, leading them to the bedroom door.

Candace smiled. "Come in," she said, feebly. And Alma and Wilson entered and stood beside the bed. Candace continued to look at them, the smile straining her lips.

"Wilson!"

"What is it, Aunt Candace?"

"I ain't altered that—will. You an' Alma can—come here an'—live —when I'm—gone. Your mother won't mind livin' alone. Alma can have—all—my things."

"Don't, Aunt Candace." Tears were running over Wilson's cheeks, and Alma's delicate face was all of a quiver.

"I thought—maybe—Alma 'd be willin' to—sing for me," said Candace.

"What do you want me to sing?" Alma asked, in a trembling voice.

" 'Jesus, lover of my soul.' "

Alma, standing there beside Wilson, began to sing. At first she could hardly control her voice, then she sang sweetly and clearly.

Candace lay and listened. Her face had a holy and radiant expression. When Alma stopped singing it did not disappear, but she looked up and spoke, and it was like a secondary glimpse of the old shape of a forest tree through the smoke and flame of the transfiguring fire the instant before it falls. "You flatted a little on—'soul'," said Candace.

5

PHYSICAL DEVELOPMENT

Social and psychological development in infancy, childhood, and adolescence are often related to the rapid physical changes characteristic of preadulthood. Most of the physical changes in adulthood are far less dramatic and not as easily detected. For most people, young adulthood is a time of optimal health, physical strength, coordination, and endurance. Decline from the peak physical state of young adulthood is gradual, rarely noticed before the late forties or early fifties. Physical decline also varies widely from person to person, and many adults experience good health and retain their strength and vigor well into late life. The physical dimension of adult development thus offers no real means of charting psychological growth and change over time. Even the single biological event common to all men and women — the loss of reproductive powers — does not present a reliable developmental marker. Most menopausal-aged women report that the end of reproductive capacity does not affect them in any important way, and the male climacterium may be so gradual as to go unnoticed.

Since most physical *changes* in adulthood occur slowly over many years, their effect upon behavior is minimal. By contrast, a person's physical *condition* — how one feels and how one looks at any point in time — may greatly affect one's life-style, view of the self, or interactions with others. Being at peak condition in young adulthood allows one to engage in activities not possible in late life. Changes in appearance that characterize middle age often lead to self-assessment and changes in life-style. Finally, older persons who are at an age most likely to experience physical deterioration and ill health develop their own unique ways of adjusting and compensating.

THE VIGOR OF YOUNG ADULTHOOD

The unlimited energy, physical stamina, and sexual prowess of young adulthood is taken for granted by the young, envied by the middle-aged, and fondly remembered by the elderly. The physical attributes of young adulthood may be both a blessing and burden, however. The urge to test the limits of one's power, the desire to give reign to inner forces must be checked and expressed in socially acceptable ways. Balancing one's physical drives with social norms often results in psychosocial conflicts characteristic of a person's adjustment to the adult world. Stephen Dedalus from James Joyce's novel *A Portrait of the Artist as a Young Man* and Holden Caulfield in J. D. Salinger's *Catcher in the Rye* (not included in this anthology) are two well-known protagonists who struggle with such conflicts. Stephen's sexual experiences bring about a spiritual conflict that he attempts to resolve through confession. And from Holden's confusion of values and sexual experimentation a social consciousness and sense of personal identity gradually emerge.

In the selection from James T. Farrell's novel *Studs Lonigan* presented in this anthology, we encounter the prototype of a "young Turk." Studs is twenty-one, street-wise, tough, and very proud of his strong body. Even after several years of "drinking and carousing . . . he was still pretty hard and tough." In this selection, Studs plays tackle in a football game that degenerates into a brawl. At the poolroom afterwards he is visibly proud of his part in both the game and the fight. Momentarily he regrets the serious injury he did to another player and for an instant realizes that physical prowess will not carry him throughout life; he wishes he had finished high school. He is too caught up in the flush of his success as a football star and fighter to dwell on such thoughts, however. He is "proud of himself, and his body. In his prime right now."

MIDDLE AGE—THE AWARENESS OF AGING

Unlike the young person whose life stretches ahead almost indefinitely, the middle-aged person begins to realize that life is finite. One becomes aware of physical aging, an irreversible process. There is a tendency to gain weight, body fat becomes redistributed, hair turns grey and hairlines recede, and skin loses its elasticity. Gradual changes in appearance combined with the realization that one has only a limited number of years left may precipitate a mid-life crisis or at least a reassessment of body and self. In some cases the awareness of aging leads to attempts to recapture the vigor of youth, to prove that one is not really older. George Babbitt, in Sinclair Lewis's novel, is a middle-aged man becoming aware of his age. In the scene selected for this anthology, we see Babbitt taking care with his clothes, being concerned about how he looks, the extra weight he has put on, his receding hairline, and his digestive system. He eventually tries to break out of his proper but boring middle-aged life stage and, temporarily at least, feels rejuvenated by having an affair. He does not, however, have the energy to keep up with family, wife, and lover, and in the end accepts his middle-aged self.

One's sexuality plays an important part in defining the self, whatever one's chronological age. Self-love comes in part from feeling physically attractive, lovable, and desired by others. Middle age, with the accompanying changes in physical appearance, is a time when both men and women may feel insecure about their desirability. Our society is particularly harsh on women as they age. In a thought-provoking article, Susan Sontag (1977) points out the existence of a double standard of aging. As men age they often are thought to become distinguished-looking, seasoned, or statesmanlike — in short, more desirable. Women, however, are thought to become old, wrinkled, asexual, and less desirable. It is only men who look very old who are viewed as physically unattractive. In the short story "Front Man in Line," by Nancy Packer, forty-six-year-old Miriam's flirtations with a handsome old man rejuvenate them both. At the close of one of his weekly visits to the office where she works, Miriam feels "pretty and sweet." "His need was insatiable," she muses, "but so too was her own. She hoped he would live forever."

OLD AGE AND THE END
OF THE PHYSICAL SELF

Life expectancy has dramatically increased within the past hundred years. In 1860, for example, the average life expectancy for men and women was 39.1 years. In 1900 it was 47.3 years. Today men and women can usually expect to live into their late seventies. Most people desire to live a long, healthy life. Literature is full of immortality-seekers and of stories of the bargains people have tried to make to avoid the inevitable end of life. The overwhelming desire for self-preservation, for life, often overshadows questions about the quality of life. Living to a very old age is desirable only if one is in good health both physically and psychologically. In the selection from *Gulliver's Travels*, Jonathan Swift offers one picture of eternal life. He suggests that immortality is far from desirable if one must live as the Struldbrugs do, physically deteriorated and socially ostracized.

It is not always possible to determine whether a physical problem affects one's mental health or whether psychological problems manifest themselves in sickness. Older adults experience repeated losses: friends die, living arrangements change, outside contacts and activities are reduced, loss of hearing or sight may make one feel insecure. Old age can be a very stressful time of life, a period when multiple adjustments need to be made. It is little wonder that older people sometimes seem confused, fearful, or depressed. Unfortunately society dismisses many such persons as senile rather than attempting to uncover and perhaps alleviate the social or physical causes for such behavior. Sometimes dramatic changes can be brought about through a change in medication or increased human contact. True senile dementia — disorientation caused by organic brain damage — affects only a very small number of older persons. In "GTT," by Carolyn Osborn, Grandmother Moore is in a nursing home. Daughter and granddaughter come to take her for a ride. Grandmother Moore's spirited personality emerges in spite of her deteriorating body. Her situation triggers feelings of guilt and fear on the part of the younger visitors.

Death signifies the end of physical being. Whether from accident in young adulthood or disease in old age, dying is, ultimately, a physical act. In the poem "There, on the Darkened Deathbed," by John Masefield, death as the end to physical existence is emphasized. Both the ravages of time and the inevitability of death put an end to beauty, laughter, youthful follies, and functioning brains.

The acceptance of death as a natural part of the total life cycle is an attitude not all can subscribe to. Elizabeth Kübler-Ross (1969) has suggested that there are stages through which a dying person moves in coming to accept death. These stages, which may also be applied to feelings surrounding a loss, are denial, anger, bargaining, depression, and finally, acceptance. In the last two selections in this chapter we see older people who have learned to accept their own deaths as a natural end to the life cycle. In "The President of Flowers," by Sydney Lea, and Arna Bontemps' "A Summer Tragedy," the question of the quality of life also arises. The couple in "A Summer Tragedy" would rather die than face starvation, and the old man in "The President of Flowers" accepts and prepares for his death with the same care that he has used in cultivating his gardens.

So, while physical development in adulthood is far less dramatic than the physical changes of childhood, our physical *condition* very much affects how we interact with others, carry out our social roles, and view life. Young adulthood is characterized by robust health, vigor, and sexual energy. A middle-aged person may still have good health, but becoming aware of the finiteness of life leads to concern with physical appearance and other signs that the body will not last forever. Old age is a time often beset by physical problems. It is a time when physical and social losses and adjustments interact with one another, causing many older adults to be erroneously labeled as senile. Death makes the physical life cycle complete.

From THE YOUNG MANHOOD
OF STUDS LONIGAN

James T. Farrell

I

Watching himself in the mirror, Studs hitched up his football pants, carefully arranging the cotton hip pads around his sides. Wished he had better ones. Wouldn't be much protection from a boot in the ribs. He touched the schimmels under his blue jersey, and put on his black helmet. Every inch a football player!

He thought of himself going out to play with old street pants, a jersey, and football shoes. Dressed that way, tackling so hard he'd knock them cuckoo; jumping up ready to go on, no matter how hard he was slammed. No use to be senseless and play without sufficient padding. Only it was swell thinking of being reckless that way, having the crowd recognize such gameness.

He flexed and unflexed his arm muscles. Even with the drinking and carousing he'd done these last couple of years, he was still pretty hard and tough. He slapped his guts. They were hard enough, too, and there was no alderman yet, or not enough anyway to be noticed. And there never would be, because he'd take care of himself before that ever happened.

He'd never have a paunch like his old man had. Iron Man Lonigan! The bigger they are, the harder they fall. He lit a cigarette and sat on the bed, thinking proudly of his body, good and strong, even if he was small; powerful football shoulders, good for fighting. And this afternoon, he'd prove that it was a good body, and that there was heart and courage inside of it.

But there wouldn't be any girls out there for him to be playing for. Other guys had girls. Wished he had a girl, Lucy, a girl coming out only to see him play . . . Goofy! . . . But he still loved Lucy even if he hadn't seen her in about four years. And if she was coming out there to see him play, because she loved him, he would play much better, and instead of being in it just for the fun and the glory, and to show them all what he was made of, he'd be playing for her also. And he wanted to. Christ sake, he was getting like a clown, all mush inside. He tried to laugh at himself; it was forced.

Smells of the cooking Sunday dinner came tantalizingly from the kitchen. His mother came to the bedroom door, and said that she had a bite ready for him.

"I can't! I'm going to play football," he snapped in uncontrolled exasperation.

"I certainly don't think much of a game that deprives you of your food," she replied.

Jesus Christ! Couldn't she understand anything!

She nagged and persuaded. He got up, and walked towards the door, with her following, still wanting him to eat. He said that he couldn't play with a belly full of food, and as she dipped her hand in the holy water fount on the wall, and showered him, he slammed the door. The father, hearing him, called that he wouldn't have such vulgar language used around the home; but Studs was gone.

He went down the steps two and three at a time, thinking why they always had to be like that, never open to reason and sense, wanting you to do whatever they wished in everything. Felt like leaving home, and living in a room by himself; some day he'd have to, if they didn't keep from trying to run everything he did.

It was humid and sunless. He liked the click of his cleats on the sidewalk. He felt so good, and in such condition, that he had an impulse to run. He checked himself, and took his time. Studs Lonigan was going to use his noodle, and conserve his energy. He was a wise guy, and in everything in life he was going to be that way, always with a little stuff left in him for a pinch.

Jim Clayburn's dude father came along, dressed in snappy gray, wearing a derby, and tapping a cane on the sidewalk. With his gray bush of hair, his face looked soft, almost like a woman's. Must have been something of a sissy and teacher's pet in his own day at school, just as Jim had been. He bowed stiffly to Studs, and Studs nodded, hoping he noticed the football outfit. Jim was studying law now, clerking for a measly ten or fifteen bucks a week. Well, by the time Clayburn, with all his studying and kill-joy stuff was in the dough, Studs Lonigan would be running his old man's business, and be in the big dough too.

He saw Tubby Connell and Nate Klein flinging passes in the street in front of the poolroom. Nate muffed one, and Studs told him to get a bushel basket. He lit a cigarette and laughed at Nate's scenery; an old-fashioned square black helmet that must have come down from Walter Eckersall's day; tight green jersey with holes in the sleeves; pants so big that he swam in them; shoes turned up at the toes because of their size. He looked more closely at the shoes; they were spiked baseball ones. He told Nate they'd never let him play in those, because he might cut somebody to ribbons. Tubby said that Klein was wearing them to show that he had the Fifty-eighth Street fighting spirit.

"This ain't tiddledy-winks; the guy I cut up will be a Monitor, and that's his tough tiddy," Nate said, hard-boiled.

He and Tubby disregarded Stud's advice to save themselves, and went on fooling around with the ball. Studs turned his back to them, and let his hand fall on his hips; his helmet was over his right elbow, and his blond hair was a trifle curly. His broad face revealed absorption. A middle-aged guy with a paunch doped along; Studs hoped that the guy had noticed him, wished he was young like he was, and able to go out and play a game of football, still full of the vim and vitality of youth. A quick feeling of contrition came over him. Suppose he should get hurt? Suppose he should never come back alive? His mother would always remember how he had slammed the door in her face. But damn it, couldn't they be reasonable?

"Hell, Flannel Mouth! How's the brother?" asked Studs, as Young Fat Malloy showed up.

"He'll be there, and he was saying that if you guys lose your first game of the season, he was going to kick your tails around the block to hell and gone. And don't think he can't! He may be a little runt, but let me tell you, Hugo was one of the toughest sergeants they ever had in the army."

"I know it," Studs said, thinking that it was another case of a good little man.

"Look at Klein, that crazy hebe! He's liable to break his neck trying to catch that football!" Fat said.

"Yeah, he's that way because he got gassed in the war."

"But he has guts. You know, Studs, you guys ought to have a crack team this year. And with a good coach like Hugo, you oughtn't to lose a game."

Studs nodded. He thought that maybe, this year, they would all get to working together like a well-oiled machine, and then, next season they could join the Mid-West League. He saw himself flashing through that semi-pro circuit like a comet, and getting himself signed up to play in the backfield with Paddy Driscoll on the Chicago Cardinals.

There was excitement; a wild fling of Nate's nearly hit a baby being wheeled along. The father crabbed like hell, but finally pushed his buggy on. Nate told Studs that wise guys like that bird needed to be punched full of holes.

More players came around, and a gang of them started over to the football field in Washington Park.

II

Wearing a large white sweater, and his old army breeches, bow-legged Coach Hugo Zip Malloy stood with arms folded, his tough mug intent, as he watched the Fifty-eighth Street Cardinals clown through signal practice.

"Come on over here, you birds, and sit on your cans a minute. That's what they're for," he yelled, regally waving his short right arm.

The players dragged over and planked themselves down, facing him. Strangers collected to gape at them. He glared at the strangers.

"Everybody not associated with the team, please fade!" he commanded; some obeyed; others dropped backwards a few feet, and then commenced to inch forwards again. Courageous gawkers stood in their tracks.

Kenny Kilarney suddenly appeared, and did a take-off on a college cheer leader:

> We ain't rough!
> We ain't tough!
> But oh! . . . are we determined?

"Say, Monkey Face!" Coach Hugo said to Kenny.

"No hope for him," Bill Donoghue said.

"Now I want you birds to listen to what I tell you!"

"But say, Hugo?" Bill Donoghue called.

"That's my name."

"Would you mind taking the cigar out of your mouth so we can see you?"

"Sonnyboy, the playground is on the other side of the drive, in back of me," Coach Hugo replied.

"Another thing, coach. Don't you think we ought to give Klein a rising vote? He hasn't been hurt yet this season."

"Jesus, wouldn't the squirrels make mince-pie out of you?" Coach Hugo said, darting a no-hope look at Bill.

"Now, when the clowns get finished pulling the whiskers off their jokes, I'll talk. . . . And by the way, can't you guys leave the cigarettes alone for a minute. It takes wind to win a football game, and you don't get wind eating them coffin nails!"

"You tell 'em, coach, I stutter," said Shrimp Haggerty, lurching drunkenly into their midst; he was thin and sallow, and dogged out in classy clothes. He wore a black band on his top-coat sleeve.

"Haggerty! The other team needs a couple of mudguards. Go on over there," Coach Hugo said.

"Now that the children have finished throwing spitballs around, teacher will talk. . . . Haggerty, get the hell out of here before I have to throw your pieces away! . . . "

Haggerty saw that Coach Hugo was really sore. He staggered away, singing.

"All right, you birds, keep your dirty ears open! I ain't gonna repeat myself! You're goin' out there now for your first crack of the season, and you're gonna play a man's game. There's only one way to play it. Play hard! Hard! Get the other guy, before he gets you! Knock him down! Let them drag him out! If you don't, you might be the unlucky chump that's dragged out. And if any of you birds are carried off that gridiron, cold, don't expect me to break down and weep for you like I was your old lady! Because you won't get knocked cuckoo if you keep your heads up, and play hard! It's the soft guy that gets knocked silly in this game. And if there's any soft babies on this team, the sooner they get it in the neck, the better off they will be, and we too! You guys got to go in there and hit hard, hit often, and every time you hit, make the guy you hit think he's collided with a battleship. Don't worry about giving the ambulance drivers work; they got wives and kiddies to support, and need it. . . . ''

"Hey, Hugo, what undertaker's giving you a rakeoff?'' interrupted Arnold Sheehan.

"Sheehan, step into the second grade. You're too bright a boy for first. . . . And now, you birds, you're goin' in that football game in about a minute. If you want to win it, you got to do it yourself. I can't win it for you. That's your job, and if you want this game, you'll have to get it by fighting (he slammed his right fist demonstratively into his left palm). I watched you guys go through signal practice. You stunk! If you go into this game like that, it'll be like the Fort Dearborn massacre. And get me, if you guys don't fight, you can get an old lady to coach you. I won't. All right, snap into it. And, oh, yes, a final word. If any bird on this other team starts dirty work . . . give him the works!''

The team arose. Nate tore forwards. The others walked slowly towards the football field, Coach Hugo making up the rear.

"Say, coach, that's a ripe husky bunch of boys you got there. Tell 'em to try center rushes, and they'll win as easy as taking candy from a baby. Now, when I was a kid. . . . ''

"Say, fellow, will you do me a favor?''

"Sure, glad to, coach!''

"All right. See that automobile drive. Well, walk across it, and keep on going until you lose yourself in the lagoon.''

Coach Hugo roughly yelled gangway, as he went through a crowd, and stepped over the ropes. He clapped his hands together, and yelled to his team:

"All right, you guys, show me if you got any guts in your veins.''

III

C
Nate Klein

LG   RG
Harold Dowson   *Carroll Dowson*
LT   RT
Red Kelly   *Dan Donoghue*

FB
Hink Weber

LE   LHB   RHB   RE
Weary Reilley   *Arnold Sheehan*   *Art Hahn*   *Jim Nolan*

QB
Studs Lonigan

waited, while the ball was put into position for the kick. It fell off the little mound on the forty-yard line four times, so a Monitor stretched himself out and held it in position.

Referee Charlie Bathcellar, wearing an astrakhan coat and a new derby, importantly signalled the two captains. Studs felt a thrill of pride as he signalled the readiness of his team; hundreds of people were watching, saw that he was captain. The whistle blew. A thin fellow in street pants and an old red jersey booted the ball on a line. Studs muffed it. The Fifty-eighth Street Cardinals formed disorganized interference. Studs scooped the ball up on the go, and thundered forwards, head down as if he were bucking the line, knees pumping. One Monitor clutched at his left sleeve. Another pulled at his pants from behind. A third dragged at his jersey from the right side. A fourth leaped to make a flying tackle around his ears. The whistle declared the ball dead. Nate Klein and a Monitor player were in the center of the field, bucking each other with arms folded together chest high.

The Cardinals lackadaisically took position in a balanced line formation. The defensive Monitor line crowded together, both tackles kneeling down inside of Dan Donoghue and Red Kelly. Hink Weber told Kelly not to play standing up. Red knelt down. Hink told him to crouch low so that he could charge. Red gave Hink a soreheaded look, but squatted in a weak position.

"Signals," Studs yelled huskily, leaning with hands on knees, eyes on the ground.

Studs tossed a lateral pass to Arnold Sheehan, who went through a mile-wide hole at right tackle. The fellow in the red jersey, Jewboy Schwartz, plugged up the hole. Arnold started to pivot, and Jewboy Schwartz got him while off balance. Three Monitors piled on, and Arnold groaned.

"Watch that piling on!" Weary yelled, rushing up.

"We ain't piling on!" Jake Schaeffer, the big Monitor captain, retorted.

"Well, he was down, wasn't he?"

"He might have crawled."

Hink Weber drew Weary back to avoid a fight.

Arnold limped, his face twisted with pain. Nate angrily asked if they had played dirty, because if they did—the works. Taking short, ziggedy steps, Coach Hugo appeared. Arnold was helped to the sidelines, and as he sat down, Fat Malloy told him that he'd played a swell game.

Weary Reilley switched to left halfback, and Tubby Connell took Weary's end. On the next play, Studs slapped the ball into Hink's guts as Hink thundered at center, hitting like a ton of bricks. He fell over Nate Klein. Getting up, he just looked at Nate and shook his head. Nate said he had been holding out his man, hadn't he? Weary Reilley was tackled by Jewboy Schwartz after a three-yard gain. When the players picked themselves up, Nate Klein was stretched out, ostensibly hurt. Coach Hugo strode importantly onto the field, followed by Fat Malloy, who lugged a water bucket. Fat rushed to Nate, and doused him.

"For Jesus sake!" Nate protested.

"Well, you were out, weren't you?"

Nate groaned weakly, rose to tottering feet, and moved dazedly, with his head hanging as if his neck were broken. But he told Coach Hugo he would stick in the game and get those bastards. Coach Hugo called it the old ginger. Nate floundered into position over the ball, and his face became a mirror of jungle ferocity.

Hink Weber punted down the field, and it was the Monitors' ball.

Studs took a defensive position, twenty yards behind the scrimmage line, and placed his hands on his hips. People in the crowd might notice how collected he seemed to be. He might get his chance to be spectacular. A fellow might break through, and Studs would stave off a touchdown with a flying tackle. Jewboy Schwartz started around the end, outran Tubby, who was boxed in, dodged Weary's lunge with a side leap, graceful as an antelope, and tore towards Studs. Studs dashed forwards a few paces, arms encircled outwards and tensed himself. Schwartz came, fast. Five yards from Studs, Jewboy Schwartz performed a feint with his right foot. Studs lunged. Schwartz would have been free had he not slipped, and Studs, in his lunge, caught Schwartz's foot. Jewboy dragged Studs along, and slipped free, but Dan Donoghue was up to make the tackle.

They patted Studs' back for such nice work. Studs' glow of pride quickly faded. He had been out-smarted, and the fellow would have been free to make a touchdown if he hadn't slipped. He was only wearing street shoes. With cleats, he wouldn't have slipped. Studs waited in back of the scrimmage line. Next time, the guy might make a monkey of him. If he was playing the other half, he might not break through as easily because Jim Nolan and Dan were better than Red and Tubby. Studs' confidence seemed gone. The Jew was too speedy and clever for him. No, goddamn it, he'd leave his feet next time before that feint! Nail him! Studs moved forwards a few feet with the pass from center. Dan smeared the play for a loss. The teams lined up and Nate staggered into his place as defensive center.

The game see-sawed through the first quarter, slow, argumentative, marred by fumbles. On the last play of the period, Studs took a punt, ran forwards, swinging the ball from side to side for effect, running forwards, thinking he was making a long run, hearing cheering from the side, and . . . Jewboy Schwartz dove into him, his shoulder smashing Studs in the solar plexus. Studs went down with a thud, and lost the ball. His guts pained; he gasped. He slowly picked himself up, a sick expression on his face. The whistle saved him from having to call time out.

IV

Early in the second quarter, Jewboy Schwartz broke loose, and fleeted down the side line. Studs ran over, left his feet, smashed through the air as Schwartz sidestepped, and picked up speed again, rolled over offside four times in a histrionic effort to show the crowd that his try had been fearless and desperate, sat up and yelled to get him. Schwartz was over for a touchdown.

Studs' shame and disappointment was lessened a little when he heard Tommy Doyle call that it was a good try. The kick for extra point was missed. Hink and Weary walked by Studs, into position. Hink said that they would have to slow the Jew up with some rough tackling. Weary declared that if he got his guts slapped a couple of times, he'd slow down because Jews were yellow. Nate ran awkwardly to Studs and started bawling him out. Studs told Nate to freeze it. Nate megaphoned to all of them that they had to fight now. Studs waited, hands on knees, worrying himself, forgetting the crowd, thinking that they had to win, had to stop that fast Jew.

The Cardinals pepped up and shouted after taking the ball to the Monitor thirty-yard line on four plays. They were going over now, but on the next play Art Hahn went through tackle, and he was stopped by Red Kelly who stood in his way. Nate yelled to Red that it wasn't a sanitarium, and Red told him shut up while he was all together. Weary yelled to can the beefing and play football. Studs flung a pass. Jewboy Schwartz picked it neatly out of the air, and ran in the clear. Studs, playing safety, went for him without confidence, left his feet in a blind dive, opened his eyes as he encircled the Jew's slippery, powerful thighs, clenched them, tumbled him down. Hearing a cheer, he realized it had been neat work. He jumped up, forgetting that it had been lucky in the glory of being cheered. He walked casually away. The thrill of leaving his feet, rushing through the air, hitting him, dragging him down so nicely, lingered. He wanted to do it again. Weary patted his back, and called it a sweet tackle in the most genuine words he'd uttered to Studs since their fight. Studs felt good again. But, boy, that Jew was built like steel. Light and fast, and hard as nails. They'd need a club, or a tank, to put him out. Still, the memory of that tackle, a split second of keen release and thrill, hung with him.

Jim Nolan recovered on a bad pass from the Monitor center. Hink Weber took the ball on the first play, and ran forty yards down the left side of the field for a touchdown. He kicked the point after touchdown. The Fifty-eighth Street Cardinals talked to each other like happy children.

Jewboy Schwartz took the kickoff. His own men got in his way, and Weary tackled him. There was a pile on, and Weary jammed his knee into Schwartz's groin. They got off, and Schwartz lay there, moaning and rolling, with both hands gripping his crotch. Schaeffer rushed to Reilley and told him to cut it out. Weary snarled back that he didn't like people to talk with their tongues; fists spoke a harder language. Hink pulled Weary aside, and again avoided a fight.

Jewboy Schwartz tried to play. When he had to punt, his kick went weakly to Art Hahn. He limped off the field, and at the half, the Fifty-eighth Street Cardinals led seven to six.

V

Between halves, Coach Hugo Zip Malloy told his team they weren't hitting hard enough. He promised to buy a drink for every one who laid out a Monitor so that the guy stayed out. He told Austin McAuliffe to go in at quarter and unleash their trick plays, because Austin, a thin, weak-faced, red-haired chap, was a scientific player. Studs took Art Hahn's half, Arnold was to go back in, and Weary was to play end in place of Tubby. Bill Donoghue was to take Kelly's tackle.

Jewboy Schwartz was back and returned the kickoff twenty yards. Weary grouped the team together after the play, and said this time, they had to put that Jew out for keeps. Studs took his position at defensive half, keen to be more in the game, tackling, running the ends, bucking the line, smearing passes. Only they couldn't let the Jew get loose. Austin was a poor safety man. But they'd stop him dead now. He waited for the play, suddenly wishing he'd gone to high school and been a star like Dan had. Studs smashed in with the play, but Dan nabbed Schwartz behind the line. Schaeffer carried the ball on the next play. Arnold Sheehan was clipped from behind, and Schaeffer got twenty yards before Hink sliced into him from the side. Arnold went out with a wrenched knee, and Art Hahn came on the field. Nolan recovered a fumble. Austin called a trick play. The ball was passed from Austin to Studs to Hahn to Nolan, and eighteen yards were lost. Austin called another trick play, a quarterback sneak, and he circled backwards, running wide. Tacklers closed in on him. He outran them to the sideline for a twenty-five yard loss. Hink punted.

Schwartz took the ball on first down and came flying through tackle without interference. Dodging to break into the open, he was hit simultaneously by Studs, Weary, and Hink. He arose groggy.

"They'll be picking up the kike's pieces now," Weary said, walking off with Studs.

Schwartz started a wide end run. Nolan smashed in, and made a flying tackle, catching Jewboy by the heels to dump him on his head. The crowd could hear the thud. He lay unconscious. He was revived and insisted on playing. Jewboy dropped back to punt. Weary and Nate Klein broke through, and piled into him blocking the kick. He got up with a bloody nose, and a hand slightly scratched from Nate's spikes. There was a row, but Hink Weber sent Nate to the sidelines to borrow another pair of shoes.

Hink took the ball through the line. Schwartz dove for him, and was stiff-armed on the chin, his head jerking back as he flopped. Hink scored another touchdown.

Hink kicked off to Schwartz. Five Cardinals hit him. He was out again, bleeding from the mouth, his upper lip crusted with congealed blood from his nose. A Monitor yelled that he was dead. Jake Schaeffer helped carry him off and walked back onto the field in tears, vowing he'd get the sonsofbitches. Weary recovered a Monitor fumble, and Schaeffer piled on him.

"What's the idea?" Weary challenged, arising.

"Play football, and quit squawking. You half killed my buddy!"

"And I'll kill you too, kike!" Weary said, clipping Schaeffer on the jaw. Before he knew what hit him, Schaeffer got two more clouts, and went down.

"Get up and fight, louse!" Weary sneered, hovering over him.

Both teams started swinging. Spectators and substitutes rushed onto the field. The three cops, at the game, struggled in vain. One of them whistled loudly. Another fled to call for reenforcements. Hugo Malloy parted through the crowd with a billy. Three Monitors went for Weary. He laid two of them cold with punches, and picked the third up and tossed him four yards away. Studs caught him as he stumbled, and he went down. A fellow stepped on his face. Nate Klein kicked him, and was smacked in the eye from behind. He slunk towards the edge of the crowd. Weary shoved about, swinging when he had to, trying to find Schaeffer. He caught him, and let him have both guns. A billy came down on his shoulder. He wheeled around, getting force, and belted the guy with the billy, flush in the mouth, closed in, and gave him the knee. He kicked the guy for good measure.

A park cop grabbed Weary. He wriggled loose, slipped behind him, and gave him a rabbit punch. A bruiser, guard on the Monitors, slugged wildly at Studs. Studs ducked, in desperation at the guy's size, and swung blindly, landing in the guts. The ham's guard dropped, and he whittled down to Studs' size. Studs let an uppercut go from his heels and caught the fellow under the chin. The bruiser fled. Slug Mason came into action, pumping with both fists. He caught two guys, and crashed their heads together.

"The cops!" somebody yelled.

The cry was taken up. The mob separated in all directions. Police reenforcements came across the park, and clubs were swung, as everybody ran. Studs, running, passed a group carrying Schwartz.

"You bastards, come down to Forty-seventh Street!"

Studs turned and thumbed his nose. An opened pocketknife zizzed by his ears. He ran.

"Swell work, Studs!" said Fat Malloy ranging alongside of him. Shots in the distance were heard.

Studs came out of the park at Fifty-sixth Street, out of breath, his side paining.

VI

The poolroom was crowded. Rumors spread quickly. Talk went of arrests, broken heads, people dead. Studs passed along from one excited group to another, liking it all, the praise, the talk, the excitement. He came upon Arnold Sheehan, who had a sprained ankle, a twisted knee, and a shiner. He had been sitting down, and when the fighting came close, he had arisen and hobbled along the ropes. It had been just his luck to get sloughed in the eye. Weary tried to stir Studs up to go down to Forty-seventh. Nobody was interested. Fifty-eighth Street had won the game and the fight anyway, they all said. Nate came to tell Studs how he'd gloriously gotten his shiner. Young Rocky Kansas interrupted to tell how he had mashed in a big baboon. Studs knew they were liars. Guys always lied like that about how they fought, how they drank, how they jazzed. He told of hitting the big guy, and lied, too, saying he had knocked the guy cold with a punch. It was like being on a glorious jag, a little bit like it had been on Armistice Day.

He heard Dan Donoghue near him ask Danny O'Neill what he thought of the game.

"Most of them don't know how to play. They tackle high, can't block, don't even know how to play their position."

"Well, they are uncoached, but don't you think it was a fair bunch for an uncoached team?" ask Dan Donoghue.

Studs frowned when O'Neill superciliously answered yes. Remembered the punk when he ran around with his stockings falling and snot running out of his nose. Uncoached! Ought to slap his teeth! Seemed to think his was gold, droopy punk!

"That Schwartz is a player. I never tackled anybody as hard to get in my high school career with Loyola and I played against some tough men," Dan said.

"He was good. But some of the guys, Kelly, McAuliffe, and Klein, for instance, were jokes."

"What do you think of Studs?" asked Donoghue.

Studs tensed. Waited, Oughtn't to care what the punk thought. Waited.

"A bit slow, but he knows what to do, leaves his feet when he tackles and handles himself well."

"Studs is a natural-born football player," Donoghue said.

O'Neill wasn't so bad. Heard too that he was a high school star. Studs sidled to them.

"Now that you're a star on the team at the Saint Stanislaus high school, what did you think of our, . . amateur game?" Studs asked, fatuously.

Before O'Neill could answer, the rumor spread that Schwartz had died on the way to the hospital. Everybody gabbed and shouted at the same time.

"Will anything be done about it?" Studs asked Kelly.

"They might hold us for manslaughter."

"Why? We played a fair game. The fight was afterwards."

"Well, they might, only, of course, we'll get out of it, and anyway, besides, we were in the right. We can get drag through my old man, who's sergeant down at Fiftieth now, and your old man knowing politicians, and some other guys the same way," Red said.

"We can get enough witnesses," said Studs.

The rumor was still being discussed when Studs left for home. If they did throw them all in the jug! He saw himself in the pen for a manslaughter charge. But they couldn't get him. He'd played a clean game.

He realized how tired he was, and his shoulders drooped. But it had been a great game, and a great fight, and he could feel proud of his part in both. He'd showed them all. He remembered that first clean tackle he had made, leaving his feet, the way he smashed into the runner, that sudden rush of his body through the air for a split second, and bang, the guy was down. Hundreds of people, too, had seen it. He was nostalgic to be still playing, making tackles like that.

Dumb, too, not to have gone to high school. If punks like O'Neill could make the grade, what couldn't he have done? He cursed, though, realizing that they would lose their permit to play in Washington Park, and that they couldn't get up a good team to travel, particularly after a fight like this; because if they traveled and didn't have a big enough mob along, they'd get the clouts plenty somewhere. Damn Reilley! And just when the scrap had started, he had been getting into top form, he felt. But the fight, too, had been a wow. The way he had hit that big yellow bastard. Only, gee, he might have been a bigger star in the game than even Schwartz, if it hadn't started.

He stuck his shoulders back, and forced himself to walk briskly. Proud of himself and his body. In his prime right now.

He became aware that it was dark, and an autumn mist was settling over Fifty-eighth Street. Street lights were on at the alley between Indiana and Michigan. There were lights in windows. He heard the scrape of shoes in back of him, and the rumble of an elevated train. Down at State Street a street car was going, the bell donging. An automobile passed. The lonesome part of the day.

If Lucy had seen it, him! Well, what if he did admit to himself; he had played and acted like a hero!

That poor bastard Schwartz, game, had to grant that, lying dead in a hospital or morgue. It could have been him, perhaps. No, he knew he wouldn't die that way; he knew that he had some kind of a destiny to live for, and that he would live until that destiny was fulfilled. Maybe he would be a damn important guy later on, politician or something. That poor Jew bastard in a morgue. On the impulse, he mumbled a prayer for the guy!

The street around him seemed gloomy, and he was gloomy too. He couldn't get the thought of that dead Jew out of his mind. He didn't feel so cocky. He felt now like he wanted something in life, and didn't know what. That game and fight now, it had been swell. But there was something more he wanted than the glory of it, and he didn't even know what it was. Funny that he kept coming back to thoughts like this.

From BABBITT

Sinclair Lewis

Myra Babbitt—Mrs. George F. Babbitt—was definitely mature. She had creases from the corners of her mouth to the bottom of her chin, and her plump neck bagged. But the thing that marked her as having passed the line was that she no longer had reticences before her husband, and no longer worried about not having reticences. She was in a petticoat now, and corsets which bulged, and unaware of being seen in bulgy corsets. She had become so dully habituated to married life that in her full matronliness she was as sexless as an anemic nun. She was a good woman, a kind woman, a diligent woman, but no one, save perhaps Tinka her ten-year-old, was at all interested in her or entirely aware that she was alive.

After a rather thorough discussion of all the domestic and social aspects of towels she apologized to Babbitt for his having an alcoholic headache; and he recovered enough to endure the search for a B.V.D. undershirt which had, he pointed out, malevolently been concealed among his clean pajamas.

He was fairly amiable in the conference on the brown suit.

"What do you think, Myra?" He pawed at the clothes hunched on a chair in their bedroom, while she moved about mysteriously adjusting and patting her petticoat and, to his jaundiced eye, never seeming to get on with her dressing. "How about it? Shall I wear the brown suit another day?"

"Well, it looks awfully nice on you."

"I know, but gosh, it needs pressing."

"That's so. Perhaps it does."

"It certainly could stand being pressed, all right."

"Yes, perhaps it wouldn't hurt it to be pressed."

"But gee, the coat doesn't need pressing. No sense in having the whole darn suit pressed, when the coat doesn't need it."

"That's so."

"But the pants certainly need it, all right. Look at them—look at those wrinkles—the pants certainly do need pressing."

"That's so. Oh, Georgie, why couldn't you wear the brown coat with the blue trousers we were wondering what we'd do with them?"

"Good Lord! Did you ever in all my life know me to wear the coat of one suit and the pants of another? What do you think I am? A busted bookkeeper?"

"Well, why don't you put on the dark gray suit to-day, and stop in at the tailor and leave the brown trousers?"

"Well, they certainly need—Now where the devil is that gray suit? Oh, yes, here we are."

He was able to get through the other crises of dressing with comparative resoluteness and calm.

His first adornment was the sleeveless dimity B.V.D. undershirt, in which he resembled a small boy humorlessly wearing a cheesecloth tabard at a civic pageant. He never put on B.V.D.'s without thanking the God of Progress that he didn't wear tight, long, old-fashioned undergarments, like his father-in-law and partner, Henry Thompson. His second embellishment was combing and slicking back his hair. It gave him a tremendous forehead, arching up two inches beyond the former hair-line. But most wonder-working of all was the donning of his spectacles.

There is character in spectacles—the pretentious tortoiseshell, the meek pince-nez of the school teacher, the twisted silver-framed glasses of the old villager. Babbitt's spectacles had huge, circular, frameless lenses of the very best glass; the ear-pieces were thin bars of gold. In them he was the modern business man; one who gave orders to clerks and drove a car and played occasional golf and was scholarly in regard to Salesmanship. His head suddenly appeared not babyish but weighty, and you noted his heavy, blunt nose, his straight mouth and thick, long upper lip, his chin overfleshy but strong; with respect you beheld him put on the rest of his uniform as a Solid Citizen.

The gray suit was well cut, well made, and completely undistinguished. It was a standard suit. White piping on the V of the vest added a flavor of law and learning. His shoes were black laced boots, good boots, honest boots, standard boots, extraordinarily uninteresting boots. The only frivolity was in his purple knitted scarf. With considerable comment on the matter to Mrs. Babbitt (who, acrobatically fastening the back of her blouse to her skirt with a safety-pin, did not hear a word he said), he chose between the purple scarf and a tapestry effect with stringless brown harps among blown palms, and into it he thrust a snake-head pin with opal eyes.

A sensational event was changing from the brown suit to the gray the contents of his pockets. He was earnest about these objects. They were of eternal importance, like baseball or the Republican Party. They included a fountain pen and a silver pencil (always lacking a supply of new leads) which belonged in the righthand upper vest pocket. Without them he would have felt naked. On his watch-chain were a gold penknife, silver cigar-cutter, seven keys (the use of two of which he had forgotten), and incidentally a good watch. Depending from the chain was a large, yellowish elk's-tooth—proclamation of his membership in the Brotherly and Protective Order of Elks. Most significant of all was his loose-leaf pocket note-book, that modern and efficient note-book which contained the addresses of people whom he had forgotten, prudent memoranda of postal money-orders which had reached their destinations months ago, stamps which had lost their mucilage, clippings of verses by T. Cholmondeley Frink and of the newspaper editorials from which Babbitt got his opinions and his polysyllables, notes to be sure and do things which he did not intend to do, and one curious inscription—D.S.S.D.M.Y.P.D.F.

But he had no cigarette-case. No one had ever happened to give him one, so he hadn't the habit, and people who carried cigarette-cases he regarded as effeminate.

Last, he stuck in his lapel the Boosters' Club button. With the conciseness of great art the button displayed two words: "Boosters—Pep!" It made Babbitt feel loyal and important. It associated him with Good Fellows, with men who were nice and human, and important in business circles. It was his V.C., his Legion of Honor ribbon, his Phi Beta Kappa key.

With the subtleties of dressing ran other complex worries. "I feel kind of punk this morning," he said. "I think I had too much dinner last evening. You oughtn't to serve those heavy banana fritters."

"But you asked me to have some."

"I know, but—I tell you, when a fellow gets past forty he has to look after his digestion. There's a lot of fellows that don't take proper care of themselves. I tell you at forty a man's a fool or his doctor—I mean, his own doctor. Folks don't give enough attention to this matter of dieting. Now I think— Course a man ought to have a good meal after the day's work, but it would be a good thing for both of us if we took lighter lunches.''

"But Georgie, here at home I always do have a light lunch."

"Mean to imply I make a hog of myself, eating down-town? Yes, sure! You'd have a swell time if you had to eat the truck that new steward hands out to us at the Athletic Club! But I certainly do feel out of sorts, this morning. Funny, got a pain down here on the left side—but no, that wouldn't be appendicitis, would it? Last night, when I was driving over to Verg Gunch's, I felt a pain in my stomach, too. Right here it was—kind of a sharp shooting pain. I—Where'd that dime go to? Why don't you serve more prunes at breakfast? Of course I eat an apple every evening—an apple a day keeps the doctor away—but still, you ought to have more prunes, and not all these fancy doodads.''

"The last time I had prunes you didn't eat them."

"Well, I didn't feel like eating 'em, I suppose. Matter of fact, I think I did eat some of 'em. Anyway—I tell you it's mighty important to—I was saying to Verg Gunch, just last evening, most people don't take sufficient care of their diges—''

"Shall we have the Gunches for our dinner, next week?"

"Why sure; you bet."

"Now see here, George: I want you to put on your nice dinner-jacket that evening."

"Rats! The rest of 'em won't want to dress."

"Of course they will. You remember when you didn't dress for the Littlefields' supper-party, and all the rest did, and how embarrassed you were."

"Embarrassed, hell! I wasn't embarrassed. Everybody knows I can put on as expensive a Tux. as anybody else, and I should worry if I don't happen to have it on sometimes. All a darn nuisance, anyway. All right for a woman, that stays around the house all the time, but when a fellow's worked like the dickens all day, he doesn't want to go and hustle his head off getting into the soup-and-fish for a lot of folks that he's seen in just reg'lar ordinary clothes that same day."

"You know you enjoy being seen in one. The other evening you admitted you were glad I'd insisted on your dressing. You said you felt a lot better for it. And oh, Georgie, I do wish you wouldn't say 'Tux.' It's 'dinner-jacket.' ''

"Rats, what's the odds?"

"Well, it's what all the nice folks say. Suppose Lucile McKelvey heard you calling it a 'Tux.'"

"Well, that's all right now! Lucile McKelvey can't pull anything on me! Her folks are common as mud, even if her husband and her dad are millionaires! I suppose you're trying to rub in *your* exalted social position! Well, let me tell you that your revered paternal ancestor, Henry T., doesn't even call it a 'Tux.'! He calls it a 'bobtail jacket for a ringtail monkey', and you couldn't get him into one unless you chloroformed him!"

"Now don't be horrid, George."

"Well, I don't want to be horrid, but Lord! you're getting as fussy as Verona. Ever since she got out of college she's been too rambunctious to live with—doesn't know what she wants—well, I know what she wants!—all she wants is to marry a millionaire, and live in Europe, and hold some preacher's hand, and simultaneously at the same time stay right here in Zenith and be some blooming kind of a socialist agitator or boss charity-worker or some damn thing! Lord, and Ted is just as bad! He wants to go to college, and he doesn't want to go to college. Only one of the three that knows her own mind is Tinka. Simply can't understand how I ever came to have a pair of shillyshallying children like Rone and Ted. I may not be any Rockefeller or James J. Shakespeare, but I certainly do know my own mind, and I do keep right on plugging along in the office and—Do you know the latest? Far as I can figure out, Ted's new bee is he'd like to be a movie actor and—And here I've told him a hundred times, if he'll go to college and law-school and make good, I'll set him up in business and —Verona just exactly as bad. Doesn't know what she wants. Well, well, come on! Aren't you ready yet? The girl rang the bell three minutes ago."

FRONT MAN IN LINE

Nancy Huddleston Packer

"Dapper Dan, the ladies' man, here comes your boyfriend, Miriam, here comes your boyfriend ugh." That was Sherry Wilkins, not quite twenty, still supporting (it gave Miriam pleasure to note) that hill country Baptist preacher voice that was the perfect vehicle, God-made, for reprimand and outrage. Oh, if you turned around to see her, you saw certain natural and undeniable attractions encased in what you could not distinguish from any Hollywood tart. That unbeatable combination of being young, glamorous, and right.

But why should Miriam waste her moments, her nerves vilifying the girl? Because Miriam was deeply implicated and it sickened her. For, indeed, there he did come, Dapper Dan, the ladies' man, straight at Miriam, his destination, his destiny as he sometimes said.

Helped to the curb by the chauffeur, his powder-blue, pouter-pigeon wife issuing last-minute cautions from the back seat, he dragged along behind his silver-headed cane, frail and salacious. He was gallant, wanton, and over eighty. His black shoes, his cream suit, his vast pearl stickpin, his lifeless wisps of yellowed hair floating in the breeze were advertisement of him. He fairly glistened, inside and out. He considered himself a rake. Nearly everyone else considered him a bother and an old fool. However, he was Daniel Shirer, Dapper Dan Shirer, and his name rang like a cash register in the city. No one swept him off the doorstep when he made his biweekly pilgrimage to his money.

Miriam Labadie, born Sims in better days and now forty-six, a widow, a receptionist-stenographer in an investment house, was never caught napping by the old reprobate, although he tried to sneak in noiselessly to steal a free pat on her arm. Always she heard his cane tip-tapping along the vinyl floor, and she turned before he could touch her. The office manager accepted the old man's attentions to her and pretended to think that Miriam deserved the credit for the old man's account. The girl, Sherry Wilkins, accepted nothing, pretended nothing, credited no one.

Miriam wished the old man would forget her, devil take the firm. It was a biweekly ordeal a fastidious woman ought not to endure. She tried to be distant and courteous, but her smiles felt like trapped dying mice. Her most casual good-mornings were assumed by him to be offerings, seductions. Mr. Shirer's hand, raised, seemed to ache to pat her on the bottom. Sometimes her hand ached to slap his hand; sometimes, God help her, her bottom ached to be patted. Time and circumstance had reduced Daniel Shirer to this and her to Daniel Shirer. Imminent humiliation dampened her spirits. She liked the old man.

She kept at her typewriter until he was almost upon her. Cat and mouse, but she didn't want that hand plying at her flesh. And yet she was, and admitted it, still coquette enough to be glad to see a bit of expectancy rise on a man's face, even that man's. She saved herself from his touch at the last moment, came swiveling around to face him across the mahogany railing.

"Why, Mr. Shirer," she said, "I was afraid you weren't coming."

"Am I late? Am I late?" Distracted, he hauled from his watch pocket a giant gold timepiece, as old as himself, and peered through faded eyes at its faded face. He loathed being late on his rounds about the city. He had once confided in her: I'm rich for being on time, I'm watching the old ticker tape while the slugabeds are going broke.

"Right on the button as always," she said. "I set my watch by you."

"Time is money," he said. And then something—a visceral ticking, a pain in his leg, the skipping of a heartbeat—brought him back to what was now more important than time and money. His eyes glinted. Lust, Miriam thought, he can't stay off it. "I've brought you something," he said, jerking his shoulder to indicate the hand held behind his back. Another stolen offering, she thought, but before she could pretend any interest, the young righteous voice behind her said, "Mr. O'Neal said when and *if* you get free, Miriam."

Shirer stepped back as if someone had shoved him. "I'm keeping you," he said, sagging. "You'd rather be doing something else."

Forget her, Miriam wanted to say, she's just young. "Rather work than talk to you? Never," she answered, giving him her very kind smile. He stared at her, wanting more. She gave more. "I'd rather talk to you than most anything."

"Ah, now, Mrs. Labadie, most anything?" he said quite quickly, leering at her, as sly as a rat, a nasty old man once again.

Surely he was more than that. Something had guided him safely over the eighty years to here. Intelligence, they said, not just money-shrewd but real intelligence, a moderate man, quite the gentleman, reserved like his time, but, they said as sadly they shook their heads, he just didn't have time to get done with his skirt-chasing. Of course not, Miriam thought ruefully, save the skirt-chasing until too late and inappropriate, and then, even then, direct it at a middle-aged woman who was insulted and grateful.

And with that thought, she felt compelled to remove herself from him, to show that she was not conniving with him and, God forbid, enjoying his advances. "I do have work to do," she said.

"Did I offend you?" he asked, in bewildered innocence. "I didn't go to do it. Why would an old codger like me ever offend a pretty young lady like yourself?" He gleamed at his words and eagerly pressed the advantage he thought he had gained. "Why if I got paid I don't think I could, it'd be asking too much of an old man who thinks as highly of you as I do. You know I think highly of you, don't you?" His gaze pinched her and he waited for an answer.

"I know," she said, and she did, and she was ashamed of herself for the anger, slight as it was, and she was angry with everyone. She flashed him her middle-aged gaiety smile, and pointed at his concealed hand. Get on with it, hand me the withered chrysanthemums you snitched from your wife's centerpiece. But this time it wasn't flowers.

"This is for you," he said, holding forth a two-pound box of candy. His grand proud gesture justified a diamond of equal size. "All chocolate, every one of them chocolate. Didn't you say any flavor was all right just so long as it was chocolate?"

"I did," she said, "I made that clever remark." He missed that and she was glad. Always, it seemed, she had a smart-aleck comment and always she regretted it. The box had no cellophane wrapping, which he instantly became aware of.

"I took the cover off, to be sure it was chocolate," he explained. "Can't trust the merchants these days."

She knew he had not bought it but merely slipped it out from home. He never really bought her anything, apparently he was too close-fisted for that. Instead, he robbed his own or his wife's possessions and brought Miriam the loot. And what a sorry loot it usually was.

Once he had brought her a little silver bonbon dish, slightly tarnished, wrapped in a wrinkled grocery sack and tied with string. Written across the sack in his large bold quavering hand was: To Miriam Labadie with highest esteem, from her no longer secret admirer. Feeling foolish and disloyal, Miriam telephoned his wife, herself approaching eighty but no less formidable for that, and reported the gift which she then sent out by the firm's messenger. From then on she had known where the withered flowers and the half-eaten boxes of candy and the yellowing handkerchiefs came from, but she did not betray him again. She did not want to hear his wife again say, "He's gotten a little senile is why he bothers you." "Oh we all just love him," said Miriam. "He doesn't bother me."

And who knew, really, if there was more bother than pleasure in his gallant attentions? Not Miriam Labadie, alone in her apartment, arranging withered flowers, tasting stale chocolates, and laughing to herself over her crazy senile gallant old and only beau, God help her.

As she opened the box and dug among the candies, avidly he watched her, and as he watched he raised his hand toward and above her. She feared that hand coming down on her, her shoulder, her breast, seeking payment for the candy she accepted only out of kindness. She pushed herself from the railing and Mr. Shirer's hand fell back upon himself, fingering his pearl stickpin, and the disappointment on his face turned to confusion. She had seen it happen before. Thwarted, he seemed to lose direction and become helpless, an old man no longer dapper, merely pitiful.

"Let me call Mr. O'Neal for you," she said, placing him. "You want Mr. O'Neal now, don't you?"

"I want you," he said. His intention reformed and he stayed her with a gesture. Slyly he finished, "for a bit of lunch perhaps?" His hands, palms toward her, begged her to be gentle for he was at her mercy. No harm meant, he seemed to say, and yet his demands, his desires, grew each week, as if fed on her refusals. A walk to the bus stop, or coffee, a ride home with him and his chauffeur, and now lunch. What would it be next time? Would he finally march in and say Let's go to bed?

"If you keep bringing me candy like this I'll never be able to eat lunch again."

Usually he accepted defeat gracefully, as if even a No from her was pleasure.

"I won't be bringing you candy much longer," he said. He gazed around the room and spoke, not directly to her, but more to himself, in a very private voice.

"I'm sorry you feel that way about it, Mr. Shirer," said Miriam. "I always lunch with the other girls and . . . "

"I'll be dead," he said, "I won't be in this race much longer." His expression was vague and unfocused and his voice was self-pitying and begging pity. But to acknowledge that was to involve herself more deeply, which she resented very much. She said, in an airy casual voice, "What a thing to say. Your kind lasts forever, you'll be here long after the rest of us are gone."

Empty, idle, lying words, but he liked them. Perceptibly he brightened, straightened, tightened. His hand rose toward her and as it did she had a vision.

A long long endlessly long chain of bedraggled people, walking without rhythm and out of step, more like a fleeing mass than an army. She saw herself somewhere near the middle, rather tall and erect and staring and perhaps set apart just a little. The mass thinned out toward the front, looked worn and old and exhausted, walked in staggers, barely upright, as dry as winter trees. And out in front of all, a high step or two ahead, was Daniel Shirer, going on and on and on, jaunty as he staggered, lustful, pursuing, eager, his raised searching hand falling back upon his pearl stickpin and then rising again and again and again.

"You're the leader of the whole band of us," she said. "What would we do without you?"

"I like to hear you say that," he said, as grateful as a child. He reached to touch her hand, so gently that she did not move it. "You've got a way with you a man likes, Mrs. Labadie. I talk with you and by God I decide maybe I'll just live forever. You stay as pretty and sweet as you are and they'll have to send down a brigade of armed angels to get me. Yessir, at least a brigade." His hand went to her wrist and she said, withdrawing her hand, "I'll lose my job if I don't get to work. You better go see Mr. O'Neal."

"Quite right," he said. Out came the gold watch and off he dragged.

Just before disappearing into O'Neal's office, he cocked his head back to Miriam. "I'll be back for a little piece of chocolate, though."

"He means a little piece of you," said Sherry Wilkins. "I just wouldn't put up with that. I just wouldn't."

Miriam did not respond. Twice a week she had to endure the two of them, the wheedling of the old, the contempt of the young. Did they quarrel through her? When she turned back to her work, letters announcing the purchase of this, the sale of that, she could not concentrate. She was not exactly ruffled, but she had felt a flutter of sensitivity with the old man, as if unwanted feeling had almost surfaced. And yet she was accustomed to the old man and their ritual of tease and flirtation and titillation and rejection. That was hardly new.

Pretty and sweet he had called her. Was that it? And she had called him the leader of the band. She saw him that way, the leader, the front man, the oldest man she knew, it was no lie. Nor, by the same token, had he done more than say for that moment what he saw. He had laid no claim to immortal truth. He merely saw her pretty and sweet, instead of forty-six and atrophied in widowhood and lonely. Sweet, yes, perhaps. Perhaps even pretty. A little. Still. Still a little pretty. Miriam thought that she would like to wash her hands where he had touched her.

"I think I'll wash my hands," she announced to no one.

"I don't blame you," said Sherry.

"O hush," said Miriam. "Leave him be, he's just a harmless old man." She sat back down.

"Dirty old man, I think they call it. Honestly, Miriam, you just ask for it. Not that you asked me but in my experience a man . . ."

"What experience?" asked Miriam.

"What?"

"A nineteen-year-old Romeo? Some thirty-year-old sophisticate you wrestled best two out of three in the back seat of a taxi? Or your grandfather, that dirty old man?"

"I never claimed . . ."

"You're young," said Miriam. "You don't know anything. You have no idea what it means to be nearly fifty and alone."

"Fifty? Why he hasn't been anywheres near fifty in over thirty years." She paused, ignored her stupidity, prissed her lips and prepared her face for a venture into wit. "In thirty years the nearest he's been to fifty is trying to put his hands all over you."

"I'm nearly fifty," said Miriam. She felt she wore the soiled look of an old lascivious woman.

"Oh you," said the girl, forgiving the quarrel. Her smile condescended to the difference between them.

Carrying with her the damaged image of herself, Miriam turned away. Did the girl not hear the whisperings of time and circumstance? Apple breasts she had, high on a stiff proud body, and a firm ungirdled untouched bottom. Hands off, everybody. And not from prudery or a desire to barter, but from arrogance and ignorance, as if what counted was the body and the hand, objects, without meaning until there was a touch between. A murky, smeared, and far-distant picture flicked in Miriam's fantasy—hinting sex between herself and Daniel Shirer—and was thrust away instantly, violent, so that seconds later she would have sworn she had not seen it.

Not fifteen minutes had passed when Shirer came out of Mr. O'Neal's office, with alacrity, as if sprung from jail, aiming right for her. Miriam thought that none of the men of her generation, surely not a younger one, would ever know how to flatter a woman with an approach like that, shy, eager, gallant, his expression begging sufferance. Miriam was preparing to give him back a little appreciation and welcome when a sound like a snort-sneer came from the girl. Miriam looked down at her typewriter. I live in this office, in this world, Dapper Dan, she said very distinctly to herself, with the likes of her, leave me alone, Dapper Dan, pass me by with barely a nod.

"Why, Mr. Shirer, back so soon?" she said.

"Soon? Why, time's winged chariot just won't move when I'm away from you, Mrs. Labadie." He grinned at her expectantly, demanding a response.

"You have world enough and time," she said.

"Ah, Miriam," he said, chewing on her name, tasting it in his mouth, and inviting her to invite him to use it. "Miriam, Miriam, a fine old name. They don't seem to use the good ones any more. Candace O'Brien, Sharon Cohen, Michele Jones, names that don't mean a thing any more. But then the young ones don't amount to much either, never will be the woman you are, Miriam, Mrs. Labadie. You're a real woman and they're just the rouge and perfume they wear, that's all."

Miriam enjoyed the discomfort that would cause the girl behind her, and momentarily she wondered if the old man had been deliberately mean. But she knew what he was really doing, persuading her to let him enjoy the intimacy of her given name.

"What's your wife's name?" she asked, like a foolish young girl on guard against the blandishments of married men. She felt so silly.

"Ruth," he said with a dismissing wave of his hand. He looked shrewd. "Which reminds me, she's been after me to get you to take supper with us one night real soon. How does that strike you?"

"I don't even know your wife," said Miriam.

"She knows you, though. You think I don't talk about you at home?" He smirked a bit and leaned closer to her. "Why, you won't believe it but she's a jealous woman, as old as we are, and it's you got her going these days." He stepped back to see his effect.

"How perfectly foolish," said Miriam, and she meant it two ways, the social disclaimer and the deep disgust.

"I wouldn't say that," said Mr. Shirer. He came again to the railing and leaned across, balanced so precariously at his belt that Miriam was afraid his legs would fly up and she'd have him in her lap. He whispered, "She's not much wife to me these days and she knows it."

His breath, metallic and stale with dentures and age, flowed over her and she drew back. "I won't tolerate that kind of talk," she said. With the flush rising through her neck, she whipped her chair around and commenced to pick at the typewriter. She saw from the outside range of her vision that Mr. Shirer had slumped, barely upright, against the railing with his head abjectly on his chest.

"I don't know why I say things like that," he said. "I don't mean to offend you. What is it happens to a man that he goes around insulting young ladies? And we do, almost all of us old men do. Is it a way of proving we're alive?"

His face was as intelligent and moderate, as focused and thoughtful, as she was sure it had been in his good years. Miriam felt awkward and indecisive and she was torn between wanting to comfort and forgive him and wanting to use this for a final break with him.

"Mr. O'Neal just rang for you," said the voice behind her, condescending again, saving Miriam from her own weakness. In a stroke of outrage and pride, Miriam swung toward the voice.

"O'Neal can wait," she said, "and you too." The young face, pretty, righteous, and petty, filled her with rage. What good were the young to her, she had lost them long ago. "You just mind that little self of yours, you hear?"

She swiveled back to Mr. Shirer, expecting to see that his spirits had ascended on the power of her words, her acceptance of him. Apparently they had not registered on him, for he looked whipped and thoughtful, musing on himself.

"First you forget the names," he said. "Then you forget the faces. Then you forget to button your pants, and then you forget to unbutton them. That has happened to me. And some place along the line you want the young women, you begin dreaming of the young women. To keep you alive, I guess. Like Solomon."

"None of that," said Miriam, cheery and coy. "I won't have that talk from a gallant old . . . buzzard like you. Why, it's a reflection on me, don't you see, a terrible reflection. If it's only because you're old, then it's not because I'm . . . well, because I'm what I hope I am anyway."

His smile was bleak, knowing, self-pitying. She recognized her failure and she rose from her chair and leaned across the railing to pull him closer to her. She pecked at his cheek with her lips.

"I never did thank you for the chocolates," she said. She thought she had done quite a nice thing and she was annoyed when his nod of gratitude was perfunctory.

"They were my wife's," he said. "I look generous at her expense. Your expense. Her expense. At my age you stay alive at somebody else's expense. If I were God I wouldn't let us."

You just keep on staying alive, she wanted to say to him. She sought for a clue, a better word, a gesture to redeem the moment. Calculations and plans flashed through her mind, inane, pointless, selfish, as perfunctory as her kissing gift had been, and as doomed to failure. She watched him slowly dying before her eyes. And, helpless, at last instinct happened to her and in its darkness she went unerringly to her own inviting and submissive heart, and thus to his.

"If I were your wife, I'd feed you chocolates all day long and at night I'd just eat you up."

She thought someone else had spoken the words, their echo sounded so abandoned and shameless. Miriam Labadie? Never. But his face shifted toward lust and longing again and she knew that she had served him well. With malice he appraised her, and as he pressed across the railing, her instinct guttered and she was her prim proud self again. But she determined to be staunch. The instant before she closed her eyes she saw his hand flick out like a claw, willful and greedy. In her deliberate blindness, she felt his squeezing pat on her thigh.

When seconds later she opened her eyes, he was already departing, a look on his face of triumph and dominance and liberty and lust.

"See you Thursday," said Miriam. He glanced back and winked at her and that wink promised more more more. His need was insatiable, but so too was her own. She hoped he would live forever.

Outside the door, one hand grasping his cane, the other fingering his pearl stickpin, he joined the mass of people moving by her window. He was frail and jaunty and dapper and alive. Gaily she waved her hand for all her world to see. Pretty and sweet she felt, and safe for the time. Intently she watched him until he was out of sight.

From GULLIVER'S TRAVELS

Jonathan Swift

The Luggnaggians are a polite and generous people, and although they are not without some share of that pride which is peculiar to all Eastern countries, yet they show themselves courteous to strangers, especially such who are countenanced by the court. I had many acquaintance among persons of the best fashion, and being always attended by my interpreter, the conversation we had was not disagreeable.

One day in much good company I was asked by a person of quality, whether I had seen any of their *Struldbrugs*, or *Immortals*. I said I had not, and desired he would explain to me what he meant by such an appellation applied to a mortal creature. He told me, that sometimes, though very rarely, a child happened to be born in a family with a red circular spot in the forehead, directly over the left eyebrow, which was an infallible mark that it should never die. The spot, as he described it, was about the compass of a silver three pence, but in the course of time grew larger, and changed its colour; for at twelve years old it became green, so continued till five and twenty, then turned to a deep blue: at five and forty it grew coal black, and as large as an English shilling, but never admitted any further alteration. He said these births were so rare, that he did not believe there could be above eleven hundred *struldbrugs* of both sexes in the whole kingdom, of which he computed about fifty in the metropolis, and among the rest a young girl born about three years ago. That these productions were not

---

Reprinted from *Gulliver's Travels*, by Jonathan Swift. Norwood, Mass.: Norwood Press, 1917. Copyright 1917 by the Macmillan Company.

peculiar to any family, but a mere effect of chance; and the children of the *struldbrugs* themselves, were equally mortal with the rest of the people.

I freely own myself to have been struck with inexpressible delight upon hearing this account, and the person who gave it me happening to understand the Balnibarbian language, which I spoke very well, I could not forbear breaking out into expressions perhaps a little too extravagant. I cried out as in a rapture; Happy nation where every child hath at least a chance of being immortal! Happy people who enjoy so many living examples of ancient virtue, and have masters ready to instruct them in the wisdom of all former ages! but, happiest beyond all comparison are those excellent *struldbrugs*, who being born exempt from that universal calamity of human nature, have their minds free and disengaged, without the weight and depression of spirits caused by the continual apprehension of death. I discovered my admiration that I had not observed any of these illustrious persons at court; the black spot on the forehead being so remarkable a distinction, that I could not have easily overlooked it: and it was impossible that his Majesty, a most judicious prince, should not provide himself with a good number of such wise and able counsellors. Yet perhaps the virtue of those reverent sages was too strict for the corrupt and libertine manners of a court. And we often find by experience that young men are too opinionative and volatile to be guided by the sober dictates of their seniors. However, since the King was pleased to allow me access to his royal person, I was resolved upon the very first occasion to deliver my opinion to him on this matter freely, and at large by the help of my interpreter; and whether he would please to take my advice or no, yet in one thing I was determined, that his Majesty having frequently offered me an establishment in this country, I would with great thankfulness accept the favour, and pass my life here in the conversation of those superior beings the *struldbrugs*, if they would please to admit me.

The gentleman to whom I addressed my discourse, because (as I have already observed) he spoke the language of Balnibarbi, said to me with a sort of a smile, which usually ariseth from pity to the ignorant, that he was glad of any occasion to keep me among them, and desired my permission to explain to the company what I had spoke. He did so, and they talked together for some time in their own language, whereof I understood not a syllable, neither could I observe by their countenances what impression my discourse had made on them. After a short silence, the same person told me, that his friends and mine (so he thought fit to express himself) were very much pleased with the judicious remarks I had made on the great happiness and advantages of immortal life; and they were desirous to know in a particular manner, what scheme of living I should have formed to myself, if it had fallen to my lot to have been born a *struldbrug*.

I answered, it was easy to be eloquent on so copious and delightful a subject, especially to me who have been often apt to amuse myself with visions of what I should do if I were a king, a general, or a great lord: and upon this very case I had frequently run over the whole system how I should employ myself, and pass the time if I were sure to live for ever.

That, if it had been my good fortune to come into the world a *struldbrug*, as soon as I could discover my own happiness by understanding the difference between life and death, I would first resolve by all arts and methods whatsoever to procure myself riches. In the pursuit of which by thrift and management, I might reasonably expect in about two hundred years, to be the wealthiest man in the kingdom. In the second place, I would from my earliest youth apply myself to the study of arts and sciences, by which I should arrive in time to excel all others in learning. Lastly, I would carefully record every action and event of consequence that happened in the public, impartially draw the characters of the several successions of princes and great ministers of state, with my own observations on every point. I would exactly set down the several changes in customs, language, fashions of dress, diet, and diversions. By all which acquirements, I should be a living treasury of knowledge and wisdom, and certainly become the oracle of the nation.

I would never marry after threescore, but live in an hospitable manner, yet still on the saving side. I would entertain myself in forming and directing the minds of hopeful young men, by convincing them from my own remembrance, experience and observation, fortified by numerous examples, of the usefulness of virtue in public and private life. But my choice and constant companions should be a set of my own immortal brotherhood, among whom I would elect a dozen from the most ancient down to my own contemporaries. Where any of these wanted fortunes, I would provide them with convenient lodges round my own estate, and have some of them always at my table, only mingling a few of the most valuable among you mortals, whom length of time would harden me to lose with little or no reluctance, and treat your posterity after the same manner; just as a man diverts himself with the annual succession of pinks and tulips in his garden, without regretting the loss of those which withered the preceding year.

These *struldbrugs* and I would mutually communicate our observations and memorials through the course of time, remark the several gradations by which corruption steals into the world, and oppose it in every step, by giving perpetual warning and instruction to mankind; which, added to the strong influence of our own example, would probably prevent that continual degeneracy of human nature so justly complained of in all ages.

Add to all this, the pleasure of seeing the various revolutions of states and empires, the changes in the lower and upper world, ancient cities in ruins, and obscure villages become the seats of kings. Famous rivers lessening into shallow brooks, the ocean leaving one coast dry, and overwhelming another: the discovery of many countries yet unknown. Barbarity over-running the politest nations, and the most barbarous become civilized. I should then see the discovery of the longitude, the perpetual motion, the universal medicine, and many other great inventions brought to the utmost perfection.

What wonderful discoveries should we make in astronomy, by outliving and confirming our own predictions, by observing the progress and returns of comets, with the changes of motion in the sun, moon, and stars.

I enlarged upon many other topics, which the natural desire of endless life and sublunary happiness could easily furnish me with. When I had ended, and the sum of my discourse had been interpreted as before, to the rest of the company, there was a good deal of talk among them in the language of the country, not without some laughter at my expense. At last the same gentleman who had been my interpreter said, he was desired by the rest to set me right in a few mistakes, which I had fallen into through the common imbecility of human nature, and upon that allowance was less answerable for them. That this breed of *struldbrugs* was peculiar to their country, for there were no such people either in Balnibarbi or Japan, where he had the honour to be ambassador from his Majesty, and found the natives in both those kingdoms very hard to believe that the fact was possible; and it appeared from my astonishment when he first mentioned the matter to me, that I received it as a thing wholly new, and scarcely to be credited. That in the two kingdoms above mentioned, where during his residence he had conversed very much, he observed long life to be the universal desire and wish of mankind. That whoever had one foot in the grave, was sure to hold back the other as strongly as he could. That the oldest had still hopes of living one day longer, and looked on death as the greatest evil, from which nature always prompted him to retreat; only in this island of Luggnagg the appetite for living was not so eager, from the continual example of the *struldbrugs* before their eyes.

That the system of living contrived by me was unreasonable and unjust, because it supposed a perpetuity of youth, health, and vigour, which no man could be so foolish to hope, however extravagant he may be in his wishes. That the question therefore was not whether a man would choose to be always in the prime of youth, attended with prosperity and health, but how he would pass a perpetual life under all the usual disadvantages which old age brings along with it. For although few men will avow their desires of being immortal upon such hard conditions, yet in the two kingdoms before mentioned of Balnibarbi and Japan, he observed that every man desired to put off death for some time longer, let it approach ever so late; and he rarely heard of any man who died willingly, except he were incited by the extremity of grief or torture. And he appealed to me whether in those countries I had travelled as well as my own, I had not observed the same general disposition.

After this preface, he gave me a particular account of the *struldbrugs* among them. He said they commonly acted like mortals, till about thirty years old, after which by degrees they grew melancholy and dejected, increasing in both till they came to fourscore. This he learned from their own confession: for otherwise there not being above two or three of that species born in an age, they were too few to form a general observation by. When they came to fourscore years, which is reckoned the extremity of living in this country, they had not only all the follies and infirmities of other old men, but many more which arose from the dreadful prospect of never dying. They were not only opinionative, peevish, covetous, morose, vain, talkative, but uncapable of friendship, and dead to all natural affection, which never descended below their grandchildren. Envy and impotent desires are their prevailing passions. But those objects against which their envy seems principally directed, are the vices of the younger sort, and the deaths of the old. By reflecting on the former, they find themselves cut off from all possibility of pleasure; and whenever they see a funeral, they lament and repine that others have gone to a harbour of rest, to which they themselves never can hope to arrive. They have no remembrance of anything but what they learned and observed in their youth and middle age, and even that is very imperfect. And for the truth or particulars of any fact, it is safer to depend on common traditions than upon their best recollections. The least miserable among them appear to be those who turn to dotage, and entirely lose their memories; these meet with more pity and assistance, because they want many bad qualities which abound in others.

If a *struldbrug* happen to marry one of his own kind, the marriage is dissolved of course by the courtesy of the kingdom, as soon as the younger of the two comes to be fourscore. For the law thinks it a reasonable indulgence, that those who are condemned without any fault of their own to a perpetual continuance in the world, should not have their misery doubled by the load of a wife.

As soon as they have completed the term of eighty years, they are looked on as dead in law; their heirs immediately succeed to their estates, only a small pittance is reserved for their support, and the poor ones are maintained at the public charge. After that period they are held incapable of any employment of trust or profit, they cannot purchase lands or take leases, neither are they allowed to be witnesses in any cause, either civil or criminal, not even for the decision of meers and bounds.

At ninety they lose their teeth and hair, they have at that age no distinction of taste, but eat and drink whatever they can get, without relish or appetite. The diseases they were subject to still continue without increasing or diminishing. In talking they forget the common appellation of things, and the names of persons, even of those who are their nearest friends and relations. For the same reason, they never can amuse themselves with reading, because their memory will not serve to carry them from the beginning of a sentence to the end; and by this defect they are deprived of the only entertainment whereof they might otherwise be capable.

The language of this country being always upon the flux, the *struldbrugs* of one age do not understand those of another, neither are they able after two hundred years to hold any conversation (farther than by a few general words) with their neighbours the mortals; and thus they lie under the disadvantage of living like foreigners in their own country.

This was the account given me of the *struldbrugs*, as near as I can remember. I afterwards saw five or six of different ages, the youngest not above two hundred years old, who were brought to me at several times by some of my friends; but although they were told that I was a great traveller, and had seen all the world, they had not the least curiosity to ask me a question; only desired I would give them *slumskudask*, or a token of remembrance, which is a modest way of begging, to avoid the law that strictly forbids it, because they are provided for by the public, although indeed with a very scanty allowance.

They are despised and hated by all sorts of people; when one of them is born, it is reckoned ominous, and their birth is recorded very particularly: so that you may know their age by consulting the registry, which however hath not been kept above a thousand years past, or at least hath been destroyed by time or public disturbances. But the usual way of computing how old they are, is by asking them what kings or great persons they can remember, and then consulting history, for infallibly the last prince in the mind did not begin his reign after they were fourscore years old.

They were the most mortifying sight I ever beheld, and the women more horrible than the men. Besides the usual deformities in extreme old age, they acquired an additional ghastliness in proportion to their number of years, which is not to be described; and among half a dozen, I soon distinguished which was the eldest, although there was not above a century or two between them.

The reader will easily believe, that from what I had heard and seen, my keen appetite for perpetuity of life was much abated. I grew heartily ashamed of the pleasing visions I had formed, and thought no tyrant could invent a death into which I would not run with pleasure from such a life. The King heard of all that had passed between me and my friends upon this occasion, and rallied me very pleasantly, wishing I would send a couple of *struldbrugs* to my own country, to arm our people against the fear of death; but this it seems is forbidden by the fundamental laws of the kingdom, or else I should have been well content with the trouble and expense of transporting them.

I could not but agree that the laws of this kingdom, relating to the *struldbrugs*, were founded upon the strongest reasons, and such as any other country would be under the necessity of enacting in the like circumstances. Otherwise, as avarice is the necessary consequent of old age, those immortals would in time become proprietors of the whole nation, and engross the civil power, which, for want of abilities to manage, must end in the ruin of the public.

GTT

Carolyn Osborn

So it has come to this. What did I expect? That's what happens to old people in the last stage of life. I'd seen it in other families, a dozen anguished documentaries, known that house of the dead, euphemistically called a nursing home, was waiting for her—for me.

"Go up front and look for Mother. See if she recognizes you." Trial by recognition—Aunt Lucy's idea of how I should meet my eighty-one-year-old grandmother. I live in Texas and have not seen her for three years. Outside it is springtime, May in Tennessee; purple and yellow iris bloom by the wall. Inside it could have been winter anywhere, warm and dark; naked light bulbs dangling from high ceilings disperse the light before it can reach human level. I repeat to myself a promise made before coming, "I will not be morbid."

I found her seated with a cluster of old ladies around a TV set. Grandmother Moore was not looking at the picture. She was staring into space, either a limitless void or some memory of her long past. I hoped she was seeing her private show, a brilliant colored reel unwinding. She had married at sixteen, beneath her—she never said so, but her obsession with respectability proved it. She was from an old Virginia family and he was a mule trader, brother to a moonshiner, nephew to a convict. Her achievement can be measured by the fact that I never knew of the existence of my grandfather's relatives until I was thirty. Aunt Lucy's husband, mellowed by the strain of his own life, told me about "the other Moores" in a bourbon-flavored moment.

She settled the mule trader down on a farm, had three children, and was widowed at forty by a train, an electric trolley running back and forth from Nashville, the nearest city. The tracks bordered some of my grandfather's farmland and he often rode the trolley home from the fields to his front gate. Mr. Moore—she always called him that, never your grandfather, but my husband, Mr. Moore—was lying on the train tracks. Did he get a foot stuck? Was he drunk? Did he commit suicide? No one seemed to know. I was three at the time and believed what they told me: he was waiting for the trolley and got run over. Grandmother moved to town for good. She'd always hated the farm and even before Mr. Moore died she'd had a house in town. She lived on the mule trader's canny investments. Hayfever sent her sneezing out of the state every fall. She went by train and she never went to the same place twice. She did not venture abroad. Her only son, George, lived with her after his first marriage until his second. It was a long time between. Once she wanted to marry again, a man she'd met on her travels. He sent her a dozen red roses and a box of chocolate-covered cherries every birthday. I ate the candy, smelled the roses, and sighed with my grandmother over romantic impossibilities. George disliked the man, a fortune hunter he said. Grandmother said he was a gentleman.

I stood in the midst of the semicircle of women before she saw me. "Marianne," she smiled. "I knew you'd come."

I bent to kiss her. I could have picked her up by myself and carried her out of there. Three years before she'd stood in front of me stiffly wrapped in her corset and fully dressed commanding, "Look!" Then, as if preparing me for some sort of secret religious rite, she'd lifted her arms slowly above her head and bent double to touch the toes of her bright red shoes. Red was her favorite color, but only as an accessory. She wore red shoes or red hats, never red dresses. Mr. Moore's black cane and a black pocketbook are her accessories now. The pocketbook, Lucy had already told me, had nothing in it, not even a handkerchief.

"Did she recognize you?" My aunt flutters like a giant gray moth behind me. Her shades are pale, her hair wispy, her nerves thin filaments on top of her skin. I am very careful with her. I nod yes and tell Grandmother I want to take her for a ride, not knowing what I want except to get her out of the dark place.

The other old women sit mesmerized by the television show while we help Grandmother to her feet. I feel the bone of her arm under the soft folds of unresisting flesh in my hand. On the way out we stop for a moment in her room. There is no privacy; every room is shared. I am introduced to a Mrs. Overton, an old lady in a white cotton nightgown sitting up in bed on the far side of the room. Mrs. Overton starts a monologue about various members of her family who haven't been to see her lately. I light a cigarette and look around wildly for an ashtray.

"They don't give you anything here," says Grandmother. "Look in that cabinet. There's a bedpan you can use."

I find the bedpan and put it on the floor beside my chair.

"Every morning the doctor looks in here and says, 'How are my lovely girls?' The next time he does it I'm going to throw that bedpan at him."

"Now, Mother," Aunt Lucy restrains a sigh. The threat is evidently an old one. She is looking for a sweater. The bureau is rickety and seems about to topple over on her every time she pulls out a drawer.

"I've got nineteen great-grandchildren. Oldest one is thirty-five." Mrs. Overton talks in the direction of Aunt Lucy's back.

I turn toward her slightly, trying to give her some attention. "That's a lot of great-grandchildren."

Mrs. Overton does not bother to agree with the obvious. As I lean down to flick ashes into gleaming white porcelain, Grandmother whispers, "Don't ever let them put you in a place like this."

There is no time for me to answer. Aunt Lucy has found the sweater she was searching for and is draping it around Grandmother's shoulders. Neither one of us suggests she should leave her pocketbook behind, though Lucy has managed to wedge a handkerchief through the handle. Mrs. Overton begins naming her great-grandchildren and their parents as we start out of the room, and in the hall I can still hear her reciting the names of generations like someone permanently stuck in Genesis's begats.

Though the place is generally clean, wallpaper is peeling in a giant swag from the hall ceiling, and the window by my grandmother's bed is so filthy I doubt she can see through it. Over everything—the photographs of children, vases of wilting peonies, fly swatters with plastic flowers attached, and the rest of the useless gilded trash relatives had chosen as gifts —hanging in the air of every room is the unappreciated yet practical suggestion, *You have lived too long. Bless the living by dying.*

We creep out through the sunroom with Grandmother's cane tapping a path before us, a nurse on one side, Aunt Lucy on the other. I follow, keeping my eyes on the car waiting immediately outside the door at the far end of the room.

"Just think, Mother, if you were in a wheelchair, you could zip right

along here!'' says Lucy too cheerfully in the same voice I use when trying
to get my children to eat their vegetables. Grandmother would have to be
confined to one soon; she is barely able to shift one foot in front of the
other and the cane wavers badly.

''Lucy, I've always told you, you have to use your muscles or you won't
have any to use.'' Her opinions on physical fitness are well known to us all:
if you can touch your toes without bending your knees you're in good
shape, and sleeping on a hard floor is better for you than a soft bed. In the
years between sixty and seventy she'd slept on the floor beside her bed
more often than in it. She'd fall asleep in bed, then sometime later in the
night get out of it and lie down on the rug with a sheet and pillow. In the
mornings after my rare overnight visits her bed would be made up before I
saw it. She didn't need witnesses to her stoicism—I doubt she would have
called it that—sleeping on the floor was good because she slept better
there.

''Now, Mrs. Moore, if you'll just be careful about the doorsill,'' the
nurse warns.

Grandmother cranes her neck and looks up at me, ''A pack of old
fools!'' She steps over the doorsill with a lot of unwanted help, then sinks
into the front seat of the car I rented at the airport last night.

Aunt Lucy tucks herself in the back seat and I start the motor. ''Where
do you want to go?''

''What does it matter?'' Her voice is petulant. ''I've lived in this
town all my life. There's no use wasting gasoline driving me around. You
go where you want to go.''

There is no place I want to go. The only reason I'd ever come to the
town was to go to my grandmother's house. I drive down Main Street,
which hasn't changed much since my childhood. All the buildings are
small and so wedged together it seems any one of them might pop out into
the street propelled by the others' anxiety to continue facing the short
thoroughfare. I drive slowly, but even then most of the fronts blur. The
only difference I notice is that the liquor stores switched sides of the street.

I remind Grandmother, ''When I was a child walking with you down
this street I stared in all the windows, but when we got near that store
you'd twitch my hand and tell me, 'Ladies don't look in whiskey shop
windows.' ''

''I know it! Now the whiskey shop's in the building I own.'' She kept
looking straight ahead.

Now I walk into a liquor store and buy a month's supply of whiskey when my husband's too busy to go. The man behind the counter calls me by name and takes my check without asking to see my driver's license. I've looked in and been in liquor stores all over the world, from those that let you sample their wares in Mexico to English wine shops where the vintage year is a matter of great importance. I take a good long look at the window. There is nothing in it but a row of bourbon bottles and a plastic crow dressed up in an evening suit, but that forbidden territory of childhood is still invested with the allure of the sinful, mysterious, and unladylike qualities Grandmother had given it.

"Oh look! There's May Morgan going down the street with a sack of groceries." Aunt Lucy struggles to roll the window down.

"Don't be silly! She's been in her grave for a week!"

"Mother, I tell you it's May Morgan. Look, there she is walking along carrying a scak of groceries." Aunt Lucy succeeded in getting the window down and was flapping her hand. She speaks to everybody. If she acknowledges others they will greet her. Every hello strengthens her existence.

The lady with the groceries conforms to the code by giving her a lavish smile.

"Lucy, she's been buried a week now." Grandmother refuses to turn her head.

"One of you is seeing a ghost," I suggest. They both hush.

We turn up one of the side streets leading to Grandmother's house, a reflex action I realize when I feel Aunt Lucy tensing behind me. Of Grandmother's children she and Uncle George are the only ones left. They both wanted to take their mother home with them, and both were unable to. George's health had been broken by a terrible automobile accident. Aunt Lucy would have to spend the rest of the day in bed, her guilt smothered by tranquilizers, after a visit to the nursing home. Uncle Phillip, well aware of her frailty, could not let her bring Grandmother to their house. Though they had tried they could not find anyone to stay with her at her own house. They dragged in one woman after another, women old enough to be companions, young enough to do the cooking and a little housework, and hopeless enough to have no other means of livelihood. Grandmother complained about each one. None of them were, to her mind, genteel enough. Gentility, that all-enveloping nebulous characteristic admired by her and other ladies of her age, could not be bought. A hired companion was condemned by her wages.

When she was seventy-nine she suffered a cerebral hemorrhage and had to be taken to the nursing home. Ever since she'd left she'd been plotting to get back to her own home again.

We pass the house, an ornate white frame with curlicues of woodwork embroidering the front and side porches and more gingerbread work dripping from the second-story eaves. Grandfather Moore hung a sign on his gate, "Trade in Your Old Mules for New," and settled down on the farm, but Grandmother hated farms then as much as she hated nursing homes now. This was her town house and there was room for the whole family in it, even the second and third generations. I lived here with my mother during part of World War II, and have spent more days than I can remember swinging on the front porch swing.

"The house looks good," I said.

"I spent a good deal of money getting it painted this year. There are renters in it now. They're not what I would call genteel!" Grandmother lapsed into an alarming silence.

Aunt Lucy sighs quietly and I know the battle has been temporarily suspended in my honor. I pull into a driveway across the street to turn around and see that the house which had once stood there on a half-acre lot is gone. Nothing remains but some doorsteps surrounded by trees.

"What happened to Mrs. Laurel's—"

"She passed away." Aunt Lucy has never, in my presence, said that anyone died.

"And after she did they tore her house down," says Grandmother in a raddled voice.

"Mother, Mrs. Laurel's house burned down. Don't you remember?"

Grandmother didn't turn her head to answer. "Anyway, it's gone!"

I don't know of any other place to go and want to do something cheerful so I suggest driving out to my street. I've never thought Marianne St. was a very good name for a street, but Uncle George, who was a real estate man before he drove into his own stone gatepost and smashed himself up, developed the area and named the street after me. We drive through the older neighborhoods out to the edge of town and find Marianne St. I've always secretly wished it could have at least been Marianne Ave., but it is St., and it is suburbia and rather poor at that.

"Nice little houses," Aunt Lucy offers.

"They keep their lawns well," I say, trying to say as little as possible.

"Tacky!" Grandmother pronounces.

Leaving Marianne St., which is mercifully short, I start back to town again. We go around the square where Uncle George still keeps an office on the side opposite the courthouse. He handles a little real estate and the

few letters I receive from him are written on his business stationery. He
keeps the office, I think, mainly because it's his place to go. Every day his
wife takes him to it at ten and picks him up at noon. He goes home for
lunch and a nap; then she drives him back to the office at three. Like his
father he admires slogans. On top of a file sits a stuffed owl, and underneath the owl on the square wooden base there's a sign which says, "Be
Wise, Buy Moore." Uncle George and the owl sit together in the office
glaring at the huge granite obelisk in the middle of the square. A memori-
al to the Confederate dead, it's bigger and even more permanent than his
gatepost.

"There's the statue of the Confederacy. Isn't it lovely?" said Aunt
Lucy.

I don't know why she had to say that. We had all been seeing it all
our lives and no one could have thought it was lovely.

"It's in the way!" says Grandmother, who couldn't possibly have
been thinking about civil rights. She meant it was in the middle of the
street as it had always been. Contrary to myths about old Southern ladies,
she never wasted any grief crying over the lost cause. Gentility interested
her; history didn't.

We return to the nursing home and ease her back into her half of the
room. Fearing Mrs. Overton will start talking again, none of us look in her
direction though I see, with a shifty glance, she's sitting up in bed as still
as carved white marble. I sit down beside Grandmother and Aunt Lucy
goes to the closet to inspect clothes. Now and then she holds up a dress
and shakes her head over a spot.

"How are your children?"

"All right."

"Tell them about me." Her eyes wander toward her bed, but she re-
sists. She tries to sit up straighter in the chair. "What will you tell them?"

I wait awhile before answering, trying to think what would please her
best. The facts I know about her life seem meager, and, to her, probably
disappointing.

"I will tell them about your house in town with a front porch swing.
Those hardly exist anymore."

"Neither do I."

I want to cry, to say yes, you do, to throw out all the junk, and tear
the draggling paper off the walls, but I only say goodbye, and take Aunt
Lucy home.

All the way to the house she weeps into an embroidered linen handkerchief and I feel a momentary sympathy for Uncle Phillip. I was born in-

to the family; he has had to spend all of his life adjusting to the Moores. I attempt to comfort Aunt Lucy though I am incapable of giving her anything other than an audience to grieve before. I love her, but her trembling is as great as my anger. We are both too prone to excessive emotions.

After leaving her stretched on her bed, I drive back to Uncle George's office. Crippled as he is, he's the only head of the family. He looks startled when I come in. I have been there only twice in my life, once when I was a child and thought I'd make him a surprise visit downtown. He sent me home. The other time was for the reading of my mother's will. She was killed in a plane crash when I was eighteen. Her lawyer, a friend of George's, decided we should meet in my uncle's office, possibly to make it easier on me—the familiar-place idea. It wasn't familiar, and nothing from that day on was easy between me and Uncle George. He had been named as my guardian until I was twenty-one. My father was killed in the war. He'd left everything to Mother, and she, in turn, left it all to me.

I had one wish then, to leave, to go as far away as possible. Uncle George allowed me to go eighteen miles away to Nashville to college. I told my husband when he asked me to marry him I certainly would if he planned to take me back with him to Texas. He laughed and promised to take me as far away as I wanted to go. To him, my family was archetypal Southern in an interesting state of decay. To me, they were everything I wanted to escape; I longed to be uprooted, to be torn from Uncle George's domination, Aunt Lucy's clinging, my grandmother's determination to mold one more lady. Some people marry into families—I married out of mine. Now I have my own family, and to them their Tennessee relatives are vague people who send them Christmas gifts.

Uncle George asks me about the children.

"They're fine."

"When are you going to bring them to see me? I sure would like to see them before they grow up."

He is a benign-looking old man with thick white hair. His body, so tough once, is cradled in his chair, his arms rest on the chair's arms. A desk, almost bare, is between us, and the owl stares at me from the top of the file cabinet. The feathers are dusty; the glass eyes are eternally bright.

"Will Grandmother ever be able to go home?"

"No. She's in a bad state, honey, and we can't get anybody to live with her. It's impossible these days. Anyway, she runs them all off."

"I know." I smile, trying to be tactful. "The place where she is . . . it's depressing."

"It's the best in town. People are waiting in line to get in there."

When he says this I see a line of wheelchairs full of old people, and behind every chair stands a younger person with a positive smile on his face. My reflections make me shudder in the middle of a warm day. The past, my present grief, my children with their lives before them, morbid ideas about my own old age, have all coalesced in one moment.

I will take her home with me, I decide, take her back to Texas. I could give her a more pleasant place to die. But where in my house, in my life, is there room for the dying? All the reasons for not doing what I feel I should do rush by and fall in a muddled heap in my mind. Our house is small, the children need constant attention, Grandmother needs twenty-four-hour vigilance. I do not have the strength required to meet all those needs.

My stay is short. Before I leave I go to see her for the last time. The photographs of Mr. Moore, my mother, Uncle George, Aunt Lucy and Uncle Phillip, their one child and his children, and the one of me and my children, all on top of the bureau smile like conspirators at each other. It was as though Grandmother wasn't sitting beside me, but Sorrow herself was on the edge of the bed holding a cane. I thought she was indomitable, but she wasn't. She was old, tired, and a little mad.

"Tell the children . . . " She stops because she cannot remember their names. Four or five times in the last week she has called me by my mother's. I wasn't even sure whether she was speaking of her children or mine, but I know what I will tell mine. Your Grandmother Moore boarded the train every fall and went to thirty-eight states, including Texas, at a time when people still counted the states they'd been to. When asked if she ever returned to one of them she usually answered, "No! Why go back to the same old place!" She did not approve of a lady drinking anything more than a glass of sherry, and one glass only, to be "sociable." Her trick for remembering names was to imagine those easily forgotten ones perched on top of her dresser, but toward the end of her life she forgot nearly all. She loved any kind of party, especially card parties, and she had no interest in history, particularly family history. She hated the country, and she lived in town until the day she died.

I left. For a week I'd been living with the Moores again and I'd almost quit thinking; I reacted. The old instincts rose—fear, rebellion, rage, and the overwhelming desire to escape. People on the run used to leave Tennessee in such a hurry all the notice they gave their neighbors was GTT scratched on the doorstep. I left my notice on Aunt Lucy's bed: Gone To Texas. Love, Marianne. So I ran, clutching my guilt to my heart.

THERE, ON THE DARKENED DEATHBED

John Masefield

There, on the darkened deathbed, dies the brain
That flared three several times in seventy years;
It cannot lift the silly hand again,
Nor speak, nor sing, it neither sees nor hears.
And muffled mourners put it in the ground
And then go home, and in the earth it lies,
Too dark for vision and too deep for sound,
The million cells that made a good man wise.
Yet for a few short years an influence stirs,
A sense or wraith or essence of him dead,
Which makes insensate things its ministers
To those beloved, his spirit's daily bread;
Then that, too, fades; in book or deed a spark
Lingers, then that, too, fades; then all is dark.

THE PRESIDENT OF FLOWERS

Sydney Lea

His wife referred to him as "Honey-Dripper,"
and it's true, in memory there is a sweet
association—sugared talk and whiff
of Sweet William, citric tang of the compost heap
in which his soft black hand threw everything,
even jars and bottles, for "glass ain't a thing
but sand blowed up, and sand it's bound to be
again one day." By which he must have meant,
though I was full of adolescent rage
and couldn't know it then, that death
was a thing too individual to count
for much among so many grander patterns.

                                          I only
sought to tell the old man truth: "Great God!
The black man in this land has no damned power!"
He warned me not to curse, then laughed like wind
along my parents' cherry orchard, nights:
"Son, I am the President of Flowers."
Poppies showed him, as they showed to no one else,
their bashful tongues. I swore that apples hung
in clusters before their blossoms fell away.
Exotic currants swelled our silver platter.
He grew a Pennsylvania avocado,

the only one I've ever seen, or heard of.
And then, toward fall, that strangest bloom—his cancer.

But he bent with it as he was used to bending,
and grapes came on more purple than before.
He gave up water, told me how the pain
would die of drought. He drove his truck to Georgia,
a visit to the family. There, he dug
a payload full of Dixie loam because
our Iris bed was full of bugs with claws.
"That red will quick-walk those old rascals down."
And *something* made them go. His death was like him,
slow: in alien odors of his darkened
house I sensed him—temples falling in,
a boyish skin, hands kneading at the folds—
and inhaled the jab of ruined marigolds.

In mem. Alex Lewis

A SUMMER TRAGEDY

Arna Bontemps

Old Jeff Patton, the black share farmer, fumbled with his bow tie. His fingers trembled and the high, stiff collar pinched his throat. A fellow loses his hand for such vanities after thirty or forty years of simple life. Once a year, or maybe twice if there's a wedding among his kinfolks, he may spruce up; but generally fancy clothes do nothing but adorn the wall of the big room and feed the moths. That had been Jeff Patton's experience. He had not worn his stiff-bosomed shirt more than a dozen times in all his married life. His swallow-tailed coat lay on the bed beside him, freshly brushed and pressed, but it was as full of holes as the overalls in which he worked on weekdays. The moths had used it badly. Jeff twisted his mouth into a hideous toothless grimace as he contended with the obstinate bow. He stamped his good foot and decided to give up the struggle.

"Jennie," he called.

"What's that, Jeff?" His wife's shrunken voice came out of the adjoining room like an echo. It was hardly bigger than a whisper.

"I reckon you'll have to he'p me wid this heah bow tie, baby," he said meekly. "Dog if I can hitch it up."

Her answer was not strong enough to reach him, but presently the old woman came to the door, feeling her way with a stick. She had a wasted, dead-leaf appearance. Her body, as scrawny and gnarled as a string bean, seemed less than nothing in the ocean of frayed and faded petticoats that surrounded her. These hung an inch or two above the tops of her heavy unlaced shoes and showed little grotesque piles where the stockings had fallen down from her negligible legs.

"You oughta could do a heap mo' wid a thing like that'n me—beingst as you got yo good sight."

"Looks like I oughta could," he admitted. "But my fingers is gone democrat on me. I get all mixed up in the looking glass an' can't tell wicha way to twist the devilish thing."

Jennie sat on the side of the bed, and old Jeff Patton got down on one knee while she tied the bow knot. It was a slow and painful ordeal for each of them in this position. Jeff's bones cracked, his knee ached, and it was only after a half dozen attempts that Jennie worked a semblance of a bow into the tie.

"I got to dress maself now," the old woman whispered. "These is ma old shoes an' stockings, and I ain't so much as unwrapped ma dress."

"Well, don't worry 'bout me no mo', baby," Jeff said. "That 'bout finishes me. All I gotta do now is slip on that old coat 'n ves' an' I'll be fixed to leave."

Jennie disappeared again through the dim passage into the shed room. Being blind was no handicap to her in that black hole. Jeff heard the cane placed against the wall beside the door and knew that his wife was on easy ground. He put on his coat, took a battered top hat from the bed post, and hobbled to the front door. He was ready to travel. As soon as Jennie could get on her Sunday shoes and her old black silk dress, they would start.

Outside the tiny log house, the day was warm and mellow with sunshine. A host of wasps were humming with busy excitement in the trunk of a dead sycamore. Gray squirrels were searching through the grass for hickory nuts, and blue jays were in the trees, hopping from branch to branch. Pine woods stretched away to the left like a black sea. Among them were scattered scores of log houses like Jeff's, houses of black share farmers. Cows and pigs wandered freely among the trees. There was no danger of loss. Each farmer knew his own stock and knew his neighbor's as well as he knew his neighbor's children.

Down the slope to the right were the cultivated acres on which the colored folks worked. They extended to the river, more than two miles away, and they were today green with the unmade cotton crop. A tiny thread of a road, which passed directly in front of Jeff's place, ran through these green fields like a pencil mark.

Jeff, standing outside the door, with his absurd hat in his left hand, surveyed the wide scene tenderly. He had been forty-five years on these acres. He loved them with the unexplained affection that others have for the countries to which they belong.

The sun was hot on his head, his collar still pinched his throat, and the Sunday clothes were intolerably hot. Jeff transferred the hat to his right hand and began fanning with it. Suddenly the whisper that was Jennie's voice came out of the shed room.

"You can bring the car round front whilst you's waitin'," it said feebly. There was a tired pause; then it added, "I'll soon be fixed to go."

"A'right, baby," Jeff answered. "I'll get it in a minute."

But he didn't move. A thought struck him that made his mouth fall open. The mention of the car brought to his mind, with new intensity, the trip he and Jennie were about to take. Fear came into his eyes; excitement took his breath. Lord, Jesus!

"Jeff . . . O Jeff," the old woman's whisper called.

He awakened with a jolt. "Hunh, baby?"

"What you doin?"

"Nuthin. Jes studyin'. I jes been turnin' things round 'n round in ma mind."

"You could be gettin' the car," she said.

"Oh yes, right away, baby."

He started round to the shed, limping heavily on his bad leg. There were three frizzly chickens in the yard. All his other chickens had been killed or stolen recently. But the frizzly chickens had been saved somehow. That was fortunate indeed, for these curious creatures had a way of devouring "poison" from the yard, and in that way protecting against conjure and black luck and spells. But even the frizzly chickens seemed now to be in a stupor. Jeff thought they had some ailment; he expected all three of them to die shortly.

The shed in which the old T-model Ford stood was only a grass roof held up by four corner poles. It had been built by tremulous hands at a time when the little rattletrap car had been regarded as a peculiar treasure. And, miraculously, despite wind and downpour, it still stood.

Jeff adjusted the crank and put his weight upon it. The engine came to life with a sputter and bang that rattled the old car from radiator to tail light. Jeff hopped into the seat and put his foot on the accelerator. The sputtering and banging increased. The rattling became more violent.

That was good. It was good banging, good sputtering and rattling, and it meant that the aged car was still in running condition. She could be depended on for this trip.

Again Jeff's thought halted as if paralyzed. The suggestion of the trip fell into the machinery of his mind like a wrench. He felt dazed and weak. He swung the car out into the yard, made a half turn, and drove around to the front door. When he took his hands off the wheel, he noticed that he was trembling violently. He cut off the motor and climbed to the ground to wait for Jennie.

A few minutes later she was at the window, her voice rattling against the pane like a broken shutter.

"I'm ready, Jeff."

He did not answer, but limped into the house and took her by the arm. He led her slowly through the big room, down the step, and across the yard.

"You reckon I'd oughta lock the do'?" he asked softly.

They stopped and Jennie weighed the question. Finally she shook her head.

"Ne' mind the do'," she said. "I don't see no cause to lock up things."

"You right," Jeff agreed. "No cause to lock up."

Jeff opened the door and helped his wife into the car. A quick shudder passed over him. Jesus! Again he trembled.

"How come you shaking so?" Jennie whispered.

"I don't know," he said.

"You mus' be scairt, Jeff."

"No, baby, I ain't scairt."

He slammed the door after her and went around to crank up again. The motor started easily. Jeff wished that it had not been so responsive. He would have liked a few more minutes in which to turn things around in his head. As it was, with Jennie chiding him about being afraid, he had to keep going. He swung the car into the little pencil-mark road and started off toward the river, driving very slowly, very cautiously.

Chugging across the green countryside, the small battered Ford seemed tiny indeed. Jeff felt a familiar excitement, a thrill, as they came down the first slope to the immense levels on which the cotton was growing. He could not help reflecting that the crops were good. He knew what that meant, too; he had made forty-five of them with his own hands. It was true that he had worn out nearly a dozen mules, but that was the fault of old man Stevenson, the owner of the land. Major Stevenson had the odd notion that one mule was all a share farmer needed to work a thirty-acre plot. It was an expensive notion, the way it killed mules from overwork, but the old man held to it. Jeff thought it killed a good many share farmers as well as mules, but he had no sympathy for them. He had always been strong, and he had been taught to have no patience with weakness in men. Women or children might be tolerated if they were puny, but a weak man was a curse. Of course, his own children—

Jeff's thought halted there. He and Jennie never mentioned their dead children any more. And naturally, he did not wish to dwell upon them in his mind. Before he knew it, some remark would slip out of his mouth and that would make Jennie feel blue. Perhaps she would cry. A woman like Jennie could not easily throw off the grief that comes from losing five grown children within two years. Even Jeff was still staggered by the blow. His memory had not been much good recently. He frequently talked to himself. And, although he had kept it a secret, he knew that his courage had left him. He was terrified by the least unfamiliar sound at night. He was reluctant to venture far from home in the daytime. And that habit of trembling when he felt fearful was now far beyond his control. Sometimes he became afraid and trembled without knowing what had frightened him. The feeling would just come over him like a chill.

The car rattled slowly over the dusty road. Jennie sat erect and silent with a little absurd hat pinned to her hair. Her useless eyes seemed very large, very white in their deep sockets. Suddenly Jeff heard her voice, and he inclined his head to catch the words.

"Is we passed Delia Moore's house yet?" she asked.

"Not yet," he said.

"You must be drivin' mighty slow, Jeff."

"We just as well take our time, baby."

There was a pause. A little puff of steam was coming out of the radiator of the car. Heat wavered above the hood. Delia Moore's house was nearly half a mile away. After a moment Jennie spoke again.

"You ain't really scairt, is you, Jeff?"

"Nah, baby. I ain't scairt."

"You know how we agreed—we gotta keep on goin'."

Jewels of perspiration appeared on Jeff's forehead. His eyes rounded, blinked, became fixed on the road.

"I don't know," he said with a shiver, "I reckon it's the only thing to do."

"Hm."

A flock of guinea fowls, pecking in the road, were scattered by the passing car. Some of them took to their wings; others hid under bushes. A blue jay, swaying on a leafy twig, was annoying a roadside squirrel. Jeff held an even speed till he came near Delia's place. Then he slowed down noticeably.

Delia's house was really no house at all, but an abandoned store building converted into a dwelling. It sat near a crossroads, beneath a single black cedar tree. There Delia, a cattish old creature of Jennie's age, lived alone. She had been there more years than anybody could remember, and long ago had won the disfavor of such women as Jennie. For in her young days Delia had been gayer, yellower, and saucier than seemed proper in those parts. Her ways with menfolks had been dark and suspicious. And the fact that she had had as many husbands as children did not help her reputation.

"Yonder's old Delia," Jeff said as they passed.

"What she doin'?"

"Jes sittin' in the do'," he said.

"She see us?"

"Hm," Jeff said. "Musta did."

That relieved Jennie. It strengthened her to know that her old enemy had seen her pass in her best clothes. That would give the old she-devil something to chew her gums and fret about, Jennie thought. Wouldn't she have a fit if she didn't find out? Old evil Delia! This would be just the thing for her. It would pay her back for being so evil. It would also pay her, Jennie thought, for the way she used to grin at Jeff—long ago, when her teeth were good.

The road became smooth and red, and Jeff could tell by the smell of the air that they were nearing the river. He could see the rise where the road turned and ran along parallel to the stream. The car chugged on monotonously. After a long silent spell, Jennie leaned against Jeff and spoke.

"How many bale o' cotton you think we got standin'?" she said.

Jeff wrinkled his forehead as he calculated.

"'Bout twenty-five, I reckon."

"How many you make las' year?"

"Twenty-eight," he said. "How come you ask that?"

"I's jes thinkin'," Jennie said quietly.

"It don't make a speck o' difference though," Jeff reflected. "If we get much or if we get little, we still gonna be in debt to old man Stevenson when he gets through counting up agin us. It's took us a long time to learn that.''

Jennie was not listening to these words. She had fallen into a trance-like meditation. Her lips twitched. She chewed her gums and rubbed her gnarled hands nervously. Suddenly, she leaned forward, buried her face in the nervous hands, and burst into tears. She cried aloud in a dry, cracked voice that suggested the rattle of fodder on dead stalks. She cried aloud like a child, for she had never learned to suppress a genuine sob. Her slight old frame shook heavily and seemed hardly able to sustain such violent grief.

"What's the matter, baby?" Jeff asked awkwardly. "Why you cryin' like all that?"

"I's jes thinkin'," she said.

"So you the one what's scairt now, hunh?"

"I ain't scairt, Jeff. I's jes thinking 'bout leavin' eve'thing like this—eve'thing we been used to. It's right sad-like."

Jeff did not answer, and presently Jennie buried her face again and cried.

The sun was almost overhead. It beat down furiously on the dusty wagon-path road, on the parched roadside grass and the tiny battered car. Jeff's hands, gripping the wheel, became wet with perspiration; his forehead sparkled. Jeff's lips parted. His mouth shaped a hideous grimace. His face suggested the face of a man being burned. But the torture passed and his expression softened again.

"You mustn't cry, baby," he said to his wife. "We gotta be strong. We can't break down."

Jennie waited a few seconds, then said, "You reckon we oughta do it, Jeff? You reckon we oughta go 'head an' do it, really?"

Jeff's voice choked; his eyes blurred. He was terrified to hear Jennie say the thing that had been in his mind all morning. She had egged him on when he had wanted more than anything in the world to wait, to reconsider, to think things over a little longer. Now she was getting cold feet. Actually, there was no need of thinking the question through again. It would only end in making the same painful decision once more. Jeff knew that. There was no need of fooling around longer.

"We jes as well to do like we planned," he said. "They ain't nothin' else for us now—it's the bes' thing."

Jeff thought of the handicaps, the near impossibility, of making another crop with his leg bothering him more and more each week. Then there was always the chance that he would have another stroke, like the one that had made him lame. Another one might kill him. The least it could do would be to leave him helpless. Jeff gasped—Lord, Jesus! He could not bear to think of being helpless, like a baby, on Jennie's hands. Frail, blind Jennie.

The little pounding motor of the car worked harder and harder. The puff of steam from the cracked radiator became larger. Jeff realized that they were climbing a little rise. A moment later the road turned abruptly, and he looked down upon the face of the river.

"Jeff."

"Hunh?"

"Is that the water I hear?"

"Hm. Tha's it."

"Well, which way you goin' now?"

"Down this-a way," he said. "This road runs 'long 'side o' the water a lil piece."

She waited a while calmly. Then she said, "Drive faster."

"A'right, baby," Jeff said.

The water roared in the bed of the river. It was fifty or sixty feet below the level of the road. Between the road and the water there was a long smooth slope, sharply inclined. The slope was dry, the clay hardened by prolonged summer heat. The water below, roaring in a narrow channel, was noisy and wild.

"Jeff."

"Hunh?"

"How far you goin'?"

"Jes a lil piece down the road."

"You ain't scairt, is you, Jeff?"

"Nah, baby," he said trembling. "I ain't scairt."

"Remember how we planned it, Jeff. We gotta do it like we said. Brave-like."

"Hm."

Jeff's brain darkened. Things suddenly seemed unreal, like figures in a dream. Thoughts swam in his mind foolishly, hysterically, like little blind fish in a pool within a dense cave. They rushed again. Jeff soon became dizzy. He shuddered violently and turned to his wife.

"Jennie, I can't do it. I can't." His voice broke pitifully.

She did not appear to be listening. All the grief had gone from her face. She sat erect, her unseeing eyes wide open, strained and frightful.

Her glossy black skin had become dull. She seemed as thin, as sharp and bony, as a starved bird. Now, having suffered and endured the sadness of tearing herself away from beloved things, she showed no anguish. She was absorbed with her own thoughts, and she didn't even hear Jeff's voice shouting in her ear.

Jeff said nothing more. For an instant there was light in his cavernous brain. The great chamber was, for less than a second, peopled by characters he knew and loved. They were simple, healthy creatures, and they behaved in a manner that he could understand. They had quality. But since he had already taken leave of them long ago, the remembrance did not break his heart again. Young Jeff Patton was among them, the Jeff Patton of fifty years ago who went down to New Orleans with a crowd of country boys to the Mardi Gras doings. The gay young crowd, boys with candy-striped shirts and rouged brown girls in noisy silks, was like a picture in his head. Yet it did not make him sad. On that very trip Slim Burns had killed Joe Beasley—the crowd had been broken up. Since then Jeff Patton's world had been the Greenbriar Plantation. If there had been other Mardi Gras carnivals, he had not heard of them. Since then there had been no time; the years had fallen on him like waves. Now he was old, worn out. Another paralytic stroke (like the one he had already suffered) would put him on his back for keeps. In that condition, with a frail blind woman to look after him, he would be worse off than if he were dead.

Suddenly Jeff's hands became steady. He actually felt brave. He slowed down the motor of the car and carefully pulled off the road. Below, the water of the stream boomed, a soft thunder in the deep channel. Jeff ran the car into the clay slope, pointed it directly toward the stream, and put his foot heavily on the accelerator. The little car leaped furiously down the steep incline toward the water. The movement was nearly as swift and direct as a fall. The two old black folks, sitting quietly side by side, showed no excitement. In another instant the car hit the water and dropped immediately out of sight.

A little later it lodged in the mud of a shallow place. One wheel of the crushed and upturned little Ford became visible above the rushing water.

6

ADULT LEARNING

Learning occurs throughout the life span. It does not end with graduation, starting a family, or becoming employed. Assuming the adult roles of parent, worker, and community member in fact stimulates the need for new knowledge or skill, as does coping with the inevitable changes and transitions of adulthood. Some of the changes that adults undergo are brought about by planned events such as marriage or retirement. Other transitions occur when unplanned events, such as a late-life pregnancy or loss of a job, necessitate adjustments. Whether changes in one's life are planned or unplanned, all offer opportunities for learning and self-assessment. While for children the "teachable moment" is closely linked to physical and cognitive development, the teachable moments for men and women are inextricably linked to the tasks and social roles characteristic of adulthood.

Adult learning can be studied separately from childhood learning. Malcolm Knowles (1980) has proposed four specific assumptions about the factors that underlie adult learning: (1) adults have a more independent self-concept than children; (2) adult learning is related to the developmental tasks and social roles of adulthood; (3) adults are present-oriented rather than future-oriented, and thus learning is desired for immediate use and problem solving; and (4) adults have an accumulation of life experiences that can be both a resource and a hindrance to learning. When linked to practice, these assumptions can facilitate adult learning that is self-directed and problem-centered.

In addition to exploring the differences between adult and child learning, researchers and educators have been interested in the adult's ability to learn and the ways in which adults learn best. With regard to the ability to learn, age is much less of a factor than other variables. Adults retain the ability to think, solve problems, and acquire new information regardless of age. Differences in learning ability between adults of the same age and differences observed between younger and older adults are most likely due to one or more of the following factors:

- Physical condition: ill health can impede learning, as can sensory impairment. For example, an older person may not remember, not because his or her memory is failing but because the information has not been recorded due to poor vision or hearing loss.
- Relevance: as mentioned earlier, an adult learns when there is a need to solve a problem, learn something new, or cope with change. As one ages, there is little tolerance for learning anything that appears to be meaningless or irrelevant.
- Speed: adults under pressure of timed tasks do not do as well as younger people. However, when allowed to pace their own learning, adults of all ages do as well as their younger counterparts.
- Personality and socioeconomic status: personality characteristics such as flexibility or rigidity, previous formal education, and social status are factors correlated with learning ability throughout adulthood. Thus a young adult learner who is open to new ideas, who has had some formal education, and whose work is engaging will continue to learn as an older adult.

Age, in and of itself, therefore has little to do with learning.

How adults learn can be investigated in several ways. One might be interested in how the brain processes information, or how the environment can be arranged to facilitate learning, or how psychological variables affect learning. One could also look at learning settings, types of instruction, or learning style. The selections in this anthology illustrate two of the ways in which adults learn: "learning from experience" and "structural learning in formal settings."

LEARNING FROM EXPERIENCE

Learning is an integral part of everyday living. Throughout the life span we learn by experiencing the people, activities, and objects that make up our environment. Learning occurs when we reflect upon concrete experience and form generalizations about those experiences. The generalizations gleaned from one situation are then tested by applying them to new situations. Of course not all adults are alike in their ability to learn from experience. Some of the factors discussed earlier that modify the ability to learn in formal situations also affect experiential learning. There are some people who do not know how to learn from their experiences, or their past experiences may interfere with absorbing new ways of doing or thinking about things. On the other hand, we consider a wise person to be one who has maximized learning from past experience and can thus be a guide to others.

Prospero, the old magician in Shakespeare's play *The Tempest*, is in a powerful position to seek vengeance from his scheming brother Antonio. Antonio and others who deposed Prospero, duke of Milan, become shipwrecked on the island ruled by the deposed duke where Prospero and his daughter have lived, with several nonhuman creatures, for the past twelve years. The tempest brought about by Prospero's magic brings the evildoers under his control. Rather than exact the revenge he has long sought, Prospero, in talking to Ariel, a spirit, allows "nobler reason" to overcome passion, for he knows that "the rarer action is in virtue than in vengeance." The "sole drift of his purpose" becomes one of leading the men to true repentance.

Wisdom is only achieved through learning acquired from experience over time. It is not an attribute gained in youth. Sara Teasdale's poem "Wisdom" expresses the notion that wisdom is achieved in exchange for youth: "When I can look Life in the eyes,/Grown calm and very coldly wise, /Life will have given me the Truth,/And taken in exchange—my youth."

The contrast between learning something cognitively and understanding it experientially is vividly illustrated in the selection from *The Minister*, by Charles Mercer. Kathy Judson is a college junior intellectually committed to the Civil Rights Movement. The excerpt opens with her joining a freedom ride to Montgomery, Alabama. It is her first experience of putting her convictions into practice. Through her own experience and through observing a minister accompanying her group, she discovers that living one's convictions can be both inspiring and dangerous.

One of the most common ways we learn in everyday life is by observing and perhaps modeling ourselves after another. In "The Last Day in the Field," by Caroline Gordon, Aleck is the master hunter, Joe the apprentice. The story is about both men, a careful balancing of Aleck against Joe. Aleck is old, wise, experienced, skilled; Joe is young, arrogant, inexperienced, eager. As the story progresses, Joe realizes that he can learn from Aleck, and Aleck realizes that experience has its advantages over youth. Interchange of knowledge between master and apprentice, mentor and protégé, constitutes a form of experiential learning in which the raw material of youth can be transformed into the experience of age.

Learning can also occur through reminiscing, reflecting, or dreaming.

Sometimes knowledge is intuitive. In the short story "The Odd Old Lady," by Thyra Samter Winslow, Mrs. Quillan begins to "know" about events before they occur. She reflects upon her intuitive knowledge, tests it out in the world around her, and then tries to use what she knows to help others. The final use of her powers is to prepare for her own death.

Experiential learning can thus take many forms, from the accumulated wisdom of Prospero to learning from intense involvement in a cause, to learning from apprenticing to a master, to learning in a more private, subconscious mode.

STRUCTURED LEARNING
IN FORMAL SETTINGS

In contrast to experiential learning, structured learning experiences are those embarked upon with the intent of gaining new knowledge, skills, or attitudes. The three selections used to illustrate structured learning are very different from one another. What they have in common is the fact that learning has not been left to chance; it has been planned for and arranged with specific outcomes in mind.

In the selection from *The Paper Chase*, by John Osborn, we encounter Mr. Hart, a first-year law student at Harvard Law School. He is about to attend his first class. Hart and the reader get a glimpse into the nature of the educational process in a very formal, professional-school setting.

Behavioral psychology, especially that popularized by B. F. Skinner, has had a significant impact on education. Such concepts as positive reinforcement, programmed instruction, and behavior modification have been incorporated into school systems, curricula, and individual classrooms since the 1950s. At the heart of this approach is the systematic arrangement of the environment so as to bring about the desired learning. In *Walden Two*, Skinner offers a fictional account of a whole society based upon behavioral engineering. The educational system is discussed in the selection chosen for this anthology. The entire educational system is tightly controlled and structured by the community planners, who plan learning experiences based upon the needs and life of the community.

The final selection in this section is from the *The Autobiography of Malcolm X*. While not fiction, this account of the black leader's learning vividly exemplifies another type of structured learning — that which is self-directed. In prison Malcolm becomes aware of his ability to learn and, once inspired, systematically sets out to become educated. He reads books from the prison library, writes letters to practice his composition skills, and participates in debates arranged by a local college. The resources of the institution for learning are used by Malcolm to the fullest in his intense effort to become educated.

In conclusion, adult learning is a complex phenomenon arising from the needs, tasks, and social roles inherent in being an adult member of society. Sometimes the learning that we need to do occurs as a by-product of everyday living. It is serendipitous, spontaneous, and so much a part of our lives that it may go unnoticed. At other times adults seek answers to questions, solutions to problems, or further training by taking advantage of the opportunities and resources available for structuring their learning.

From THE TEMPEST

William Shakespeare

ACT V. Scene I.

Before Prospero's cell. Enter Prospero in his magic robes, and Ariel.

PROS.   Now does my project gather to a head:
  My charms crack not; my spirits obey; and time
  Goes upright with his carriage. How's the day?
ARI.   On the sixth hour; at which time, my lord,
  You said our work should cease.
PROS.   I did say so,
  When first I raised the tempest. Say, my spirit,
  How fares the king and's followers?
ARI.   Confined together
  In the same fashion as you gave in charge,
  Just as you left them; all prisoners, sir,
  In the line-grove which weather-fends your cell:
  They cannot budge till your release. The king,
  His brother and yours, abide all three distracted,
  And the remainder mourning over them,
  Brimful of sorrow and dismay; but chiefly
  Him that you term'd, sir, "The good old lord, Gonzalo";
  His tears run down his beard, like winter's drops

Reprinted from *Shakespeare's Complete Works*, edited by William George Clark and William
Aldis Wright. New York: A. L. Fowle, c. 1902.

From eaves of reeds. Your charm so strongly works 'em,
That if you now beheld them, your affections
Would become tender.

PROS.   Dost thou think so, spirit?

ARI.   Mine would, sir, were I human.

PROS.   And mine shall.
Hast thou, which art but air, a touch, a feeling
Of their afflictions, and shall not myself,
One of their kind, that relish all as sharply
Passion as they, be kindlier moved than thou art?
Though with their high wrongs I am struck to the quick,
Yet with my nobler reason 'gainst my fury
Do I take part; the rarer action is
In virtue than in vengeance: they being penitent,
The sole drift of my purpose doth extend
Not a frown further. Go release them, Ariel:
My charms I'll break, their senses I'll restore,
And they shall be themselves.

ARI.   I'll fetch them, sir.   [*Exit.*]

PROS.   Ye elves of hills, brooks, standing lakes and groves,
And ye that on the sands with printless foot
Do chase the ebbing Neptune, and do fly him
When he comes back; you demi-puppets that
By moonshine do the green sour ringlets make,
Whereof the ewe not bites, and you whose pastime
Is to make midnight mushrooms, that rejoice
To hear the solemn curfew; by whose aid,
Weak masters though ye be, I have bedimm'd
The noontide sun, call'd forth the mutinous winds,
And 'twixt the green sea and the azured vault
Set roaring war: to the dread rattling thunder
Have I given fire, and rifted Jove's stout oak
With his own bolt; the strong-based promontory
Have I made shake, and by the spurs pluck'd up
The pine and cedar; graves at my command
Have waked their sleepers, oped, and let 'em forth
By my so potent art. But this rough magic
I here abjure, and when I have required
Some heavenly music, which even now I do,

To work mine end upon their senses that
This airy charm is for, I'll break my staff,
Bury it certain fathoms in the earth,
And deeper than did ever plummet sound
I'll drown my book.   [*Solemn music.*]

WISDOM

Sara Teasdale

When I have ceased to break my wings
Against the faultiness of things,
And learned that compromises wait
Behind each hardly opened gate,
When I can look Life in the eyes,
Grown calm and very coldly wise,
Life will have given me the Truth,
And taken in exchange—my youth.

Reprinted with permission of Macmillan Publishing Co., Inc. from *Collected Poems* by Sara Teasdale. Copyright 1917 by Macmillan Publishing Co., Inc., renewed 1945 by Mamie T. Wheless.

THE MINISTER

Charles Mercer

Name: Katherine Judson. Age: twenty-one. Home: New York City. Occupation: junior, Wellesley College, Wellesley, Massachusetts. Affiliation: Student Nonviolent Coordinating Committee.

In the heat and turmoil of the Nashville bus terminal the young, bespectacled black took down the information carefully, then looked Kathy up and down. "Honey, you sure you're twenty-one?"

"I will be in a few days."

He grinned. "So you want to spend your birthday in jail. You doing this to duck your year's finals?"

"I finished them yesterday," Kathy said. "I had to fly to get here on time."

"Plenty of time," the black said. "This bus don't keep much of a schedule. The drivers keep funkin' out. So you're a SNICK." Thus the Student Nonviolent Coordinating Committee was called. "We got five SNICK's, eight CORE's, three SCLC's, seven independents, and not a single N double ACP." He looked around at the next bench. "Suzie Polk over there's a SNICK from Howard. Hey, Suzie!" he yelled above the din at a stout young Negro woman. "Here's an ofay to keep you company."

Suzie Polk treated Kathy coolly. What was SNICK doing at Wellesley? Kathy sometimes had wondered herself. A gang of Nashville white youths, jeering and yelling obscenities at the group planning an integrated bus ride to Montgomery, Alabama, made conversation almost impossible

Reprinted by permission of the author and International Creative Management, Inc. from *The Minister*, by Charles Mercer, © 1969 by Charles Mercer. New York: G. P. Putnam's Sons.

anyway. When a couple of youths began throwing tomatoes, shirt-sleeved sheriff's deputies stepped in front of the gang and said, ''Cut it out, boys, now just take it easy.'' Kathy wanted to tell Suzie that *this* was why she had come here, that they were sisters, that all citizens must have equal rights. But of course, those sentiments, which had seemed convincing on the Wellesley campus, would have sounded banal in the Nashville bus terminal.

''There's Dave Murchison.'' Suzie pointed to a tall, husky-looking young white man who had just come in carrying an airline flight bag and was being greeted warmly by a couple of the black leaders. ''He's one ofay Dr. King trusts. Last year during the Greensboro sit-ins he spent a week in jail.''

Kathy found it hard to believe. She thought him sort of handsome in an Ivy League biscuit-cutter way: cropped hair, lean face, deadpan demeanor. He stared at her over the heads of the blacks, then made his way to her.

''I'm Dave Murchison. Who are you?''

''Kathy Judson, New York.''

He sat down beside her. ''I'm at Union Seminary.''

Suddenly he interested her. ''My father's a minister in New York.''

He looked at her more closely. ''Martin Judson?'' Yes. ''Martin Judson of Old Fourth,'' he said slowly. ''So we have a daughter of the Protestant Establishment with us.''

She narrowed her eyelids at him. ''What Establishment are you talking about, preacher boy?''

He grinned suddenly. ''The New York Protestant Establishment begins at the Cathedral and goes south to Trinity at Wall, then curves through the prettier parts of Long Island and up into Westchester. They wear the sword of liberalism but take care never to join any expedition south of the Mason-Dixon Line.''

Father a member of the Protestant Establishment? It was ridiculous. Because he had pulled Old Fourth up by its bootstraps and built it into a strong church, he apparently had become a target for the little preacher boys. Good heavens, Father was a radical! When she had phoned him from Wellesley and asked for money to join the freedom ride, he had not demurred for an instant. ''I'll send a check right away, Kathy. Glad you want to act on your convictions. Just do me one favor. If you land in jail and SNICK doesn't have the bail money promptly, send me a wire.''

At last they climbed on the bus, and Kathy sat down beside Suzie.

David Murchison took the seat across the aisle from Kathy. As the bus rolled through the suburbs of Nashville, he talked endlessly, practically telling her the story of his life.

He had been graduated from the University of Michigan, where he had worked at trying to be a writer. "Only thing wrong with that is I don't have any real talent for it." Then why Union Theological? His answer to her question was vague.

"Well, maybe just to irritate my old man. He's dead and doesn't know it. Dead and buried in Scarsdale. I hadn't seen him in three years when I tried to raise some money from him to go to Union. Gosh, it made him mad. He hates Christianity—everything, me included. Says I'm a goddamn Communist."

His father and mother had divorced when he was fifteen, and now she was married to a kooky art dealer and living in Paris. It was his mother who financed him at Union. "She'd like to spoil me. Compensation, I suppose, for walking out on the old bastard in Scarsdale and going off with the art dealer." Did he hate her, too? "No, I sort of like her and feel sorry for her."

There were six white and seventeen black passengers on the bus which sped south through a parched-looking land of yellow clay. The country was as Kathy had expected from her reading about the South. But the atmosphere in the bus was wholly unexpected. In Wellesley and Boston she had heard much about the warm fraternity of fighters for civil rights, but on this bus there was a restraint amounting to coolness between blacks and whites. Dave, a veteran of the new civil war, was the only white whom the blacks trusted fully.

Early in the afternoon the bus stopped where there was a roadside stand, a dilapidated house above a clay bank, a mangy dog asleep in the dust. An old man began padlocking an outhouse as Kathy walked to the stand where a thin woman with a weathered face stared at her grimly. There was nothing to eat, nothing to drink, the woman cried shrilly.

Dave shared his sandwiches and thermos of iced tea with Kathy, who had not thought to bring food or drink. After they climbed onto the bus, he sat down beside her and at once fell asleep. She marveled at him. When she remembered having read that instant sleep was a capacity possessed by most persons who fought oppressive society, she even began to admire him. In midafternoon the black leader called to him, and he awakened as instantaneously as he had slept.

Following a short conference with Dave, the leader addressed the riders. Montgomery was their destination, but first they must pass through Birmingham. He advised them to segregate themselves by color, remain passive, and not try to leave the bus when it paused at the Birmingham terminal. "But Dave has other ideas. He's going to tell you his, and you're free to act as you please. After all, this is a *freedom* ride."

Dave's voice rose easily, and Kathy realized he must be a persuasive public speaker. "My thought is that the Battle of Montgomery is no more important than the Battle of Birmingham. In fact, the more Southern battlefields the better. I think the police may stop us at the Birmingham city limits and arrest any who refuse to segregate their seats. Personally, this ofay plans to get arrested. They say the Birmingham city jail has nice clean sheets and ice cold drinks." There were jeering cheers. "Is there a black man on this bus willing to go to jail with me?" After a lengthy silence a young CORE man said he would be honored. "Anybody else want to see how the better half lives in a Southern jail?"

Kathy wondered if he was gazing at her. Remembering suddenly a line from one of her childhood prayers—"Let's get on with it, Lord"—she stood up.

Dave smiled at her and called, "Bless thee, Katherine, in the names of Peter, Titus, and Paul. Kathy Judson of New York is looking for a cellmate. Any takers?"

Suzie looked around at her and exclaimed, "Well, I'll be! Come sit with me, Kathy."

"You're a pretty dispirited-looking bunch," Dave said. "Let's put some oil on this tired machine. Let's *lubricate* democracy and make freedom hum. Everybody remembers that rascal John Brown. . . ."

As he led them in the well-known song, Kathy thought: *My gosh, an old-time Gospel singing preacher, turned inside out and twisted all around, with different aims and a language part new, part old, but all tuned to strange ears.*

Half an hour later, as they entered Birmingham, the wailing of a police siren made her neck chill. The driver pulled to the side and stopped the bus. Kathy, thinking of what she had heard about Southern police brutality, was scared. Yet she had asked for whatever might happen to her, so there was no reason to William Blake it and think with the poet: "and the bitter groan of a martyr's woe/Is an arrow from the Almighty's bow."

To her surprise, the policeman who stepped onto the bus was young, good-looking. In a courteous tone he said they had entered the city limits of Birmingham. Then he recited the local ordinance on segregation of bus riders and asked them to conform with the law. When Kathy, Dave, and their black seat partners failed to move, the policeman said he would have to take them into custody. Unprotesting, they left the bus with him. Kathy and Suzie rode to police headquarters in the rear seat of one squad car while Dave and his companion rode in another.

At headquarters they pleaded guilty and were booked. After searching through a sheaf of papers, a lieutenant said Dave and his seat companion had criminal records; if they could not post bail of one thousand dollars each, they would be remanded to jail. Dave laughed, and they were led away. Suzie's bail was set at five hundred dollars, and she left with a matron.

"Now look here," the lieutenant said to Kathy. Why should a nice girl like her mess around in things that didn't affect her? It was the most paternal lecture she ever had received. Repent—and go home. She thought of a couple of eloquent remarks but could not bring herself to make them. Instead, she insisted she was guilty, and lacking five hundred dollars' bail, she followed the matron to a reasonably clean cell in the women's block.

A drunken woman yammered down the block, and two cockroaches paraded on the ceiling. After a while Suzie called out her name, and Kathy answered. Having anticipated arrest, Kathy had brought along a paperback edition of *Walden*, which she had started twice in years past but never finished. Now, beginning it again while curled up on her cot, she found herself understanding for the first time why Thoreau went to the pond.

Around six o'clock the matron brought her corned-beef hash, bread, and canned peaches. When she came for the dishes, she lingered for a long time—not to converse, but to lecture. What did Kathy think she was accomplishing? On and on the matron ranted. Didn't she at least want to notify her parents so they could bail her out? No, she had given the lieutenant money for a telegram notifying SNICK headquarters of Suzie's and her arrests, but she was beginning to wonder if the telegram had been sent.

Later in the evening five women who had been on the bus were brought into the block. They said there had been roughing at the bus terminal, and they had been put under something called protective custody. Kathy slept poorly, and the next day she began to understand why the verb "languish" applied to jail. After finishing *Walden*, she started it again and found that the pond had grown stagnant to her.

On the second morning, following a breakfast of bread, powdered eggs, and coffee, she and the six black women riders were taken to the room where they had been arraigned. Two black men riders were brought from their cells and joined them. Kathy inquired about Dave, but the men did not know what had become of him. When the nine were led out and placed by threes in police cars, she assumed they were being taken to court.

But the cars sped north out of Birmingham along the highway which the freedom riders had followed into the city two days previously. At last Kathy asked, "Where are we going?" Neither of the two policemen in the front seat answered her. It was bewildering and a little frightening, like being caught up in a Kafka creation in which the subject could not relate to the object. She had been arrested and jailed under due process of law, but now the authorities were violating law as flagrantly as the freedom riders. On the police cars raced for what seemed hours.

At last the car began to slow down on a lonely stretch of road fringed by clay banks and pine barrens. When they stopped, one of the policemen spoke for the first time: "Get out!" The woman beside Kathy began to shake and weep. Her terror was infectious, raising unreasonable images of the law gone berserk, of massacre by police guns on the hot and piny clay. Kathy's legs shook as she climbed out.

The policemen stared out at her contemptuously, ignoring the blacks. "This is the state line," one said. "Start walking, and never come back to Alabama."

As they walked north in the heat, cars passed them in both directions. Drivers stared at them curiously, but none stopped. Eventually, Kathy thought, they would reach a town where they could board a bus back to Nashville. It was a sad, a ridiculous ending to her brave protest, her great adventure. Before long the heat began to dissipate her anger into a sullen weariness.

The blaring of a horn behind them warned of some new danger. She looked around at an old outsized limousine such as served airport passengers. Seated beside the black driver was David Murchison, who managed to look at the same time surprised, pleased, sad, and angry. Thus possibly General Nathan Bedford Forrest had looked when surrounded in these parts before issuing his famous order: "We'll charge both ways!" But when Dave climbed out of the swaybacked limousine, his order was: "Hop in! Back to Birmingham!"

Not Bedford Forrest, but Tom Sawyer, Kathy thought. Into jail, out of jail, back to jail again—and like Huck Finn, she wondered to what purpose. "Now wait a minute," she said.

"You've had enough?"

"Not necessarily. I'd just like some explanation of what's being accomplished."

"We've got 'em on the run."

"I'd say they had us on the walk. How did you get out of jail?"

"My outfit raised bail. Reinforcements are pouring in. Our intelligence network is really cracking. We knew the minute you people were run out of town. Both President Kennedy and the Attorney General are trying to get the governor of Alabama on the phone. We're gathering strength at the Birmingham bus terminal. Before long they'll weaken, and we'll bus it on to Montgomery. Climb in!"

After they climbed into the swaybacked limousine and headed back to Birmingham, Kathy asked him, "Have you ever considered an Army career?"

"No dice. I'm a pacifist."

Some pacifist! Like Uncle Tubby, with his medals, or Father, with his Korean adventures. Onward, Christian soldiers, marching on to jail.

More than a score of freedom riders were gathered at the Birmingham bus terminal when they arrived there. Kathy expected momentarily that they would be arrested, but General Bedford Forrest Murchison proved himself the wiser tactician. They were too numerous now; such a large number of arrests would flood the jail and draw more national attention to Birmingham than the city authorities cared to receive.

Now the police gave them a protective screen against the toughs who wanted to assault them. Now, too, Kathy began to realize that patience was the most important weapon of the resistance fighter. As the hours crept by, she struggled against boredom, fatigue, and—worst of all—a feeling of personal uncleanliness. She would have given almost anything for a shower, a change of clothing, a few quiet moments away from the din—anything, of course, except giving up the effort and going home.

It was a long night on benches which seemed to grow harder as time passed. Their effort to integrate the terminal lunchroom failed when the employees closed it and left. Dave and a white professor from Princeton attempted a sortie out for coffee and food, but they were attacked by a gang of youths and retreated to the terminal somewhat battered. At an early hour of morning, however, a strong force of allies brought them coffee and dry bologna sandwiches.

Wheels were turning in other places, Dave maintained cheerfully. Eventually the governor of Alabama would have to pick up the phone and answer the President of the United States. Eventually something must indeed have happened someplace else, for, about ten o'clock in the morning, they climbed onto a bus and set out for Montgomery.

Ah, Montgomery, first capital of the Old Confederacy, rising from the Alabama River, white columns gleaming through catalpa, sweet gum and magnolia, haunt of Jefferson Davis and the professional auctioneers wearing beaver hats and black tailcoats as they cried, "Niggers is cheap, niggers is cheap . . . " swollen now to one hundred and thirty-four thousand black and white skins, industries capitalized by the North, yet still unreconstructed Confederate. Thus Kathy tried to alleviate her weariness. Thus, too, a black man ahead of her said, "We'll bring those bastards to their knees."

It happened with terrifying suddenness after the bus pulled into the Montgomery terminal. The mob gathered there was much larger, its outraged cries more menacing than the crowds had been in Nashville and Birmingham. Dave led the way off the bus. Kathy, not far behind, saw him suddenly engulfed by several youths. He disappeared, as if the earth had swallowed him. Those behind him began trying to struggle back on, but those still aboard were screaming that the mob was trying to set fire to the bus. Kathy found herself flung into the roaring crowd as by a kind of centrifugal force. She glimpsed a man swing a baseball bat at her and tried to dodge, but someone else shoved her into its arc. There was a numbing pain in her right side, and she went down, struggling for consciousness. . . .

The events that followed always remained vague to her. Somehow she struggled free of the fierce riot and finally was seized by two policemen. When arraigned the pain in her chest was so severe that she begged for the attention of a doctor. What bail was set she could not remember; neither could she recall whether she gave Father's name and address. She kept asking about Dave, but no one seemed to understand her. And then she found herself in a cell with two Negro women.

Perhaps it was that day, perhaps the next, that a doctor came to her cell. Almost at once he had her carried out on a stretcher and transported by ambulance to a women's ward of a hospital. After a time she was rolled off for X rays, and eventually, at some hour of daylight or darkness, a physician came to her bedside. He was a kindly, competent man named Grey, who talked with her as if she were a close friend. She had four broken ribs and a torn liver, besides cuts and contusions about the head and both arms. Her ribs would heal; so would her liver without surgery if she remained immobile, Dr. Grey believed. She gave him Father's name, and he promised to find out what had happened to Dave.

The next afternoon she awakened from a doze to see Dave standing beside her bed. Both his eyes were blackened, his lip cut, his jaw swollen.

He said something corny: "But you ought to see those other guys." He assumed a John L. Sullivan stance and swung his fists. "Take that, Jeff Davis! Take that, Pierre Beauregard! And you that, Braxton Bragg! Not a scratch on 'em." Incredibly, his eyes filled with tears. Even more incredibly, he leaned over and kissed her gently on the forehead. "Kathy, I'm so sorry about that beautiful face of yours. But the doctor says you're going to be all right." Blinking back his tears, he pulled up a chair and sat down gingerly, wincing. "The greatest indignity came when somebody gave me a tremendous boot in the ass."

"Why aren't you in jail?" she asked.

"Released on bail again. Things are really popping. . . . " Montgomery was under martial law. Martin Luther King, Jr., had arrived from Chicago, and when he tried to address a black mass meeting at a church, there had been an even worse riot than at the bus terminal. Reinforcements for the freedom riders were pouring in from the North, as were federal marshals.

THE LAST DAY
IN THE FIELD

Caroline Gordon

That was the fall when the leaves stayed green so long. We had a drouth in August and the ponds everywhere were dry and the watercourse shrunken. Then in September heavy rains came. Things greened up. It looked like winter was never coming.

"You aren't going to hunt this year, Aleck," Molly said. "Remember how you stayed awake nights last fall with that pain in your leg."

In October light frosts came. In the afternoons when I sat on the back porch going over my fishing tackle I marked their progress on the elderberry bushes that were left standing against the stable fence. The lower, spreading branches had turned yellow and were already sinking to the ground but the leaves in the top clusters still stood up stiff and straight.

"Ah-h, it'll get you yet!" I said, thinking how frost creeps higher and higher out of the ground each night of fall.

The dogs next door felt it and would thrust their noses through the wire fence scenting the wind from the north. When I walked in the back yard they would bound twice their height and whine, for meat scraps Molly said, but it was because they smelled blood on my old hunting coat.

They were almost matched liver-and-white pointers. The big dog had a beautiful, square muzzle and was deep-chested and rangy. The bitch, Judy, had a smaller head and not so good a muzzle but she was springy loined too and had one of the merriest tails I've ever watched.

Reprinted from *The Forest of the South* by Caroline Gordon. New York: Charles Scribner's Sons, 1934.

When Joe Thomas, the boy that owned them, came home from the hardware store he would change his clothes and then come down the back way into the wired enclosure and we would stand there watching the dogs and wondering how they would work. Joe said they were keen as mustard. He was going to take them out the first good Saturday and wanted me to come along.

"I can't make it," I said, "my leg's worse this year than it was last."

The fifteenth of November was clear and so warm that we sat out on the porch till nine o'clock. It was still warm when we went to bed towards eleven. The change must have come in the middle of the night. I woke once, hearing the clock strike two, and felt the air cold on my face and thought before I went back to sleep that the weather had broken at last. When I woke again at dawn the cold air was slapping my face hard. I came wide awake, turned over in bed and looked out of the window.

There was a scaly-bark hickory tree growing on the east side of the house. You could see its upper branches from the bedroom window. The leaves had turned yellow a week ago. But yesterday evening when I walked out there in the yard they had still been flat with green streaks showing in them. Now they were curled up tight and a lot of leaves had fallen on to the ground.

I got out of bed quietly so as not to wake Molly, dressed and went down the back way over to the Thomas house. There was no one stirring but I knew which room Joe's was. The window was open and I could hear him snoring. I went up and stuck my head in.

"Hey," I said, "killing frost."

He opened his eyes and looked at me and then his eyes went shut. I reached my arm through the window and shook him. "Get up," I said, "we got to start right away."

He was awake now and out on the floor stretching. I told him to dress and be over at the house as quick as he could. I'd have breakfast ready for us both.

Aunt Martha had a way of leaving fire in the kitchen stove at night. There were red embers there now. I poked the ashes out and piled kindling on top of them. When the flames came up I put some heavier wood on, filled the coffee pot, and put some grease on in a skillet. By the time Joe got there I had coffee ready and some hoe cakes to go with our fried eggs. Joe had brought a thermos bottle. We put the rest of the coffee in it and I found a ham in the pantry and made some sandwiches.

While I was fixing the lunch Joe went down to the lot to hitch up. He was just driving Old Dick out of the stable when I came down the back steps. The dogs knew what was up, all right. They were whining and surging against the fence and Bob, the big dog, thrust his paw through and into the pocket of my hunting coat as I passed. While Joe was snapping on the leashes I got a few handfuls of straw from the rack and put it in the foot of the buggy. It was twelve miles where we were going; the dogs would need to ride warm coming back late.

Joe said he would drive. We got in the buggy and started out, up Seventh Street and on over to College and out through Scufftown. When we got into the nigger section we could see what a killing frost it had been. A light shimmer over all the ground still and the weeds around the cabins dark and matted the way they are when the frost hits them hard and twists them.

We drove on over the Red River bridge and up into the open country. At Jim Gill's place the cows had come up and were standing waiting to be milked but nobody was stirring yet from the house. I looked back from the top of the hill and saw that the frost mists still hung heavy in the bottom and thought it was a good sign. A day like this when the earth is warmer than the air currents is good for the hunter. Scent particles are borne on the warm air and birds will forage far on such a day.

It took us over an hour to get from Gloversville to Spring Creek. Joe wanted to get out as soon as we hit the big bottom there but I held him down and we drove on to the top of the ridge. We got out there, unhitched Old Dick and turned him into one of Rob Fayerlee's pastures—I thought how surprised Rob would be when he saw him grazing there—put our guns together, and started out, the dogs still on leash.

It was rough, broken ground, scrub oak, with a few gum trees and lots of buckberry bushes. One place a patch of corn ran clear up to the top of the ridge. As we passed along between the rows I could see the frost glistening on the north side of the stalks. I knew it was going to be a good day.

I walked over to the brow of the hill. From here you can see off over the whole valley—I've hunted every foot of it in my time—tobacco land, mostly. One or two patches of corn there on the side of the ridge. I thought we might start there and then I knew that wouldn't do. Quail will linger on the roost a cold day and feed in shelter during the morning. It is only in the afternoon that they will work out to the open.

The dogs were whining. Joe bent down and was about to slip their leashes. "Hey, boy," I said, "don't do that."

I turned around and looked down the other side of the ridge. It was better that way. The corn land of the bottoms ran high up on to the hill in several places there and where the corn stopped there were big patches of ironweed and buckberry. I knocked my pipe out on a stump.

"Let's go that way," I said.

Joe was looking at my old buckhorn whistle that I had slung around my neck. "I forgot to bring mine."

"All right," I said, "I'll handle 'em."

He unfastened their collars and cast off. They broke away, racing for the first hundred yards and barking, then suddenly swerved. The big dog took off to the right along the hillside. The bitch, Judy, skirted a belt of corn along the upper bottomlands. I kept my eye on the big dog. A dog that has bird sense will know cover when he sees it. This big Bob was an independent hunter, all right. I could see him moving fast through the scrub oaks, working his way down toward a patch of ironweed. He caught first scent just on the edge of the weed patch and froze with every indication of class, head up, nose stuck out, and tail straight in air. Judy, meanwhile, had been following the line of the corn field. A hundred yards away she caught sight of Bob's point and backed him.

We went up and flushed the birds. They got up in two bunches. I heard Joe's shot while I was in the act of raising my gun and I saw his bird fall not thirty paces from where I stood. I had covered the middle bird of the larger bunch—that's the one led by the boss cock—the way I usually do. He fell, whirling head over heels, driven a little forward by the impact. A well-centered shot. I could tell by the way the feathers fluffed as he tumbled.

The dogs were off through the grass. They had retrieved both birds. Joe stuck his in his pocket. He laughed. "I thought there for a minute you were going to let him get away."

I looked at him but I didn't say anything. It's a wonderful thing to be twenty years old.

The majority of the singles had flown straight ahead to settle in the rank grass that jutted out from the bottomland. Judy got down to work at once but the big dog broke off to the left, wanting to get footloose to find another covey. I thought of how Trecho, the best dog I ever had—the best dog any man ever had—used always to be wanting to do the same thing and I laughed.

"Naw, you don't," I said, "come back here, you scoundrel, and hunt these singles."

He stopped on the edge of a briar patch, looked at me and heeled up promptly. I clucked him out again. He gave me another look. I thought we were beginning to understand each other better. We got some nice points among those singles but we followed that valley along the creek bed and through two or three more corn fields without finding another covey. Joe was disappointed but I wasn't beginning to worry yet; you always make your bag in the afternoon.

It was twelve o'clock by this time, no sign of frost anywhere and the sun beating down steady on the curled-up leaves.

"Come on," I said, "let's go up to Buck's spring and eat."

We walked up the ravine whose bed was still moist with the fall rains and came out at the head of the hollow. They had cleared out some of the trees on the side of the ravine but the spring itself was the same: a deep pool welling up between the roots of an old sycamore. I unwrapped the sandwiches and the piece of cake and laid them on a stump. Joe got the thermos bottle out of his pocket. Something had gone wrong with it and the coffee was stone cold. We were about to drink it that way when Joe saw a good tin can flung down beside the spring. He made a trash fire and we put the coffee in the can and heated it to boiling.

It was warm in the ravine, sheltered from the wind, with the little fire burning. I turned my game leg so that the heat fell full on my knee. Joe had finished his last sandwich and was reaching for the cake.

"Good ham," he said.

"It's John Ferguson's," I told him.

He had got up and was standing over the spring. "Wonder how long this wood'll last, under water this way."

I looked at the sycamore root, green and slick where the thin stream of water poured over it, then my eyes went back to the dogs. They were tired, all right. Judy had gone off to lie down in a cool place at the side of the spring, but the big dog, Bob, lay there, his forepaws stretched out in front of him, never taking his eyes off our faces. I looked at him and thought how different he was from his mate and like some dogs I had known—and men too—who lived only for hunting and could never get enough no matter how long the day. There was something about his head and his markings that reminded one of another dog I used to hunt with a long time ago and I asked the boy who had trained him. He said the old fellow he bought the dogs from had been killed last spring, over in Trigg—Charley Morrison.

Charley Morrison! I remembered how he died, out hunting by him-self and the gun had gone off, accidentally they said. Charley had called his dog to him, got blood over him and sent him home. The dog went, all right, but when they got there Charley was dead. Two years ago that was and now I was hunting the last dogs he'd ever trained. . . .

Joe lifted the thermos bottle. "Another cup?"

I held my cup out and he filled it. The coffee was still good and hot. I drank it, standing up, running my eye over the country in front of us. Af-ternoon is different from morning, more exciting. It isn't only as I say that you'll make your bag in the afternoon, but it takes more figuring. They're fed and rested and when they start out again they'll work in the open and over a wider range.

Joe was stamping out his cigarette: "Let's go."

The dogs were already out of sight but I could see the sedge grass ahead moving and I knew they'd be making for the same thing that took my eye: a spearhead of thicket that ran far out into this open field. We came up over a little rise. There they were, Bob on a point and Judy back-ing him not fifty feet from the thicket. I saw it was going to be tough shoot-ing. No way to tell whether the birds were between the dog and the thicket or in the thicket itself. Then I saw that the cover was more open along the side of the thicket and I thought that that was the way they'd go if they were in the thicket. But Joe had already broken away to the left. He got too far to the side. The birds flushed to the right and left him standing, flat-footed, without a shot.

He looked sort of foolish and grinned.

I thought I wouldn't say anything and then I found myself speaking: "Trouble with you, you try to out-think the dog."

There was nothing to do about it, though. The chances were that the singles had pitched in the trees below. We went down there. It was hard hunting. The woods were open, the ground everywhere heavily carpeted with leaves. Dead leaves make a tremendous rustle when the dogs surge through them. It takes a good nose to cut scent keenly in such noisy cover. I kept my eye on Bob. He never faltered, getting over the ground in big, springy strides but combing every inch of it. We came to an open place in the woods. Nothing but hickory trees and bramble thickets overhung with trailing vines. Bob passed the first thicket and came to a beautiful point. We went up. He stood perfectly steady but the bird flushed out fif-teen or twenty steps ahead of him. I saw it swing to the right, gaining alti-

tude very quickly—woods birds will always cut back to known territory—
and it came to me how it would be.

I called to Joe: "Don't shoot yet."

He nodded and raised his gun, following the bird with the barrel. It
was directly over the treetops when I gave the word and he shot, scoring a
clean kill.

He laughed excitedly as he stuck the bird in his pocket. "My God,
man, I didn't know you could take that much time!"

We went on through the open woods. I was thinking about a day I'd
had years ago in the woods at Grassdale, with my uncle, James Morris, and
his son, Julian. Uncle James had given Julian and me hell for missing just
such a shot. I can see him now standing up against a big pine tree, his face
red from liquor and his gray hair ruffling in the wind: "*Let him alone! Let
him alone!* And establish your lead as he climbs."

Joe was still talking about the shot he'd made. "Lord, I wish I could
get another one like that."

"You won't," I said, "we're getting out of the woods now."

We struck a path that led due west and followed it for half a mile. My
leg was stiff from the hip down now and every time I brought it over, the
pain would start in my knee, Zing! and travel up and settle in the small of
my back. I walked with my head down, watching the light catch on the
ridges of Joe's brown corduroy trousers and then shift and catch again.
Sometimes he would get on ahead and then there would be nothing but
the black tree trunks coming up out of the dead leaves.

Joe was talking about some wild land up on the Cumberland. We
could get up there on an early train. Have a good day. Might even spend
the night. When I didn't answer he turned around: "Man, you're sweating."

I pulled my handkerchief out and wiped my face. "Hot work," I said.

He had stopped and was looking about him. "Used to be a spring
somewhere around here."

He had found the path and was off. I sat down on a stump and mopped
my face some more. The sun was halfway down through the trees now, the
whole west woods ablaze with the light. I sat there and thought that in another hour it would be good and dark and I wished that the day could go
on and not end so soon and yet I didn't see how I could make it much farther with my leg the way it was.

Joe was coming up the path with his folding cup full of water. I hadn't thought I was thirsty but the cold water tasted good. We sat there awhile and smoked, then Joe said that we ought to be starting back, that we must be a good piece from the rig by this time.

We set out, working north through the edge of the woods. It was rough going and I was thinking that it would be all I could do to make it back to the rig when we climbed a fence and came out at one end of a long field that sloped down to a wooded ravine. Broken ground, badly gullied and covered with sedge everywhere except where sumac thickets had sprung up—as birdy a place as ever I saw. I looked it over and knew I had to hunt it, leg or no leg, but it would be close work, for me and the dogs too.

I blew them in a bit and we stood there watching them cut up the cover. The sun was down now; there was just enough light left to see the dogs work. The big dog circled the far wall of the basin and came up wind just off the drain, then stiffened to a point. We walked down to it. The birds had obviously run a bit into the scraggly sumac stalks that bordered the ditch. My mind was so much on the dogs I forgot Joe. He took one step too many. The fullest blown bevy of the day roared up through the tangle. It had to be fast work. I raised my gun and scored with the only barrel I had time to peg. Joe shouted; I knew he had got one too.

We stood there trying to figure out which way the singles had gone but they had fanned out too quick for us, excited as we were, and after beating around awhile we gave up and went on.

We came to the rim of the swale, eased over it, crossed the dry creek bed that was drifted thick with leaves, and started up the other side. I had blown in the dogs, thinking there was no use for them to run their heads off now we'd started home, but they didn't come. I walked on a little farther, then I looked back and saw Bob's white shoulders through a tangle of cinnamon vine.

Joe had turned around too. "They've pinned a single out of that last covey," he said.

I looked over at him quick. "Your shot."

He shook his head. "No, you take it."

I limped back and flushed the bird. It went skimming along the buckberry bushes that covered that side of the swale. In the fading light I could hardly make it out and I shot too quick. It swerved over the thicket and I let go with the second barrel. It staggered, then zoomed up. Up, up, up, over the rim of the hill and above the tallest hickories. It hung there for a second, its wings black against the gold light, before, wings still spread, it came whirling down, like an autumn leaf, like the leaves that were everywhere about us, all over the ground.

THE ODD OLD LADY

Thyra Samter Winslow

The first time that old Mrs. Quillan knew anything was, well, different, was the night at dinner when Winnie came into the dining room wearing her new blue dress.

Winnie was seventeen and the prettiest of the old lady's grandchildren. She had soft, light hair and a tip-tilted nose, and had just got over the sloppy-sweater stage. Now she wore a dress that fitted closely her slim, young body.

"I'm so glad you got the spot out of your dress," the old lady said, in her gentle voice with just a suggestion of a quaver in it.

"What spot do you mean, Grandma?" asked Winnie. "This is my new dress. I never had a spot on it."

"Why, didn't Ralph Miller spill chocolate ice-cream soda on it and we couldn't . . . " Grandma began and stopped suddenly.

"You must have dreamed that, Mother," said Julia Latham a bit uncertainly. It wasn't like Mrs. Quillan to imagine things. Everybody was always saying how clear her mind was.

"Of course, I . . . I guess I dreamed it," said the old lady quickly. She put some raspberry jam on a piece of bread for Bobby and was glad he didn't say anything. Bobby was a great one for repeating things. So was Evan, her son-in-law. They never meant anything by it, Grandma knew that. But they liked family jokes. If . . . if they took this up . . . Grandma gave a sigh of relief when they began talking about something else.

For, as soon as she had said it, Grandma knew! She knew as definitely as she knew that on the table stood the old teapot and sugar bowl that Grandpa had brought her when he'd gone to St. Louis many years ago. It wasn't a dream! She knew something no one else could know. And it had never happened to her before. Winnie didn't know about the spot on her dress because she hadn't yet spotted her dress! Ralph Miller hadn't yet spilled the chocolate soda down the front of it. Poor Winnie! Her lovely new dress to be ruined like that! Grandma couldn't warn her.

There was nothing she could do, for Grandma didn't know how she knew about the spot. Sometimes, here of late, she'd got sort of mixed up about things. Like when she thought she'd seen Mrs. Willis on the street —and Mrs. Willis had been dead for three years! Oh, Grandma knew, all right, when she thought hard. And she tried to think before she said things, but this had sort of tumbled out. Oh, well, maybe she was wrong! Maybe Winnie wouldn't spot her dress after all.

Grandma tried to pretend to herself that she hadn't said anything.

There were lots of things to do. Dishes to wash. Beds to make. Helping her daughter, Julia, so that Julia could have time for the things she liked to do. Doing the things Winnie was supposed to do, because Winnie hated housework. A young girl has to have some fun!

Three days later Winnie flew into the house.

"That awkward goon of a Ralph Miller!" she wailed. "He spilled a whole glass of chocolate ice-cream soda all over my dress! He said Chester Alden shoved his arm. It never will come out, I know!"

"You'd better take it right to the cleaners," her mother said, "unless Grandma . . ."

"I'm afraid I can't," said Grandma, knowing the spot would always show.

"It's my new dress!" said Winnie. And then she remembered. "Grandma, didn't you say I'd get chocolate soda on my dress?"

"Oh, Grandma was just imagining things. She wasn't even with you. Rush out to the cleaners with that dress," Julia said.

Winnie ran away and Grandma took a deep breath of thankfulness. Maybe they wouldn't mention what she'd said about the spot ever again. It was too bad, though, it's coming true. Winnie didn't get many pretty things. Grandma made a resolution to be more careful.

It was odd about life anyway. One time everything had run along so smoothly. There'd been the little cottage and Grandpa, and then the children. There wasn't even time to think about things, then. Everything was in its right order—just the way it happened. Breakfast to get—hearty breakfasts, for Grandpa worked hard and liked hot biscuits and a nice piece of fried ham in the morning. And there was bread to bake—fat, fragrant loaves, and coffee roasting in the oven and bacon frying. Grandma liked nice smells. And sewing for the whole family—you couldn't buy good, ready-made things in those days. And long rides with Grandpa in the surrey behind Nelly, the steady old mare. And then this big house, and a girl to help with the cleaning, though Grandma liked to do the cooking herself. And the children growing up . . .

And now Grandpa was dead and little Josephine was dead. And Arthur was married and living in Chicago, and he never forgot to send a check every month and a letter, too, though being married to a wife none of them knew very well sort of separated them.

Grandma shook her head. Everything was all right! Here she was, living with Julia and Evan, who were so good to her. Of course the house was hers, and Arthur's check went into the family coffers, but she knew Evan did the best he could. Grandma did her share, too. And she was glad she could help in the house and with the neighbors when she had a chance. Dr. Clement was mighty good about coming by, and picking her up, and letting her do things when he had a patient who was too poor to hire a nurse.

Yes, everything was all right, except knowing things. And even that might be all right, if she could remember to keep things straight in her mind.

It was last year when things began to get mixed up. Things that had happened a long time ago seemed to have happened only yesterday. And things that had happened only yesterday she couldn't remember at all. She asked Dr. Clement about it—as if it were happening to someone else, and he said that's the way it was sometimes when you got old.

It wasn't much fun getting old. Grandma knew she took little, short steps, and the others had to walk slowly when they went to church. And there were her teeth . . . and her eyes. And it was lonely without Grandpa, though she never let the others know. There weren't many men like Grandpa. She'd been lucky having him all those years. The year they planted the lilac bush . . . It seemed odd when she forgot it had been planted many years ago.

But that was all right, remembering things that happened so long ago and forgetting the things that happened just yesterday. It was this new thing that worried Grandma, knowing things before they happened at all. But maybe it was an accident—knowing about the stain on the blue dress. She must be careful and keep her mind on what she was saying.

But she forgot that day at breakfast. The rest of the family drank coffee, but Grandma liked tea.

"Bring in Grandma's tea," Julia called to Winnie, who was carrying things in from the kitchen.

"Just bring my tea in a cup," said Grandma, "as long as the teapot's broken." But she was sorry about the teapot, for she loved it.

"The teapot's not broken, Mother," said Julia.

"But Bobby broke it," said Grandma. "Don't you remember? I don't mind, really. He couldn't help it."

"Here's your teapot," said Winnie and put it on the table in front of Grandma.

"I'm sorry," Grandma said, "I just imagined it, I guess."

But she hadn't imagined it. She just hadn't realized that the teapot hadn't yet been broken! She picked it up lovingly and watched the clear amber stream pour into her cup.

"You're getting odd notions, Mother," said Evan, "the way you imagine things!"

"I know," said Grandma, "maybe things that I dream of. . . . "

She put her hands into her lap suddenly. They were trembling so she couldn't have held the pot another minute.

A couple of days later, Bobby came home from school and reached for the cookie jar, high on the shelf, and the teapot careened onto the floor and lay there, broken.

"I couldn't help it!" wailed Bobby. "Maybe, because what Grandma said about my breaking the teapot . . . "

"Of course," comforted Grandma, "I sort of put it into your mind. You couldn't help it at all." She gave Bobby some of the Jordan almonds Mrs. Rogers had brought her on her birthday. No one said anything else about the teapot—after all, it was just an old teapot that only Grandma cared about.

"I'll be more careful after this!" Grandma told herself. But it worried her. It was all right the days she took an umbrella when the skies were still clear, because old ladies were apt to carry umbrellas. And going to see old Mrs. Hodges when she was lying alone and ill, because Grandma always had gone to see Mrs. Hodges. Only that day Grandma took a basket of provisions and wore her old clothes, the way she did when Dr. Clement took her to see sick people. But no one thought anything about it, because no one but Grandma was interested in Mrs. Hodges.

It was different about Winnie's new beau. Grandma knew about him as if it had already happened. But she couldn't seem to see clearly the people he was mixed up with. It couldn't be Winnie! Winnie couldn't get into anything like that!

Grandma thought it over and she knew she had to warn Evan, though she usually stayed out of things.

"That new boy from Chicago—I wouldn't let Winnie go out with him," she said.

"Why, Mother, he's a cousin of the Dillmans," Evan said. "He's been ill, came here to build up. A fine young man!"

"He's not a fine young man," Grandma said. "He'll . . . he'll get into trouble. I don't want Winnie . . ."

"The way you talk!" said Winnie. "Honest, Grandma, he couldn't be nicer—not like these dull home-town boys I'm used to."

The others agreed—a nice young man, Sid Forrest.

They never knew that when Sid telephoned, and Grandma answered the call, she didn't tell Winnie. And she gave Winnie the wrong directions the day Sid was to meet her at the library.

But when Winnie continued to see Sid, Grandma knew she had to do something. She even worried about it at night in bed.

Finally, she made up her mind. One day she put on her best black dress, with a little, white-embroidered collar, and the brooch Grandpa had given her and her rather shapeless little black hat, and went to see Morris Dillman.

Mr. Dillman was a tall, lanky gentleman, with a lined face. He had known Grandma Quillan all of his life.

"What can I do for you, Mrs. Quillan?" he asked kindly.

"It's about Sid Forrest," Grandma said. "He's going with Winnie, my granddaughter. I don't want him to come to the house any more."

"Why, Mrs. Quillan, he's my own second cousin. We're very fond of him. Did the family send you?"

"Oh, no, they don't know anything about it. I thought, if we talked it over . . ."

"I'll see what I can do," said Dillman, as if he were talking to a child. "Now, you go home and forget all about it."

"Oh, thank you," Grandma said. And stayed on to talk about little things, so Mr. Dillman wouldn't think she was odd or anything.

Morris Dillman must have gone right over to see Evan Latham, for by the time Grandma got home—she had stopped in to see Mrs. Morrison and the twins—the whole family knew about her call.

"Why, Mama," Julia said, "I don't know what's got into you lately. It isn't like you at all."

"Dillman thought it was odd," said Evan, who looked worried, too, "his cousin and all . . . "

"Why, Mother," Julia said quite sternly, "you'll ruin Winnie's chances . . . "

"I've never done anything like this before. And she'll have other chances. She's only seventeen."

Winnie was in tears. She didn't say anything.

But Sid kept on seeing Winnie. Grandma didn't know what to do. If there were only some way she could tell them what she knew. And right on the heels of that, there was that thing she said, without thinking, on the way to church.

"They're certainly neglecting the Kerner house since old man Kerner died," Grandma said.

They all looked at her curiously.

"Why, what makes you think he's dead?" Evan asked.

"Why, he died that day we had the rainstorm . . . " She began, then stopped, remembering!

"He's as alive as any of us." Evan said. "But they do neglect their place, all right—too lazy to keep it up. You mustn't get notions like that in your mind, Mother."

Old man Kerner died a few weeks later, and it rained hard the day he died. It was funny, Grandma saying that.

And when she said that about the Bates's apple tree being struck by lightning, weeks beforehand. Just a coincidence, of course, but it was odd . . .

Grandma began to be afraid to say anything. She had to think over carefully what she was going to say, and try to remember if a thing had happened twenty years ago—or yesterday—or was going to happen to-morrow. It was like, well, being up in a balloon, or maybe an airplane. Grandma didn't know about airplanes. She'd never been up in a balloon, either. But an airplane winged so swiftly through the sky, surely it couldn't get a view of the whole country at one time. A balloon seemed sort of stationary. She could see everything all stretched out at one time, though not too clearly, sometimes.

Yesterdays, a long way back, were clear. But recent yesterdays were dimmed, with just a few things plain. Today was clear enough. And tomorrow was like yesterday—certain things standing out bright and real and shining, the rest of it sort of dim, as if it were still in Time.

Sometimes Grandma knew, by the way the family looked at her, that she had said things she didn't mean to say, even when she didn't know what she had said. Only Bobby didn't seem to care. She loved Bobby; she loved all her children and grandchildren. If there was only something she could do . . .

If she'd only cared about big events! If only she'd been smarter when she was young! And had read the first pages of the newspapers and all of the serious books Grandpa had read, instead of darning children's stockings in the evening. If she knew about things, maybe now she'd be able to see things ahead that would help people. But when she tried to see ahead —to big things—she saw only confusion, and never anything she could tell anyone. But, if the little things just stayed in their proper places . . .

Julia Latham was awfully worried about her mother. She talked things over with Evan.

"I don't know what we can do," she said. "Mother acts all right most of the time, but some of the things she says . . . And she has such odd explanations . . . "

"It's too bad," Evan said. "She's been such a wonderful person, but now . . . she's odd. There's no denying it. Perhaps if you saw Dr. Clement . . . "

"That's what I thought I'd do," Julia said. "He's known Mother longer than any of us, and being a doctor and all. . . . "

Julia sat in the doctor's office and pretended to read the magazines that were as old as the cartoons said magazines in doctors' offices were. She tried to keep her mind on what she was reading and on the people in the office, until the nurse said Dr. Clement could see her.

Dr. Clement was hearty and red-faced, kind and wise.

"Nothing wrong, I hope," he said. "I saw Evan yesterday. He looked fine. And Grandma Quillan. . . . "

"It's about Mother I want to see you," Julia said. "She's not really ill. She's always been so well, but here lately . . . we're worried about her."

"But she seemed fine! She stopped in just a few weeks ago, to tell me about the Bosleys down on Graham Road. Said the older boy was going to die, but that we could save the other two. As good a diagnosis as a doctor could have given. The boy died of rheumatic fever, but we're getting the other two on their feet. With the right care. . . . She's a remarkable woman, Grandma Quillan. Many's the time she's helped me out."

"Mother is wonderful," said Julia. "You don't have to tell me that. But, well, like knowing about the Bosley boy. . . . Maybe that isn't just what I mean. But her mind is all confused. She doesn't remember what happened yesterday, but something that happened twenty years ago. . . . "

"Sure!" Dr. Clement said. "A lot of old people get that way. She asked me about that condition some time ago, but I wasn't certain she meant herself. Usually people don't realize their own condition. But I don't think that's serious."

"I'm glad of that," Julia said. "But that isn't all. She gets all kinds of hallucinations. She imagines things."

"What kind of things?"

"She thinks they've happened. But they haven't happened at all."

"Oh, I see!" Dr. Clement was more serious now.

"Sometimes she tries to pretend she didn't say them, and then gets more mixed up than ever. And sometimes she frightens us—things happen just the way she says they've already happened. I don't know if you see what I mean. A coincidence, of course, but it worries us."

"Of course," Dr. Clement said.

"And there's Bobby. She's devoted to him and he loves her, too, but he's only seven. And after school she's frequently alone with him . . . "

"Oh, I feel she's perfectly safe."

"I hope so, doctor. But we can't help worrying. The other day she said Bobby would cut himself with a new knife somebody had given him. And the next day he did cut himself. It may be the power of suggestion on a child, for Bobby hangs on every word she says. And she went to a friend of ours and complained about one of Winnie's boy friends. Isn't there something, doctor?"

"There aren't any drugs, if that's what you mean. I'm afraid it's senile dementia. But let me come in and look her over. She ought to have a good physical and mental check-up. And it may be, if you can't take care of her at home, that she ought to go to a sanitarium or a nursing home."

"There must be some other way!" Julia began to sob.

"Don't cry, child," said Dr. Clement. "If the old lady is . . . odd, it might be the best way all around. She'd be perfectly comfortable. There's a place just out of town run by trained nurses—a series of little white cottages and very pleasant. There are some old schoolteachers there—a nice class of people. I could send her to a hospital for observation, or have a couple of psychiatrists pass on her, unless she wants to go voluntarily. But don't worry about it until I talk to her. And don't let her know; I'll just drop in. . . . "

The next afternoon, Dr. Clement came to call. Grandma liked and admired him. She gave him a glass of sherry and some homemade cookies.

"You work too hard," she said. "But I could have helped with Mrs. Bronson. She told me what you did for her."

"I didn't think you were up to it."

"I'm as good as I was twenty years ago."

"I hope you are, but you look . . . peaked. Maybe you need a good overhauling—a good tonic."

"Nonsense, never felt better!"

"Well, I'm going to look you over anyhow."

"If you've nothing better to do with your time."

He listened to Grandma's heart and her lungs. He asked her questions. And Grandma sat on the sofa, very still, like a little girl, and answered everything. Some of the questions were peculiar, but after all, he was her friend. When he'd first come to town, she'd thought he was a fine young man. Grandpa had thought so, too.

She hoped she said the right things. A couple of times she got so interested in what he was saying she sort of forgot. . . . Oh, well, he knew her pretty well. He'd understand.

They talked about little things then, people they both knew, the weather, spring was nearly here . . .

"I see you found your bag all right," said Grandma when Dr. Clement picked it up and started to leave.

"Found my bag?"

"Why, yes. Didn't you leave it at the Plunketts' out on Talbot Road?"

"Why, yes, of course," said Dr. Clement. But when he was in his car he had to admit that Mrs. Latham was right. For the old lady was odd when she spoke of old man Brewster, who had been dead for ten years, and of the Corning boy having measles when he wasn't sick, and the lost bag.

Why, he hadn't been near the Plunketts' in a couple of months! Maybe it would be better if the old lady went to a nursing home. The psychiatrists could examine her there. He'd make arrangements. . . .

Grandma was in her room when she heard a lot of excitement downstairs. She went down at once to find the family assembled in the living room, and Winnie in tears.

"It's Sid Forrest!" she sobbed.

"So, they found out about him!" said Grandma.

"What do you mean?" Evan asked.

"About the checks and the girl in the bakery shop . . . "

"That's not it, Grandma! He eloped with Irene Jessup. If I'd only treated him nicer," Winnie wailed.

"Then they don't know about the checks?"

"What checks?" asked Julia.

"Why . . . why . . . " Grandma didn't go on.

"It's bad enough that he eloped," said Winnie, "without your saying terrible things . . . "

"Just forget him!" said her father. "There's other good fish!"

"Not in this town!" Winnie sobbed.

"You're only seventeen! You're just a child!" Julia said.

Grandma put her arms around her granddaughter and drew her down on the couch next to her.

"You'll meet someone else," she said, "a fine man, you'll see!"

"Will he be good-looking?"

"Yes," said Grandma, "and you'll be very much in love."

It wasn't until two days later that the family found out about the forged checks.

The very next day Grandma woke up earlier than usual. She dressed quickly, not in her neat housedress, but in her best black dress, with a fresh collar, and Grandpa's pin to hold it in place. There were so many things to do. . . .

She straightened her bureau drawers, though they were already in apple-pie order—the pile of clean handkerchiefs; her collars; her decent, plain underthings.

"What are you doing?" Julia called. She was so worried about her mother—about Winnie—about so many things. But there was nothing she could do. . . .

"I thought I'd go over to Mrs. Hodges. Take her a few things. . . . "

"If you feel well enough. . . . "

"Never felt better in my life!"

Grandma made half a dozen neat little bundles: her pearl beads—not real, but mighty pretty; the cameo pin Julia thought old-fashioned; the bracelet with the onyx ornament. After the breakfast dishes were finished, and she'd made her bed, she'd give these little packets to some of her old friends. They weren't much. She didn't have much to give—for she wanted Julia and Winnie to have her ring and her gold bracelet, her other things. Well, these would bring a little pleasure—folks didn't have too much pleasure these days.

She was tired when she came home, but not too tired to help get dinner. She'd had a bite of lunch with Mrs. Burgess, to whom she'd given her real-lace collar-and-cuff set. Mrs. Burgess had always admired it, and she didn't have a lot, poor thing. Grandma smiled. She herself always had had nice things; not grand, exactly, but nice—the moonstone pin Julia liked to wear, the little, enameled watch Arthur's wife had given her, and the house . . . Wouldn't it be awful to be old and not have things to give anyone?

In the excitement of finding out about Sid Forrest's activities, Winnie had already got over her heartbreak. She was a bit tragic at dinner, but Grandma gathered she was rather enjoying herself.

Grandma went to her room as soon as the dishes were in the cupboard. All of the running around and the excitement and all. . . .

She heard the telephone ring and Julia's voice answering:

"Dr. Clement, you went to the Plunketts' on Talbot Road? And you left your bag there. And you didn't know where you left it when you stopped in to see the Corning boy who had the measles. And then you remembered what Grandma Quillan had said. I don't quite understand, but of course I'll tell her. She's gone to bed now, but in the morning. . . ."

Grandma smiled to herself. So Dr. Clement had found out about the bag and the measles. They'd find out a lot of things. . . .

The telephone rang again. This time it was for Winnie. Her voice was excited and loud.

"Isn't it dreadful!" she said. "But I'm not surprised at all. Grandma told me weeks ago what would happen—warned me! She's got second sight or something. She can tell fortunes. She told me I was going to marry a rich, handsome man and be happy! Sure! Come over tomorrow and she'll tell you everything. . . ."

That would be terrible, almost the last straw! Grandma smiled wryly. But she knew she wouldn't have to worry about it. There didn't have to be a last straw!

Julia and Evan were fine . . . and Winnie, once she got some sense into her head . . . and Arthur's family . . . none of them needed her any more . . . not even Bobby, who was growing up.

Grandma puttered around the room, arranging things the way she wanted them, climbed into the old-fashioned double bed she'd kept for herself when Julia refurnished the house.

Very carefully, so as not to break them—as if it mattered any more— she put her glasses on the little bed table, turned out the light and closed her eyes. She was never one for reading in bed or lying awake at night. She'd always been too tired for that. And then she said the prayers she'd learned from her own mother, the way she always said them, "Our Father, which art in Heaven" and "Now I lay me down to sleep."

She wished she could have helped them more . . . Julia and Evan . . . Winnie, with her new idea about fortune-telling . . . all of them . . . if there only had been some way . . .

She wiped a tear from her cheek with the back of her hand. The views from the balloon—a long-ago view of yesterday, and the view of today, and tomorrow—all began to merge and grow dim. Grandma gave a long sigh of relief as she fell asleep. There wasn't a thing she had to worry about any more.

From THE PAPER CHASE

John Osborn

In the few days between arrival at Harvard Law School and the first classes, there are rumors. And stories. About being singled out, made to show your stuff.

Mostly, they're about people who made some terrible mistake. Couldn't answer a question right.

One concerns a boy who did a particularly bad job. His professor called him down to the front of the class, up the podium, gave the student a dime and said, loudly:

"Go call your mother, and tell her you'll never be a lawyer."

Sometimes the story ends here, but the way I heard it, the crushed student bowed his head and limped slowly back through the one hundred and fifty students in the class. When he got to the door, his anger exploded. He screamed:

"You're a son of a bitch, Kingsfield."

"That's the first intelligent thing you've said," Kingsfield replied. "Come back. Perhaps I've been too hasty."

Professor Kingsfield, who should have been reviewing the cases he would offer his first class of the year, stared down from the window forming most of the far wall of his second story office in Langdell Hall and watched the students walking to class.

He was panting. Professor Kingsfield had just done forty push-ups on his green carpet. His vest was pulled tight around his small stomach and it seemed, each time his heart heaved, the buttons would give way.

A pyramid-shaped wooden box, built for keeping time during piano lessons, was ticking on his desk and he stopped its pendulum. Professor Kingsfield did his push-ups in four-four time.

His secretary knocked on the door and reminded him that if he didn't get moving he'd be late. She paused in the doorway, watching his heaving chest. Since Crane had broken his hip in a fall from the lecture platform, Professor Kingsfield was the oldest active member of the Harvard Law School faculty.

He noticed her concern and smiled, picked up the casebook he had written thirty years before, threw his jacket over his shoulder and left the office.

Hart tried to balance the three huge casebooks under one arm, and with the other hold up his little map. He really needed two hands to carry the casebooks—combined, they were more than fifteen inches thick, with smooth dust jackets that tended to make the middle book slide out—and he stumbled along, trying to find Langdell North and avoid bumping into another law student.

Everything would have been easy if he had known which direction was North. He had figured out that the dotted lines didn't represent paths, but instead tunnels, somewhere under his feet, connecting the classrooms, the library, the dorms and the eating hall in Harkness. He knew that the sharp red lines were the paths—little asphalt tracks winding along through the maze of granite buildings.

Some of the buildings were old. Langdell was old: a three-story dark stone building, built in neoclassical renaissance. It stretched for a block in front of and behind him, with the library on the third floor. Hart had been circling it for ten minutes trying to find an entrance that would lead to his classroom.

The other buildings he'd passed were more modern but in an attempt to compromise with Langdell had been given the library's worst features. They were tall concrete rectangles, broken by large dark windows, woven around Langdell like pillboxes, guarding the perimeter of the monolith. It seemed that everything was interconnected, not only by the tunnels, but also by bridges which sprung out from the second and third floors of Langdell like spider legs, gripping the walls of the outposts.

Hart took a reading on the sun, trying to remember from his Boy Scout days where it rose. He absolutely refused to ask anyone the way. He disliked being a first year student, disliked not knowing where things were. Most of all, he disliked feeling unorganized, and he was terribly unorganized on this first day of classes. He couldn't read his map, he couldn't carry his casebooks. His glasses had fallen down over his nose, and he didn't have a free hand to lift them up.

He had expected to have these troubles, and knew from experience that he wouldn't want to ask directions. Thus, he had allowed a full twenty minutes to find the classroom. His books were slowly sliding forward from under his arm, and he wondered if he should reconsider his vow never to buy a briefcase.

He moved into a flow of red books, tucked on top of other casebooks. Red. His contracts book was red. He followed the flow to one of the stone entrances to Langdell, up the granite steps. In the hallway, groups of students pushed against each other, as they tried to squeeze through the classroom door. Every now and then books hit the floor when students bumped. A contagious feeling of tension hung in the corridor. People were overly polite or overly rude. Hart pulled his books to his chest, let his map drop to the floor, and started pushing toward the red door of the classroom.

Most of the first year students, in anticipation of their first class at the Harvard Law School, were already seated as Professor Kingsfield, at exactly five minutes past nine, walked purposefully through the little door behind the lecture platform. He put his books and notes down on the wooden lectern and pulled out the seating chart. One hundred and fifty names and numbers: the guide to the assigned classroom seats. He put the chart on the lectern, unbuttoned his coat, exposing the gold chain across his vest, and gripped the smooth sides of the stand, feeling for the indentations he had worn into the wood. He did not allow his eyes to meet those of any student—his face had a distant look similar to the ones in the thirty or so large gilt-framed portraits of judges and lawyers that hung around the room.

Professor Kingsfield was at ease with the room's high ceiling, thick beams, tall thin windows. Though he knew the room had mellowed to the verge of decay, he disliked the new red linoleum bench tops. They hid the mementos carved by generations of law students, and accented the fact that the wooden chairs were losing their backs, the ceiling peeling, and the institutional light brown paint on the walls turning the color of mud. He could have taught in one of the new classrooms with carpets and programmed acoustics designed to hold less than the full quota of a hundred and fifty students. But he had taught in this room for thirty years, and felt at home.

At exactly ten past nine, Professor Kingsfield picked a name from the seating chart. The name came from the left side of the classroom. Professor Kingsfield looked off to the right, his eyes following one of the curving benches to where it ended by the window.

Without turning, he said crisply, "Mr. Hart, will you recite the facts of *Hawkins* versus *McGee*?"

When Hart, seat 259, heard his name, he froze. Caught unprepared, he simply stopped functioning. Then he felt his heart beat faster than he could ever remember its beating and his palms and arms broke out in sweat.

Professor Kingsfield rotated slowly until he was staring down at Hart. The rest of the class followed Kingsfield's eyes.

"I have got your name right?" Kingsfield asked. "You are Mr. Hart?" He spoke evenly, filling every inch of the hall.

A barely audible voice floated back: "Yes, my name is Hart."

"Mr. Hart, you're not speaking loud enough. Will you speak up?"

Hart repeated the sentence, no louder than before. He tried to speak loudly, tried to force the air out of his lungs with a deep push, tried to make his words come out with conviction. He could feel his face whitening, his lower lip beat against his upper. He couldn't speak louder.

"Mr. Hart, will you stand?"

After some difficulty, Hart found, to his amazement, he was on his feet.

"Now, Mr. Hart, will you give us the case?"

Hart had his book open to the case: he had been informed by the student next to him that a notice on the bulletin board listed *Hawkins* v. *McGee* as part of the first day's assignment in contracts. But Hart had not known about the bulletin board. Like most of the students, he had assumed that the first lecture would be an introduction.

His voice floated across the classroom: "I . . . I haven't read the case. I only found out about it just now."

Kingsfield walked to the edge of the platform.

"Mr. Hart, I will myself give you the facts of the case. *Hawkins* versus *McGee* is a case in contract law, the subject of our study. A boy burned his hand by touching an electric wire. A doctor who wanted to experiment in skin grafting asked to operate on the hand, guaranteeing that he would restore the hand 'one hundred percent.' Unfortunately, the operation failed to produce a healthy hand. Instead, it produced a hairy hand. A hand not only burned, but covered with dense matted hair.''

"Now, Mr. Hart, what sort of damages do you think the doctor should pay?''

Hart reached into his memory for any recollections of doctors. There were squeaks from the seats as members of the class adjusted their positions. Hart tried to remember the summation he had just heard, tried to think about it in a logical sequence. But all his mental energy had been expended in pushing back shock waves from the realization that, though Kingsfield had appeared to be staring at a boy on the other side of the room, he had in fact called out the name Hart. And there was the constant strain of trying to maintain his balance because the lecture hall sloped toward the podium at the center, making him afraid that if he fainted he would fall on the student in front of him.

Hart said nothing.

"As you remember, Mr. Hart, this was a case involving a doctor who promised to restore an injured hand.''

That brought it back. Hart found that if he focused on Kingsfield's face, he could imagine there was no one else in the room. A soft haze formed around the face. Hart's eyes were watering, but he could speak.

"There was a promise to fix the hand back the way it was before,'' Hart said.

Kingsfield interrupted: ''And what in fact was the result of the operation?''

"The hand was much worse than when it was just burned . . . ''

"So the man got less than he was promised, even less than he had when the operation started?''

Kingsfield wasn't looking at Hart now. He had his hands folded across his chest. He faced out, catching as many of the class's glances as he could.

"Now, Mr. Hart,'' Kingsfield said, ''how should the court measure the damages?''

"The difference between what he was promised and what he got, a worse hand?'' Hart asked.

Kingsfield stared off to the right, picked a name from the seating chart.

"Mr. Pruit, perhaps you can tell the class if we should give the boy the difference between what he was promised and what he got, as Mr. Hart suggests, or the difference between what he got, and what he had.''

Hart fell back into his seat. He blinked, trying to erase the image of Kingsfield suspended in his mind. He couldn't. The lined white skin, the thin rusty lips grew like a balloon until the image seemed to actually press against his face, shutting off everything else in the classroom.

Hart blinked again, felt for his pen and tried to focus on his clean paper. His hand shook, squiggling a random line. Across the room, a terrified, astonished boy with a beard and wire-rimmed glasses was slowly talking about the hairy hand.

From WALDEN TWO

B. F. Skinner

The living quarters and daily schedules of the older children furnished a particularly good example of behavioral engineering. At first sight they seemed wholly casual, almost haphazard, but as Frazier pointed out their significant features and the consequences of each, I began to make out a comprehensive, almost Machiavellian design.

The children passed smoothly from one age group to another, following a natural process of growth and avoiding the abrupt changes of the home-and-school system. The arrangements were such that each child emulated children slightly older than himself and hence derived motives and patterns for much of his early education without adult aid.

The control of the physical and social environment, of which Frazier had made so much, was progressively relaxed—or, to be more exact, the control was transferred from the authorities to the child himself and to the other members of his group. After spending most of the first year in an air-conditioned cubicle, and the second and third mainly in an air-conditioned room with a minimum of clothing and bedding, the three- or four-year-old was introduced to regular clothes and given the care of a small standard cot in a dormitory. The beds of the five- and six-year-olds were grouped by threes and fours in a series of alcoves furnished like rooms and treated as such by the children. Groups of three or four seven-year-olds occupied small rooms together, and this practice was continued, with frequent change of roommates, until the children were about thirteen, at which time they took temporary rooms in the adult building, usually in pairs. At marriage, or whenever the individual chose, he could participate in building a larger room for himself or refurnishing an old room which might be available.

A similar withdrawal of supervision, proceeding as rapidly as the child acquired control of himself, could be seen in the dining arrangements. From three through six, the children ate in a small dining room of their own. The older children, as we had observed on our first day at Walden Two, took their meals at specified times in the adult quarters. At thirteen all supervision was abandoned, and the young member was free to eat when and where he pleased.

We visited some of the workshops, laboratories, studies, and reading rooms used in lieu of classrooms. They were occupied, but it was not entirely clear that the children were actually in school. I supposed that the few adults to be seen about the building were teachers, but many of them were men, contrary to my conception of schoolteachers at that age level, and more often than not they were busy with some private business. Since Frazier had requested that we avoid questions or discussions in the presence of the children, we proceeded from one room to another in growing puzzlement. I had to admit that an enormous amount of learning was probably going on, but I had never seen a school like it before.

We inspected a well-equipped gymnasium, a small assembly room, and other facilities. The building was made of rammed earth and very simply decorated, but there was a pleasant ''non-institutional'' character about it. The doors and many of the windows stood open, and a fair share of the schoolwork, or whatever it was, took place outside. Children were constantly passing in and out. Although there was an obvious excitement about the place, there was little of the boisterous confusion which develops in the ordinary school when discipline is momentarily relaxed. Everyone seemed to be enjoying extraordinary freedom, but the efficiency and comfort of the whole group were preserved.

I was reminded of children on good behavior and was on the point of asking how often the pressure reached the bursting point. But there was a difference, too, and my question slowly evaporated. I could only conclude that this happy and productive atmosphere was probably the usual thing. Here again, so far as I could see, Frazier—or someone—had got things under control.

When we returned to our shade tree, I was primed with questions, and so, I am sure, was Castle. But Frazier had other plans. He had either forgotten how remarkable was the spectacle we had just witnessed, or he was intentionally allowing our wonderment and curiosity to ferment. He began from a very different point of view.

"When we discussed the economics of community life," he said, "I should have mentioned education. Teachers are, of course, workers, and I'm willing to defend all that I said about our economic advantage as specifically applied to education. God knows, the outside world is not exactly profligate in the education of its children. It doesn't spend much on equipment or teachers. Yet in spite of this penny-wise policy, there's still enormous waste. A much better education would cost less if society were better organized.

"We can arrange things more expeditiously here because we don't need to be constantly re-educating. The ordinary teacher spends a good share of her time changing the cultural and intellectual habits which the child acquires from its family and surrounding culture. Or else the teacher duplicates home training, in a complete waste of time. Here we can almost say that the school *is* the family, and vice versa.

"We can adopt the best educational methods and still avoid the administrative machinery which schools need in order to adjust to an unfavorable social structure. We don't have to worry about standardization in order to permit pupils to transfer from one school to another, or to appraise or control the work of particular schools. We don't need 'grades'. Everyone knows that talents and abilities don't develop at the same rate in different children. A fourth-grade reader may be a sixth-grade mathematician. The grade is an administrative device which does violence to the nature of the developmental process. Here the child advances as rapidly as he likes in any field. No time is wasted in forcing him to participate in, or be bored by, activities he has outgrown. And the backward child can be handled more efficiently too.

"We also don't require all our children to develop the same abilities or skills. We don't insist upon a certain set of courses. I don't suppose we have a single child who has had a 'secondary school education', whatever that means. But they've all developed as rapidly as advisable, and they're well educated in many useful respects. By the same token we don't waste time in teaching the unteachable. The fixed education represented by a diploma is a bit of conspicuous waste which has no place in Walden Two. We don't attach an economic or honorific value to education. It has its own value or none at all.

"Since our children remain happy, energetic, and curious, we don't need to teach 'subjects' at all. We teach only the techniques of learning and thinking. As for geography, literature, the sciences—we give our children opportunity and guidance, and they learn them for themselves. In that way we dispense with half the teachers required under the old system, and the education is incomparably better. Our children aren't neglected, but they're seldom, if ever, *taught* anything.

"Education in Walden Two is part of the life of the community. We don't need to resort to trumped-up life experiences. Our children begin to work at a very early age. It's no hardship; it's accepted as readily as sport or play. And a good share of our education goes on in workshops, laboratories, and fields. It's part of the Walden Two Code to encourage children in all the arts and crafts. We're glad to spend time in instructing them, for we know it's important for the future of Walden Two and our own security."

"What about higher education?" I said.

"We aren't equipped for professional training, of course," said Frazier. "Those who want to go on to graduate study in a university are given special preparation. Entrance requirements are always tyrannical, though perhaps inevitable in a mass-production system. So far, we've been able to find graduate schools that will take our young people as special students, and as they continue to make excellent records, we expect fewer difficulties. If worse comes to worst, we shall organize as a college and get ourselves accredited. But can you imagine the stupid changes we should have to make?" Frazier snorted with impatience. "Oh, well. Tongue in cheek. Tongue in cheek."

"Don't you mean 'chin up'?" I asked.

"We'd have to set up a 'curriculum', require a 'C average', a 'foreign language', 'so many years of residence', and so on, and so on. It would be most amusing. No, 'tongue in cheek' was what I meant."

"Your people don't go to college, then?"

"We have no more reason to distinguish between college and high school than between high school and grade school. What are these distinctions, anyway, once you have separated education from the administration of education? Are there any natural breaks in a child's development? Many of our children naturally study more and more advanced material as they grow older. We help them in every way short of teaching them. We give them new techniques of acquiring knowledge and thinking. In spite of the beliefs of most educators, our children are taught to think. We give them an excellent survey of the methods and techniques of thinking, taken from logic, statistics, scientific method, psychology, and mathematics. That's all the 'college education' they need. They get the rest by themselves in our libraries and laboratories.''

''But what about libraries and laboratories, though?'' I said. ''What can you actually provide in that line?''

''As to a library, we pride ourselves on having the best books, if not the most. Have you ever spent much time in a large college library? What trash the librarian has saved up in order to report a million volumes in the college catalogue! Bound pamphlets, old journals, ancient junk that even the shoddiest secondhand bookstore would clear from its shelves—all saved on the flimsy pretext that some day someone will want to study the 'history of a field'. Here we have the heart of a great library—not much to please the scholar or specialist, perhaps, but enough to interest the intelligent reader for life. Two or three thousand volumes will do it.''

Frazier challenged me with a stare, but I did not wish to fight on such difficult terrain.

''The secret is this,'' he continued. ''We subtract from our shelves as often as we add to them. The result is a collection that never misses fire. We all get something vital every time we take a book from the shelves. If anyone wants to follow a special interest we arrange for loans. If anyone wants to browse, we have half a barnful of discarded volumes.

''Our laboratories are good because they are real. Our workshops are really small engineering laboratories, and anyone with a genuine bent can go farther in them than the college student. We teach anatomy in the slaughterhouse, botany in the field, genetics in the dairy and poultry house, chemistry in the medical building and in the kitchen and dairy laboratory. What more can you ask?''

''And all this is just for the fun of it? You don't feel that some disciplined study is necessary?'' said Castle.

''What for?'' asked Frazier in unsuccessfully pretended surprise.

''To provide techniques and abilities which will be valuable later,'' said Castle. ''For example, the study of a language.''

''Why 'late'? Why not acquire a language *when* it's valuable? We acquire our own tongue that way! Of course, you're thinking of an educational process which comes to a dead stop sometime around the middle of June in one's last year in college. In Walden Two education goes on forever. It's part of our culture. We can acquire a technique whenever we need it.

''As to languages,'' Frazier continued, ''you must know that even in our largest universities a language department considers itself very well off if two or three students at any one time approach fluency. We can do better than that. A member of Walden Two who once lived in France has interested several of our members, from ten to fifty years old, in the language. You may run into them during your stay. I hear them buzzing around the dining room every now and then, and they add a pleasantly cosmopolitan touch. And I'm told they're developing a good feeling for the French language and French literature. They'll never get any grades or credits, but they're getting French. Is there really any choice? Either French is worth learning, *at the time you learn it*, or it's not. And let's be sensible.''

"I'm still skeptical," said Castle. "Of course, I'm still at a disadvantage in arguing against an accomplished fact.'' Frazier nodded his head violently. ''But not everything has been accomplished,'' Castle went on. "Your pleasant schoolrooms, your industrious and contented children—these we must accept. But it would take us a long time to find out how well-educated your children really are according to our standards.'' Frazier made a move to speak, but Castle hurried on. ''I'll admit these standards won't tell us everything. We couldn't ask your children to take our examinations, because they haven't been learning the same things, even in such a field as French. Your students would probably do no better on a second-year French examination than the average Parisian. I'll admit that, and I confess with all the humility I can muster that the kind of learning you've described is the better—if a comparison is possible. It's the ideal which every college teacher glimpses now and then when he looks up from the dance of death in which he has been caught. But I can't swallow the system you've described because I don't see what keeps the motors running. Why do your children learn anything at all? What are your substitutes for our standard motives?''

"Your 'standard motives'—exactly,'' said Frazier. "And there's the rub. An educational institution spends most of its time, not in presenting facts or imparting techniques of learning, but in trying to make its students learn. It has to create spurious needs. Have you ever stopped to analyze them? What are the 'standard motives', Mr. Castle?''

"I must admit they're not very attractive,'' said Castle. "I suppose they consist of fear of one's family in the event of low grades or expulsion, the award of grades and honors, the snob value of a cap and gown, the cash value of a diploma.''

"Very good, Mr. Castle,'' said Frazier. "You're an honest man.

And now to answer your question—our substitute is simply the absence of these devices. We have had to *uncover* the worthwhile and truly productive motives—the motives which inspire creative work in science and art outside the academies. No one asks how to motivate a baby. A baby naturally explores everything it can get at, unless restraining forces have already been at work. And this tendency doesn't die out, it's *wiped* out.

"We made a survey of the motives of the unhampered child and found more than we could use. Our engineering job was to *preserve* them by fortifying the child against discouragement. We introduce discouragement as carefully as we introduce any other emotional situation, beginning at about six months. Some of the toys in our air-conditioned cubicles are designed to build perseverance. A bit of a tune from a music box, or a pattern of flashing lights, is arranged to follow an appropriate response—say, pulling on a ring. Later the ring must be pulled twice, later still three or five or ten times. It's possible to build up fantastically perseverative behavior without encountering frustration or rage. It may not surprise you to learn that some of our experiments miscarried; the resistance to discouragement became almost stupid or pathological. One takes some risks in work of this sort, of course. Fortunately, we were able to reverse the process and restore the children to a satisfactory level.

"Building a tolerance for discouraging events proved to be all we needed," Frazier continued. "The motives in education, Mr. Castle, are the motives in all human behavior. Education should be only life itself. We don't need to create motives. We avoid the spurious academic needs you've just listed so frankly, and also the escape from threat so widely used in civil institutions. We appeal to the curiosity which is characteristic of the unrestrained child, as well as the alert and inquiring adult. We appeal to that drive to control the environment which makes a baby continue to crumple a piece of noisy paper and the scientist continue to press forward with his predictive analyses of nature. We don't need to motivate anyone by creating spurious needs."

"I've known a few men with the kind of motivation you mean," I said.

"The contemporary culture produces a few by accident," said Frazier quickly, "just as it produces a few brave or happy men."

"But I've never understood them," I said rather faintly.

"Why should you, any more than unhappy people can understand the happy ones?"

"But isn't there a real need for the spurious satisfactions?" I said.

"Little signs of personal success, money—personal domination, too, if you like. Most of what I do, I do to avoid undesirable consequences, to evade unpleasantnesses, or to reject or attack forces which interfere with my freedom."

"All the unhappy motives," said Frazier.

"Unhappy, perhaps, but powerful. I think the very thing which seems most unpromising in your system is its happiness. Your people are going to be too happy, too successful. But why won't they just go to sleep? Can we expect real achievements from them? Haven't the great men of history been essentially unhappy or maladjusted or neurotic?"

"I have little interest in conclusions drawn from history," said Frazier, "but if you must play that game, I'll play it too. For every genius you cite whose greatness seems to have sprung from a neurosis, I will undertake to cite similar acts of greatness without neurosis. Turn it around and I'll agree. A man with a touch of genius will be so likely to attack existing institutions that he'll be called unbalanced or neurotic. The only geniuses produced by the chaos of society are those who do something about it." Frazier paused, and I wondered if he were thinking of himself. "Chaos breeds geniuses. It offers a man something to be a genius about. But here, we have better things to do."

"But what about the cases where unhappiness has led to artistic or scientific achievement?" I asked.

"Oh, I daresay a few first-rate sonnets would have remained unwritten had the lady yielded," said Frazier. "But not so many, at that. Not many works of art can be traced to the lack of satisfaction of the basic needs. It's not plain sex that gives rise to art, but personal relations which are social or cultural rather than biological. Art deals with something less obvious than the satisfaction to be found in a square meal." Frazier laughed explosively, as if he had perhaps said more than he intended.

"We shall never produce so satisfying a world that there will be no place for art," he continued. "On the contrary, Walden Two has demonstrated very nicely that as soon as the simple necessities of life are obtained with little effort, there's an enormous welling up of artistic interest. And least of all do we need to fear that simple satisfactions will detract from the scientific conquest of the world. What scientist worth the name is engaged, as scientist, in the satisfaction of his own basic needs? He may be thinking of the basic needs of others, but his own motives are clearly cultural. There can be no doubt of the survival value of the inquiring spirit—of curiosity, of exploration, of the need to dominate media, of the urge to control the forces of nature. The world will never be wholly known, and man can't help trying to know more and more of it.''

The topic seemed to have grown too vague to stimulate further discussion, but Castle soon offered a substitute.

"I'm torn between two questions which seem incompatible yet equally pressing,'' he said. "What do you do about differences among your children in intellect and talent? And what do you do to avoid producing a lot of completely standardized young people? Which question should I ask, and what's your answer?''

"They're both good questions,'' said Frazier, "and quite compatible.'' I made a move to speak and Frazier said, "I see that Mr. Burris wants to help with the answers.''

"My guess is,'' I said, "that differences are due to environmental and cultural factors and that Mr. Frazier has no great problem to solve. Give all your children the excellent care we have just been witnessing and your differences will be negligible.''

"No, you're wrong, Burris,'' said Frazier. "That's one question we have answered to our satisfaction. Our ten-year-olds have all had the same environment since birth, but the range of their IQ's is almost as great as in the population at large. This seems to be true of other abilities and skills as well.''

"And of physical prowess, of course,'' said Castle.

"Why do you say 'of course'?'' said Frazier, with marked interest.

"Why, I suppose because physical differences are generally acknowledged.''

"All differences are physical, my dear Mr. Castle. We think with our bodies, too. You might have replied that differences in prowess have always been obvious and impossible to conceal, while other differences have customarily been disguised for the sake of prestige and family pride. We accept our gross physical limitations without protest and are reasonably happy in spite of them, but we may spend a lifetime trying to live up to a wholly false conception of our powers in another field, and suffer the pain of lingering failure. Here we accept ourselves as we are.''

"Aren't the talented going to be unhappy?''

"But we don't go in for personal rivalry; individuals are seldom compared. We never develop a taste much beyond a talent. Our parents have little reason to misrepresent their children's abilities to themselves or others. It's easy for our children to accept their limitations—exactly as they have always accepted the gross differences which Mr. Castle called physical prowess. At the same time our gifted children aren't held back by organized mediocrity. We don't throw our geniuses off balance. The brilliant but unstable type is unfamiliar here. Genius can express itself.''

We had shifted our positions from time to time to stay within the shade of our tree. We were now centered due north and crowding the trunk, for it was noon. The schoolwork in the area near the building had gradually come to an end, and the migration toward the dining room had taken place. Frazier stood up and straightened his knees with care. The rest of us also got up—except Castle, who stayed stubbornly in his place.

''I can't believe,'' he began, looking at the ground and apparently not caring whether he was heard or not, ''I can't believe you can really get spontaneity and freedom through a system of tyrannical control. Where does initiative come in? When does the child begin to think of himself as a free agent? What is freedom, anyway, under such a plan?''

''Freedom, freedom,'' said Frazier, stretching his arms and neck and almost singing the words, as if he were uttering them through a yawn. ''Freedom is a question, isn't it? But let's not answer it now. Let's let it ring, shall we? Let's let it ring.''

From THE AUTOBIOGRAPHY
OF MALCOLM X

Malcolm X, with Alex Haley

Out of the blue one day, Bimbi told me flatly, as was his way, that I had some brains, if I'd use them. I had wanted his friendship, not that kind of advice. I might have cursed another convict, but nobody cursed Bimbi. He told me I should take advantage of the prison correspondence courses and the library.

When I had finished the eighth grade back in Mason, Michigan, that was the last time I'd thought of studying anything that didn't have some hustle purpose. And the streets had erased everything I'd ever learned in school; I didn't know a verb from a house. My sister Hilda had written a suggestion that, if possible in prison, I should study English and penmanship; she had barely been able to read a couple of picture post cards I had sent her when I was selling reefers on the road.

So, feeling I had time on my hands, I did begin a correspondence course in English. When the mimeographed listings of available books passed from cell to cell, I would put my number next to titles that appealed to me which weren't already taken.

Through the correspondence exercises and lessons, some of the mechanics of grammar gradually began to come back to me.

After about a year, I guess, I could write a decent and legible letter. About then, too, influenced by having heard Bimbi often explain word

From *The Autobiography of Malcolm X*, by Malcolm X, with the assistance of Alex Haley. Copyright © 1964 by Alex Haley and Malcolm X, copyright © 1965 by Alex Haley and Betty Shabazz. Reprinted by permission of Random House, Inc.

derivations, I quietly started another correspondence course—in Latin.

Under Bimbi's tutelage, too, I had gotten myself some little cell-block swindles going. For packs of cigarettes, I beat just about anyone at dominoes. I always had several cartons of cigarettes in my cell; they were, in prison, nearly as valuable a medium of exchange as money. I booked cigarette and money bets on fights and ball games. I'll never forget the prison sensation created that day in April, 1947, when Jackie Robinson was brought up to play with the Brooklyn Dodgers. Jackie Robinson had, then, his most fanatic fan in me. When he played, my ear was glued to the radio, and no game ended without my refiguring his average up through his last turn at bat.

. . . . .

It was because of my letters that I happened to stumble upon starting to acquire some kind of a homemade education.

I became increasingly frustrated at not being able to express what I wanted to convey in letters that I wrote, especially those to Mr. Elijah Muhammad. In the street, I had been the most articulate hustler out there—I had commanded attention when I said something. But now, trying to write simple English, I not only wasn't articulate, I wasn't even functional. How would I sound writing in slang, the way I would *say* it, something such as, "Look, daddy, let me pull your coat about a cat, Elijah Muhammad—"

Many who today hear me somewhere in person, or on television, or those who read something I've said, will think I went to school far beyond the eighth grade. This impression is due entirely to my prison studies.

It had really begun back in the Charlestown Prison, when Bimbi first made me feel envy of his stock of knowledge. Bimbi had always taken charge of any conversations he was in, and I had tried to emulate him. But every book I picked up had few sentences which didn't contain anywhere from one to nearly all of the words that might as well have been in Chinese. When I just skipped those words, of course, I really ended up with little idea of what the book said. So I had come to the Norfolk Prison Colony still going through only book-reading motions. Pretty soon, I would have quit even these motions, unless I had received the motivation that I did.

I saw that the best thing I could do was get hold of a dictionary—to study, to learn some words. I was lucky enough to reason also that I should try to improve my penmanship. It was sad. I couldn't even write in a straight line. It was both ideas together that moved me to request a dictionary along with some tablets and pencils from the Norfolk Prison Colony school.

I spent two days just riffling uncertainly through the dictionary's pages. I'd never realized so many words existed! I didn't know *which* words I needed to learn. Finally, just to start some kind of action, I began copying.

In my slow, painstaking, ragged handwriting, I copied into my tablet everything printed on that first page, down to the punctuation marks.

I believe it took me a day. Then, aloud, I read back, to myself, everything I'd written on the tablet. Over and over, aloud, to myself, I read my own handwriting.

I woke up the next morning, thinking about those words—immensely proud to realize that not only had I written so much at one time, but I'd written words that I never knew were in the world. Moreover, with a little effort, I also could remember what many of these words meant. I reviewed the words whose meanings I didn't remember. Funny thing, from the dictionary first page right now, that ''aardvark'' springs to my mind. The dictionary had a picture of it, a long-tailed, long-eared, burrowing African mammal, which lives off termites caught by sticking out its tongue as an anteater does for ants.

I was so fascinated that I went on—I copied the dictionary's next page. And the same experience came when I studied that. With every succeeding page, I also learned of people and places and events from history. Actually the dictionary is like a miniature encyclopedia. Finally the dictionary's A section had filled a whole tablet—and I went on into the B's. That was the way I started copying what eventually became the entire dictionary. It went a lot faster after so much practice helped me to pick up handwriting speed. Between what I wrote in my tablet, and writing letters, during the rest of my time in prison I would guess I wrote a million words.

I suppose it was inevitable that as my word-base broadened, I could for the first time pick up a book and read and now begin to understand what the book was saying. Anyone who has read a great deal can imagine the new world that opened. Let me tell you something: from then until I left that prison, in every free moment I had, if I was not reading in the library, I was reading on my bunk. You couldn't have gotten me out of books with a wedge. Between Mr. Muhammad's teachings, my correspondence, my visitors—usually Ella and Reginald—and my reading of books, months passed without my even thinking about being imprisoned. In fact, up to then, I never had been so truly free in my life.

The Norfolk Prison Colony's library was in the school building. A variety of classes was taught there by instructors who came from such places as Harvard and Boston universities. The weekly debates between inmate teams were also held in the school building. You would be astonished to know how worked up convict debaters and audiences would get over subjects like ''Should Babies Be Fed Milk?''

Available on the prison library's shelves were books on just about every general subject. Much of the big private collection that Parkhurst had willed to the prison was still in crates and boxes in the back of the library—thousands of old books. Some of them looked ancient: covers faded, old-time parchment-looking binding. Parkhurst, I've mentioned, seemed to have been principally interested in history and religion. He had the money and the special interest to have a lot of books that you wouldn't have in general circulation. Any college library would have been lucky to get that collection.

As you can imagine, especially in a prison where there was heavy emphasis on rehabilitation, an inmate was smiled upon if he demonstrated an unusually intense interest in books. There was a sizable number of well-read inmates, especially the popular debaters. Some were said by many to be practically walking encyclopedias. They were almost celebrities. No university would ask any student to devour literature as I did when this new world opened to me, of being able to read and *understand*.

I read more in my room than in the library itself. An inmate who was known to read a lot could check out more than the permitted maximum number of books. I preferred reading in the total isolation of my own room.

When I had progressed to really serious reading, every night at about ten P.M. I would be outraged with the ''lights out.'' It always seemed to catch me right in the middle of something engrossing.

Fortunately, right outside my door was a corridor light that cast a glow into my room. The glow was enough to read by, once my eyes adjusted to it. So when ''lights out'' came, I would sit on the floor where I could continue reading in that glow.

At one-hour intervals the night guards paced past every room. Each time I heard the approaching footsteps, I jumped into bed and feigned sleep. And as soon as the guard passed, I got back out of bed onto the floor area of that light-glow, where I would read for another fifty-eight minutes—until the guard approached again. That went on until three or four every morning. Three or four hours of sleep a night was enough for me. Often in the years in the streets I had slept less than that.

BIBLIOGRAPHY

A. ADULT DEVELOPMENT AND RELATED WORKS

Atchley, Robert. *The Sociology of Retirement.* Cambridge, Mass.: Schenkman, 1975.

Berger, Morroe. *Real and Imagined Worlds.* Cambridge, Mass.: Harvard University Press, 1977.

Butler, Robert N. "The Life Review: An Interpretation of Reminiscence in the Aged." *Psychiatry* 26 (1963):65–76.

Channels, Vera. "Family Life Education Through the Use of Novels." *The Family Coordinator* Vol. 20, No. 3 (1971):225–30.

Erikson, Erik. *Childhood and Society.* New York: W. W. Norton, 1950.

Gasarch, Pearl, and Gasarch, Ralph. *Fiction: The Universal Elements.* New York: Van Nostrand Reinhold, 1972.

Gould, Roger. *Transformations.* New York: Simon & Schuster, 1978.

_____. "Transformations During Early and Middle Adult Years." In *Themes of Work and Love in Adulthood*, edited by Neil J. Smelser and Erik H. Erikson. Cambridge, Mass.: Harvard University Press, 1980.

Hale, Nathan. "Freud's Reflections on Work and Love." In *Themes of Work and Love in Adulthood*, edited by Neil J. Smelser and Erik H. Erikson. Cambridge, Mass.: Harvard University Press, 1980.

Hall, Elizabeth. "Acting One's Age: New Rules for Old" (interview with Bernice Neugarten). *Psychology Today* Vol. 13, No. 11 (1980):66, 68, 70, 72, 74, 77, 78, 80.

Jourard, Sidney. *The Transparent Self.* Princeton: Van Nostrand Reinhold, 1964.

Knowles, Malcolm. *The Modern Practice of Adult Education.* Chicago: Follett, 1980.

Knox, Alan. *Adult Development and Learning.* San Francisco: Jossey-Bass, 1977.

Kübler-Ross, Elizabeth. *On Death and Dying.* New York: Macmillan, 1969.

Levinson, Daniel. *The Seasons of a Man's Life.* New York: Alfred A. Knopf, 1978.

Lowenthal, Marjorie Fisk, Thurnher, Majda, and Chiriboga, David. *Four Stages of Life.* San Francisco: Jossey-Bass, 1975.

McKenzie, Leon. "Analysis of *Bildungsroman* Literature as a Research Modality in Adult Education: An Inquiry." *Adult Education* 25 (1975):209–16.

Neugarten, Bernice L. "Adaptation and the Life Cycle." In *Counseling Adults*, edited by Nancy Schlossberg and Alan Entine. Monterey, Calif.: Brooks/Cole, 1977.

Neugarten, Bernice, and Datan, Nancy. "Sociological Perspectives on the Life Cycle." In *Life-span Developmental Psychology: Personality and Socialization*, edited by Paul Baltes and K. Warner Schaie. New York: Academic Press, 1973.

Sheehy, Gail. *Passages: The Predictable Crises of Adult Life.* New York: E. P. Dutton, 1976.

Somerville, Rose. "Death Education as Part of Family Life Education: Using Imaginative Literature for Insights into Family Crises." *The Family Coordinator* Vol. 20, No. 3 (1971):209–23.

Sontag, L. Susan. "The Double Standard of Aging." In *Readings in Adult Psychology: Contemporary Perspectives*, edited by Lawrence R. Allman and Dennis T. Jaffe. New York: Harper & Row, 1977.

Troll, Lillian E. *Early and Middle Adulthood.* Monterey, Calif.: Brooks/Cole, 1975.

Vaillant, George. *Adaptation to Life.* Boston: Little, Brown, 1977.

B.   LITERARY WORKS

Albee, Edward. *Who's Afraid of Virginia Woolf?* New York: Atheneum, 1963.

Baldwin, James. *Nobody Knows My Name.* New York: Dial Press, 1961.

Beckett, Samuel. *Krapp's Last Tape.* New York: Grove Press, 1958.

Bellow, Saul. *Herzog.* New York: Viking Press, 1964.

Chekhov, Anton. "Heartache." In *The Image of Chekhov.* New York: Alfred A. Knopf, 1963. Translated by Robert Payne.

Connell, Evan S. *Mr. Bridge.* New York: Alfred A. Knopf, 1969.

Fitzgerald, F. Scott. *Tender Is the Night.* New York: Charles Scribner's Sons, 1934.

Hesse, Herman. *Steppenwolf.* New York: Modern Library, 1963.

Gold, Herbert. "The Heart of the Artichoke." In *American Short Stories Since 1945*, edited by John Hollander. New York: Harper & Row, 1968.

Joyce, James. *A Portrait of the Artist as a Young Man.* New York: Viking Press, 1964.

Kazan, Elia. *The Arrangement.* New York: Stein & Day, 1967.

Malamud, Bernard. *Dubin's Lives.* New York: Avon Books, 1977.

Miller, Arthur. *Death of a Salesman.* New York: Penguin Books, 1949.

Olsen, Tillie. "I Stand Here Ironing." In *Tell Me A Riddle.* New York: Delacorte Press, 1956.

Salinger, J. D. *The Catcher in the Rye.* Boston: Little, Brown, 1951.

Updike, John. *A Month of Sundays.* Greenwich, Conn.: Fawcett Publications, 1975.

———. *Rabbit, Run.* New York: Alfred A. Knopf, 1970.

INDEX